A WORLD FOR ALL?

Center of
THEOLOGICAL INQUIRY

This volume of essays has been sponsored
by the Center of Theological Inquiry in
Princeton as part of its mission to foster
fresh thinking on global and ecumenical
questions. The editors and many of the
contributors are members of the Center.
For more information, go to CTI's website
at: www.ctinquiry.org

A WORLD FOR ALL?

Global Civil Society in Political Theory and Trinitarian Theology

Edited by

William F. Storrar,
Peter J. Casarella, &
Paul Louis Metzger

WILLIAM B. EERDMANS PUBLISHING COMPANY
GRAND RAPIDS, MICHIGAN / CAMBRIDGE, U.K.

© 2011 Wm. B. Eerdmans Publishing Co.

Published 2011 by
Wm. B. Eerdmans Publishing Co.
2140 Oak Industrial Drive N.E., Grand Rapids, Michigan 49505 /
P.O. Box 163, Cambridge CB3 9PU U.K.

Printed in the United States of America

17 16 15 14 13 12 11   7 6 5 4 3 2 1

Library of Congress Cataloging-in-Publication Data

A world for all?: global civil society in political theory and Trinitarian theology /
    edited by William F. Storrar, Peter J. Casarella & Paul Louis Metzger.
        p.   cm.
    Includes bibliographical references and index.
    ISBN 978-0-8028-2742-5 (pbk.: alk. paper)
    1. Christian sociology.   2. Religion and civil society.
    3. Globalization — Religious aspects — Christianity.   4. Trinity.
    I. Storrar, William.   II. Casarella, Peter J.   III. Metzger, Paul Louis.

BT738.W67   2010
261.8′7 — dc22

                                        2010040500

www.eerdmans.com

Contents

Foreword

In 2007, I addressed a UN global forum in Vienna on the challenges governments face when engaging with civil society. I said then:

> First, there is a definitional challenge, because in many countries today, we still use the terms "NGO" and "civil society" interchangeably. It is important that we recognize that the term "civil society" is a much broader rubric that includes social movements, faith-based institutions, trade unions, professional associations, and so on. A failure to understand that full spectrum of associational life will lead policymakers not to be able to unleash the full potential of all these different elements of civic life. The other issue is that we make an assumption that civil society is all good . . . the question about addressing the "uncivil civil society" or "the dark side of the civil society," as it's sometimes called, is a challenge that we have to deal with.

That is why I welcome *A World for All?* It addresses this challenge to think clearly and honestly about global civil society. What is it? Does it really promise a world for all? These are important questions to consider, not only for governments but also for citizens and civil society actors, including faith-based institutions. They are asked here with illumination

---

Kumi Naidoo is the Executive Director of Greenpeace International and was formerly Secretary-General of CIVICUS. He is widely recognized and respected as a leader of global civil society. He writes here in a personal capacity.

and insight. I found the opening essays by John Keane and Kimberly Hutchings particularly helpful in understanding global civil society in all its social complexity and moral ambiguity. And I welcome the other chapters in this volume that explore the role of the churches in civil society. They provide one example from the world's religions of the contribution of faith-based institutions to a world for all. But they also show how self-critical religious traditions need to be in examining their own mixed record on civil society, as argued by J. Carter in his epilogue. This makes for a healthy debate within these pages.

Many of the essays in this book were first presented at a conference I addressed in Edinburgh in 2005, on how we create a world for all. In the years since then, that question has become all the more urgent. We have seen the failure of governments and bankers to tackle the problems of the global environment and economy. Now we are seeing again the spontaneous power of ordinary people to mobilize for political change. It has become all the more important to see the potential and the problems of global civil society and its faith-based institutions as agents of change. This book helps us do that with its distinctive blend of critique and conviction. I commend it to a wide readership.

Kumi Naidoo

The Editors' Preface

A Contribution to a Conversation

A World for All? is a distinctive volume of essays on global civil society by scholars in politics, philosophy, Christian ethics, and theology. It is a timely contribution to a growing conversation on globalization, ethics, and religion in the academy, church, and public life. In Part I, leading social theorists consider the contested concept of global civil society and the role of religion in its emergence. The editors are grateful to thinkers of the distinction of John Keane, Kimberly Hutchings, Max Stackhouse, and Alexander Broadie for introducing the concept of civil society and opening it up to such insightful analysis for a global era. In Part II, an ecumenical range of theologians draw on the Christian tradition to consider the relationship between civil society and the Church that worships a trinitarian God, providing theological perspectives, historical resources, and local case studies from around the world.

The question mark in the title of this volume shows the purpose of its essays. The aim of *A World for All?* is not to offer one theoretical or theological account of global civil society. It is to encourage the kind of interdisciplinary and ecumenical discussion on this topic to be found in these pages and to inform the thinking of those asking its central question: does global civil society offer hope of a world for all? Amid debate and disagreement, all contributors are united in the conviction that a global civil society must foster and not foil that inclusive social vision.

As a theological volume of essays on global civil society, this is an ecumenical venture. The three editors of *A World for All?* come from different parts of the church in the West: William Storrar is in the Scottish Reformed tradition, Peter Casarella is a Latino Catholic, and Paul Louis Metzger is an American Evangelical. Their collaboration grew out of their residency together as visiting scholars at the ecumenical Center of Theological Inquiry in Princeton, where this project was first envisioned in 2004. Their joint editorship also expresses a shared conviction that Christians must show among themselves the same attitude that is vital to the flourishing of an inclusive global civil society, the grateful recognition of different viewpoints on common concerns. In that spirit, each of the editors sets out below his particular ecclesial perspective on the theme of this book. In doing so, they are launching the ecumenical dialogue and interdisciplinary debate that run from their respective Introductions to Parts I and II and on through each contributor's chapter to the guest epilogue by the African American theologian J. Kameron Carter. In his Epilogue, Carter critically reviews the whole volume and questions its concept of the global and Trinitarian theological assumptions. He does so at the editors' invitation, reflecting their commitment to fostering a genuine inquiry on global civil society that will extend far beyond these pages into seminar rooms, church halls, and public forums around the world.

An Ecumenical Protestant Perspective

The publication of this volume of essays on global civil society follows the centenary of the Edinburgh 1910 World Missionary Conference. That landmark gathering is widely recognized as the birthplace of the modern ecumenical movement. It led to the formation of the World Council of Churches (WCC) in 1948, linking Protestant, Anglican, and Orthodox churches (and more recently some Evangelical and Pentecostal churches from the global South). Edinburgh 1910 also prepared the way for the WCC's later conversations on mission and unity with the Roman Catholic Church in the wake of the Second Vatican Council in the 1960s and with Evangelicals associated with the Lausanne Covenant in the 1970s. William Storrar stands in this Edinburgh tradition of ecumenism. He is a minister of the Church of Scotland, in whose General Assembly Hall the Edinburgh 1910 conference was held. He was also Professor of Christian Ethics and Practical Theology and Director of the Centre for Theology and Public Issues at the University of Edinburgh from 2000 to 2005.

With this Edinburgh centenary in mind, he considers it timely as an ecumenical Protestant (a Reformed Catholic) to note three features of the relationship between the World Council of Churches and global civil society.

First, it is an empirical relationship. The modern ecumenical movement is itself an institutional expression of the forces of globalization operating from the late nineteenth century through to the early twenty-first century. The missionaries who gathered in Edinburgh in 1910 to discuss future cooperation in the world missionary movement were largely Anglo-American and European Protestants, with few non-western and no Catholic or Orthodox representatives in their midst. Their missionary presence in Africa, Asia, and the Pacific region was inseparable from the colonial, commercial and imperial presence of their sending countries in these parts of the non-western world. Their ability to travel and communicate across these vast regions of the globe was made possible by the new technologies of telegraph, steam ship, and railways connecting the continents. Their commitment to holding international conferences and establishing organizations with a global reach was part of a much wider social phenomenon in this turn-of-the-century era: the establishing of many such international bodies and gatherings for varied intergovernmental, political, economic, social, and religious purposes.[1] The rise of the modern ecumenical movement is an early and integral part of these processes of globalization that led in the later twentieth century to the reality of a global civil society, that vast inter-locking network of non-governmental structures, non-violent activities, and independent actors described by John Keane in the opening chapter of Part I. The ecumenical movement can be seen as one set of those self-directed and yet interdependent civil structures, activities, and actors across the globe.

The last point is important. Christianity is a now a world religion. Empirically, it is becoming a religion of the global South, where a growing proportion of Christians now live, many in poverty and some in conflict with neighbors of other faiths.[2] This demographic shift has been accompanied by a change in the way Christianity's witness in the world is understood in ecumenical thinking. Some have described it as the move from

1. John Keane, *Global Civil Society?* (Cambridge: Cambridge University Press, 2003), pp. 50-57.

2. See Philip Jenkins, *The Next Christendom: The Coming of Global Christianity* (New York: Oxford University Press, 2007); Sebastian Kim and Kirsteen Kim, *Christianity as a World Religion* (London: Continuum, 2008).

world mission to world Christianity.[3] The ecumenical movement represented by the WCC is therefore a participant observer in the civil and religious processes of globalization, and this shift must influence the thinking of churches and theologians from within its ranks on the question of global civil society.

But that is not the whole account of the relationship of these ecumenical churches to the emergence of a global civil society. It is also, secondly, an ethical relationship. Like the international socialist movement in the same period, the British, American, and German church leaders and missions that had gathered in Edinburgh in 1910 to strengthen international cooperation across borders proved powerless to hold together their international cause with the outbreak of a world war in 1914 or again in 1939. Their hopes for a "Christian century" of world evangelism and peace were shattered by these global conflicts among nation states and the rise of totalitarian regimes. Chastened by these violent events in the "Christian West" and challenged in their western missionary assumptions by independence movements in colonies and churches around the world, the mid-century ecumenical movement that met to form the World Council of Churches in 1948 was asking more self-critical moral and theological questions about its own confusion of mission with colonialism. Increasingly, the Christians and churches of Africa, Asia, Latin America, and the Pacific were represented in its meetings and structures and found their own theological voice in its deliberations. This led to more critical reports and programs on world affairs emerging from WCC General Assemblies and conferences in the second half of the twentieth century, addressing global problems of poverty, violence, racism, sexism, environmental degradation, international law, and human rights in the ecumenical quest for a world for all.[4]

In other words, the modern ecumenical movement has offered a reflexive ethical critique as well as having been an empirical expression of globalization in the course of the twentieth century. As part of that ethical assessment, it eventually considered the nature and role of civil society within the wider context of globalization. In 1995 the WCC held a consulta-

3. See, for example, the three-year research program of the Irish School of Ecumenics, Trinity College Dublin, on "Visioning 21st Century Ecumenism: Diversity, Dialogue and Reconciliation," 2009-2011.

4. See Nicholas Lossky et al., eds., *Dictionary of the Ecumenical Movement,* 2nd ed. (Geneva: WCC Publications, 2002), for the WCC's engagement with these global problems: including "Ecumenical Conferences," pp. 359-73; "International Law," pp. 591-95; "WCC Assemblies," pp. 1231-38.

tion on theology and civil society in partnership with the Evangelical Academy in Loccum, Germany, which published its papers as *God's People in Civil Society: Ecclesiological Implications,* 1996. As the Puerto Rican scholar Helio Gallardo has commented on such developments in ecumenical thinking:

> Slowly the churches are becoming aware that (as Israel Batista has put it) "whatever we call civil society, be it an old idea, a new paradigm or an easy slogan, society is becoming a testing place for alternatives, the reorganization of social movements and the space for the healing witness of local churches and ecumenical groups in the face of the predominance of the market economy and the weakness of the state."[5]

Third, the ecumenical movement has had its own evolving theological understanding of the meaning of the local and the global in relation to mission, and of civil society in relation to the Church. We noted above the move of Christians, churches, and theologians in the global South into full membership and leadership in the world ecumenical movement. This has been accompanied by the recognition that theology is local and contextual and that its universality lies in the "global flow" of local and contextual theological ideas and methods in a new catholicity (as Robert Schreiter has put it).[6] This understanding of the contextual nature of theology has arisen in part out of the insight of a religious movement conceived in the spatial terms of the whole inhabited earth:

> Theology, as a human activity, is subjected to the limitations of space and time. The ecumenical movement makes us recognize that we live in the same space, on the same earth, but not in the same time. A universal theology presupposes simultaneity, which only oppression and domination can achieve.[7]

If its origins lie in a more Christocentric concern for world mission and evangelism among western Protestants at the start of the twentieth century, by the early twenty-first century the ecumenical movement associ-

---

5. Helio Gallardo, "Civil Society," p. 212.

6. See Stephen B. Bevans, *Models of Contextual Theology* (Maryknoll, NY: Orbis, 2002); David Bosch, *Transforming Mission: Paradigm Shift in Theology of Mission* (Maryknoll, NY: Orbis, 1991), pp. 420-32; for Robert Schreiter's evolving understanding of the local and the global in relation to catholicity, see nn. 19, 21 below.

7. Konrad Raiser, "Theology in the Ecumenical Movement," in *Dictionary of the Ecumenical Movement*, p. 1119.

ated with the WCC had been through its own theological paradigm shift "to an intentionally more expansive Trinitarianism, from the history of salvation to care for the planet, from reconciliation among Christians to common life in the entire human household," raising the need for a theology of religions as well as mission in a religiously pluralist world.[8] A key feature of the ecumenical movement's evolving intellectual response to globalization and global civil society has been this creative tension in its thinking between the local and the global, the contextual and the universal, the recognition of difference and the realization of the common good.

Among the most perceptive and influential ecumenical thinkers on these theological developments is Konrad Raiser, a former General Secretary of the World Council of Churches. Writing in 1996 on the challenge of globalization for the churches, he notes that for all its achievements, "it symbolizes a form of human power that cannot be controlled and thus becomes self-destructive."[9] Only God sees the earth as an integrated whole, a conviction humans express in prayer and adoration. This theological conviction leads Raiser to a moral and political conviction that the "potentially self-destructive dynamics of the process of globalization can only be met if humans, individually and collectively, learn again to live within limits."[10] To that end, Raiser sees a key role for the churches within local and global civil society:

> In the present situation of increasing fragmentation as the reverse side of the trend towards globalization, the primary task of Christian churches is to further the process of reconstructing sustainable human communities. This is reflected in the growing interest in processes of strengthening civil society over against the formal structures on the political, social, and economic levels. For centuries, churches have shaped their structured life in correspondence to the prevailing structures of the state, or more recently the patterns of the business world. The challenge as we move into the twenty-first century will be to understand the churches as a vital part of civil society transcending the potentially exclusive claims of culture, racial origin, or ethnic loyalties.[11]

8. Raiser, *Dictionary of the Ecumenical Movement,* "Preface to the Second Edition."
9. Konrad Raiser, "The World in the Twenty-First Century," in *The Future of Theology: Essays in Honour of Jürgen Moltmann,* ed. Miroslav Volf et al. (Grand Rapids: Eerdmans, 1996), p. 7.
10. Raiser, *The Future of Theology,* p. 8.
11. Raiser, *The Future of Theology,* p. 9.

This volume of essays offers examples of churches around the world doing just that, playing a vital part in creating a more inclusive local and global civil society. Such churches reflect this shift in the ecumenical understanding of mission from an exclusive concern for world evangelism in 1910 to a more inclusive concern for the well-being of God's world in 2010.[12] In taking seriously Raiser's ecumenical challenge to understand the churches in relation to civil society, *A World for All?* does not reduce them to that empirical or ethical relationship. Rather, it argues for the theological contribution of the churches to wider conversations on global civil society in the academy and public life, including the critical voice of some theologians in this volume like Johnson and Carter who would challenge the concept itself on theological grounds.

A Roman Catholic Perspective

Since at least the latter half of the twentieth century, the Roman Catholicism to which Peter Casarella belongs has had to engage the question of a global civil society. Already in 1963, Pope John XXIII, the convener of the Second Vatican Council, spoke in his Encyclical *Pacem in Terris* of "an immense task" that faced the contemporary church. He was thinking about the daunting challenge of calling for peace in the midst of the Cold War and other pressing global conflicts. The optimistic pope hoped to direct civil societies in the world towards the common good so that people could begin to see a closer connection between the exercise of political authority and the realization of the common good.[13] The global realization of a common good is what led John XXIII to underscore *the immensity of the task:*

> Hence among the very serious obligations incumbent upon persons of high principles, we must include the task of establishing new relationships in human society, under the mastery and guidance of truth, justice, charity and freedom — relations between individual citizens, between citizens and their respective States, between States, and finally between individuals, families, intermediate associations and States on the one hand, and the world community on the other. There is surely

12. See Bosch, *Transforming Mission*, pp. 409-420, for an authoritative account of this shift in ecumenical thinking on evangelism and mission.
13. *Pacem in Terris*, #136.

no one who will not consider this a most exalted task, for it is one which is able to bring about true peace in accordance with divinely established order.[14]

The pope who realized the opening up of the Catholic Church to the modern world was also the forger of a global Catholic social ethic of justice and peace. He saw that a global vision does not fall from the sky into the hands of global actors. On the contrary, it requires paying close attention to the individual, the family, intermediate associations, the state, and finally to the notion of a human family that theoretically should bind nations into a common purpose. His insight into the need for individual agents of civil society and for global institutions to preserve and administer this lofty vision continues to inspire church leaders today and still needs to be brought into the everyday parlance of lay Catholics throughout the world.[15]

Every new engagement with the idea of promoting a civil society will accentuate different aspects of the Catholic view of the world. Recently, Jeanne Heffernan Schindler published a fascinating and superbly edited collection of essays by Catholic and Reformed thinkers entitled *Christianity and Civil Society: Catholic and Neo-Calvinist Perspectives*.[16] The Catholic contributors to this volume effectively communicate that the preservation of the civil society from a Catholic perspective is a distinct alternative to an abstract social theory of liberal democracy founded only upon the triad of individual, state, and market. On both the theoretical and practical level, Catholicism has contributed impressively to the promotion and establishment of institutional values and entities that *mediate for individuals* in the face of the competing interests of the state and of expansively global markets. These authors join their vision to social and legal theorists in the U.S. such as Robert Putnam, Michael Sandel, and Mary Ann Glendon who decry the diminished role of mediating institutions in North America and tout their preservation as the key to maintaining what is worth preserving in the Anglo-European traditions of a Christian democracy. Heffernan

14. *Pacem in Terris*, #163.

15. Cf. Symposium "Peace on Earth," United Nations Headquarters, October 7, 2003, Intervention by H. E. Archbishop Renato R. Martino, President of the Pontifical Council for Justice and Peace, on Universal Common Good and World Authority, accessed on-line on July 2, 2009, at http://www.holyseemission.org/pacem-martino.html.

16. Jeanne Heffernan Schindler, ed., *Christianity and Civil Society: Catholic and Neo-Calvinist Perspectives* (Lanham, MD: Lexington Books, 2008).

and her colleagues highlight the Catholic principle of subsidiarity, i.e. the notion that the dignity of the individual cannot be subsumed into the logic of larger entities like the state and market as well as the notion that peoples and nations have to have their own rightful autonomy respected even as the global order is acknowledged to be more tightly interconnected and more dependent on a vision of civil society that is palpably global.[17]

The present volume extends the modern Catholic tradition of addressing the issue of a global civil society in a somewhat different but not altogether divergent direction. This volume highlights the contemporary articulation of the principle of catholicity itself.[18] Since the publication in 1997 of Robert Schreiter's *The New Catholicity: Theology between the Global and the Local*, it has become increasingly common for Catholic theologians to consider communication across diverse cultures as the new context for thinking about the principle of catholicity.[19] Whereas economic globalization has a compressing effect on global cultures (ponder the amount of information that can be compressed into the computer chip or iPod), a genuine and differentiated unity of cultures preserves their unique identities into a whole.[20] Catholicity understood in these terms is not a new abstraction. Casarella, for example, contributes a piece to this volume on the social analogy of the Trinity and makes this contribution as a Latino Catholic. Highlighting one's social, economic, or cultural location, one's race, and/or one's ethnicity is not a move that is performed as an addition to a pre-existing idea of a new catholicity. Such difference as an inculturation of the faith is itself the warp and woof of that which is integrated in the whole.

More recently, Schreiter has acknowledged that his earlier forays into the question of catholicity that focus on the notion of catholicity as spatial extension now need to be brought into conversation with "Neo-Augustinian" theologies of culture that focus more on the integrity of the faith. Here Schreiter is bringing into the global conversation important

17. See especially the compelling contributions by Russell Hittinger and Kenneth L. Grasso to that volume.

18. See, for example, Avery Dulles, S.J., *The Catholicity of the Church* (Oxford: Clarendon, 1985) for a magisterial treatment of the theme.

19. Robert Schreiter, *The New Catholicity: Theology between the Global and the Local* (Maryknoll, NY: Orbis, 1997).

20. Schreiter, *The New Catholicity*, p. 11 on globalization as compression. See also Robert J. Schreiter, *Constructing Local Theologies* (Maryknoll, NY: Orbis, 1985), for the semiotic analysis of culture that undergirds Schreiter's ecclesiology.

voices like those of Hans Urs von Balthasar, Joseph Ratzinger (now Pope Benedict XVI), David L. Schindler, Tracy Rowland, and Graham Ward.[21] This conversation concerning the multiple discourses of catholicity in contemporary Catholic theology stands only at the beginning, but its outcome promises to be fruitful. The Neo-Augustinian task of questioning the abstract nature of the discourse of global civil society in the name of a concrete witness of the church is, in a sense, already underway in the contributions made by at least three of the non-Catholic contributors to this volume: Kristin Deede Johnson, Daniela Augustine, and J. Kameron Carter.

On June 29, 2009, Pope Benedict XVI promulgated *Love in Truth*, the third encyclical of his pontificate. Here we see how the proposal initiated by John XXIII of fostering truly global values can be extended to confront the crisis of economic globalization and how globalization becomes a challenge to all believers. The pope's concept of truth allied to and incarnated in charity is taken directly from St. Augustine. He states: "Truth — which is itself gift, in the same way as charity — is greater than we are, as St. Augustine teaches."[22] Proposals for a just re-ordering of society need to take into account, says the Augustinian pope, the truth that *the human person is first of all gift*. Only in this light, he argues, can one avoid both the cultural dictatorship of sheer relativism and the leveling of all cultures into a mirror image of markets that operate solely on the basis of the redistribution of commercial goods. Citing his predecessor John Paul II, the pope argues for a view of global civil society in which economic activity does not "prescind from gratuitousness."[23] Gratuitousness is a requirement for global economic justice, and the implementation of such gratuitousness requires more than just a mere sentiment for change: "Today's international economic scene, marked by grave deviations and failures, requires a *profoundly new way of understanding business enterprise*."[24] In short, the fu-

---

21. Robert Schreiter, "Forms of Catholicity in an Age of Globalization," unpublished address delivered at the Catholicity Colloquium organized on January 15, 2009, by the Center for World Catholicism and Intercultural Theology at DePaul University. An earlier version of this paper was accessed on-line on July 2, 2009, at http://www.mission-preciousblood.org/Docsfiles/2008/schreiter_two_forms_catholicity.pdf.

22. *Charity in Truth*, Encyclical Letter of Pope Benedict XVI dated June 29, 2009, #34, citing St. Augustine, *De Libero Arbitrio* 2.3.8ff, accessed on-line on July 14, 2009, at http://www.vatican.va/holy_father/benedict_xvi/encyclicals/documents/hf_ben-xvi_enc_20090629_caritas-in-veritate_en.html.

23. *Charity in Truth*, #38.

24. *Charity in Truth*, #40.

ture of a global civil society that is truly open to genuine difference cannot look merely to individual needs, bureaucratic proposals made by nation-states and transnational agencies, and the inexorabilities of globalizing markets. The truly complex interaction of political and economic actors in our world must also be viewed in terms of a notion of human persons acting in a communion that remains open to transcendence.[25] In other words, Pope Benedict is challenging his own flock and all others who wish to listen to deepen their understanding of and commitment to social justice in light of the complex problem of economic globalization and in the very same breath underscoring the perduring centrality of the question of God.

An American Evangelical Perspective

"A World for All?" The Evangelical Christian movement of which Paul Louis Metzger is a part in the United States has a difficult time answering this question. Evangelicals have often felt as if they have been left behind as a persecuted remnant in the United States.[26] They have also been accused of leaving others behind with manifest destiny ambitions of taking back

---

25. Cf. *Charity in Truth*, #42: "Sometimes *globalization* is viewed in fatalistic terms, as if the dynamics involved were the product of anonymous impersonal forces or structures independent of the human will. In this regard it is useful to remember that while globalization should certainly be understood as a socio-economic process, this is not its only dimension. Underneath the more visible process, humanity itself is becoming increasingly interconnected; it is made up of individuals and peoples to whom this process should offer benefits and development, as they assume their respective responsibilities, singly and collectively. The breaking-down of borders is not simply a material fact: it is also a cultural event both in its causes and its effects. If globalization is viewed from a deterministic standpoint, the criteria with which to evaluate and direct it are lost. As a human reality, it is the product of diverse cultural tendencies, which need to be subjected to a process of discernment. The truth of globalization as a process and its fundamental ethical criterion are given by the unity of the human family and its development towards what is good. Hence a sustained commitment is needed so as to *promote a person-based and community-oriented cultural process of world-wide integration that is open to transcendence*."

26. George Marsden addresses this problematic situation and psyche in his work, *Fundamentalism and American Culture: The Shaping of Twentieth-Century Evangelicalism — 1870-1925* (Oxford: Oxford University Press, 1980). See, e.g., p. 184. See also chapter one, "A Faulty Order: Retreating Battle Camps and Homogeneous Units," in Paul Louis Metzger's work, *Consuming Jesus: Beyond Race and Class Divisions in a Consumer Church* (Grand Rapids: Eerdmans, 2007), pp. 13-38.

America for God from the pagan secularists.[27] When Clarence Darrow humiliated William Jennings Bryan at the Scopes Monkey Trial in 1925, evangelicals mourned the loss of their seat of honor in the public square, which they had occupied since their forefather Jonathan Edwards in the 1700s. Forced out of the Promised Land, they dreamed of the time when God would bring them home to rebuild the walls and the temple. The Moral Majority types thought they had fulfilled this dream as fundamentalist-evangelical leaders like the late Jerry Falwell, Timothy LaHaye of *Left Behind* series fame, and James Dobson lobbied and politicked to put righteous judges and rulers back in power, only to find that the left has been raised from the dead with a vengeance. So, where does the evangelical movement stand or fall today?

On March 10, 2009, *The Christian Science Monitor* published an opinion piece by Michael Spencer titled "The Coming Evangelical Collapse." The sub-heading of the article read, "An anti-Christian chapter in Western history is about to begin. But out of the ruins, a new vitality and integrity will rise." Spencer furthermore maintains in the article that

> this collapse will herald the arrival of an anti-Christian chapter of the post-Christian West. Intolerance of Christianity will rise to levels many of us have not believed possible in our lifetimes, and public policy will become hostile toward evangelical Christianity, seeing it as the opponent of the common good.[28]

While many common, ordinary evangelical Christians seek to live quiet, compassionate lives among their fellow citizens, and evangelical churches and ministries are playing increasing roles in compassionate outreach in addressing the AIDS, poverty, and hunger and thirst epidemics, the mainstream media often enjoys drawing attention to the extreme voices in the evangelical movement who appear to preach a gospel of hate

27. Jeff Sharlet speaks to the complex and problematic nature of the Evangelical movement and its engagement of the society at large in his article on Ted Haggard and New Life Church in Colorado Springs, Colorado. See Jeff Sharlet, "Inside America's Most Powerful Megachurch," *Harper's* 310, no. 1860 (May 2005): 42–44.

28. See Michael Spencer's opinion piece in *The Christian Science Monitor* titled, "The Coming Evangelical Collapse," with a subheading that reads, "An anti-Christian chapter in Western history is about to begin. But out of the ruins, a new vitality and integrity will rise." It can be found in the March 10, 2009, edition of *The Christian Science Monitor* and can be accessed at http://www.csmonitor.com/2009/0310/p09s01-coop.html (accessed on July 24, 2009).

and excess rather than extreme love.[29] In this light, *it is all the more important* that the movement take seriously the call to bear witness to Christ in grace and truth. The evangelical community must create the space through a living witness for the views of evangelicals to be heard. This involves sacrificially living out the gospel, not trying to take back America from their enemies (as they are often accused of doing), but laying down their lives for their "enemies" as an overflow of Christ's holy incarnate love.

Why would an evangelical theologian serve as an editor to this volume? As an evangelical leader, Metzger believes that it is critically important that the evangelical movement of which he is a part develop a public theology of the common good in which evangelicals are able to dialogue and work with those from very different perspectives in view of the belief that all people are created in the image of God and have inherent dignity and value. He also maintains that evangelicals need to move through their own convictions rather than stopping short at those convictions and refusing to listen to those from radically different points of view. Generally speaking, evangelicals are wary of ecumenical dialogue, fearing that it compromises biblical truth and evangelical distinctives. Metzger contends that evangelicals must not compromise their convictions by going around them in search of common ground. But given the evangelical belief that all people are created in the image of the triune God, he maintains that the movement must not stop short and refuse to enter into dialogue either. Thus, he argues that evangelicals must enter into open and

29. In an interview with *Rolling Stone,* Bono speaks of how evangelicals are becoming an increasingly redemptive force in society at large. See Jann S. Wenner, "Bono: The Rolling Stone Interview," *Rolling Stone,* Nov. 3, 2005, where Bono says, "I'm wary of faith outside of actions. I'm wary of religiosity that ignores the wider world. In 2001, only seven percent of evangelicals polled felt it incumbent upon themselves to respond to the AIDS emergency. This appalled me. I asked for meetings with as many church leaders as would have them with me. I used my background in the Scriptures to speak to them about the so-called leprosy of our age and how I felt Christ would respond to it. And they had better get to it quickly, or they would be very much on the other side of what God was doing in the world. Amazingly, they did respond. I couldn't believe it. It almost ruined it for me — 'cause I love giving out about the church and Christianity. But they actually came through: Jesse Helms, you know, publicly repents for the way he thinks about AIDS. I've started to see this community as a real resource in America. I have described them as 'narrow-minded idealists.' If you can widen the aperture of that idealism, these people want to change the world. They want their lives to have meaning." This portion of the interview is excerpted from the website: Jann S. Wenner, *Rolling Stone: Bono* (http://www.jannswenner.com/Archives/Bono.aspx, accessed on July 29, 2009).

honest dialogue that involves sustained consideration of particular truth claims of various traditions, including their own, building on those convictions in search of common ground.[30] Lastly, evangelicals need to develop a theology of engagement that promotes sacrificial co-existence, one in which evangelicals lay down their lives for their alternative belief system and lifestyle neighbors and the common good in view of the belief in the uncommon love of God revealed as Jesus Christ. Only when evangelicals create the space with laid-down lives of sacrificial co-existence in a world for all can they rightfully hope that their views of the *evangel* will be heard by all.

30. This is largely an American evangelical cultural phenomenon. However, given the influence of the American evangelical church worldwide, other segments of the evangelical movement find it difficult to enter into ecumenical dialogue. Two constructive attempts at engaging the broader Christian community are the proceedings of the Lausanne Covenant and the work of "Evangelicals and Catholics Together." It is worth noting that historically British evangelical leaders such as Thomas Chalmers, Lord Shaftesbury, and William Wilberforce were influential voices who pioneered strategies and outcomes addressing the common good of the global community. In the States, evangelical thinkers like Jonathan Edwards and Carl F. H. Henry spoke of the pressing need for regeneration for optimal benefit in sustained social action while also favoring work with non-Christians who shared the same moral convictions for the sake of promoting the common good. See Gerald R. McDermott, *One Holy and Happy Society: The Public Theology of Jonathan Edwards* (University Park: The Pennsylvania State University Press, 1992), pp. 180-81; Carl F. H. Henry, *The Uneasy Conscience of Modern Fundamentalism* (Grand Rapids: Eerdmans, 1947; reprint, with foreword by Richard J. Mouw, 2003), p. 79. The Princeton Proposal for Christian Unity is an important document that challenges evangelicals to partner with other Christian movements for the sake of the church at large, and includes reflections on how evangelicals demonstrate certain qualities and strengths that are very beneficial to the health and well-being of the entire Christian community. See Carl E. Braaten and Robert W. Jenson, ed., *In One Body through the Cross: The Princeton Proposal for Christian Unity* (Grand Rapids: Eerdmans, 2003), pp. 55-56. Generally speaking, it has been American evangelical missiologists (more so than American evangelical theologians) who have been concerned for ecumenical discourse (in part because of pragmatic concerns on the ground). American evangelical theology largely lags behind due to a lack of awareness of the need for a theology of the common good rooted in the image of God and the triune God's compassionate engagement of the world at large. Notable exceptions to this tendency in American evangelical theology would be those evangelical theologians from the Reformed tradition; they are generally more sensitive and engaged in ecumenical discourse given Reformed theology's robust theology of the common good. An example of a growing ecclesiological concern for ecumenical discourse among evangelical theologians is Brad Harper's and Paul Louis Metzger's *Exploring Ecclesiology: An Evangelical and Ecumenical Introduction* (Grand Rapids: Brazos, 2009).

Acknowledgments

The editors would like to thank all those who have helped in the preparation of this volume. Above all, the contributors deserve recognition for their willingness to collaborate, for their learned productivity, and especially for their understanding and patience. The project was born during the academic year 2003-2004 at the Center of Theological Inquiry in Princeton, and the then Director, Dr. Wallace Alston, Jr., deserves much credit for hosting the three editors as visiting scholars at the Center. The other supportive institutions along the way were the University of Edinburgh's Centre for Theology and Public Issues (CTPI), and the Irish School of Ecumenics (ISE), Trinity College Dublin. They jointly organized an international, interdisciplinary conference at the University of Edinburgh School of Divinity on September 4-7, 2005, entitled "A World for All? The Ethics of Global Civil Society." It was the culmination of a five-year program on citizenship and civil society at CTPI under the direction of one of the editors, William Storrar, who chaired the Edinburgh conference. Original drafts of a number of the papers that appear in this volume were presented at that gathering, and all three editors are extremely grateful to the organizers for what they did to make this volume possible, especially Dr. Cecelia Clegg (CTPI) and Dr. Gillian Wylie (ISE). They also wish to thank a leading global civil society advocate of a world for all, Kumi Naidoo, then of CIVICUS, for his inspiring address to the Edinburgh conference, connecting the concerns of scholars and practitioners.

With William Storrar's move from the Chair of Christian Ethics and Practical Theology at the University of Edinburgh to the Directorship of the Center of Theological Inquiry in 2005, it has continued to offer the support for this project begun by his predecessor, including making possible the editorial assistance of Ms. Atria Larson, Ph.D. candidate in Medieval Studies at The Catholic University of America. We would like to express our sincere gratitude to Ms. Larson for her considerable and considerably patient efforts to redeem us of our stylistic shortcomings. The final product owes much to her able assistance and perseverance to the end. As the editors and the majority of contributors to *A World for All?* are members of the Center, the whole volume exemplifies its ecumenical program of interdisciplinary theological inquiry for a global era.

A special word of thanks goes to William B. Eerdmans, Jr., as well as to Jon Pott, editor-in-chief of the William B. Eerdmans Publishing Company, and to our editor, Jenny Hoffman, for her professional work on our behalf. Bill accompanied this project in many ways, in many places, and over a long period of time. His support was generous and immediate from the beginning. We wish to honor him and all that he has given us with this humble offering. We also dedicate it to Max Stackhouse, a pioneer in the theological study of globalization and an opening contributor in Part I. Max was the leader of a major inquiry on *God and Globalization* at the Center of Theological Inquiry. The editors hope that *A World for All?* will build on Max's groundbreaking collaborative work. Above all we hope that this book will be welcomed by the global civil society practitioners whom we had the privilege of meeting at the *World for All?* conference in 2005. The fitting threefold dedication of this book is finally to them and to all their practitioner colleagues in churches and civil societies around the world who struggle daily to achieve a world for all, often at the risk of their lives.

The outline for this book started with some jottings on a napkin at a lunch with the three editors in Princeton. It first took form in some of the papers presented at an international conference in Edinburgh, where they were discussed with participants from around the globe. Many others have enriched the project along the way in ways that could not have been imagined then. These concentric circles of conversation on our theme will continue to grow with its publication. In the end we take responsibility for what appears here. Given that the authors have been so patient to see the final outcome, we also hope that our readers will indulge us the benefit of knowing that we too consider the idea of a global conversation as ambitious as it is urgent. Hopefully, our offerings will be judged a fruitful beginning to a conversation that needs to be extended considerably in both time and space.

WILLIAM F. STORRAR,
PETER J. CASARELLA,
PAUL LOUIS METZGER

Political Theory, Ethics, and Global Civil Society

Introduction to Part I

William F. Storrar

The four essays on global civil society in Part I began their life as conference and colloquium addresses in Edinburgh. Their key concept of civil society has only lately come back into public and academic prominence, but its origins are centuries-old. The city of Edinburgh can fairly lay claim to being one of civil society's intellectual and institutional homes. It was here in the eighteenth century that Scotland gave up its parliamentary independence but gained its intellectual eminence in the flourishing civic culture of the Scottish Enlightenment. Without its own state, Scotland continued as an autonomous civil society through its surviving national institutions and civic elites, especially in its law courts, universities, and national church. It was here in 1767 that Adam Ferguson, a former army chaplain, wrote his seminal work, *An Essay on the History of Civil Society,* while professor of moral philosophy at the University of Edinburgh. It was here that the university's Principal, William Robertson, a leading Church of Scotland minister, wrote his influential histories of the Americas and India, seeing these other cultures sympathetically through the lenses of his own moderate Presbyterian assumptions about civil society. It was here that Edinburgh's greatest minds, David Hume and Adam Smith, enjoyed the conviviality and conversation of the city's philosophical clubs and societies, thereby constituting what Jürgen Habermas would later call the bourgeois public sphere.[1] Out of this Enlightenment world of civic ideas,

---

1. Jürgen Habermas, *The Structural Transformation of the Public Sphere* (Cambridge: Polity Press, 1989).

3

institutions, and discourses, the fabric of Scottish civil society was woven — but only for some of Edinburgh's residents.

Two hundred years later, in the 1970s, I supported my studies at the University of Edinburgh by working as a night cleaner in its arts and social science buildings, including those named after Scottish Enlightenment luminaries: the David Hume Tower, and the Adam Ferguson and William Robertson Buildings. Early one morning, taking a tea break in the David Hume Tower with my fellow cleaners, we looked out over the city. Beside me stood an older man from an Irish Catholic immigrant family background who had grown up in the working class tenements of Edinburgh's Old Town: "Aye, son," he said, apropos of nothing, "This is no' a poor man's city!" Born and brought up in the city of Adam Ferguson, William Robertson and David Hume, he knew that he was not part of Edinburgh's bourgeois and Presbyterian civil society. This comment from thirty years ago captures the problematic at the heart of this collection of essays: when contemplating the ambiguous civic and religious realities of globalization, the fellow migrant workers of that Edinburgh cleaner around the world may also want to cry out, "This is still not our civil society!"

Three sets of questions are raised by this hermeneutic of suspicion from below. Does the emergence of civic ideas, institutions, and movements around the world necessarily represent a more inclusive and just social order or do they only serve to reinforce existing inequalities of power and wealth among peoples and nation states? Does the globalization of this civil society represent the emergence of a world for all or only serve to impose a further western hegemony over other cultures? And does religion reinforce the divisions or strengthen the dynamism of civil society, preventing or promoting its inclusive existence around the world?

To address these pressing empirical, theoretical, and moral questions, an international, interdisciplinary conference for researchers, policy-makers and practitioners was held at the University of Edinburgh in September 2005. Its theme was: "A World for All? The Ethics of Global Civil Society." This conference was the culmination of a five-year research program on citizenship and civil society at the university's Centre for Theology and Public Issues, which I directed from 2000 to 2005.[2] The

2. For publications from this CTPI program, 2000-2005, see William F. Storrar and Andrew R. Morton, *Public Theology for the 21st Century* (London: T&T Clark, 2004); and three volumes in the Public Concerns series, Saint Andrew Press, Edinburgh, series editors,

program included collaboration with the Irish School of Ecumenics, Trinity College Dublin, in running conferences on local civil society in Scotland and Northern Ireland ("A Place for All?"), held in Belfast, 2004, and on global civil society ("A World for All?"), held in Edinburgh, 2005. The plenary papers from the Edinburgh conference by the political theorists John Keane and Kimberly Hutchings and the Christian ethicist Max Stackhouse now reach a wider audience as the introductory essays in Part I of this volume. They open up the debate about the nature and normative character of the concept of global civil society. Their varied theoretical accounts of civil society and globalization are followed in Part II by a series of theological studies on how the worship of a trinitarian God by churches across history and around the world influences the Christian understanding of local and global civil society. Many of these studies were first presented at the Edinburgh 2005 conference by scholars who were in residence with me as fellow members of the Center of Theological Inquiry in Princeton, New Jersey, in 2004.

In particular my editorial colleagues Peter Casarella and Paul Louis Metzger played the leading part in conceiving and planning this work with me over many lunches together in Princeton. While we did not reach the dizzy conversational heights of the eighteenth-century Edinburgh dining clubs of Ferguson, Smith, Hume, and Robertson, we shared their conviction about the vital bond between sociability and intellectual inquiry. Casarella and Metzger's skill in commissioning, editing, and introducing the major second part of this volume pays tribute to their scholarly judgment and inclusive civic and global vision as Catholic and Evangelical theologians. Their collaboration across different Christian traditions also reflects their own virtues of civility and mutual respect and a shared spiritual commitment to the church's constructive but diverse roles in civil societies through time and around the world.

William Storrar and Alison Elliot: William Storrar and Peter Donald, eds., *God in Society: Doing Social Theology in Scotland Today* (2003); Kathleen Marshall and Paul Parvis, *Honouring Children: The Human Rights of the Child in Christian Perspective* (2004); and Johnston R. McKay, ed., *Netting Citizens: Exploring Citizenship in the Internet Age* (2004). This body of work on citizenship is dedicated to the memory of the late Professor Robina Goodlad, University of Glasgow, whose inspiring lecture at the Belfast conference, 2004, shared the wisdom of a life dedicated to the cause of social justice and participatory democracy, especially in deprived urban communities.

Religion and Civil Society: The Missing Link

But one question remains before I introduce the opening theoretical essays of Keane, Hutchings, and Stackhouse: what holds the two parts of this volume together, the theoretical and the theological, apart from their intellectual origins in the Presbyterian Edinburgh of the Scottish Enlightenment and their institutional occasion in an Edinburgh University conference on global civil society? The clue lies in the fourth and final essay in Part I: Alexander Broadie's study of philosophical rhetoric and the role of the preacher in Scottish Enlightenment social thought. It bridges the ethical and the ecclesial banks of this book by going back to Enlightenment Scotland, where the role of the Presbyterian minister and the idea of a civil society were inseparably linked. All the elements of Scottish Enlightenment social theory are embodied in the preacher.

Broadie's seminal essay was first presented as a paper at a colloquium on "Theology and Social Theory in the Scottish Enlightenment," which I ran at the Centre for Theology and Public Issues, Edinburgh University in March 2004, in collaboration with the Center of Theological Inquiry, Princeton. After identifying rhetoric as "a prominent field of philosophical inquiry in the Scottish Enlightenment," Broadie then considers some preparatory notes for a lecture on preaching by Thomas Reid that he discovered in the papers of this major eighteenth-century Scottish philosopher. After serving as a Presbyterian parish minister, Reid was a professor of moral philosophy, first at King's College, Aberdeen and then at the University of Glasgow. As the leading exponent of common sense philosophy against Hume's skepticism, Reid saw the preacher in the pulpit as having the pivotal public role in holding together civil society. Unlike the lawyer or politicians, who used their rhetorical skills to appeal to the specialized and educated audiences of the law court or the public assembly, the preacher had the far more intellectually demanding and complex rhetorical task of commending the common moral sense of Christian and civic virtues to all ranks and conditions of society. Gathered in the one parish church, the socially diverse congregation was to be edified by the sacred and civic rhetoric of the central liturgical act in Reformed worship, the sermon. Here, at the heart of what we may reasonably call the Christian Enlightenment of eighteenth-century Scotland, the social theory and theology of civil society meet in the one emblematic figure, the minister in the pulpit of the local parish church.

Broadie's essay on Reid thus provides the lost philosophical bridge in the eighteenth-century history of ideas to support this book's interdisciplinary linking of theoretical and theological studies of civil society in the context of globalization in the twenty-first century. More than that, Broadie shows how the reflections of the scholar are inseparable from the responsibilities of the practitioner: Thomas Reid the moral philosopher is inseparable from Reid the parish minister and lecturer on homiletics to students for the parish ministry. In Thomas Reid and his fellow Church of Scotland minister, university professor of rhetoric, and lecturer on preaching, Hugh Blair of Edinburgh University, we find the all but unknown Scottish Enlightenment roots of my own academic discipline of Practical Theology. It was this enduring Scottish philosophical and theological conviction about the importance of reflective practice in church and society that shaped the Edinburgh conference in 2005, bringing together as it did local and global civil society practitioners and policymakers as well as academic researchers. This linking of the theoretical and the practical also helps us to understand the complex interactions of a now global civil society. And so Part II will offer local case studies as well as historical and theological perspectives on the church's civic involvement. But we begin in Part I with three essays that consider the multi-layered concept of global civil society, its contested nature, and the role of religion in its creation.

Conceptualizing Global Civil Society

In the opening essay, leading civil society theorist John Keane offers a clear but complex and nuanced account of the relatively new concept of global civil society. It is a term that has only come into use in the last twenty years or so. The term has gained currency in part because of the revival of the language of civil society itself, first among dissident intellectuals in Eastern Europe in the late 1980s and then more widely among various progressive movements in Europe and around the world, including, for example, the successful civic campaign for a Scottish Parliament in the 1990s (thus democratizing and bringing home that eighteenth-century Scottish bourgeois idea through this global flow of intellectual currents across time and space). But in larger part, the concept of global civil society has gained purchase because of the impact of the more powerful economic forces of globalization on civic institutions, networks, and movements around the world.

Once more, Keane starts his account of global civil society among the thinkers of Enlightenment Scotland. He contrasts Adam Smith's analysis in *The Wealth of Nations* (1776) of the emerging market economies of the Atlantic region in the later eighteenth century with what is happening today through the impact of now global markets on human social experience. Smith described an economic world of "shallow integration," where western manufacturing industries enjoyed a "natural protection" from foreign competition thanks to the oceans of the world and what Keane calls "arms length trade in raw materials, goods, and services among independent firms and by means of international movements of capital." According to Keane, this market economy of shallow integration remained in operation well into the twentieth century but has now been replaced by what he calls "the processes of deep integration." Describing the social impact of these market forces of deep integration in a global economy, he writes,

> Business is a bridge, and often enough a battering ram, a force that breaks down barriers among peoples, cultures, and geographic regions. There are other globalizing forces at work, including efforts at cross-border political and legal integration and civic initiatives and social movements, but business is undoubtedly a prime mover in fostering strong images of ourselves as involved in a great human adventure, one that not only is carried out on a global scale but also stimulates a new awareness that we are being drawn into a global civil society.

To make sense of the impact of these globalizing economic forces on the social, cultural, and political fabric of civic life around the world, Keane offers an ideal-type description of global civil society and then systematically reflects on each of six key elements of his definition. When we speak of global civil society we are thinking of non-governmental structures, activities, and actors. It is a term that describes a vast "society of interlocking societies" across the globe that are self-directed and yet interdependent. To function effectively, the social actors of global civil society must both refrain from violence and observe certain norms, especially that of civility, "a respect for others expressed as the acceptance of strangers and the willingness to live and work with them." But in "harboring many ways of life," global civil society is also characterized by strong pluralism *and* strong conflict potential, both with governments and within its own "vast, interconnected, and multi-layered non-governmental space." Finally, global civil society is truly *global,* "the most complex society in the history of the human species." And yet, for that reason, it is "riddled with power relations," as civil society movements and actors compete to get what they want at the local, regional, and global levels of political order.

8

Keane concludes by addressing some of the public and academic mis-understandings, and identifying some of the normative advantages of global civil society, calling in turn for "new languages of interpretation to help us to picture and understand its intricate social linkages stretched across vast distances." Surely one of his challenges to the Christian theologians who write in the second part of this volume, and to thinkers in all religions, is to bring such new languages of interpretation into the global public sphere from the rich storehouse of their own scriptures, traditions, and communities of faith and practice. For his own part, Keane sees the greatest threat to an ethically shaped and socially sustainable global civil society as a lack of political imagination and will to establish effective, efficient, and legitimate structures of global governance. The flourishing of "the web of civil society institutions that presently cover the earth" urgently requires a political theory of global civil society that will refute the fatalism of many in the face of the unconstrained power of economic and environmental globalization. Fresh political thinking is needed to empower citizens to fashion the necessary global political institutions in order to ensure a world for all. Typically, Keane, as a theorist of democracy, ends with a challenge to his readers: "Whether and to what extent it can or does succeed is for you and others to decide." More than any other research scholar or public intellectual, John Keane has helped us to respond to that challenge as informed, realistic, but not fatalistic, global citizens and people of faith.

Contesting Global Civil Society

By way of contrast with Keane's ultimately hopeful analysis, placing its confidence in the political agency of citizens, Kimberly Hutchings questions the assumption that global civil society is a necessarily civilizing force in the world, countering the violence of the international order of nation states.[3]

---

3. As Hutchings is the dissenting voice on global civil society in Part I, I shall give her arguments more detailed attention in this Introduction. For an extended theological critique of Keane's understanding of global civil society, and a different reading of the Scottish Enlightenment and civil society, readers should turn to the essays by Kristen Deede Johnson and William J. Danaher, respectively, in Part II. A salutary history or genealogy of the racialist notions underpinning trinitarian theologies of the global in the west since Columbus can be found in J. Kameron Carter's Epilogue, a Christological challenge to the trinitarian thinking on civil society in Part II of this volume. All of which confirms the editors' claim to be convening a conversation and not presenting a consensus among the contributors to *A World for All?*

At the outset, she asks a fundamental question of politics at any level: "what it means for politics to be genuinely civil." As an opening response, she offers a telling quotation from Hobbes' *Leviathan* that "covenants without the sword are words." But that is exactly her problem with the civilizing claims of the global civil society ideal. It is "an ideal of covenants (words) without the sword." Those who believe in the civilizing power of civil society at the global level of international politics are mistaken at both the conceptual and ontological level. The academic and civic advocates of this "progressivist hypothesis" operate with binary oppositions that do not hold up to close examination, whether in principle or in practice.

In particular, Hutchings questions the binary oppositions between state and non-state, global and international, civil and uncivil, which are embedded in the assumptions and actions of civil society theorists and actors. Each one does not bear scrutiny in her judgment. The distinction between state and non-state civil society spheres is too restrictive and prescriptive to allow for the reality of "more complex and dialectical modes in which they are mutually entangled." She acknowledges that there is a persuasive spatial distinction to be made between state and non-state, as "different kinds of political 'spaces.'" But even here there are problems in this binary distinction for Hutchings: "In literal terms, the spaces of civil society activism, from the streets to the internet to the conference platform, depend on enabling conditions, which in turn depend on economic, legal, and political conditions which are mediated through states." Similarly, she questions the distinction between the global and the international: the notion that a "world of thickening interdependence across borders of state and nation, mediated through explicitly trans-state or super-state mechanisms (market, media, technology)" will civilize the international order of inter-state relations, "the network of interaction, violent and non-violent, between sovereign entities." Again, she sees these two realms as interacting far more than the binary thinking of global civil society theorists and practitioners will allow:

> The idea that the global could civilize the international clearly depends on conceiving the global and international as distinct but simultaneously co-existing dimensions of world politics. Yet, on examination, the international mediates the global and the global mediates the international. As many scholars have pointed out, the state has been the leading international actor in globalization processes, as well as being influenced in turn by those processes. This is true in relation to economic as well as cultural globalization processes, from the globaliza-

tion of capital, to global transport and communication networks to international human rights regimes.

Finally, Hutchings considers what she regards as the most important and problematic distinction in the civilizing case for global civil society: the normative distinction between civil and uncivil, the civilized and the un-civilized. This binary distinction prevents us from recognizing and think-ing critically about the presence of violence in global civil society as well as in the international political order of sovereign states. The complex and cultivated presence of forms of violence and coercion in civilized societies is just as real as the violent state of nature that is often ascribed to the in-ternational order of nation states. For Hutchings, we have to "understand better the conditions of possibility of both violence and non-violence within the multiple contexts of world politics, including those contexts identified with global civil society, such as the activities of nongovern-mental organizations, transnational social movements, and cultural and religious organizations." On that point, her analysis challenges the theolo-gians writing in the second part of this volume to look self-critically at the violent history and tendencies of their own religious civilizations.

In conclusion, Hutchings offers a different moral vision for a civi-lized, non-violent life together amid the mediating and mixing worlds of state and non-state, global and international, civil and uncivil. Her con-cern is an ethical one:

> To the extent that the international is bad and global civil society is good, then we do not have to worry about potential exclusivity, hierar-chy, and coercion within the civil society realm — witting or unwitting — nor about the ways in which civil society activism and global gover-nance are interconnected as well as opposed. What I am trying to sug-gest . . . is that for those of us concerned with the inclusivity of the eth-ics of global civil society referred to in the title of this volume of essays, rather than asking the question of whether global civil society can civi-lize the international, we would be better advised to start by asking what a "civil," fundamentally non-coercive and non-violent global civil society might look like and what its conditions of possibility might be.

Drawing on the work of the American philosopher Judith Butler, she is con-cerned with what constitutes "the conditions of possibility of a liveable hu-man life," amid the complex and dialectical interdependencies of global civil society and the international political order "in the post 9/11 world." For Butler an individual human life is constituted by the norms of recognition operating in the larger society. A human life is liveable in both a physical and a psychic sense only if an individual is recognized as fully human. The norms of recognition on which the liveable human life depend are therefore both socially given and inseparable from the political question of power and power relations in society. A flourishing human life is possible only if that individual and her fully human identity are morally affirmed by other individuals in the wider culture. Such an inclusive social ethic is usually seen as depending on either the moral universalism deriving from the western liberal Enlightenment or the countervailing perspective of cultural and moral relativism. Both ethical bases are seen as inadequate by Butler and Hutchings for nurturing liveable human lives in global civil society.

Taking the example of the transnational feminist movement, they criticize western feminists for the maternalism of imposing the supposedly universal moral claims of the liberal Enlightenment about women's rights on women in postcolonial societies:

> From Butler's point of view, feminist global civil society activism may take on either an uncivil or a civil form. Feminist activism takes on a form of uncivility, when it seeks to reify one set of norms of recognition and leaves no space for the conceptions of "liveability" bound up with those forms to be challenged and transformed.

This is an example of the coercive nature of civil society ideas and actors, something not admitted by the "progressive hypothesis" of global civil society as an intrinsically non-violent and non-coercive phenomenon. As an alternative to liberal universalism as the ethical basis of a truly inclusive world for all, Hutchings affirms Butler's strategy of "mutual translation" for nurturing the contingent, not necessary, civility of global civil society. Continuing with her critique of trans-national feminism, Hutchings writes:

> ... "civil" civil society activism is about submitting to the "difficult labor" of cultural translation. And what this means is that feminist trans-national activists must ensure that they leave space to listen to as well as speak on behalf of women, and that they leave open the possibility of their own transformation as well as that of others.

In the politics of mutual translation, different civic groups and discourses in local and global civil society must seek to find common ground or at least map the limits of their mutual understanding. This is to be done through the honest admission of their unequal power relations and conflicting interests *within* civil society. Mutual translation in an inclusive civil society requires the recognition of the humanity of the other and the discipline of listening to and being transformed by the other. It seeks to translate different convictions to one another in civil ways, by trial and error rather than rational conformity to an *a priori* universal norm of an "authoritative meta-language."

Hutchings welcomes Butler's more realist understanding of the coercive nature of civil society, requiring a more robust civil politics of mutual translation and transformation. Here Hutchings returns to her opening, Hobbesian text, "Butler's work is helpful in forcing us to reflect on the difficulties of separating words from the sword even in civil society contexts." She is, however, critical of Butler's limiting of her "civil" politics of mutual recognition, translation, and trial and negotiation to civil society, conceived still in an all too idealized way. Hutchings closes with a plea for its extension to the international political order as well, seen not as a counter to but as a dialectical partner with global civil society.

Before leaving Hutchings's critical but not hostile questioning of the over-simplified assumptions of global civil society advocates, I want to highlight the importance of one key part of her argument from Butler for theology's conversation with this theoretical debate in the second part of this volume. It concerns Butler's understanding of the relationship between the universal and the particular:

> For Butler, "the relation of the universal to its cultural articulation is insuperable." She illustrates this by demonstrating how different substantive and procedural moral universalisms are only intelligible to the extent that they articulate their claims in terms that are drawn from available frameworks of meaning. Such frameworks inevitably reflect certain patterns and norms of recognition as opposed to others, and their universalizability is therefore dependent on the universalization of particularity (culturally, historically and socially).

And, we might add, religiously. Here is a critical link between the political theoretical and the Christian theological sections of the book. Butler does not see the universal as "a transcendental ground in which the meaning of being 'human' is known *a priori*." It is rather a commitment to having "the terms of the universal" re-signified "through challenges from the excluded." This is what makes the work of cultural translation for Butler a difficult labor:

> Moreover, there is no cultural consensus on an international level about what ought or ought not to be a claim to universality, who may make it, and what form it ought to take. Thus, for the claim to work, for it to compel consensus, and for the claim performatively to enact the very universality it enunciates, it must undergo a set of translations into the various rhetorical and cultural contexts in which the meaning and force of universal claims are made. (Butler, "Restaging the Universal")

In what follows in Part II, this could be seen as what is happening to the universal claims of the Christian Church to worship a triune God within civil society. In the various theological essays and contextual studies, these universal Christian theological claims about the nature of God and the world are being translated into various rhetorical and cultural contexts in which their meaning and force are operative in churches and local civil societies around the world today. In as much as the feminist civil politics of Butler and Hutchings is highlighting the importance of negotiating universal claims to human liveability through the recognition of particular local contexts and voices, then there is common ground for a conversation with Christian theologies of civil society that seek to do the same: recognizing the universal claims of Jesus Christ in the particular rhetorical and cultural contexts of churches committed to the excluded around the world. The extent to which such a *civil* Christian trinitarian theology can also rise to the challenge of civil dialogue and co-existence beyond the divided world of global Christianity, with other religious and secular traditions making equally universal claims, remains to be seen. That vital question of inter-religious civility for a liveable human future in a global era is beyond the more modest scope of this book but not beyond the agenda for further inquiry set by its theological contributors (as can be seen, for example, in the essays by Jayakiran Sebastian and Paul Louis Metzger).

Creating Global Civil Society

Finally, Max Stackhouse suggests ways in which religion and, in particular, certain Christian traditions of social thought are playing a constructive role in the creation of a global civil society. He first considers the historical

origins of the term "civil society" and the different interpretations of it offered by western thinkers such as Locke and Hegel and, more recently,
Jürgen Habermas. All are interested in that social zone where people develop voluntary relationships and institutions. Stackhouse sees three areas
of agreement between Locke and Hegel on the nature and character of civil
society, despite their basic disagreement on whether civil society (Locke)
or political society (Hegel) is paramount in human affairs. First, they are
both interested in those social relationships and mediating institutions
that lie between what they see as the two primary agents in society: the individual in the family and the collective in the state. Second, both Locke
and Hegel see the economic world of commerce as part of civil society, unlike the later Habermas, who has argued strongly to the contrary, seeing
modern forms of economic rationalization as a coercive and colonizing
threat to civil society. Stackhouse relates this economic question about
civil society to contemporary American debates on whether civic participation is declining, growing or just changing its character in the United
States. Third, and more importantly for Stackhouse's own argument on
global civil society, both Locke and Hegel assume "that religion will have a
role in forming persons and associations in civil society." Stackhouse bases
this claim on more recent scholarship on the neglected importance of religious influences on their social thought. This leads him to make a more
fundamental claim for the formative role of religion in history, and in social and political theory generally, a role too often ignored by contemporary advocates of civil society.

Stackhouse sets out to support this central thesis in his essay by considering first what Christianity did historically for civil society and then
asking which Christian social theories are best equipped to understand a
global future that will be "pluralistic in both religion and social structure."
For Stackhouse, the distinctive historical contribution of Christianity towards the rise of civil society in the West was its formation of self-
governing moral communities outside the structures of ethnicity or empire, fostering a sense of the common good beyond these particular loyalties. Whether in the monastic orders of the feudal era, the lay movements
of the Reformation, the independent congregations of Revolution-era
New England, the multiple social agencies and agendas of the ecumenical
movement of the twentieth century or in the new Evangelical, Pentecostal,
and liberationist forms of the church in the global South, Stackhouse sees
recurring institutional evidence for the ways in which Christianity has
shaped and is shaping a social order populated by self-regulating organiza-

tions with a variety of social forms and goals, the very kernel of a civil society. Stackhouse goes beyond that historical argument to make a further and more controversial assertion. He sees modernity and the forces of globalization, including global civil society, as emerging only out of a western culture shaped in significant part by the social theories of two particular Christian traditions, Roman Catholic and Reformed. He writes: "These two branches of the faith, the Catholic and the Reformed, see it as part of the duty of Christianity . . . to form and sustain the social ecology of the common life for the well-being of all." What they have in common is "a capacity to cultivate pluralism while preserving a sense of unity," although the historical impact of this piety on polity and policy only happens "over decades, generations, and centuries." They do so with different social models. Stackhouse calls the Catholic model of this social ecology the "hierarchical-subsidiarity" view and the Reformed model the "federal-covenantal" view. Together in some adaptive combination, these two social models could provide the theoretical and institutional resources to shape a new civilization for a global era, according to Stackhouse, one that manifests "a fresh view of responsible citizenship in a global civil society" and "a promising vision of the catholicity of the churches and the ecumenicity of the great faiths."

This last inclusive, inter-religious note should be heard and not forgotten in reading Stackhouse's account of the Christian elements shaping civil society or the Christian theological essays on global civil society that follow in Part II. As the editors say in the Preface, this volume is only one interdisciplinary contribution from political theory and Christian theology to a much wider conversation on global civil society. In that wider discussion, far beyond these pages, inter-religious scholarship has a vital contribution to make, one that we welcome. Whatever the verdict in the wider debate on the role of religion in forming a global civil society, all four of these opening essayists ask the question that haunted Thomas Reid and his fellow preachers in the Scottish Enlightenment and my fellow university cleaner in his native city of Edinburgh: how can we make a world for all, one that affirms both our differences and our common humanity?

A World for All? Thoughts on Global Civil Society

John Keane

When historians look back on our times, they are sure to note a most remarkable development: the end of the world that was familiar to Adam Smith. When Smith, in *Wealth of Nations* (1776), famously analyzed the market economies of the Atlantic region, he supposed that industries and services of all kinds enjoyed a "natural protection" from foreign competition, thanks to geographical distance. The world of Adam Smith was influenced by a political economy in which business was mainly "homespun," and it remained so well into the twentieth century. It was a world of *shallow integration:* arm's length trade in raw materials, goods, and service among independent firms and by means of international movements of capital.

Our world, by contrast, is caught up in processes of *deep integration.* This intensive integration — I have argued in *Global Civil Society?* (2003) — is heavily responsible for stimulating a new global awareness. Business is a bridge, and often enough a battering ram, a force that breaks down barriers among peoples, cultures, and geographic regions. There are other globalizing forces at work, including efforts at cross-border political and legal integration and civic initiatives and social movements, but business is undoubtedly a prime mover in fostering strong images of ourselves as involved in a great human adventure, one that not only is carried out on a global scale but also stimulates a new awareness that we are being drawn into a global civil society.

These three unfamiliar words, global civil society — a neologism of the last twenty years — were born at the confluence of a number of overlapping streams of concern among publicly-minded intellectuals at the end of the 1980s. Of special importance were the revival of the old language of civil society, especially in central-eastern Europe, after the military crushing of the Prague Spring; the heightened appreciation of the revolutionary effects of the new galaxy of satellite/computer-mediated communications (captured in Marshall McLuhan's famous neologism, "the global village"); the new awareness, stimulated by the peace and ecological movements, of ourselves as members of a fragile and potentially self-destructive world system; and the world-wide growth spurt of neoliberal economics and market capitalist economies structured by deep integration.[1] Fed by such developments, talk of global civil society has become popular among citizens' campaigners, bankers, diplomats, nongovernmental organizations, and politicians. World Bank documents welcome "the opportunity to work with civil society"; the Asian Development Bank similarly speaks of the need to "strengthen cooperation with civil society"; and even the World Trade Organization (WTO) declares its support for dialogue with the world's civil society institutions.[2] In these and other contexts, the phrase "global civil society" tends to become protean and promiscuous, to the point where some observers understandably grow skeptical and begin to ask: what do these words actually mean?

There is general agreement that talk of global civil society is a re-

1. Among the earliest expressions of these concerns is the theory of a "world civic culture" in Elise Boulding, *Building a Global Civic Culture: Education for an Interdependent World* (New York: Teachers College Press, 1988); the idea of "global civilization" in the working paper by Richard Falk, "Economic Dimensions of Global Civilization" (Global Civilization Project, Center for International Studies, Princeton University, 1990); the theory of the "internationalisation" of civil society and the terms "cosmopolitan civil society" and "global" or "transnational" civil society in John Keane, "The Future of Civil Society," in Tatjana Sikosha, *The Internationalisation of Civil Society* (The Hague, 1989) and *The Media and Democracy* (Cambridge: Polity Press, 1991), pp. 135ff.; and Morten Ougaard, "The Internationalisation of Civil Society" (Center for Udviklingsforskning, Copenhagen, June 1990). Among the first efforts to draw together this early work is Ronnie Lipschutz, "Reconstructing World Politics: The Emergence of Global Civil Society," *Millennium* 21, no. 3 (1992): pp. 389-420.

2. Each case is cited in Aziz Choudry, "All this 'civil society' talk takes us nowhere" (http://globalresearch.ca/articles/AZ1201A.html), p. xxi; cf. the call for "a new international social covenant between markets, states and civil society" in Gerhard Schröder, ed., *Progressive Governance for the XXI Century: Contribution to the Berlin Conference* (Munich: C. H. Beck, 2002), p. xxi; "The United Nations: Partners in Civil Society," www.un.org/partners/civil_society/home.htm; Madeleine Albright, *Focus on the Issues: Strengthening Civil Society and the Rule of Law. Excerpts of Testimony, Speeches and Remarks by U.S. Secretary of State Madeleine K. Albright* (Washington, DC: U.S. Department of State, 2000).

sponse to rising concerns about the need for a new social and economic and political deal at the global level. And parallels are sometimes observed with the early modern European invention of the distinction between government and civil society, which emerged during the period of questioning of the transcendental foundations of order, especially of monarchic states claiming authority from God.[3] Beyond this elementary consensus, many discrepancies and disagreements are evident. Some writers, policy makers, and activists see in the idea of global civil society a way of *analyzing* and *interpreting* the empirical contours of past, present, or emergent social relationships at the world level. Others mainly view the concept in pragmatic terms, as a guide to formulating a *political strategy;* still others view it as a *normative ideal.* In practice, these different emphases often crisscross and complement each other. Yet since they can and do also produce divergent types of claims, it is important to distinguish among them and, as far as possible, to avoid mixing them up and producing confusion.

Given the versatility of the term, which is surely one of the reasons for its rising popularity, it follows that its different usages should not be conflated, as is typically done when the words global civil society are flung about in vague, simplistic, or tendentious speech. This is the point at which an attempt carefully and prudently to define global civil society must be made. Allow me to try my hand, initially by using it as ideal-type concept — as an intentionally produced mental construct or "cognitive type" (Umberto Eco) that is very useful for heuristic and expository purposes, for naming and clarifying the myriad of elements of a complex social reality, even though it cannot be found in such "pure" form anywhere within the social world itself. When the term global civil society is used in this way, as an ideal-type, it properly refers to *a dynamic non-governmental system of interconnected socio-economic institutions that straddle the whole earth, and that have complex effects that are felt in its four corners. Global civil society is neither a static object nor a fait accompli. It is an unfinished project that con-*

3. Compare my "Despotism and Democracy: The Origins and Development of the Distinction Between Civil Society and the State 1750-1850," in *Civil Society and the State: New European Perspectives,* ed. John Keane (London and New York: Verso, 1988 [reprinted 1998]), pp. 35-72, and Adam Seligman, "Civil Society as Idea and Ideal," in *Alternative Conceptions of Civil Society,* ed. Simone Chambers and Will Kymlicka (Princeton: Princeton University Press, 2002), pp. 13-33. In my view, Seligman's explanation of the rise of the ideal of a civil society suffers from the same weakness evident in Marxian accounts: their one-sided emphasis upon the growth of market economies and the corresponding search for a new ethical order in which individual interests could be reconciled with the public good.

sists of sometimes thick, sometimes thinly, stretched networks, pyramids, and hub-and-spoke clusters of socio-economic institutions and actors who organize themselves across borders, with the deliberate aim of drawing the world together in new ways. These non-governmental institutions and actors tend to pluralize power and to problematize violence; consequently, their peaceful or "civil" effects are felt everywhere, here and there, far and wide, to and from local areas, through wider regions, to the planetary level itself.

Contours

I should like to look carefully at six elements of this rather abstract definition. Considered together, these tightly coupled features of global civil society mark it off as historically distinctive. To begin with, the term global civil society refers to *non-governmental* structures and activities. It comprises individuals, households, profit-seeking businesses, not-for-profit non-governmental organizations, coalitions, social movements, and linguistic communities and cultural identities. It feeds upon the work of media celebrities and past or present public personalities — from Gandhi, Bill Gates, Primo Levi, and Martin Luther King to Bono and Aung San Suu Kyi, Bishop Ximenes Belo, Naomi Klein, and al-Waleed bin Talal. It includes charities, think tanks, prominent intellectuals (like Tu Wei-ming and Abdolkarim Soroush), campaigning and lobby groups, citizens' protests responsible for "clusters of performances,"[4] small and large corporate firms, independent media, Internet groups and websites, employers' federations, trades unions, international commissions, parallel summits, and sporting organizations. It comprises bodies like Amnesty International, Sony, Falun Gong, Christian Aid, al Jazeera, the Catholic Relief Services, the Indigenous Peoples Bio-Diversity Network, FIFA, Transparency International, Sufi networks like Qadiriyya and Naqshabandiyya, the International Red Cross, the Global Coral Reef Monitoring Network, the Ford Foundation, Shack/Slum Dwellers International, Women Living Under Muslim Laws, News Corporation International, OpenDemocracy.net. Considered together, these institutions and actors constitute a vast, interconnected, and multi-layered non-governmental space that comprises

4. Charles Tilly, "From Interactions to Outcomes in Social Movements," in *How Social Movements Matter,* ed. Marco Giugni et al. (Minneapolis: University of Minnesota Press, 1999), p. 263.

many hundreds of thousands of more-or-less self-directing ways of life. All of these forms of life have at least one thing in common: across vast geographic distances and despite barriers of time, they deliberately organize themselves and conduct their cross-border social activities, business, and politics outside the boundaries of governmental structures.

Second, we can say that global civil *society* refers to a vast, sprawling non-governmental constellation of many institutionalized structures, associations, and networks within which individual and group actors are interrelated and functionally interdependent. As a society of societies, it is "bigger" and "weightier" than any individual actor or organization or combined sum of its thousands of constituent parts — most of whom, paradoxically, neither "know" each other nor have any chance of ever meeting each other face-to-face. Global civil society is a highly complex ensemble of differently sized, overlapping forms of structured social action; like a Tolstoy novel, it is a vast scenario in which hundreds of thousands and millions of individual and group adventures unfold, sometimes harmoniously through co-operation and compromise, and sometimes conflictually. Like all societies in the strict sense, it has a marked life or momentum or power of its own. Its institutions and rules have a definite durability, in that at least some of them can and do persist through long cycles of time. Global civil society, as I try to show in *Global Civil Society?*, has much older roots. Most non-European civilizations have made contributions to it, and the effects upon our own times of early modern European developments — the ground-breaking workers' movements and pacifist traditions, and the growth spurt of globalization during the half-century before World War One — are easily observed. The institutions of present-day global civil society, like those of any functioning society, both predate the living and outlive the life-span of this society's individual members, every one of whom is shaped and carried along in life by the social customs and *traditions* of this global society. In various ways, the social actors of global civil society are both constrained and empowered by this society. These actors are enmeshed within codes of unwritten and written rules that both enable and restrict their action in the world; they come to understand that many things are possible, but that not everything goes, that some things are desirable, and that some things are not possible, or that they are forbidden. Within global civil society — which is only one particular form of society — social actors' involvement in institutions obliges them to refrain from certain actions, as well as to observe certain *norms,* for instance those that define what counts as civility.

Civility — respect for others expressed as the acceptance of strangers and the willingness to live and work with them — is a third quality of this global society. Different civilizations entertain different notions of civility — they each make civil persons, as John Ruskin said — but, because our world is comprised of intermingling civilizations that are not in any sense self-contained or "pure,"[5] global civil society is a space inhabited by various overlapping norms of *non-violent* politeness covering matters of indirection, self-restraint, and face-saving. This society is a complex and multi-dimensional space of non-violence, though it is by no means an irenic paradise on earth. On the outskirts of global civil society, and within its nooks and crannies, dastardly things go on. It provides convenient hideouts for gangsters, war criminals, arms traders, and terrorists. It contains pockets of *incivility* — geographic areas that coexist uneasily with "safe" and highly "civil" zones, dangerous areas like the Strasbourg district of Neuhof, with its crumbling buildings, walls splattered with graffiti, and streets littered with car wrecks; the Los Angeles suburb of South Central, considered by many a "no-go area," whose night streets are owned by murderous black, Latino, and Asian gangs; and whole cities like Ahmadabad in Gujarat, where in early 2002 many hundreds of people, mainly Muslims, were killed and wounded by semi-planned rioting, sabotage, and ethnic cleansing, helped by local police with blind eyes. The spaces of freedom within global civil society also enable individuals and groups to network, in the form of criminal gangs that run world-wide industries. The contemporary formation of terrorist networks that crisscross "home" and "abroad" would be unthinkable without the help of global civil society. Another example is the sale and sex trafficking of young girls and boys — an industry that is now contested by both governments (as in the 1996 Stockholm declaration of 122 countries against all forms of child sexual exploitation) and social campaign networks, like Plan International and End Child Prostitution, Pornography and Trafficking. What is interesting and important about such social initiatives is that they specialize in repairing the torn fabric of global civil society. They work for greater mutual respect, human dignity, and compromise among different ways of life. They organize against harmful prejudices (for instance, the belief that sleeping with a child can give protection against, or even cure, HIV infection), and they

5. Felipe Fernández-Armesto, *Millennium: A History of Our Last Thousand Years* (London and New York: Bantam Press, 1995), chapter 1, and *Civilizations* (London: Pan Books, 2000).

press political authorities to engage in legal and policing reforms which serve to restrict access to predator groups like tourists, businessmen, and soldiers on overseas duty. The implication of this third point is clear: global civil society is not just any old collection of ways of life that have nothing in common but their non-identification with governing institutions. Factually speaking, this society encourages compromise and mutual respect. There is (to speak literally and metaphorically) plenty of room within its walls for people who believe in God, as well as for religious people for whom the idea of a creator God is anathema, as well as for people who feel only diffuse respect for the sacred, as well as for people who believe in nothing else except themselves. Insofar as these various actors have a more or less deep sensitivity towards violence and violence-prone institutions, they enable global civil society to be "civil" in a double sense: it consists of non-governmental (or "civilian") institutions that tend to have non-violent (or "civil") effects.

Exactly because global civil society harbors many ways of life it means many different things to those who live their lives within its structures. This is its fourth quality: it contains both strong traces of *pluralism* — and *strong conflict potential*. To speak (as some do) of a "world order" or "one world" or "a global community" is misleading: the world is in fact sub-divided in two basic ways by the emergent global society. First, its civilian institutions place limits upon government. Global civil society serves as a cross-border brake or potential check upon various forms of government, and especially absolutist political rule. *All* governmental institutions, from local councils through territorial states and regional and supra-national institutions like the United Nations and the World Trade Organization, are now feeling the pinching effects of this civil society. Meanwhile, secondly, scuffles and skirmishes over the distribution of socio-economic power also regularly take place *within* global civil society itself. These contests typically become visible through media coverage, which attracts witnesses to both local and world-wide disputes concerning who gets what, when and how. In this way, global civil society functions as a monitoring and signaling platform, from which both local matters — mimicking the butterfly effect that has been held responsible for fluctuations in whole weather patterns — can assume global importance, and global-level problems (like nuclear weapons, terrorism, the environment) are named, defined, and problematized. A sense of "the world" and "humanity" as complex and vulnerable totalities consequently strengthens. But global civil society — contrary to its communitarian interpreters —

does not resemble a "global community" (Etzioni).[6] For its participants, rather, this society nurtures a culture of self-awareness about the hybridity and complexity of the world.

The heterogeneity of global civil society works against enforced unity. It throws into question presumptions about spontaneous sympathy and automatic consensus.[7] It heaps doubt upon claims (famously associated with Seneca) that all human beings are "social animals." This complex society is not a space wherein people naturally touch and feel good about the world. Certainly that happens. Dressed in the clothing of honest pilgrims, young people take time off, travel the world, odd-job, sleep rough, sleep around, wonder and marvel at the complexity and beauty of the world, just like a satisfied botanist observing and contemplating the extraordinary complexity of plant life. Others meanwhile dedicate their lives to charitable or volunteer work by putting their minds and hearts to work with others. They speak of compassion and practice it. Yet despite all this, the world of global civil society can be tough, calculating, and rough 'n' tumble. It looks and feels expansive and polyarchic, full of horizontal push and pull, vertical conflict and compromise.

The volume of this worldly self-awareness of the contested complexity of the world should not be exaggerated. It is hard to estimate its extent, but probably only five percent of the world's population has an acute awareness of the tightening interdependence of the world, its ecosystems, institutions, and peoples. Perhaps another twenty-five per cent are moderately or dimly aware of this interdependence. While most others have not (yet) thought over the matter, or do not much care, or are too cynical or self-preoccupied to open their eyes and ears, the aggregate numbers of those who are globally aware are weighty enough to spread awareness that global civil society exists; that it is a force to be reckoned with; that it both operates within, and resembles, a patchwork quilt of power relations.

This brings me to its fifth feature: global civil society is most definitely riddled with *power relations*. Its social groups and organizations and movements lobby states, bargain with international organizations, pressure and bounce off other non-state bodies, invest in new forms of production, champion different ways of life, and engage in charitable direct

6. Amitai Etzioni, "Toward A New World Architecture?" unpublished paper (Washington, DC, 2002).

7. Francis Fukuyama, *The Great Disruption: Human Nature and the Reconstitution of Social Order* (New York: Free Press, 1999), chapter 13.

action in distant local communities, for instance through "capacity-building" programs that supply jobs, clean running water, sporting facilities, hospitals, and schools. In these various ways, the members of global civil society help to conserve or to alter the power relations embedded in the chains of interaction linking the local, regional, and planetary orders. Their cross-border links and networks help to define and redefine who gets what, when, and how in the world. Of great importance is the fact that these cross-border patterns have the power to stimulate awareness among the world's inhabitants that mutual understanding of different ways of life is a practical necessity, that we are being drawn into the first genuinely bottom-up transnational order, a global civil society, in which millions of people come to realize, in effect, that they are incarnations of worldwide webs of interdependence, whose complexity is riddled with opportunity, as well as danger.

To say this is to note — this sixth and final point is obvious, but most crucial — that global civil society is *global*. To speak of a *global* civil society is to refer to politically framed and circumscribed social relations that stretch across and underneath state boundaries and other governmental forms. This "macro-society" or "society of interlocking societies" consists of a myriad of social interactions stretched across vast geographic distances. Global civil society is the most complex society in the history of the human species. It comprises a multitude of different parts, which are connected in a multitude of different ways. These diverse components interact both serially and in parallel, and they produce effects that are often both simultaneous and sequential. These effects, while normally generated by local interactions and events, have emergent properties that tend to be global. We are not exactly speaking here of a "vast empire of human society, as it is spread over the whole earth" (Wordsworth).[8] Global civil society is neither a new form of empire (a "global society of control" as Hardt and Negri have claimed) nor encompassing of the whole earth,[9] but it certainly is a special form of *unbounded* society marked by constant feedback among its many components.

The unbounded quality of this civil society arguably requires new perspectives and new languages of interpretation to help us picture and

8. From William Wordsworth's preface to *Lyrical Ballads, with Other Poems* (2nd edition, London, 1800).

9. Compare the claim that there is a spreading new form of empire — a "global society of control" — ruled by global capital in Michael Hardt and Antonio Negri, *Empire* (Cambridge, MA, and London: Harvard University Press, 2000), especially pp. 325-350.

understand its intricate social linkages stretched across vast distances. Perhaps (to take one example) this society can be likened to the tens and hundreds of thousands of "nested systems within nested systems" described in certain versions of complexity theory.[10] Seen in this way, global civil society is both integrated and de-centered, sustained by many different actually existing societies, whose members regularly interact and/or feel the effects of others' actions across political boundaries. These effects are not due to proximity alone; they are felt at great distances, usually by social actors who have no direct contact with one another, and who are otherwise fated to remain "strangers" to one another. This interdependence of global civil society — to switch for a moment to ecological similes — resembles a vast, dynamic biosphere. It comprises a bewildering variety of complex interacting habitats and species: international non-governmental organizations (INGOs), voluntary groups, businesses, civic initiatives, social movements, protest organizations, whole nations, ethnic and linguistic clusters, pyramids, and networks. To compare this society with a vast biosphere that stretches to every corner of the earth is to underscore both the great complexity of its linkages and its vulnerability to internal and external interference. Just as nearly every part of the earth, from the highest mountains to the deepest seas, supports life, so too global civil society is now found on virtually every part of the earth's surface. To be sure, everywhere it is tissue-thin — just like the natural biosphere, which resembles a paper wrapping that covers a sphere the size of a football — and its fringes, where ice and permafrost predominate, are virtually inhospitable. In the interior of the Antarctic, only restricted populations of bacteria and insects are to be found; and even on its coasts there are very few living inhabitants, among which are a handful of flowering plant species, as well as seals, whales, penguins, and other birds. Global civil society is similarly subject to geographic limits: whole zones of the earth, parts of contemporary Afghanistan, Burma, Chechenya, and Sierra Leone for instance, are no-go areas for civil society actors and institutions, which can survive only by going underground.

But in those areas of the earth where it does exist, global civil society comprises many biomes — whole areas (like North America and the Euro-

10. The vast literature includes David Bohm and F. David Peat, *Science, Order, and Creativity* (London and New York: Routledge, 2000), and John Briggs and F. David Peat, *Turbulent Mirror: An Illustrated Guide to Chaos Theory and the Science of Wholeness* (New York: Perennial Library, 1990).

pean Union and parts of the Muslim world) characterized by specific animals and plants and climatic conditions. Each biome in turn comprises large numbers of living ecosystems made up of clusters of organisms living within a non-living physical environment of rocks, soil, and climate. These ecosystems of global civil society — cities, business corridors, and regions for instance — are interconnected. And they are more or less intricately balanced, through continuous flows and recycling of efforts among (as it were) populations of individuals of the same species, which thrive within communities (such as smaller cities) that are themselves embedded within non-living geographic contexts.

Prospects

Defined in this way, as a vast, interconnected, and multi-layered non-governmental space that comprises many hundreds of thousands of self-directing institutions and ways of life that generate global effects, the ideal-type concept of global civil society invites us to improve our understanding of the emerging planetary order. It calls on us to think more deeply about it, in the hope that we can strengthen our collective powers of guiding and transforming it. This clearly requires sharpening up our courage to confront the unknown and to imagine different futures.[11] And it most definitely obliges us to abandon some worn-out certainties and outdated prejudices. Let us dwell for a moment on what the new understanding of global civil society obliges us to give up.

Among the primary needs is to question the current habit among researchers and publics of speaking of civil societies as "national" phenomena and, thus, of supposing or implying that global civil society and domestic civil societies are binary opposites. Many are still tempted to think in (architectural) terms of two different "levels" of civil society — the "national" and the "global" — as if *homo civilis* was a divided creature, strangely at odds with itself, rather like a figure in the prose of Kleist: a figure pulled simultaneously in two different directions, towards "home" and away from "home." "Global civil society," runs one version of this way of thinking, is "a transnational domain in which people form relationships

---

11. A stimulating example of such rethinking that is guided by the idea of a global civil society is Michael Edwards, *Future Positive: International Co-operation in the 21st Century* (London: Earthscan, 1999).

and develop elements of identity outside their role as a citizen of a particular state." It "represents a sphere that thus transcends the self-regarding character of the state system and can work in the service of a genuinely transnational, public interest."[12] Note the strong presumption that politically defined territory remains the ultimate foundation of civil society institutions — as if "the global" was an add-on extra, a homeless extra-territorial phenomenon. Note as well how such images of global civil society draw upon architectural metaphors of up and down, here and there. They imply that the world of civil societies is split into two levels — that "domestic" civil society is "self-regarding," whereas the other-regarding global civil society is "above and beyond national, regional, or local societies," or "above the national level."[13] Exactly how the two "levels" are related, or how "citizens" climb up and down the ladders in between, is left unclear.

In fact — the exemplary case is that of Ireland, easily the most globalized country in the world — the language of "domestic" and "foreign" or "the local" and "the global," as well as the architectural simile of "above and beyond," are downright misleading. Within the forces and processes that operate from within global civil society there is no clear line separating the "national" from the "global"; the two dimensions, the "inside" and the "outside," constantly intersect and co-define each other. Take a simple example: jeans. This item of clothing is worn world-wide, and one might even say, with just a touch of exaggeration, that jeans are the prized uniform of millions of people who live, work, and play within civil societies. As an item of clothing, everybody knows that it had local American origins, and that as an American commodity jeans have traveled well. They are today a relatively cheap and popular form of casual dress on every continent, in over a hundred countries. Yet this globalization of jeans has not been synonymous with the homogenization of meaningful ways of life. Jeans are not worn in identical ways with identical connotations — the Marlboro Man on his ranch competes for attention with Thai youths on motorcycles and Lebanese young women, veiled and unveiled, relaxing together in esplanade cafés, all wearing jeans, in non-standard ways. All these

12. Paul Wapner, "The Normative Promise of Nonstate Actors: A Theoretical Account of Global Civil Society," in Paul Wapner and Lester Edwin J. Ruiz, eds., *Principled World Politics: The Challenge of Normative International Relations* (Lanham, MD: Rowman and Littlefield, 2000), p. 261.

13. Helmut Anheier et al., "Introducing Global Civil Society," in *Global Civil Society 2001,* ed. Helmut Anheier et al. (Oxford and New York: Oxford University Press, 2001), pp. 4, 3.

figures are incarnations of worldwide cultural webs that are themselves bound up with latticed global networks of production that deliver raw and processed materials like copper from Namibia, cotton from Benin and Pakistan, zinc from Australia, thread from Northern Ireland and Hungary, synthetic dye from Germany, pumice from Turkey, polyester tape from France, and steel zips machined in Japan.

The simple example of jeans highlights the normal patterns of complexity in the globalization of civil society. It drives home the point that the so-called domestic and the global — to draw upon similes from the field of physics — are marked by strong interactions of the kind that hold together the protons and neutrons inside an atomic nucleus; or, to switch to the language of complexity theory, the domestic and the global are normally linked together in complex, cross-border patterns of looped and re-looped circuitry. When it comes to understanding the dynamics of global civil society, there is no definable or decidable boundary between interiority and exteriority. The "micro" and the "meso" and the "macro" dimensions of this society are both interconnected and co-determinant of each other. The tiniest and the largest operations and events are implicated in loops that produce feedback — ranging from system-simplifying and system-upsetting (or negative) forms through to feedback that is more positive, in that it produces effects that are disproportionate to their causes, so adding to the overall heterogeneity and dynamism of the components of the global social system.

To repeat: the use of ecological similes and themes drawn from complexity theory may be questionable, but they serve the basic purpose of identifying the urgent need to develop theoretical imagery for better imagining global civil society, as it is and as it might become. The rule of thumb, both in the past and in the present, is that the liveliest "local" civil societies are those enjoying the strongest worldwide links. To speak of a global civil society is to highlight the intricate patterns of interdependence and co-dependence of its many different parts, their implication as nodal points within an open system of networks fueled by feedback and feed-forward loops. It is important to see that, just as within locally bounded societies larger social aggregates like trade unions often reinforce (rather than simply subsume) the power and status of smaller social units, like households, so the relationship between these more local civil society units and their more distant or globalizing connectors is not a zero-sum relationship.

Another misunderstanding has to do with whether or not, or to what extent, talk of global civil society is a wooden horse for "Westernization." It is significant, and profoundly ironical, that descriptive usages of the concept of global civil society have now spread to every continent of the globe. The birth and maturation of global civil society have been riddled with many ironies. I have tried to show in various writings that its civil institutions can even be understood and defended as the condition of a healthy, publicly shared sense of irony, but for the moment here is among the strangest ironies of all: an originally European way of life, some of whose members set out brutally to colonize the world in the name of a civil society, helped lay the foundations for its own universal appeal and, with that, strengthened civil resistance to colonizing forms of power and prejudice originally traceable to the European region. The revolts of the colonized in the name of a "civilized society" against British imperial power in the eighteenth-century American colonies was the first-ever case in point of this unintended consequence. There have subsequently been many more and recent instances of these ironic, failed attempts to crush the willpower of a (potentially) self-governing civil society through armed state or imperial power that once prided itself on its own "civilizing mission." Examples range from the gentle and prolonged resistance to imperial power by locally formed civil societies (as in Australia and New Zealand) to the volcanic upheavals against colonial and post-colonial power in contexts otherwise as different as Haiti, India, South Africa, and Nigeria.

One important effect of such unintended developments is observable: the contemporary "emigration" of the language of civil society, from its original birthplace in Europe to all four corners of the earth.[14] In recent years, the family of terms "civil society" and "global civil society" have proved to be good travelers. After making a first appearance in Japan and then developing vigorously in the European region, including its eastern fringes, the terms spread to the United States and Canada, and throughout central and South America. They have appeared as well throughout sub-Saharan Africa, Oceania, and all regions of Asia and the Muslim world.[15]

14. See my *Civil Society: Old Images and New Visions* (Stanford: Stanford University Press, 1998), especially pp. 32ff.

15. The literature is vast and still growing rapidly. Among the best-known contributions are *Civil Society: History and Possibilities,* ed. Sudipta Kaviraj and Sunil Khilnani (Cambridge and New York: Cambridge University Press, 2001); *Civil Society in the Middle East,* 2 volumes, ed. Richard Augustus Norton (Leiden and New York: Brill, 1995); *Civil Society: Challenging Western Models,* ed. Chris Hann and Elizabeth Dunn (London and New York: Routledge, 1996); *Emerging Civil Society in the Asia Pacific Community: Nongovernmental Underpinnings of the Emerging Asia Pacific Regional Community,* ed. Tadashi

This globalization of the concept of civil society is one aspect of the emergent global civil society, for it shows how civil society ideas and languages and institutions are spreading beyond their place of origin into new contexts, where they are in turn conceptualized or re-conceptualized in local contexts, from where the revisions, which are sometimes cast in very different terms, often feed back as "re-exports" into the original donor contexts.[16] Hence, the language of civil society is both pluralized and globalized and comes to have entangled meanings that suggest that it is not just a Western privilege (Gellner). Not only is talk of civil society now heard world-wide within circles of journalists, lawyers, and academics. Non-governmental organizations, business people, professionals, diplomats, and politicians of various persuasions also like to speak the same language. The spreading talk of civil society may well convince future historians to look back on this globalization of the term and to judge that its global extension, which is without precedent, signaled the birth of something new in the world: the unprecedented (if unevenly distributed) growth of the sense within non-governmental organizations and publics at large that civilians live in one world, that their lives dangle on ten thousand strings, and that they have common interests and obligations to other civilians living beyond their borders, simply because they are civilians.

Paradise on Earth?

These reflections on global civil society have mainly concentrated on questions of definition. Normative questions — what is so good about global civil society, why we should dream of it at night and chase after it by day — have been ignored. There is no time to work through questions of global ethics. I have dealt with them at length in *Global Civil Society?* and so it is worth just asserting here that its normative advantages are three-fold. First, carefully defined, it is the only grand "earthly" norm that strives for

Yamamoto (Singapore and Tokyo: Institute of Southeast Asian Studies and Japan Center for International Exchange, 1995); *Civil Society and the Political Imagination in Africa: Critical Perspectives,* ed. John L. and Jean Comaroff (Chicago and London: University of Chicago Press, 1999); and *Civil Society and the State: New European Perspectives,* ed. John Keane (London and New York: Verso, 1988 [1998]).

16. Makoto Iokibe, "Japan's Civil Society: An Historical Overview," in *Deciding the Public Good: Governance and Civil Society in Japan,* ed. Tadashi Yamamoto (Tokyo and New York: Japan Center for International Exchange, 1999).

universality by insisting on peoples' entitlements to be different while insisting on their duties to respect each other as equals — hence, the most powerful available shield against destructive and violent and arrogant "isms," such as xenophobia, nationalism, religious bigotry, and "fundamentalisms" of all kinds. Second, the norm of a global civil society, with its emphasis on the non-governmental, and hence the desirability of placing limits upon what governments can and should do with their subjects, is a basic ingredient of any attempt to think through what "global democracy" might mean. Third, global civil society is a norm that works in favor of what I have elsewhere called the "democratization of violence." It does so by calling into question the supposed "naturalness" or inevitability of violence and violence-prone movements, organizations, and institutions.

Although questions of strategy — the political problem of how to defend and to extend and to shake up and equalize the relations of power within global civil society — have not been central in my remarks, it goes without saying that actually existing global civil society poses big political challenges, simply because it is no paradise on earth. Global civil society enables individuals, groups and organizations to organize and to deploy their powers across borders, despite remaining barriers of time and distance. This society provides non-governmental structures and rules which enable individuals and groups to move and to decide things, to follow their inclinations, to bring governmental power-holders to heel, to engage in many kinds of mutually beneficial exchanges, even to work for the socialization of market economies so that production for social need, rather than for profit, prevails. This society makes it easier and cheaper for trades unions and campaigners against hunger to co-ordinate their actions, for companies in Seoul to ship goods to Italy, for the aboriginal peoples of northern Canada to keep in touch with their brothers and sisters in southern Africa; it enables the residents of Melbourne to visit relatives in Athens, activists in Vancouver to challenge the timber-cutting policies of Indonesians and Brazilians, and large banks in Frankfurt and Tokyo to manage their world-wide foreign-exchange positions around the globe, from one branch to another, always staying ahead of the setting sun.

Global civil society, as Michael Walzer has said so aptly,[17] resembles a project of projects. It resounds of liberty, with all its multifariousness, awkwardness, challenges, and hope. Its civilities tend to be independent-

17. Michael Walzer, "The Concept of Civil Society," in *Toward a Global Civil Society,* ed. idem (Providence and Oxford: Berghahn, 1995), p. 27.

minded and active, rather than deferential. It is rich in freedoms within and beyond borders: for example, to keep in touch with others who are loved and valued; to accumulate money and wealth; to consume products that were once considered exotic, in any season; to travel, to make friends across borders, and to reunite with others, virtually or actually; and to re-build damaged infrastructures by recovering memories, protecting the vulnerable, raising hopes, and generating new wealth and income. Global civil society offers other possibilities: "spaces of hope"[18] in which to warn the world of threats to its security and to denounce and to reduce violence and uncivil war; the freedom to press the principle that social and political power beyond borders should be subject to greater public accountability; and, generally, the opportunity to rescue the culture of "cosmopolitanism" from its negative connotations of jet-setting, leisured individuals loyal to no one and bent on selfishly sampling all cultures at will — replacing such connotations through the defense of a *worldly* politics (the Make Poverty History campaigns are a case in point) that cultivates the need for transna-tional mobility of viewpoint and action in support of justice and freedom for all of the earth's inhabitants.

In these various ways, global civil society potentially enables millions of people to *socialize* definitions of our global order — even to *imagine* its positive reconstruction. Unfortunately, such freedoms or spatial opportu-nities are currently unfolding in a hell for leather, Wild West fashion, and are also very unevenly distributed. The freedoms of global civil society are exclusionary and fail to produce equalities; in other words, global civil so-ciety is not genuinely global. It is not a *universal* society. Vast areas of the world, and certainly the large majority of the world's population, are ex-cluded from active involvement. True, they "participate" within this soci-ety in the minimal sense that they are sometimes seen fleetingly, by the privileged, mostly as anonymous television or newspaper images and bro-ken voices and reported tales of woe. In an era of rapid communications, the marginalized know that the world is a ladder on which some go up and many go down. They see and feel their abjectness refracted through their encounters with the guardians of power and prosperity. The wretched of the earth come to develop a world-wide reputation for malnutrition, dis-ease, homelessness, and death.

They are seen as well as victims robbed of a voice by the cruel facts of communication poverty. It is common knowledge that three-quarters of

18. David Harvey, *Spaces of Hope* (Berkeley: University of California Press, 2000).

the world's population (now totaling over 6 billion) are too poor to buy a book; that a majority have never made a phone call in their lives; and that only between five and ten percent currently have access to the Internet. It is less common knowledge (according to recent US State Department figures) that as many as 4 million men, women, and children annually are being bought, sold, transported, and held against their will in slave-like conditions. For its victims, global civil society means the freedom of others to exploit them — in quick time, at great distances. It means as well rising vulnerability to the destructive or infectious powers of others: whereas smallpox, first discovered in the Nile Valley 1,300 years ago, reached the continent of Australia only during the nineteenth century, the AIDS virus took merely three decades to penetrate to all four corners of the earth. The global epidemic has so far left 50 million people infected, of whom 16 million have died. Around 14 million children have consequently been orphaned; and in countries like Lesotho and Zimbabwe, where one-fifth of all children have lost their parents, whole social fabrics are torn by crumbling household structures.

From their side, the excluded and victimized "participate" within global civil society in a second minimal sense: thanks to aid programs, television, and Hollywood and Bollywood films, they know something about the lives of the rich and powerful of the world. Struggling to make ends meet, they are aware of how insubstantial is their share of the world's wealth and power and style. They sense that their lives are permanently under the shadow of "Westerners" and things "Western": they are subjected to crude and aggressive prejudices of those who shadow them. They feel scorned, as if they are the "wrongful" majority. They know that being marginal means being condemned to a much shorter life. They are made to feel like victims of a predatory mode of foreign intervention: they feel shut out from global civil society, or uprooted by its dynamism, or imprisoned within its discriminatory structures and policies, like unpayable debt-service payments, or victimized by hunger or scores of uncivil wars.[19]

Others — many Muslims say — feel profound disappointment, tinged with anger and righteous indignation. They reason that the enormous potential of global civil society to expand dialogue among civilizations, to "affirm differences through communication," is being choked to death by the combined forces of global markets and military might, mani-

19. John Keane, "On Communicative Abundance," *CSD (Center for the Study of Democracy) Perspectives* (London: University of Westminster Press, 1999).

fested for instance in the long-standing and dangerously self-destructive alliance between the United States and Israel; some deeply religious Muslims *(mutawwa)* blast that alliance as world-threatening. Still others are gripped by feelings of humiliation: of being crushed into impotence that derives from the failure to be understood, the simple inability to make their voices heard, to be recognized as the potential makers of their own histories. Then, finally, there are the damned who curse quietly or express open hatred for this civil society — or who join Dostoevsky's underground man by drawing the defiant conclusion, against all things "reasonable" and "Western," that two plus two indeed equals five. From there, it may be only a step or two to picking up a gun or packing a bomb into a rucksack — to fight for the cause of ridding the world of the hypocrisy and decadence of an immediate aggressor, or a pseudo-universal way of life.[20]

All these reactions serve to fuel the conclusion that global civil society today resembles a string of oases of freedom in a vast desert of localized injustice and resistance. The simile — familiar in the Arabic contrast between *al-mujtama' al-madani* (civil society) and *al sahara*, the desert, with its connotations of savagery, the unpolished, and unrefined — can be prolonged for a moment, in order to draw another conclusion: that it is important to see that the privileges within this oasis cannot be taken for granted. Global civil society currently suffers a serious deficit of legitimacy: not only does it generate enemies who make a fist in their pockets, but it is also marked by the absence of widely held "common values." There is certainly plenty of moral "spirit" within this society: movements, organizations, groups, and individuals project and defend ideas and values that bear crucially upon the ways the world should be organized. Yet the old rule that a common sense of belonging is necessary for a community to survive and thrive does not apply — or so far does not hold — for global civil society. It contains no "self-evident truths" (in the sense of the American revolutionaries) and indeed any attempt to project a particular bundle of norms as candidates for "Common World Values" — to do with such familiar modern versions of principles as Race, Religion, History, Nation — appears both reactionary and divisive. Global civil society is at best bonded together by norms that are strongly procedural, such as commit-

20. Fred R. Dallmayr, "Globalization from Below," *International Politics* 36 (September 1999): 321-34; Richard Falk, *Predatory Globalisation: A Critique* (Cambridge: Polity Press and Malden, MA: Blackwell, 1999), chapter 8; and Orhan Pamuk, "The Anger of the Damned," *The New York Review of Books,* November 15, 2001, p. 12.

ments to due process of law, political democracy, and social pluralism, and also by norms, like civility and the commitment to non-violence, that have a highly variable content or are revocable under certain conditions. The upshot is that this society is highly vulnerable to the charge that it contains no binding moral Esperanto or "world values," and that consequently "many people feel as though they have lost control of their lives."[21] And so, unsurprisingly, the plural freedoms of global civil society are threatened constantly by the fact that it is a breeding ground for manipulators who take advantage of its available resentments and freedoms by waving the sword of ideologies above the heads of others.

Borderless exchanges also produce strong political reactions in favor of the local and national. Sometimes these localist reactions are dogmatic. They are often led by public figures — Patrick Buchanan, Pim Fortuyn, Pauline Hanson, Vladimir Zhirinovsky, Christoph Blocher — who behave like the albatrosses of globalization. Harbingers of political storms, they rail against the whole dirty business of "Euro-globalization" (Jean-Marie Le Pen). It stands accused of robbing "us" of "our" jobs because of competition from low-paid "foreign" labor and cheap "foreign" imports. The dogmatists play on the fact that in various parts of global civil society, except Japan, the number of foreign-born workers has been rising in recent decades. More than 7 million Mexican-born people are now living in the United States; and in the European Union, there are an estimated 20 million legal (and 3 million illegal) immigrants. The "anti-globalization" dogmatists bowdlerize the point: they ignore the fact that most trade is between the richest countries, and that (for example) unskilled and low-paid jobs in these countries are typically in the service sector, which for obvious reasons is comparatively insulated from global competition, and often suffers labor shortages. The dogmatists play on protectionist impulses. They warn citizens that "their" own country is already "full," and that (as Pim Fortuyn said repeatedly before his assassination in 2002) "foreigners," with their peculiar, bigoted beliefs, are diluting the precious culture of tolerance for which civil societies are renowned.[22] Sometimes the dogmatists preach revenge. "Why should we create suffering for ourselves?" Vladimir Zhirinovsky once asked. The answer was quick: "We should create suffering for others."[23]

21. From the speech by Amitai Etzioni to the colloquium, "Diversity Within Unity" (Centre for the Study of Democracy, London, April 25, 2002).

22. On the general problem of nationalism, see my *Civil Society: Old Images, New Visions* (Stanford: Stanford University Press, 1998), pp. 79-113.

23. *Financial Times* (London), December 9, 1993.

Fatalism

In *Global Civil Society?* I called for a radical revision of prevailing theories of globalisation that think in the old-fashioned terms of (potentially) "sovereign" territorial states, or of "multi-level governance" or "cosmopolitan democracy." Beyond that probability, nothing is certain, which is why it should not be supposed that long-lasting remedies for the weaknesses of global civil society can be found within the cupboards of contemporary political acceptability. Brand new democratic thinking — implicit in the theory of global civil society — is required, even if there are no guarantees of success. That lugubrious thought prompts a final few words about historical analogies and the pitfalls of fatalism in matters of global civil society.

It is common in discussions of global politics that the complaint is heard that our so-called global system is a global non-system, a field of anarchy: it seems that no institution or body regularly occupies the seat of power. Its complex and contradictory logic seems to be: *sauve qui peut.* There seem to be no secure rules or regulations; nobody seems to be in charge, except those with the strongest muscles. Little wonder, then, that many languish in its presence. It seems to defy description, and so to induce a faint feeling — even a feeling of fatalism before the powers that be.

This fatalism is a serious opponent of global civil society. The fatalist, who comes in two types, is generally someone who feels overwhelmed or overpowered by the world. One of them, the ignoramus, is simply ignorant and confident in that ignorance, often supremely so in the straightforward conclusions that are drawn. They know alright who rules the world: it is the rich and powerful, or the big multinational corporations, or the United States of America, for instance. And that's that. Nothing more to be said — and nothing more can be done, at least for the time being. There is another species of fatalist: the more cautious type. They do not have a clue about who runs the world, and they are not much troubled or intrigued by their ignorance. This blasé fatalist does not know who rules the world; when asked, they readily admit to their ignorance, and quickly add, with a sigh, that they do not much care. They divine from their ignorance the conclusion that the effort to define who holds the reins of power is a waste of time. For — here the two species of fatalists join forces — it is said that there is no point in wasting words on the subject, for no matter what is said and attempted the governing forces always get their way. Here the two types of fatalists spread their sails and drift together in the ancient waters of Greek mythology, where fatalism appears in the shape of old women who sit patiently spinning the threads and ropes of worldly events that are bound to happen. Fate was represented as both external and internal to the individual. One's fate was "spun," and so given, from the outside; but fate was at the same time intensely personal, something experienced from the inside. It left the individual no other option but to yield to what was felt outside and inside. The Romans called this inner and outer experience of necessity *fatum*. It literally meant "a thing said," something that is reported before it actually happens. Fate is a forewarning of an event or chain of events that cannot not happen. The *fatum* is irreversible. It cannot be changed by a millimeter or a gram. Fatalists are those who believe or accept this. They embrace fate, their unfreedom, as theirs. Fate is *their* fate.

The contemporary sense that fate has power over our lives is understandable. A moment's reflection reveals that human beings are never totally in control of everything that happens to their lives. They chronically feel forced to go along with things, to accept or to do things against their will. All this is understandable. But when the recognition and acceptance of fate harden into dogma, fatalism takes hold of the individual, or group, cruelly and without mercy. Fatalism distorts and paralyzes visions and actions; it makes it seem that nothing can be done, that everything is foreordained. That is why fatalism is a curse of the project of nurturing the ethos and institutions of global civil society. Fatalism produces inattention towards the framework of governance within which this society has sprung up and today flourishes. Fatalism is the silent enemy of political thinking about global civil society and the global order. It conjures necessity from contingency. Fatalism feeds wistfulness. It turns its back on the job of naming and mapping this society and its framing institutions, in order that they may better be judged, defended, reformed, or fundamentally transformed.

We know from historians that among the principal reasons why the last major growth spurt of "globalization" failed was that no effective or efficient or legitimate structures of global government were put in place.[24] By the 1930s, people and political institutions like the League of Nations, its Economic and Financial Organization, the International Labor Organization, and the Bank for International Settlements were overwhelmed by the intense contradictory pressures of a globalized world. Governing insti-

---

24. Harold James, *The End of Globalization: Lessons from the Great Depression* (Cambridge, MA: Harvard University Press, 2001); see also Andrew Gamble, *Politics and Fate* (Cambridge: Polity Press and Malden, MA: Blackwell, 2000).

tutions were overburdened by economic crises and long-standing political resentments, including the bitter politics of reparations and war debts. Luckily, the essential ingredients of a 1920s-style endogenous revolt against democratic forms of globalization are today missing. There are today no Soviet Unions or Third Reichs on the horizon. The thought that defenders of *souverainisme* (the term used by French protesters in Seattle for the defense of the territorial state) or *al Quaeda* or the Burmese junta or Chinese-style capitalism in post-totalitarian form serve as universal counter-models to global civil society in more democratic form is laughable. Fatalism, however, is no laughing matter. It is the favorite liquor of idiots, and kicking its habits is for that reason — as de Gaulle reportedly commented after spotting a Free French tank daubed with the words "Death to Idiots!" — a vast task. Ultimately, fatalism, the lack of political imagination and will, is our principal threat. That is why its refusal initially requires a strong dose of clear thinking about the web of civil society institutions that presently cover the earth. A political theory of global civil society seeks to do just that. Whether and to what extent it can or does succeed is for you and others to decide.

Can Global Civil Society Civilize
the International? Some Reflections

Kimberly Hutchings

Civilizations explain the potential of societies to espouse new directions of development. Civil societies shape common sense and collective purposes. A strong civil society can be the inner strength of a civilization and the creative force for its development; its absence, the explanation of subordination to an expansive Other.[1]

International human rights is always in the process of subjecting the human to redefinition and renegotiation. It mobilizes the human in the service of rights, but also re-writes the human and rearticulates the human when it comes up against the cultural limits of its working conception of the human, as it does and must.[2]

Introduction

This volume of essays is symptomatic of the current popularity of the expression "global civil society" within academic, policy, and activist circles, both as an analytic and as a normative term of art. Over the past several

1. R. Cox, "Thinking About Civilizations," *Review of International Studies* 26, no. 5 (2000): 228.
2. J. Butler, *Undoing Gender* (London: Routledge, 2004), p. 33.

years a very large literature has emerged within the social sciences which has tried to describe, explain, and judge the nature of global civil society and its place within contemporary accounts of world politics, whether the latter is understood in terms of "globalization" or "international relations" (more on this distinction below).[3] I have been asked to respond to the question of whether global civil society has the capacity to civilize the international and, in my chapter, I engage in some reflections on the implications of the question of global civil society's "civilizing" power. Cox, in the first of the quotations by which this chapter is framed, is representative of a strong version of the "civil society argument,"[4] in which civil society is understood as the inner strength of civilization, and the answer to the question of the civilizing power of global civil society must therefore be a resoundingly positive one. I will argue, however, that such a view is mistaken. The argument that "global civil society" can act as a panacea for the "international" depends on conceptual and ontological distinctions that do not hold.

At the same time, however, the question of global civil society's civilizing power does take us back to a question that is fundamental to politics (whether we are talking about politics within or across the boundaries of states), that is, the question of what it means for politics to be genuinely civil. Hobbes famously asserts that covenants without the sword are but words.[5] The ideal of global civil society is an ideal of covenants (words) without the sword. What kind of meaning can such an ideal have within contemporary world politics? In the concluding section of the paper, I

3. Roughly speaking there is a distinction in the literature between those who see the world as already thoroughly globalized (Keane), and those who still see the inter-state realm as of primary importance in understanding civil society beyond the state (Colás). For recent discussions of the concept of global civil society see: H. Anheier, M. Glasius, and M. Kaldor, eds., *Global Civil Society 2001* (Oxford: Oxford University Press, 2001) and later volumes; M. Kaldor, *Global Civil Society: An Answer to War* (Cambridge: Polity Press, 2003); J. Keane, *Global Civil Society?* (Cambridge: Cambridge University Press, 2003); R. D. Germain and M. Kenny, "The Idea(l) of Global Civil Society," in *The Idea of Global Civil Society: Politics and Ethics in a Globalizing Era,* ed. Germain and Kenny (London: Routledge 2005); G. Baker, and D. Chandler, "Introduction: Global Civil Society and the Future of World Politics," in *Global Civil Society: Contested Futures,* ed. Baker and Chandler (London: Routledge, 2005); D. O'Byrne, "Globalization, Cosmopolitanism and the Problem of Civil Society," in *Global Ethics and Civil Society,* ed. Eade and O'Byrne (Aldershot: Ashgate, 2005).

4. M. Walzer, "The Civil Society Argument," in *Gramsci and Marxist Theory,* ed. C. Mouffe (London: Routledge, 1992).

5. T. Hobbes, *Leviathan,* ed. R. Tuck (Cambridge: Cambridge University Press, 1991), p. 117.

turn to the recent work of Judith Butler and her suggestion that we can find a civil, non-coercive, non-violent politics at work in challenges by civil society activists to the exclusivity of claims to universality embedded in the discourse of universal human rights (see the second opening quotation above). She associates this kind of politics with civil society actors, both within and across state boundaries, such as feminist and gay rights movements. Such a politics (of resistance) is non-violent, she claims, in that it is committed to extending the scope of norms of recognition in such a way as to maximize, globally, the lives that may be lived and the lives that may be mourned. In my view, Butler's work is helpful in articulating what a "civil" civil society politics might mean and the kind of global ethic it might require. It is also helpful in that it draws attention to the difficulties in both principle and practice of separating words from the sword, even within a civil society context. Nevertheless, I suggest that Butler's argument remains limited in its usefulness because of the ways in which it continues to rely on a strong distinction between civil society and state or inter-state, which is neither analytically nor normatively justifiable.

In my conclusions, I do not mean to suggest that the ethical promise which so many find within civil society activism in world politics is necessarily unfounded. Nevertheless, I do want to trouble and disturb frameworks of thought in which not only are distinctions between "global civil society" and the "international" assumed to be clear-cut, but the former is always already known to be morally good and the latter morally questionable.

Interpreting the Question

The question ("can global civil society civilize the international?") connects two terms via a third: *global civil society* and *international* are linked by the term *civilize*. The proposition suggested by the question, and by the majority of current scholarship on global civil society, is a progressivist one, in which global civil society is associated with claims about the betterment of world politics.[6] According to this reading, the question presents the following hypothesis for examination: that global civil society (good)

6. It should be noted that accounts of the progressive nature of global civil society do not always reflect the same views either about what global civil society is, or its normative promise. For instance, one can contrast Kaldor's vision, in which global civil society is linked to universal liberal humanist values, with that of Keane, in which global civil society is fundamentally a realm of moral pluralism (Kaldor, *Global Civil Society;* Keane, *Global Civil Society?*).

may transform the international (bad) through its (global civil society's) peculiar instrumentality (civilization). Let us go on to examine the kinds of assumptions that underpin such a progressivist hypothesis.

To begin with, although progressivist theorists of global civil society differ in the precise meaning they give to the concept, they are all agreed that: firstly, global civil society is *different* from the international; secondly, that global civil society is linked in significant ways to globalization — the growing inter-dependence of people across the world (cultural, economic, communicative); and thirdly, that global civil society has positive values embedded in it (accounts of the latter varying from moral universalisms of various kinds[7] to moral pluralism).[8] According to these kinds of accounts of global civil society, the contrast between global civil society and the international is drawn as a contrast between the ethically inflected politics of non-state actors and the, at best, amoral politics of state actors in inter-state relations. Such a view invokes an idea of the international as an anarchic, uncivilized, violent "state of nature," prior to or outside of civilization, which is identified instead with the intra-state realm or with "global civil society."[9] Unsurprisingly therefore, the verb "to civilize," which connects global civil society to the international in the question, on the progressivist reading implies that the values of peace and order currently (supposedly) exhibited in intra-state or global civil society contexts may potentially be injected into, or even replace, the international (inter-state).

The above interpretation of the meaning of the hypothesis inherent in the question poses certain problems. First, and most obviously, it requires acceptance of particular definitions of, and assumptions about

7. R. Falk, *On Humane Governance: Towards a New Global Politics* (Cambridge: Polity Press, 1995); Kaldor, *Global Civil Society.*

8. Keane, *Global Civil Society?*

9. For the purposes of this chapter, because of the nature of the question I was asked to address, my emphasis is very much on global civil society posited as an alternative to inter-state relations. This marginalizes the equally significant issue of the relation between global civil society and global economic relations, which is touched on only briefly. In its origins in seventeenth- and eighteenth-century European thought, the idea of civil society included the full range of non-state activities and organizations and was primarily associated with economic activities. In more recent years, civil society has come to be defined in distinction from the market as well as the state (see I. M. Young, *Inclusion and Democracy* [Oxford: Oxford University Press, 2000]; O'Byrne, "Globalization"). However, I would agree with Keane that to exclude the market from our sociological understanding of global civil society is unhelpful (Keane, *Global Civil Society?;* see also R. Kiely, "Global Civil Society and Spaces of Resistance," in *Global Ethics,* ed. Eade and O'Byrne).

"global civil society," "international," and "civilize," all of which are in fact highly contestable. If we take the concept of *global civil society* first, there are powerful arguments to the effect that there is no such thing as "global civil society," and, even if it is accepted as having some descriptive or analytic purchase, the predominant view that global civil society is a normatively progressive phenomenon is open to challenge. In the discipline of International Relations, for instance, there is a high degree of scepticism about the degree to which globalization processes have changed the fundamental structures of world politics. This then extends to scepticism about the existence of a genuinely *global* (trans- or super-state) civil society, except as a term that serves certain functional, political purposes for a range of state and non-state actors in the international sphere.[10] Alternatively, global civil society may be accepted as a meaningful term, but identified with elite, unaccountable actors and co-optation by states, rather than as a progressive emancipatory force.[11]

If we turn now to examine the concept of the *international,* its meaning is also highly contested. Although it is certainly the case that some theories of inter-state politics define the international realm in terms of a Hobbesian state of nature, this is by no means the only interpretation. Liberal institutionalist, international society and constructivist theorists of international politics see the international as a realm that, already and increasingly, is one of order rather than anarchy.[12] Perhaps most contentious of all, however, is the meaning of *civilize.* On the progressivist global civil society hypothesis, "to civilize" is understood unproblematically as a term of amelioration. This ignores the huge ideological weight carried by discourses of civilization, which has been used historically to describe and justify war and imperialism in the name of civilizing a barbarous "other."

But even beyond the definitional issues and the analytic and norma-

10. D. Chandler, "Constructing Global Civil Society," in *Global Civil Society,* ed. Baker and Chandler.

11. L. Amoore and P. Langley, "Global Civil Society and Global Governmentality," in *The Idea of Global Civil Society: Politics and Ethics in a Globalizing Era,* ed. Germain and Kenny (London: Routledge, 2005); R. D. Lipschutz, "Global Civil Society and Global Governmentality: Resistance, Reform or Resignation?," in *Global Civil Society,* ed. Baker and Chandler.

12. Theoretical debates concerning the nature of the international are deeply divided in the study of international relations between more and less anarchic understandings. For useful discussions of alternative theories, see S. Burchill et al., *Theories of International Relations,* 3rd ed. (Basingstoke: Palgrave Macmillan, 2005) and C. Brown with K. Ainley, *Understanding International Relations,* 3rd ed. (Basingstoke: Palgrave Macmillan, 2005).

tive debate in which they are embedded, there are problems with reading the question of whether global civil society can civilize the international. The term global civil society has a peculiar logic, in that it is presented simultaneously as something that is already the case *and* as the means through which the state of affairs signalled by the term global civil society will be brought about. As both the end and the means of global progress, global civil society bleeds into the categories of both "international" and "civilize" with which it is contrasted in the question of whether it (global civil society) can civilize the international. Because global civil society is identified both as an existing phenomenon and with that which is civilized, to ask whether global civil society can civilize the international amounts almost to a tautology. Perhaps then the question becomes not "whether" but "to what extent" global civil society has the capacity to civilize the international. But whichever way it is phrased, ultimately the question only has meaning to the extent that we can make clear conceptual and ontological distinctions between its terms. I suggest that this requires us to be able to hold fast to three binary oppositions in particular: those between state and non-state; global and international; civil and uncivil. I will now go on to examine these three conceptual oppositions in more detail. In each case, an investigation of the contrasted terms casts doubt on the ease with which they can be distinguished in principle and in practice. I will argue, however, that the most important distinction for the progressivist hypothesis posed by the question of the civilizing power of global civil society is the last; this is the distinction between civil and uncivil, and the imbrications of that distinction in the related contrasts between civilized and uncivilized, peaceful and violent, good and bad.

Challenging the Binaries:
State/Non-State; Global/International; Civil/Uncivil

State/Non-State

The identification of global civil society with non-state in opposition to state is secured in different ways by different theories, and draws on the history of conceptualizing civil society in an intra-state context.[13] Four

13. Keane, *Global Civil Society?*; Germain and Kenny, "The Idea(l) of Global Civil Society."

ways of explaining and securing the state/non-state distinction are common: first, through the differentiation of types of *actors;* second, through the differentiation of types of *action;* third, through distinguishing between orientations to different kinds of *ends;* and fourth, through differentiating between different kinds of public *spaces.* In the case of the first mode of establishing the distinction, non-state actors are taken to be individual or collective actors that are not representatives of states, states themselves or inter-state institutions or organizations. In the global context (depending on the range of activities counted as proper to civil society in particular theories)[14] non-state actors might include anyone from individual human rights activists to business entrepreneurs, as well as the organizations, movements, or companies for which they work, providing their activities cut across state borders. If we look at these actors more closely, however, in what sense precisely are they non-state? They are not, by and large, non-state in the sense that they operate independently of states in terms either of the mechanisms through which they gain recognition as actors (status under domestic and international law as an individual with a passport, or an organization recognized as commercial or charitable); or the processes through which their aims are pursued (the means through which they communicate, travel, advocate or demonstrate); or indeed in terms of those aims themselves (to influence or change state/inter-state policy or law). This is not to say that non-state actors are equivalent to state actors, but it is to suggest that the existence and identity of non-state actors are in important respects dependent on states.

If a clear distinction, however, between state and non-state is difficult to draw in terms of civil society actors, it may be that the type of action is more crucial in grounding the state/non-state distinction. Iris Marion Young provides an example of this kind of argument, in which she seeks to establish both the sociological and normative specificity of civil society.[15] She argues (following Habermas) that the distinction between state and civil society is best understood as reflecting the Habermasian distinction between strategic and communicative action.[16] Whereas the state

14. For instance, depending on whether you see market actors as civil society actors or not; see note 9 above.

15. Young, *Inclusion and Democracy.*

16. Young, *Inclusion and Democracy,* p. 160. The philosopher and social theorist, Jürgen Habermas, developed the distinction between action oriented to communicative ideals and action oriented to strategic outcomes. Essentially, the former must meet certain universal moral standards (inherent in the presuppositions of communication itself) as a

(and also the market in her argument) is characterised by instrumental rationality and the means of coercion or violence, civil society action is characterized by communicative rationality, the force of voluntary agreement or consensus through deliberation. But again, even if one accepts the analytic distinction between strategic and communicative rationality, it is not clear that it can be mapped onto the state/non-state contrast. It is not difficult to identify instances of instrumental rationality, hierarchy and coercion in civil society, and one might also argue that there is plenty of communicative rationality within states. In order to make the distinction work, one is obliged to radically restrict what can count as genuinely part of civil society. This leads to definitions that exclude violent or exclusive actors (revolutionary movements, nationalist parties as well as criminal or terrorist organizations) from civil society proper. And it also requires one to overlook state institutions oriented towards deliberation from parliaments to select committees to courts. The same kind of resolution by fiat occurs when it is the ends or aims of civil society that are held to be the key to the distinction between state and non-state. In these kinds of arguments (most strongly associated with the cosmopolitanism of thinkers such as Falk and Kaldor), the idea of civil society becomes highly prescriptive, and is held to include only those actors/actions oriented, either explicitly or implicitly, towards a universal end. Again, however, this mode of drawing the distinction is unsatisfactory. Frequently both civil society and state actors claim that they are acting in the service of universal ends of human rights and democracy. It would be hard to demonstrate definitively that such claims are always true or always hypocritical in either case.

Perhaps the most persuasive of the ways in which the distinction between state and non-state is drawn is the fourth possibility, that is, in terms of the idea of different kinds of political "spaces." According to this account, global civil society is that realm of public activity that is not the activity of states or their representatives. The advantage of this way of drawing the distinction is that it is much less restrictive and prescriptive

---

condition of success, whereas the success of the latter is determined purely technically. This distinction is embedded in Habermas's account of modern societies, which he sees as split between "lifeworld" and "system," the former being spheres of ethical and emancipatory activity, the latter of technical control (J. Habermas, *The Theory of Communicative Action,* 2 vols. [Boston: Beacon Press, 1984 and 1987]). In his more recent work, Habermas associates civil society with the "lifeworld" and the state with "system" (Habermas, *Between Facts and Norms* [Cambridge: Polity Press, 1996]). This mapping has been picked up by theorists of civil society such as Young.

than either the "types of action" or "types of end" arguments. However, as with the "types of actor" argument, it turns out to be much more difficult to disentangle state from non-state public spheres than it at first appears. In literal terms, the spaces of civil society activism, from the street to the internet to the conference platform, depend on enabling conditions, which in turn depend on economic, legal and political conditions which are mediated through states. More importantly, the spaces of global civil society activism increasingly overlap with those of the state, in particular in the fields of development, peace-building and humanitarian aid.[17] The point of the above discussion is not to suggest that there are no distinctions to be drawn between different types of actors, action, ends or locations in either domestic or international politics. Rather the point is to question dualistic readings of the meaning of both state and civil society and to indicate the complex and dialectical modes in which they are mutually entangled.[18]

Global/International

It is impossible to do justice to all of the issues raised by the contrast between "global" and "international" implicit in the hypothesis about the civilizing power of global civil society. At the level of description, the term "global" refers to a world of thickening interdependence across borders of state and nation, mediated through explicitly trans-state or super-state mechanisms (market, media, technology). Different accounts of the global see it more or less positively as the context for the evolution of planetary level solidarities or, alternatively, as a realm of tension and conflict between winners and losers in economic and cultural globalization processes.[19] When attached to the term "civil society," "global" is prescriptively more associated with the former than the latter. In contrast to "global," "international" signifies inter-state, the network of interaction, violent and non-violent, between sovereign entities. As noted above, on some accounts, the inter-state is ordered through the logic of self-interest inherent in anarchy, on analogy with a Hobbesian state of nature. On other ac-

17. M. Edwards and J. Gaventa, eds., *Global Citizen Action* (London: Earthscan, 2001).
18. Kiely, "Global Civil Society."
19. D. Held et al., *Global Transformations* (Cambridge: Polity Press, 1999); D. Held and A. McGrew, eds., *The Global Transformations Reader* (Cambridge: Polity Press, 2000).

counts, the inter-state is itself an ordered social condition, regulated by certain norms and capable of a significant degree of institutionalization. The international is antithetical to the global in analytic terms because it is tied to the settled particularity of states as a plurality of sovereign actors, though in principle particular states may have global ambitions.

In descriptive and analytic terms the idea of the global (as in global civil society) having an effect on the international clearly depends on rejection of either a strong globalization thesis or a strongly sceptical position. In the case of the former, the international is already transcended, in which case the question of the civilizing power of global civil society for the international becomes redundant. In the case of the latter, the reality of the global is in question, so again the possibility of it acting on the international could not make sense. The idea that the global could civilize the international clearly depends on conceiving the global and international as distinct but simultaneously co-existing dimensions of world politics. Yet, on examination, the international mediates the global and the global mediates the international. As many scholars have pointed out, the state has been the leading international actor in globalization processes, as well as being influenced in turn by those processes. This is true in relation to economic as well as cultural globalization processes, from the globalization of capital, to global transport and communications networks to international human rights regimes.[20]

Civil/Uncivil

Social scientific debate about the descriptive and analytic purchase of the terms "civil society," "global" and "international" is made extraordinarily difficult by the normative weight carried by these concepts. The verb "to civilize" in the hypothesis about the civilizing power of global civil society clearly implies both that global civil society is an agent of civilization and that the international is uncivilized. It draws together a contrast between that which is cultivated (civilized) and that which is natural (uncivilized) and between that which is fundamentally about words (civil) and that which is fundamentally about the sword (uncivil). Implicitly we are encouraged to identify civilization with civility and nature with violence, and to re-read contemporary world politics in terms of the Lockean story of

20. D. Held et al., *Global Transformations*.

the move from a state of nature (the international) to what he called "society" (global civil society).[21]

This mapping of the terms global civil society (civil, civilized) and international (uncivil, uncivilized), however, is misleading for two reasons. It is misleading as a characterization of global civil society and the international, which, as I have tried to suggest above, cannot be clearly demarcated and may both be civil as well as uncivil and vice versa. But perhaps more importantly, it is misleading because in identifying civil with civilized and uncivil with uncivilized, it relegates violence and coercion, along with the international, to the realm of nature. This latter has a double consequence. On the one hand, it allocates the international to a pre-moral or amoral position, one that possesses (and could possess) no resources for ethical development and thereby suggests that civil society politics possesses an unquestionable monopoly on ethics. On the other hand, in equating violent and coercive politics with that which is natural, it makes the question of the relation between civilization, violence and coercion literally unthinkable. And yet, as we all know, there is no contradiction between civilization and incivility. Violence and coercion are just as civilized as non-violent political processes in the sense that they require conditions of possibility fully as complex and cultivated. There is nothing natural about the violence of states. Moreover, violence and coercion take many different forms. Violence can be a matter of direct and intentional, foreseen but unintended, or indirect and unintended injury. Coercion can be about the exercise or threat of direct physical force or a range of mechanisms that limit and constrain what it is possible to do or say.[22] When it is linked to an imaginary "state of nature" condition, the understanding of how violence operates in and pervades social and political relations is blocked. The identification of non-violence with civilization as such, becomes a way of evading the question of violence in world politics, whether this is the violence of state or non-state actors. In order to address the question of violence properly, not only do "global civil society," the "international" and the complex ways in which they are interrelated and differentiated have to be disaggregated and understood. But we also have to understand better the conditions of possibility of both violence and non-violence within the multiple contexts of world politics, including those con-

21. J. Locke, *Two Treatises of Government*, ed. P. Laslett (Cambridge: Cambridge University Press, 1988), p. 282.

22. V. Bufacchi, "Two Concepts of Violence," *Political Studies Review* 3, no. 2 (2005): 193-204.

texts identified with global civil society, such as the activities of non-governmental organizations, transnational social movements, and cultural and religious organizations. Civil society actors may not possess the same resources for violence as states, but, in the context of radical global inequalities of power, the potential for violent and coercive practices within global civil society needs to be explicitly recognised and addressed.

To summarize the argument so far: first, I have claimed that it is hard to sustain a sharp distinction between global civil society and the international on descriptive, analytic, or normative grounds. This does not mean there are no meaningful distinctions to be drawn, but they should not be understood in simple binary terms. The politics of global civil society is part of the international and vice versa. Second, I have suggested that keeping to the binary distinction is dangerous because it encourages participants/activists involved in non-governmental or non-state transnational political action not to reflect on the politics of their own practices. To the extent that the international is bad and global civil society is good, then we do not have to worry about potential exclusivity, hierarchy, and coercion within the civil society realm — witting or unwitting — nor about the ways in which civil society activism and global governance are interconnected as well as opposed. What I am trying to suggest through the above discussion is that for those of us concerned with the inclusivity of the ethics of global civil society referred to in the title of this volume of essays, rather than asking the question of whether global civil society can civilize the international, we would be better advised to start by asking what a "civil," fundamentally non-coercive and non-violent global civil society politics might look like and what its conditions of possibility might be. In the next section of this chapter I will consider one attempt to articulate a non-violent, global civil society politics in the post-9/11 world, that of Judith Butler.

Global Civil Society, Non-Violence, and Liveable Lives

> There are no obituaries for the war casualties that the United States inflicts, and there cannot be. If there were to be an obituary, there would have to have been a life, a life worth noting, a life worth valuing and preserving, a life that qualifies for recognition.
>
> It is not simply, then, that there is a "discourse" of dehumanization that produces these effects, but rather that there is a limit

to discourse that establishes the limits of human intelligibility. It is not just that a death is poorly marked, but that it is unmarkable. Such a death vanishes, not into explicit discourse, but in the ellipses by which public discourse proceeds.[23]

In the essays in *Undoing Gender* and *Precarious Life*, Butler puts forward an account of the conditions of possibility for non-violent civil society politics as a counter to the kind of politics implicit in the "unmournability" of the lives of unrecognized others referred to in the above quotation.[24] In this sense her argument clearly shares ground with what I have referred to as the "progressivist hypothesis" about global civil society. However, unlike most progressivist civil society arguments, Butler does not make a necessary connection between civil society activism and non-violence; for her the politics of recognition is not confined to the state but is a permanent feature of all sites of political engagement. Non-violent civil society politics, in both intra-state and trans-national contexts, requires a commitment not to universal values and explicitly non-coercive means, but, much more fundamentally, to what she calls "the difficult labour of cultural translation."[25]

Butler's argument rests on two claims: first, that the meaning of any singular human life (the identity and capacities of unique individuals) is given by complex culturally and institutionally embedded patterns and norms of recognition which enable sense to be made of that singular life, by both the individual concerned and others. In this sense, individual selves are fundamentally mediated by other individuals and by embedded norms of recognition. One of the most important ways in which this is evident to Butler is in relation to gender, which is at once at the heart of the individual's sense of self and outside of individual control ("But the terms that make up one's own gender are, from the start, outside oneself, beyond oneself in a sociality that has no single author").[26] The crucial point for Butler is that every singular life is dependent on modes of recognition that are not individually authored or under the control of any specific "self" or

23. J. Butler, *Precarious Life: The Powers of Mourning and Violence* (London: Verso, 2004), pp. 34-35.

24. Butler, *Undoing Gender;* Butler, *Precarious Life*.

25. Butler, "Restaging the Universal: Hegemony and the Limits of Formalism," in J. Butler, E. Laclau, and S. Žižek, *Contingency, Hegemony, Universality: Contemporary Dialogues on the Left* (London: Verso, 2000); *Undoing Gender*, pp. 227-231.

26. Butler, *Undoing Gender*, p. 1.

"other." Secondly, Butler argues that the dependence of self on recognition is necessarily "bound up with the question of power and with the problem of who qualifies as recognizably human and who does not."[27] This is because culturally and institutionally embedded norms of recognition are not neutral reflections of what it means to be human, but rather constitute the conditions of possibility of a liveable human life.

Butler's notion of "liveability" encompasses both the literal and the psychic/social chances of surviving of any given individual. Her examples here draw on her experience of trans-national human rights activism in relation to the rights of lesbian, gay, trans-sexual, and trans-gendered humans, and the ways in which the liveability of such lives is limited, and often entirely prohibited by the dominant norms of recognition in different national and cultural contexts. Prohibition may mean literal killing or injury (reflecting a primal bodily vulnerability which Butler sees as indissolubly bound up with the self's other primal vulnerability, derived from its dependence on recognition). But prohibition may also mean the impossibility of engaging in certain practices or the necessity of concealing aspects of one's being and/or doing from others.

Traditionally, the question of which lives are allowed to be liveable has been presumed to require *either* the establishment of norms of recognition that somehow transcend the particularity of specific lives, *or*, require the acceptance of the contextually dominant norms of recognition as authoritative. Essentially this gives the global civil society activist a choice between moral universalism or cultural relativism. In an earlier essay, Butler expresses her unhappiness with both of these responses, philosophically and politically.[28] Philosophically, she argues that both responses rely on a mistaken understanding of both the "universal" and of "culture." Politically, she argues that both involve the reifying of a particular set of norms of recognition, without openness to the possibility of challenge. For Butler, "the relation of universality to its cultural articulation is insuperable."[29] She illustrates this by demonstrating how different substantive and procedural moral universalisms are only intelligible to the extent that they articulate their claims in terms that are drawn from available frameworks of meaning. Such frameworks inevitably reflect certain patterns and

27. Butler, *Undoing Gender*, p. 2.
28. J. Butler, "Restaging the Universal: Hegemony and the Limits of Formalism," in Butler, Laclau, and Žižek, *Contingency, Hegemony, Universality*.
29. Butler, "Restaging the Universal," p. 24.

norms of recognition as opposed to others, and their universalizability is therefore dependent on the universalization of particularity (culturally, historically, and socially). Nevertheless, Butler does not see the insuperability of elements of exclusivity in any norms of recognition as undermining the importance of the link between a civil society politics committed to the extension of the terms of "liveability" and the ideal of "universality." For her, however, the universal is not a transcendental ground in which the meaning of being "human" is known *a priori*, but rather a commitment to the possibility that the terms of the universal may always be re-signified, through challenges from the excluded — and this is where the notion of the labor of cultural translation comes in:

> Moreover, there is no cultural consensus on an international level about what ought and ought not to be a claim to universality, who may make it, and what form it ought to take. Thus, for the claim to work, for it to compel consensus, and for the claim performatively to enact the very universality it enunciates, it must undergo a set of translations into the various rhetorical and cultural contexts in which the meaning and force of universal claims are made.[30]

As Butler points out, translation may be understood in two different ways. It can operate as a process in which competing meanings are adjudicated in relation to an authoritative meta-language. Or, it can be understood as a process of trial and error, in which the understanding and endorsement of political claims depend crucially on the scope for recognition and negotiation between the authors, audiences and referents of the claims in question. The former understanding is the one implied by discourses of legitimization that rely on either moral universalism (the positing of an authoritative meta-language) or cultural relativism (the positing of the impossibility of translation because of the absence of a meta-language). For Butler, however, translation is not a matter of subsuming all languages under a meta-language but of forging common ground across different languages; or, in so far as this cannot be done, of recognizing the limits of mutual intelligibility. This is a process, according to Butler, which must allow for (even if it cannot guarantee) the possibility of mutual transformation and the articulation of more inclusive political vocabularies.

30. Butler, "Restaging the Universal," p. 35.

The example of feminism as a category of trans-national civil society activism can be used to illustrate the relevance of Butler's rather abstract discussion to the question of what a genuinely "civil" global civil society politics might entail. Historically, the feminist movement is an archetypal example of a trans-national movement with a self-consciously civilizing mission. Early feminists and their more recent heirs have identified themselves as carrying forward the task of improving the conditions and possibilities of women across boundaries of state and nation. In recent years, the most important discourse for this kind of trans-national activism has been that of women's human rights.[31] And this language has underpinned and provided normative force for campaigns around civil, political, and economic issues, from female genital mutilation, to women's reproductive rights, to development. The discourse of human rights is grounded in a strong ethical universalism, which has its origins in liberal enlightenment thought. This universalism is based on the notion that there are rationally accessible, universalizable ethical principles, which transcend the particularities of situation. In Butler's terms, this is a "meta-language" model of ethical universalism, in which there are standards of judgment against which any actual practice may be measured and either legitimated or shown to be wrong.

Many feminists involved in trans-national activism, in particular "third world" and postcolonial feminists, however, have taken issue with both the theory and practice of liberal enlightenment universalism within the feminist movement. In terms of practice, it has been pointed out that the discourses of liberal feminism have justified "maternalist" intervention by Western women in the lives of non-Western women of a kind that echoes the history and ideology of Western imperialism, colonialism and neo-colonialism.[32] Moreover, postcolonial feminists argue that this kind of ethical universalism treats all women as in some sense modelled on a Western norm and is therefore insensitive to the significance of specific cultural and social contexts and to differences in the issues that are most politically

31. G. Ashworth, "The Silencing of Women," in *Human Rights in Global Politics,* ed. T. Dunne and N. Wheeler (Cambridge: Cambridge University Press, 1999); C. Bunch, with P. Antrobus, S. Frost, and N. Reilly, "International Networking for Women's Human Rights," in *Global Citizen Action,* ed. Edwards and Gaventa.

32. C. T. Mohanty, A. Russo, and L. Torres, eds., *Third World Women and the Politics of Feminism* (Bloomington and Indianapolis: Indiana University Press, 1991); C. T. Mohanty, *Feminism without Borders: Decolonising Theory, Practicing Solidarity* (Durham and London: Duke University Press, 2003); Butler, *Undoing Gender,* pp. 204-31.

significant for different women. For instance, if we look at the debates that have dominated feminist international conferences, there is a pattern in which issues such as reproductive rights, poverty, or pornography are given different priorities for different reasons by different categories of women.[33]

The framework of liberal enlightenment universalism remains the most significant within feminist trans-national politics. This undoubtedly reflects the predominance of liberal values within the frameworks set by international law, international organizations and international regimes, frameworks within which feminist civil society activists are obliged to work. Nevertheless, the debate within the feminist movement between liberal feminists and a range of alternative positions has created space for a different way of thinking about the ethic underpinning feminist global civil society activism. According to this approach, the meaning of women's human rights, rather than being settled in advance according to universal standards, is used as a kind of "placeholder," the meaning of which must be negotiated. In order for this negotiation to take place, a first step must be enabling empowerment and voice for those women who are multiply silenced by the predominant politics of both global civil society and interstate social, political and economic processes. This kind of development in trans-national feminist politics reflects the ethic of Butler's ideal of cultural translation as a project of mutual transformation, rather than the subsumption of all meanings under a master narrative.[34] She writes, "It is crucial to understand the workings of gender in global contexts, in transnational formations, not only to see what problems are posed for the term 'gender' but to combat false forms of universalism that service a tacit or explicit cultural imperialism."[35]

From Butler's point of view, feminist global civil society activism may take on either an uncivil or a civil form. Feminist activism takes on a form of incivility when it seeks to reify one set of norms of recognition and leave no space for the conceptions of "liveability" bound up with those

33. A. Basu, ed., *The Challenge of Local Feminisms: Women's Movements in Global Perspective* (Boulder: Westview Press: 1995); A. C. Snyder, *Setting the Agenda for Global Peace: Conflict and Consensus Building* (Aldershot: Ashgate, 2003).

34. B. Ackerley, *Political Theory and Feminist Social Criticism* (Cambridge: Cambridge University Press, 2000); Bunch et al., "International Networking"; K. Singh, "Handing Over the Stick: The Global Spread of Participatory Approaches to Development," in *Global Citizen Action,* ed. Edwards and Gaventa.

35. Butler, *Undoing Gender*, p. 8.

forms to be challenged and transformed. In contrast, "civil" civil society activism is about submitting to the "difficult labour" of cultural translation. And what this means is that feminist trans-national activists must ensure that they leave space to listen to as well as speak on behalf of women, and that they leave open the possibility of their own transformation as well as that of others.[36]

Butler's work is helpful in forcing us to reflect on the difficulties of separating words from the sword even in civil society contexts. She provides a useful analysis of the ways in which ethical universalism may block rather than enhance a genuinely democratic and inclusive civil society politics, in particular within a trans-national context. At the same time, Butler articulates some very valuable insights into how one might think about a non-violent politics of global civil society underpinned by an ethic of inclusivity, in which no one set of the norms of recognition that render lives liveable or unliveable is ever taken as fixed and unchallengeable. Nevertheless, there are problems with Butler's analysis. In many ways, her account remains too strongly attached to an idealized conception of civil society, which is opposed to state and inter-state realms. This is evident both analytically and normatively in her argument, since the state is always described in terms of a project of domination, and the only possibilities of progress are associated with civil society, grass-roots movements. In my view, Butler's nuanced account of the complexities and difficulties of a "civil" civil society politics needs to be extended to encompass a world in which global civil society does not act as a counter to "the international," but rather is deeply and dialectically intertwined with it.

Conclusion

The idea that global civil society can civilize the international relies on a massive over-simplification of the complexity and inter-relation of state and non-state, global and international, civil and uncivil in both theory and practice. I have argued, however, that it may be more helpful not to dwell on the question I was asked to answer, but to think more deeply instead about the question of the meaning of a "civil" global politics, in which both state and non-state actors participate, and how it might be

36. K. Hutchings, "From Morality to Politics and Back Again: Feminist International Ethics and the Civil Society Argument," *Alternatives* 29 (2004): 239-264.

possible. Butler offers one kind of answer, focusing particularly on certain kinds of civil society activism as exemplifying a genuinely inclusive ethic, which contrasts with the dehumanizing discourses of both state and non-state actors. However, her answer is clearly that civility is profoundly difficult in both principle and practice. Moreover, her confinement of the answer to civil society activism tends to reinforce the unsustainable distinctions on which accounts of global civil society's civilizing potential rely. As long as the civil society argument rests on a set of claims to the moral high ground in contrast to the politics of states, then it risks rendering itself irrelevant to the very world politics that it seeks to describe and judge. If we are to move beyond an over-idealization of global civil society in contrast to the international, then proponents of global civil society must be willing not only to be self-critical about the civility of their own politics, but also to recognize the existing and potential relations between the politics of global and international, civil society and state.

Civil Society, Religion, and the Ethical Shape of Polity

Max L. Stackhouse

Several debates have been raging for more than a decade in the United States about the nature and character of civil society. One is quite academic, but it is highly pertinent to this conference. It is rooted in the historical debate as to which of the two great archetypical philosophers of the modern idea of civil society was more nearly correct. I say "modern" idea because, as John Keane has pointed out, the classic idea of *societas civilis* referred to those patterns of life characteristic of a community organized under a legal regime that guaranteed relative safety, peace, and orderly government in a given territory.[1] The modern idea assumes a differentiation between the civil society and the political regime. Was it Locke, influenced by Althusius' notion of society as a consociation of consociations, who had it right, that civil society is formed on the basis of a linked set of voluntary compacts that have a dual basis, that they are designed to protect the material interests of persons and they can be ethically made due to the human capacity to recognize overarching "self-evident" moral truths?[2] If so, then such a society can create a political order to defend the rights of citizens, to enforce just laws and to serve the common good.

The echoes of the biblical covenantal law, of the Deuteronomic praise of a righteous people anointing just rulers who followed those laws

---

1. John Keane, ed., *Civil Society and the State: New European Perspectives* (London: Verso Publishers, 1988), Introduction.

2. Especially, his *Second Treatise of Government* [1690] (Cambridge: Hackett Publishing Co., 1980), ed. C. B. Macpherson.

and of the promise of plenty and peace, are just below the surface of such claims. At least the founding fathers of colonial America, like the older Scottish Covenanters who anticipated some of these ideas and Adam Smith who was influenced by them, thought that such ideas were valid theologically, morally, and practically. They thus inferred that a civil society could constitute and could unmake what it had made. It could overthrow a government if it violated true morality and the material interests of the people. The colonies broke with the king of Britain and sought to form a new constitutional government based on a just covenant. Civil society, in this Lockean view, was functionally and ethically seen as prior to political society, and no state authority could form or justly dismantle the civil society.

Or was it Hegel, modifying some observations of Kant, who had it right, that civil society is a historical stage of bourgeois life that developed beyond the primal structures of domestic life and was, in advanced cultures, surpassed by the modern state in which the spirit of reason comes to the fuller actuality of political sovereignty? In this sense, the bourgeois of civil society dialectically both resists the comprehending authority of the state and becomes synthetically wedded to it; but in that progressive dialectic, a political authority is formed that orders and commands all subordinate relations, institutions and associations. In this one can almost hear an echo of Paul's advice in Romans 13: "Let every one be subject to the governing authorities; for there is no authority except from God . . . ," even if Hegel's governing authority strikingly resembles the Prussian State.

Hegel, to be sure, was no Hobbes, who argued that the people had to forfeit their freedom to a totalitarian ruler in order to constrain the brutish and mean conflicts among the people and to establish peace, but he did think that people could find their collective freedom in a political regime that comprehended the whole and fostered civil society when and where it served the state. He also argued that those who do not recognize the logic of history on this point would be crushed by it — a view widely held by no small number of hyper-modernist thinkers, right and left, not the least of whom was, in one way Marx, in another Lenin, and in a third those development experts in the West who advocated huge loans to new post-colonial governments with weak civil societies on the basis of their belief that governments could and would use the funds to construct the schools, medical services, economic institutions, and legal patterns that make civil societies viable. Far too often they did not do this, and the result was the debt crisis. Civil society may be prior to political society in its historical development, Hegel and the statist theorists of development argued, but the political order is prior in terms of governing and forming civil society.[3]

It is quite possible that Hegel had it right in the short run. A political order that is built on top of an existing set of institutions may have to see that various institutions and their leaders obey the law and do not disrupt the peace. And a morally, rationally, and spiritually strong government can do this in ways that could well foster a free, pluralistic, and disciplined civil society, one characterized by "Sittlichkeit" — "ethicalness." Such a government tolerates debate and dissent, differentiation and specialization, whereas a morally, rationally, and spiritually weak government tends to, indeed almost always resorts to, violent means of control and fears every other social collectivity beyond itself.

But Locke probably had it more right in the longer run: the material and moral fabric of civil society is potentially more enduring than specific governments, and such a civil society will subvert, de-legitimate, and finally overthrow any government that does not foster the flourishing of its material and moral interests. The workings of a civil society are slower but deeper. Governments can respond to crises by command, with power, quickly. Civil society must build by persuasion, voluntary compliance, and trust over time. Today, in a globalizing world, where the institutions of civil society include corporations, media, information technology, advocacy and aid NGO's, governments are compelled to cater to the formation of civil society institutions beyond any state's power to control or command, even if some can, within limits, exercise hegemonic influence.

These fathers of the modern idea of civil society fundamentally disagree about one key matter, while basically agreeing on three others. They disagree as to whether the civil society can trump the political society or whether the political order must comprehend and control the institutions of civil society. But they agree, first, on the fact that there are essentially two reference points for defining civil society: the individual, represented by household property rights, and the collective, represented by the state. To put it another way, they share, at a deep level, a two-agent theory of society consisting of the individual as embedded in family and the collective as embedded in state law. What is creative and enduring about their work

---

3. Especially his *Philosophy of Right* [1821], trans. T. M. Knox (New York: Oxford University Press, 1967). He is particularly interested in how authority is distributed by the major alternatives.

is that they are trying to account for the other relationships in which people live and work and have their being and which shape both the affections of private life and the destiny of nations. This issue of how to deal with intermediary organizations can be seen not only in the history of modern academic tensions between sociological and political perspectives, but, as several new studies show, in debates today in China and the Islamic world about the relative priority of persons and their relationships in families to the growth of religious associations, non-state economic organizations, and popular movements outside of family connections and often in the face of state authority.[4]

A second area where the Lockean and Hegelian traditions agree is that they both see commerce, markets, and the formation of corporate enterprises as a part of civil society. Of course, these were not so developed as they have become in the last century, particularly since World War II. Still, the East India trading companies of England and Holland were well known and so were the trading concerns of the Hanseatic League in what was to become Germany. These were founded and flourishing by the early 1600s, some as independent trading ventures and some as mercantilist companies. Still, they were considered to be vital parts of civil society that, often with the chartered approval of the state, expanded the activities of civil society beyond the boundaries of the existing political rule, anticipating what we now call globalization. These trading companies, for instance, had an active, if sometimes ambiguous and contentious, relationship to missions, educational and medical institutions, cultural exchange, and technological transfer.

This inclusion of the corporate-economic institutions in the category of civil society has been challenged by many, not the least by the quite influential German philosopher, Jürgen Habermas. He argues that the idea of civil society has changed so that it no longer should include the economy as it did with Locke and Smith plus Hegel and Marx. Instead the idea of civil society should be confined to non-governmental and non-

---

4. This distinction appears in debates about the nature and character of civil society in Chinese and Islamic societies today. See Timothy Brook et al., eds., *Civil Society in China* (Armonk, NY: M. E. Sharp, Inc., 1997); Sze-Kar Wan, "Christian Contributions to the Globalization of Confucianism (beyond Maoism)," in *Christ and the Dominions of Civilization*, ed. Max L. Stackhouse et al. (Harrisburg, PA: Trinity Press International, 2002); Sohail H. Hashmi, *Islamic Political Ethics: Civil Society, Pluralism and Conflict* (Princeton, NJ: Princeton University Press, 2002); and Robert W. Hefner, *Civil Islam: Muslims and Democratization in Indonesia* (Princeton, NJ: Princeton University Press, 2000).

economic institutions and practices — those that form the communicative structures of the public sphere that have an impact on the life-world of persons. The change of meaning is due to the fact that not only big government bureaucracy but also today's forms of economic rationalization have grown so large that they tend to colonize the life-world, distort the possibilities of genuinely egalitarian communication, and truncate the possibilities of meaning formation, all key tasks of civil society. The term "civil society" thus should be reserved for those organizations, associations, and movements that emerge out of the concerns of the common life and that make a direct, transformative impact on private life and practical problems.[5] This view has influenced many activists in religious circles, and, as Mary Kaldor has argued, it has been enormously influential and resonated with secular liberals in the Kantian tradition, with radicals in the Marxist tradition, and with a number of current populist movements.[6]

The debate on this matter in the United States has, over the last decade, less often taken the form of anti-capitalism or anti-corporations or anti-globalization, although such voices are present. It more often has to do with whether the long history of voluntary associational participation and democratic action can be maintained given the economic and technological changes at the beginning of this new century. The poles of this debate can be seen in a pair of recent books. One of the most cited studies is by Harvard professor Robert Putnam, and is titled *Bowling Alone.*[7] It is an expanded version and defense of a lengthy article he wrote by this title in

5. Habermas has made such arguments in a number of places, including his *The Structural Transformations of the Public Sphere: An Inquiry into a Category of Bourgeois Society* (Cambridge, MA: MIT Press, 1991). A similar view is advanced by the German sociologist Ulrich Beck, a key influence on the statement against globalization by the World Council of Churches, "Alternative Globalization: Addressing Peoples and Earth" (AGAPE), 2005, available on the World Council website, www.oikoumene.org.

6. This is the central theme of Mary Kaldor's argument in her *Global Civil Society, An Answer to War* (Cambridge: Polity Press, 2003). She argues that this entails a new kind of politics that is non-coercive. John Keane offers a more sober estimate of the prospects, and its limitations, in his *Global Civil Society?* (Cambridge: Cambridge University Press, 2003). He corrects Kaldor's vision, in my view, specifically by including the economic sphere within the orbit of civil society.

7. I refer to Robert Putnam, *Bowling Alone: The Collapse and Revival of American Community* (New York: Simon & Schuster, 2000). The main points of the argument are not entirely new and have been recognized for some time in both Europe and the USA. Useful perspectives can be found in J. F. A. Taylor's early *The Masks of Society: An Inquiry into the Covenants of Civilization* (New York: Appleton-Crofts, 1966), and Alan Wolfe, *Whose Keeper? Social Science and Moral Obligation* (Berkeley: University of California Press, 1989).

1995, one of the most discussed essays written by a social scientist in several decades. He suggests that the tradition of civil society in the USA is growing thin. He argues that while Americans are notoriously individualistic, in the sense that they want to defend individual human rights and liberties, they have historically also been joiners, forming leagues or clubs or unions or independent institutions or political parties or advocacy groups in almost every area of social activity, including the sport of bowling. But these associational activities no longer preoccupy the population. People are, and want to be, on their own. People go bowling alone; it is no longer a team sport. This is true, he argues, not only in regard to sports, but also in regard to economic activity, daily schedules, personal styles, work habits, and political attitudes. He says that fewer and fewer people creatively engage in cooperative projects for the common life.

The question Putnam poses for our question is this: insofar as America represents a globalized and globalizing force in the world, is it likely to enhance the prospects for voluntary, cooperative activity that sustains democracy, or does it erode that prospect? Certainly developments that have occurred since he wrote — the aftermath of the attack on the Twin Towers on 9/11 — has exacerbated the American temptation to become more interventionist abroad and to impose exaggerated security measures at home that are widely seen as threats to democracy and human rights. Insofar as the US is seeking to foster democracy, human rights, an open economic system, and religious freedom in lands where it did not exist before, it remains unclear as to what the effects of current policies will be on the inner value system of US civil society and the social capital that sustains and nurtures it as well as on other countries.

A contrary view of our situation was presented by *The Ladd Report.* As Director of the Roper Center for Public Opinion Research, Ladd assembled a wide range of data to demonstrate where he thinks Putnam was wrong in discerning the actual situation. True, some civic organizations have declined; but in an open, dynamic society, associational groups rise and fall with some rapidity. It may be that fraternal organizations are less active than in the past. And it is certainly true that labor unions, student activist groups, and racial advocacy organizations are in relative decline compared to a generation ago when Martin Luther King, Jr. was at his height, or when anti-Viet Nam protests were daily a focus of the news. Yet, membership in environmental organizations, advocacy groups for women and the elderly, and volunteer-service projects among the youth are increasing, and charitable giving to institutions independent of government is going up.[8] Governmental aid programs to the poverty regions of the world seem low compared to the size of the US economy, but the contributions to charitable independent NGO's are increasing, as are volunteer workers organizing to serve all over the world. And there are more missionaries supported by church organizations working internationally on programs that are concerned with social services and economic development as well as evangelism than ever before.

Moreover, many news reports indicate greater participation of more minorities and women in the economy at every level and the rapid expansion of the number and kinds of corporations in which people work together. If economic institutions are seen as part of civil society, this means that new workmates, possibilities for new friendships, fresh attitudes, and novel professional associations are increasing, especially in employment over the past two decades in corporations with five to fifty employees, where people must cooperate as a team. David Miller has also recently documented the explosion of faith-based prayer/study/ethics/support groups that are mushrooming in the corporate context.[9] Still, Putnam was partly right, for the shape of participation has shifted in important ways, as Putnam has now recognized.[10] If Ladd is correct, then America's experience suggests that civil society can flourish globally under changing conditions.[11]

The third area where Locke and Hegel agree is that they presumed that religion would have a role in forming persons and associations in civil society. In his famed *Letter Concerning Toleration*, Locke argued for the freedom of religion and against the social, ethical, and political perils of atheism. Less well known are his writings directly on religion, some of which have been neglected for a century, as political scientists and economists did not think that religion had any real effect on what interested them. Yet, now that they have been rediscovered, they are altering the com-

8. Everett Carl Ladd, *The Ladd Report* (New York: The Free Press, 1999). An extended debate on this matter from many perspectives is available in the Ethikon Series of volumes on ethics and public affairs, edited by Nancy Rosenblum et al., *Civil Society and Government* (Princeton, NJ: Princeton University Press, 2001).

9. David W. Miller, *God at Work* (New York: Oxford University Press, 2007).

10. See the interview with Putnam, "Beyond 'Bowling Alone,'" in *The Harvard Gazette* (December, 2003), p. 9. The debates are reviewed in Corwin Smidt, ed., *Religion as Social Capital* (Waco, TX: Baylor University Press, 2003).

11. I treated these debates and their implications more extensively in "Civil Society, the State, and Religion in Contemporary America," given as a lecture in Tokyo and published in the *Seigaku-in University Journal of Advanced Studies* (Summer, 2003).

mon interpretations of his political writings.[12] Moreover Hegel's work is deeply infused with religious influence, as Lawrence Dickey has recently shown. He points to the modifications made on his earlier pietistic political loyalties by the influence of the Scottish Enlightenment authors, Adam Ferguson and Adam Smith, with their accents on civil society and economics as areas of moral life.[13] Many disciples of Locke and of Hegel and most contemporary advocates of civil society still do not take the formative role of religion in history or in social and political theory seriously, but this neglect may well be fateful for our prospects with the dramatic resurgence of religion over most of the world and the collapse of the earlier secularization hypothesis.

In this regard it may be useful to remind ourselves with a brief sketch of what Christianity has done for civil society historically.[14] In one sense, Christianity gave it birth, although the incubation period was very long, and it was nourished by many philosophical and social nutrients which it tested and selectively ingested. Many religions involve the worship of the gods of the tribe or caste, or of the gods of the city or regime. Religious identity is tied to gene pool or to the empire. The early Christians, however, worshiped a transcendent God who became also immanent in human life. They formed the church, the Body of the risen Christ as an ecclesiological fellowship. This introduced a new kind of social organization into world history, one not identical to any ethnic-based or political-based deities. In struggles that lasted over centuries it carved out a new social space in the common life, finally winning the right to exist and to be self-governing, outside the control of either the leaders of Israel or those of Rome, from whom it also drew much. And by the time of Constantine and the rise of the feudal period, when it looked as if the church might be swallowed either into the patriarchal feudal order or the imperium, the church

12. See, for example, Victor Nuovo, ed., *John Locke: Writings on Religion* (Oxford: Oxford University Press, 2002). Further texts, some from non-published manuscripts, are being edited by him; and Paul Sigmund of Princeton University hosted a major conference on the impact of these re-discoveries in May, 2004. The papers are also forthcoming.

13. See Laurence Dickey, *Hegel: Religion, Economics, and the Politics of Spirit, 1770-1807* (New York: Cambridge University Press, 1987).

14. See also the delightful little volume by Jonathan Hill, *What Has Christianity Ever Done for US* (Oxford: Lion, 2005), who traces many of the intellectual and cultural contributions. His main point is that some particular traditions are more capable than others of bearing universal and enduring principles and purposes. That is the point of speaking about the Catholic and Ecumenical Protestant traditions.

established monastic orders, taking vows of poverty, chastity, and obedience, which meant that the core of the church could not be subjected to the authority of the emperor or a feudal patriarch, even if it advocated respect for those in authority and parts of the church were tempted to subject themselves to dominant institutions and their financial support.

The leaders of the Reformation later repudiated monastic orders, and the Reformed churches found their center in the congregations of the emerging, post-feudal cities. In that context, they expanded what the late medieval church had already begun — they located themselves as a part of, not apart from, society while maintaining their own normative commitments. They opposed celibacy and saw productive economic activity as a vocation in which they could and should exercise ascetic discipline. They founded schools, hospitals, charitable and business associations, civilian associations, and proto-democratic councils with "factions" — many of the institutional clusters that we now identify as part of the civil society. These pre-modern Christians in effect established in those lands where Catholic and Reformed Christianity gained influence the very idea that groups dedicated to moral purposes and to aid the common good could and should be organized, self-governing, and able to hold wealth, publish opinions, and hold public meetings without undue control by external authorities. These developments seem more remarkable when they are compared to other ways of organizing religion around the world and when noting how the religions influenced their cultures over the centuries. On the basis of comparative studies in how religion and culture shape social development, it is fair to say that many world religions tend to subordinate independent organizations, to swallow them into either caste, tribal, or national structures, to crush them as rivals, or to co-opt them for political gain.[15]

In this regard, it has been said since Tocqueville that America more clearly represents this part of the classic Christian tradition than does Continental Europe, for while Europe has a long civilization deeply stamped by Christian influences, active participation in its churches appears to be in decline, even if populist movements rise and fall with great temporary energy. Of course, since Westphalia the national churches were established by political authority. But that support evaporated and a secular statist tendency was increased by the French Revolution (and later by the Stalinist,

---

15. See, for example, Lawrence E. Harrison et al., eds., *Culture Matters; How Values Shape Human Progress* (New York: Basis Books, 2000).

Hitlerian, and Maoist ones) when new governments took control of all "subordinate" institutions. There are exceptions, of course, and it is interesting that the exceptions are precisely in those areas where the Reformed traditions were strongest and civil societies were more mature.[16]

I should point out that America underwent a milder version of the same apparent "secularization." But many argue that the United States is now in the midst of what some call a new "Great Awakening," the explosion of Evangelical, Pentecostal, and Charismatic movements that are tied to dynamic movements in Latin America, Africa, and Asia. As David Martin and Philip Jenkins have argued with regard to Latin America and Africa, and as David Aikman has suggested with regard to China, and as I have witnessed there and in India, these movements are transforming those societies from the spiritual center out as much if not more than did the Liberation movements of the post-colonial period from the bottom up or the development schemes of the last half century from the top down.[17] We do not know of course whether these dramatic movements will generate new ranges of civil society, but my own experience in these regions suggest that they could very well do so — if they develop new versions of what the Catholic and Reformation heritage did and develop a basic theology of ecclesiology and, by extension, fresh constructive theories of a just mode of social organization.

It is well known, of course, that religion in its more classical forms played a major role in the founding of the American colonies. In my home state of Massachusetts, for example, it was illegal to form a town government until a church was established by the people of the area. Churches were organized on a congregational basis, with the members electing the pastor. They could not imagine how one could possibly expect to have a decent government if the people were not already organized according to their covenanted shared convictions and their common willingness to be regularly instructed in the Word of God. Later these same congregations became advocates for the Declaration of Independence and the Bill of

16. An argument for this view was laid out by Abraham Kuyper, Prime Minister of Holland, in his 1898 *Lectures on Calvinism* (Grand Rapids: Eerdmans Publishers, 1976 [9th printing]).

17. See, for example, David Martin, *Tongues of Fire* (London: Blackwell, 1993) and *Pentecostalism* (London: Blackwell, 2001); Philip Jenkins, *The Next Christendom*, new ed. (New York: Oxford University Press, 2003); and David Aikman, *Jesus in Beijing: How Christianity Is Transforming China and Changing the Global Balance of Power* (New York: Regnery Publications, 2003).

Rights, and still later for the abolition of slavery. Further, in the struggles against Fascism and Communism, and still later against racism in the United States and in South Africa, they played a major motivational and organizational role, always against voices in the churches that opposed these stands.[18] New research by John Nurser has also shown that direct Christian influence from related denominations was decisive in the development of the United Declaration of Human Rights.[19] And while the Ecumenical Protestant voice is less influential today, Evangelical voices are growing in influence in the public debates about social issues, in spite of the fact that they have no clear social theory, although they share, with Locke, a concern for the separation of church and state, and with Hegel, a confidence in the progressive spread of religious consciousness and of morality in public life.[20] But with a basic trust, at least in parts of America, in the born-again soul, they make personal faith the test of righteous leadership. These religious movements are deeply shaping politics. No politician, judge, or top appointee in America can today be overtly anti-religious or even non-religious and gain sustained support; and every campaign involves appearances in Christian churches, Jewish synagogues, Islamic mosques, and, in some cases, Buddhist or Hindu temples, most of which have now adopted some form of a congregational or presbyterian polity, even in those church bodies with long traditions of having bishops.[21] One can see in this that the influence of the churches on public policy is less through its direct advocacy of political programs than through the way it

18. See Reinhold Niebuhr, *Christian Realism and Political Problems* (New York: Charles Scribner, 1953); Jacques Maritain, *Man and the State* (Washington, DC: Catholic University Press, 1961); Martin Luther King, Jr., *Stride Toward Freedom* (New York: Harper & Bros., 1958); and John deGruchy et al., *The Church Struggle in South Africa*, 25th anniversary edition (Minneapolis: Fortress Press, 2005).

19. John S. Nurser, *For All Peoples and All Nations* (Washington: Georgetown University Press, 2005).

20. See, for example, Ronald Sider et al., *Toward an Evangelical Public Policy* (Grand Rapids: Baker Books, 2005).

21. What has changed in this area in America is the acceptability of the kind of religion. Until John F. Kennedy, a Roman Catholic, was elected, all Presidents and Vice Presidents were Protestant of one stripe or another. In the 2000 presidential contest, the Democratic candidate for vice president, Joseph Lieberman, was an overtly practicing Jew, and the Democratic presidential candidate, Al Gore, hosted a fund-raising event in a Buddhist monastery, while the Republican candidate, George W. Bush, made campaign stops at Evangelical colleges and churches, and named Jesus Christ as his favorite political philosopher. In 2004, Bush's opponent was reticent about discussing his Roman Catholic faith, to his considerable disadvantage.

69

has shaped the polity of the civil society and thereby provided a sense of the right order and worthy purposes of social institutions in the consciousness of the population.

Indeed, in spite of what was predicted in terms of an inevitable secularization that was to come with modernization, religion is in a state of revitalization and is again a matter of political debate and social formation.[22] But there is a rather serious problem in some of these new, vigorous movements. As I have already mentioned, many of the most vital movements in America and in the developing world do not have a conscious social theory. They may be for many good things, and they certainly are against evils of various kinds, but they have no fuller vision of a polity. Many think that religion is personal, and should be kept private, and they are supported in this by many secularists. This, in my judgment, is very dangerous: it leaves the public square spiritually naked and the moral resources of the social order drawing on historic theological-ethical capital without refilling the account. Others, of course, think that, in fact, religion inevitably generates particularist, not universal or even general, ethical perspectives that must be allowed expression in public life simply as a matter of equity since everyone speaks from a particular perspective. But this view seems to make theology merely another voice now shouted with a holy megaphone. These views, however, can easily deceive us into thinking that professing a faith guarantees the making of moral policy. Only a few, it seems, attend to the historical fact that piety shapes polity, and polity shapes policy, although it does so only over decades, generations, and centuries. The best evidence suggests, I think, that religion is a powerful force in a wide range of social matters, even if some think it should not be, and even if it is indirect and slow in the way it influences society.[23]

22. A representative group of pioneering volumes are: John Witte, Jr., *Christianity and Democracy* (Boulder, CO: Westview Press, 1993); Rodney Petersen, ed., *Christianity and Civil Society* (Maryknoll, NY: Orbis Books, 1964); T. William Boxx et al., eds., *Policy Reform and Moral Grounding* (Latrobe, PA: Center for Economic and Policy Education, 1996); Michael Perry, *Religion in Politics* (New York: Oxford University Press, 1997); Robert Audi and Nicholas Wolterstorff, *Religion in the Public Square* (New York: Rowman and Littlefield, 1997); and, more recently, William Storrar and Andrew Morton, eds., *Public Theology for the 21st Century* (London: T&T Clark, 2004).

23. This is a major hypothesis of the series I have edited with others, *Religion and the Powers of the Common Life, The Spirit and the Modern Authorities,* and *Christ and the Dominions of Civilizations,* Volumes 1, 2, and 3 of *God and Globalization* (Harrisburg, PA: Trinity Press International, 2000, 2001, and 2002). Volume 4 is my own concluding study in the series, *Globalization and Grace* (New York: Continuum, 2007).

If religion has been and is likely to be a major force in the formation and shaping of civil society in the present and, indeed, in the global future, what religion should it be, especially since the future will be quite pluralistic in both religion and social structure? The key contenders in this debate, as I have already indicated, are the Roman Catholics and the Reformed Protestants. They have theologically-refined and experience-tested ways of organizing complex systems, although they each had periods in which their complicity with tyranny and anarchy was palpable. That is true of any model of social order, I presume; but these seem to have demonstrated the capacity to self-correct. While recognizing that contributions have come from other streams of Christian thought and from non-Christian faiths, these two traditions have characteristic social theories that influenced the trajectories that are shaping the future. They both stand against anti-social sectarians and against pretentious theocrats. Most Christians in America, however critical they are of many features of modernity and global trends, see today's society as in fact more graceful, more economically successful, more democratic, more protective of human rights, and more compassionate than any other societies known to history or around the world. It is not that people are satisfied with everything that is going on; reform groups flourish in almost every venue; but they advocate reforms in the trajectory of religiously-shaped, modern society.

These two branches of the faith, the Catholic and the Reformed, see it as part of the duty of Christianity to engage and reform the recalcitrant aspects of the human soul and to advocate for just governance, but most of all to form and sustain the social ecology of the common life for the well-being of all. And in their modern form, this means promoting democracy, human rights, an open economy, and the freedom to convert and to organize. That, in my estimation, is why support for the drive to establish democracy in lands where it did not flourish, remains as strong as it is. It is a half-conscious religious thing, as well as a calculated political-economic risk. And no small number of Catholic and Protestant advisors and consultants from the think-tanks in Washington are meeting with Evangelical leaders from NGO's, voluntary associations, advocacy groups, and the offices of legislators to school them on the great Catholic and Protestant social philosophers.

Their advocates share many concerns: abortion, pornography, teen pregnancy, etc. And they are opposed to those social philosophies rooted in Marx or Darwin. They also both oppose certain secular understandings of human existence wherein legitimate social life consists only of voluntary agreements constructed by autonomous individuals on the basis of rationally calculated marginal utility or pleasure, which is how Locke is sometimes understood, or that see persons as little more than a manifestation of some collective spirit being historically manifest, which is how Hegel is sometimes read. The one view denies the ethical sociality of humans; the other obscures the moral dignity of the human person, including the capacity to transcend collective consciousness.

The Catholic and Protestant theologians of culture or society differ, however, in basic normative social theory. They have different mental maps of what the good society looks like, and what we should aim for in our social and political policies. One model may be called the "hierarchical-subsidiarity" view, most fully articulated by the Roman Catholic tradition, but held by others as well, and the other the "federal-covenantal" view, most fully articulated by the Reformed tradition, but also held by others.[24] What these two views share is a capacity to cultivate pluralism while preserving a sense of unity, although they do that differently.

While both the main models largely agree on the several threats to civil society, it may be useful to clarify the disagreement as they bear on our questions. The fundamental differences, I think, were artfully stated by F. W. Dillistone almost a half century ago. He recognized the intimate relationship of theology, ecclesiology, and social philosophy and used that relationship to compare the two models. In a sense, ecclesiology stands as the ideal model that stands between the ideal, theologically-based sense of how we think God wants us to order our lives together and the realities of social life as we live it. In *The Structure of the Divine Society,* he argues that a hierarchical-subsidiary model (which he calls "organic") presumes a naturally differentiated, vertical, complex but "singular" body, ordered by means of an internally stratified structure, spiritual and material, that aids the many parts or "organs" of the whole to fulfill their innate tendency to actualize virtue and the common good. The subsidiarity part of it indicates that the lower and local "organ" in the system has a certain priority,

24. See, for example, James Skillen and Rockne McCarthy, *Political Order and the Plural Structure of Society* (Atlanta: Scholar's Press, 1991). Parallel arguments can be found in the older book by James Hastings Nichols, *Democracy and the Churches* (Philadelphia: Westminster Press, 1951), more recently in William J. Everett, *God's Federal Republic* (New York: Paulist Press, 1988); and most masterfully in the Jewish scholar, Daniel Elazar, *The Covenant Tradition in Politics,* 4 vols. (Piscataway, NJ: Transaction Publishers, 1995-98), especially volume 3: *Covenant and Civil Society.*

because it is closer to daily life, and that the higher level authorities are designed to serve the lower ones as needed.

In contrast, the federal-covenantal view is a "pluralist" model in which religious and other institutions in society — familial, cultural, economic, educational, medical, artistic, etc. — are organized independently but work as a matrix of networked covenantal associations. Each one has its own relative sovereignty, held together by bonds of pledged agreements and a common discernment of purpose. Each sphere of human activity pursues the purposes to which it is called, while the interactive matrix of spheres is regulated by constitutionally stated principles of right and wrong.[25] Each sphere may have its own internally stratified organization for coordination purposes, but each sector within the sphere must have a substantial degree of autonomy of purpose under common regulations. Thus, the university, the hospital, and the business corporation, the church, and the art museum, and the nuclear family, for example, are free to pursue their own ends under just law, but no one of these may dictate what the other spheres do.

Both of these models avoid the perils of libertine individualism and political collectivism and both support the view that between the person and the collective are the decisive, differentiated mediating institutions that sustain life, the fabric of civil society. The technical theological, ethical difference is this: one view sees these parts of the whole as comprehended by a natural moral harmony made effective by compassionate and magisterial leadership which seeks to guide the whole to fulfill innate good ends. The other view sees various spheres of life, each constructed on the basis of a recognition of need in a broken world and a calling to meet that need. What holds the society together, indeed, is less some common, natural tendency of the whole to the good, than a working pluralism of institutions with possibly conflicting ends that are held accountable to transcendent principles of right and wrong as discerned by all the spheres.

I suspect that some combination of hierarchy with subsidiarity and the federation of covenanted groups will find their way into the future, although the efforts to combine these in the UN proposals for revising its organization or the attempts to draft an EU Constitution show that we are still on the front edge of what is required. I suspect that a formal kind of federal-covenantal model can include aspects of the hierarchical-

---

25. F. W. Dillistone, *The Structure of the Divine Society* (London: Lutterworth Press, 1951). See also Kuyper, *Lectures on Calvinism*.

subsidiarity in each one of the spheres of civil society as it is emerging in our global context, recognizing that various forms of hegemonic powers are likely to influence the actual functioning of hierarchies and the discernment and definition of normative laws of right and wrong. This, I think, can be seen as theologically valid, as practicable as any other model I can think of, and as able to form a tolerable unity in the face of an increased pluralism of faiths and organizations that global encounter is bringing. It is no accident, as the Marxists used to say, that people from many faiths and political loyalties migrate into those pluralistic societies which have embraced the modern Catholic and Reformed patterns of life.

I have sketched something of the history, development and major theories of civil society, and argued that religion is indispensable to it. If such a view is valid, it puts a special burden on clergy, community leaders, and politicians who are committed to preserving open societies and building a more just and sustainable future. It reminds us of how long any lasting transformations take and how high they must reach into transcendent realms as well as how deep into souls and societies. But such an overview may give us a mental map of where we may want to go, building on a past that provides some firm foundations for the future. This shifts the sense of role among those involved in civil society from resistance and protest to vision and construction. It also opens the door to seeing missions in a new light and seeing social participation as a kind of mission. Of course, it demands that we, as individuals, see ourselves in multiple roles in the various spheres, sectors, and areas of civil society, seeking a kind of integrity that cannot be realized by any state and only imperfectly in the human soul but which can be relatively approximated in our churches and common life. I pray it also suggests a fresh view of responsible citizenship in a global civil society, a promising vision of the catholicity of the churches and the ecumenicity of the great faiths as they can shape tomorrow's civilization.

The Place of Religion in Civil Society: Thomas Reid, Philosophical Rhetoric, and the Role of the Preacher

Alexander Broadie

Rhetoric was a prominent field of philosophical enquiry during the Scottish Enlightenment. Adam Smith lectured on the subject for about twelve years while Professor of Moral Philosophy at Glasgow University; Hugh Blair, Professor of Rhetoric and Belles Lettres at Edinburgh University, likewise lectured on the topic for many years; and George Campbell, Professor of Divinity at Marischal College, Aberdeen, and Principal of the College, published a magisterial two-volume work *The Philosophy of Rhetoric.* These were just three of the many Scots for whom philosophical rhetoric was a major subject of enquiry. A fourth leading figure of the Scottish Enlightenment who wrote on rhetoric was Thomas Reid, though his writings on the subject have gone largely unnoticed, chiefly because until very recently very few of those writings had been published.[1]

It is not surprising that Reid was interested in rhetoric, the art of persuasion by speech. He was bound to ask himself the question, firmly situated within philosophical rhetoric, what kind of argument is persuasive against philosophers who doubt or deny principles of common sense. Reid asks this in several places. Thus, for example, he writes: "How are first Principles to be defended when denied. 1 Ridicule how far proper. Mere laughing is surely no Argument & whatever force it has may be employed for Error as well as Truth. But those who deny first Principles may be often

---

1. Reid's writings on rhetoric are collected in A. Broadie, ed., *Thomas Reid on Logic, Rhetoric and the Fine Arts: Papers on the Culture of the Mind* (Edinburgh: Edinburgh University Press, 2005).

Ridiculed in a fair way by displaying the Consequences of their Opinions & the conduct in Life which they naturally lead to. The Sceptical System opens a large field for Wit Humour & Ridicule of this Kind which a Lucian[2] or a Swift would know how to improve<.> Should any such Genius ever attempt this manner of confuting Scepticks I think it would be fair dealing. For surely that opinion must be truly ridiculous which has ridiculous consequences & <implies> A Ridiculous Conduct in Life."[3] And elsewhere he writes: "Yet I do not deny that there may be occasions wherein the folly of Vice may be represented so as to be an Object of Ridicule and in like Manner where errors are to be refuted that are truly absurd and contrary to the first Principles of human Belief."[4] There is therefore no doubt that Reid expressly associated his rhetorical work with the exposition of his philosophy of common sense. The last quotation I gave is taken from a manuscript which includes what appears to be the preparatory sketch of a lecture under the title "Eloquence of the pulpit."[5] In the sketch Reid brings together reflections on rhetoric, philosophy, theology, and the place of religion in civil society.

As regards the place of religion in civil society one important detail should be noted, the fact that almost all the significant contributors to the Scottish Enlightenment were devoted members of the Kirk, Scotland's national church and a central feature of civil society in eighteenth-century Scotland. Among major figures only Hume wrote sustained hostile critiques of the church and of religion. It is true that some leading lights in the Kirk, such as William Leechman, Francis Hutcheson, John Simson, and Henry Home, Lord Kames,[6] were in more or less serious trouble with their presbyteries, or even with the General Assembly of the Church of Scotland, the Kirk's governing body; but these were men with a strong religious faith, who were judged by sharp-eyed theologians to have strayed across a

2. Lucian, Greek satirist (c. 115–c. 200 AD), author of *Dialogues of the Gods and Dialogues of the Dead.*

3. Aberdeen University Library Birkwood Collection ms 2131/4/I/8a (hereinafter Birkwood 2131/4/I/8a). The manuscript, edited and annotated, is in A. Broadie, *Thomas Reid,* p. 171.

4. Birkwood 2131/8/I/6. Broadie, *Thomas Reid,* p. 241.

5. Birkwood 2131/8/I/6. Broadie, *Thomas Reid,* pp. 240-50.

6. See Anne Skoczylas, *Mr Simson's Knotty Case: Divinity, Politics and Due Process in Early Eighteenth-Century Scotland* (Montreal: McGill-Queen's University Press, 2001). For discussion of the theological dimension of some of the travails of these ministers, see M. A. Stewart, "Religion and Rational Theology," in *The Cambridge Companion to the Scottish Enlightenment,* ed. A. Broadie (Cambridge: Cambridge University Press, 2003), pp. 31-59.

doctrinal line that would have been barely visible to many non-theologians. Indeed leading lights among the Scottish literati were not only members of the Kirk but also ordained ministers of it. Here one thinks of Francis Hutcheson, Thomas Reid, Hugh Blair, William Robertson, George Campbell, and many others. They signed the Westminster Confessions, preached the Kirk's doctrines, and in general practiced what they preached. The Enlightenment in Scotland was therefore strongly support-ive of, and in many ways was a product of, the Kirk, and of course when these ministers wrote on matters theological or otherwise ecclesiastical, it was from the distinctive Calvinist presbyterian Church of Scotland that their message came.

It may be added that the foregoing point provides strong support for the proposition that the Enlightenment in Scotland spoke with a distinc-tively Scottish accent, and that it is therefore permissible to speak of a spe-cifically Scottish Enlightenment, and not simply of Scotland as one of the places where *the* Enlightenment unfolded. In that sense the Enlightenment in Scotland was a citizen of Scotland, not a wayfarer passing through. The significance of the Scottish accent of the Scottish Enlightenment is plain if we make comparison with French discourse on religion during this same period. No one can dispute that the French Enlightenment had its own ac-cent, and it will be helpful to indicate the difference. One thinks of Voltaire's *Lettres philosophiques* (1733), which the authorities felt compelled to con-sign to the flames; of Diderot's *Pensées philosophiques* (1746) whose reprint-ing and sale were promptly made criminal offences; of his *Lettre sur les aveugles* (1749), which led to his imprisonment. There was also the *Encyclopédie* of Diderot and d'Alembert, whose publication the govern-ment attempted to stop partly for fear of the damage it would do to religion. Likewise La Mettrie was at least an agnostic, though perhaps the common judgment of him as an atheist was correct. And in his *Lettres persanes* Montesquieu wrote scathingly on the practices and beliefs of the church. Boulanger, in several of his *Encyclopédie* articles as well as in *L'Antiquité dévoilé* (1766) and Baron d'Holbach, especially in *Christianisme dévoilé* (1767) and *Le système de la nature* (1770), added their voices to the French anti-clerical chorus. These men were leading *philosophes,* and their publicly expressed ideas on religion helped to determine the character of the French Enlightenment, no less than the Scottish literati by their writings on reli-gion helped to determine the character of the Scottish Enlightenment.

When considering the question of national manifestations of the En-lightenment it is appropriate to ascribe to writings on religion a central role since religion was at the heart of the Enlightenment's all-important preoccupations with toleration and the public use of reason. On this basis we must conclude that the Scottish and the French Enlightenments were not simply different from each other but were mutually opposed. There was of course the alleged atheist Hume, who seems to have had a foot in each country but, on the basis of the considerations I have just been presenting, the *esprit* of Hume was arguably much more on the side of France than of Scotland, and the fact that he wrote the *Treatise of Human Nature* while living at La Flèche and that more than once he contemplated becoming a citizen of France, is of real significance.

In both Scotland and France we find a lively interest in the rhetoric of the pulpit. Several of Scotland's enlightened preachers reflected on the art of preaching. Hugh Blair was peculiarly well placed to engage in such reflections, since he combined the post of Professor of Rhetoric and Belles Lettres at the University of Edinburgh with that of minister of the High Kirk of St Giles in Edinburgh, thus representing in a special way the unity of theory and practice. George Campbell likewise lectured on the role of the preacher,[7] as did David Fordyce, regent at Marischal College.[8] The topic was common and indeed inevitable for many students since it had to be taught as part of the programme for the formation of Church of Scotland ministers.

As regards France, particular mention should be made of François Fénelon. His *Dialogues sur l'éloquence* (Amsterdam, 1717) opens with a discussion between three interlocutors, one of whom had just heard a sermon which he had much liked and wished to discuss with the other two. The *Dialogues* of Fénelon, as translated by William Stevenson (London, 1722), was popular in Britain in the eighteenth century, and it is perhaps particularly significant that the work was published in Glasgow in 1750 and again in 1760. Reid must have known the book well. Regarding French eloquence, it might be added that, as we shall shortly note, in a list compiled by Reid of eight famous preachers of more recent times, no fewer than four wrote in French: Valentin-Esprit Fléchier,[9] Jean-Baptiste

7. George Campbell, *Lectures on Systematic Theology and Pulpit Eloquence* (London, 1807). See Jeffrey Suderman, *Orthodoxy and Enlightenment: George Campbell in the Eighteenth Century* (Montreal: McGill-Queen's University Press, 2001).

8. David Fordyce, *Theodorus: A Dialogue Concerning the Art of Preaching* (London, 1752).

9. Valentin-Esprit Fléchier (1632-1710), Bishop of Nîmes from 1687, noted for his funeral orations.

Massillon,[10] Louis Bourdaloue,[11] and Jacques Saurin.[12] I should say, in passing, that these points indicate the need for research into the impact of French writings on Reid's rhetorical investigations, particularly in view of the fact that of the thirty books we at present know Reid to have owned, the only one that is specifically on rhetoric is *La rhétorique ou l'art de parler* (The Hague, 1725) by Gabriel Girard.[13] Here however I shall focus on Reid himself. This will at least help to define the starting point for an investigation of the kind I have just outlined.

In light of these comments it will be clear that Reid was working within a well-recognised genre when, as Professor of Moral Philosophy at Glasgow University, he lectured to his advanced class on the "eloquence of the pulpit." There is also good reason to suppose that he was well-informed about both Scottish and French writings on the subject.

In speaking of the institution of the preacher, he affirms that "it must be acknowledged by every candid Person; that this Institution, is truly worthy of God as one of the best means of carrying on the improvement of Mankind in Knowledge & Virtue."[14] The term "improvement" works hard in this passage. In an age when there was a common belief that by the exercise of intellect the human condition could be improved in all its aspects, Reid fully accepted this belief and also held that, as the mind of man is superior to the body,[15] the improvement of the mind is a nobler task than the improvement of the body. As we shall now see, he held that the preacher can play an immense role in the process of improvement.

10. Reid does not name Massillon here; he simply writes "the Bishops of Clermont," but it is probable that he had in mind Jean-Baptiste Massillon (1663-1742), Bishop of Clermont, a famous preacher, whose sermons were published in numerous editions in both French and English.

11. Louis Bourdaloue (1632-1704) was an outstanding preacher who delivered many sermons in the presence of Louis XIV. Several volumes of his sermons were published.

12. Jacques Saurin (1677-1730), a celebrated Protestant preacher and author of several volumes of sermons, including *Nouveaux sermons sur l'histoire de la Passion de Notre Seigneur Jesus Christ*, 2 vols. (Rotterdam, 1732).

13. Reid also owned a copy of *Synonimes françois*, 2 vols. (Paris 1780) by Bernard Lamy, a book sure to be of more than merely passing interest to a rhetorician.

14. Birkwood 2131/8/I/6. Broadie, *Thomas Reid*, p. 241.

15. "[T]he mind is a nobler work, and of a higher order than the body. . . ." Thomas Reid, *An Inquiry into the Human Mind*, ed. D. R. Brookes (Edinburgh: Edinburgh University Press, 1997), p. 11. "The mind of man is the noblest work of God which reason discovers to us." Thomas Reid, *Essays on the Intellectual Powers of Man*, ed. D. R. Brookes and K. Haakonssen (Edinburgh: Edinburgh University Press, 2002), p. 12.

Reid's reference to our improvement in "Knowledge & Virtue" has to be understood in the light of his description of the preacher as having "the Noblest & most Sublime Subjects to handle."[16] The subjects are: "The Nature, the Attributes & the Administration of the Supreme Being, the various Dispensations of his Grace & Goodness towards the Children of Men<,> a Future Judgment and State of Rewards and Punishment. The End we ought to propose to ourselves in the conduct of Life. The Wisdom & intrinsick Excellence of Virtue & the folly and Baseness of Vice." This range of subjects implies a formidable array of tasks for the preacher. Reid enumerates, "He has an Opportunity of instructing the Ignorant in things of the highest Moment. Of convincing the Infidel and those who are in dangerous Error by sound Argument<,> of comforting the dejected. Of rousing and awakening the thoughtless & secure. Of determining the resolutions of those who waver between vice & virtue, of fortifying the weak. Of open<ing> the Eyes of the most wicked to see the folly the pravity and danger of the Course they are taking."

One feature of the Aristotelian concept of rhetoric is prominent in this list, namely, the idea that the primary job of the orator is to deploy "sound Argument" in support of the position being defended. Reid accepts that one part of the preacher's task is to persuade his flock, and he thinks that one of the best ways to persuade is to produce a good argument. In this he sets to one side Plato's concept of the unscrupulous orator who is concerned solely to persuade and who is therefore willing to use falsehoods and invalid arguments if by so doing he secures his goal. As against this concept Reid acknowledges that we all have a faculty of reason and most of us respond positively to a good argument, and that, in the face of lack of faith or in the face of erroneous faith, the preacher's proper response is therefore to use sound arguments. But besides this role, Reid stresses that the preacher is also required to bring comfort, to arouse those who are thoughtless and feel secure (how Kierkegaardian!), to strengthen the will of the weak, and to instruct the wicked in the folly of their ways.

Surely a preacher able to achieve all these things must be able to exercise immense influence on society. Yet not many preachers have had such influence. Reid emphasizes the problems. He invokes a formidable list of recent and contemporary preachers, Robert South, Valentin-Esprit Fléchier, Jean-Baptiste Massillon, Louis Bourdaloue, John Tillotson, Jacques Saurin, Thomas Secker and Hugh Blair, and he adds sadly that

16. Birkwood 2131/8/I/6. Broadie, *Thomas Reid*, p. 240.

fewer preachers have attained the highest level of their art than have speakers in the political and the legal field, two other great classes of persuaders. Reid's explanation of this situation is of great interest.

First, politicians and lawyers can be successful speakers even in those cases where they do not have a reputation for exemplary virtue. The chief question asked of politicians is whether they can formulate good policies and can then carry out a sufficient number of their policies to retain the confidence of the electorate. The question whether they are good persons is less important. The same is true of courtroom lawyers; the issue of whether they are good at defending their clients is the only thing important to those who are wondering about hiring them. Whether the lawyer's life is morally exemplary would not normally appear on the radar screen.

The situation is quite different as regards the preacher. We require of him a higher degree of moral uprightness than is required of politicians, lawyers, or any other person whose job is to be a persuasive speaker. What makes the difference is that a main task of the preacher is to commend to his audience the paths of righteousness, and of course we are more likely to attend to him if he walks along those same paths that he commends to others. Reid affirms: "But of all Speakers the least Indulgence is shewn to him whose very profession and Bussiness it is to be an Authorised Censor of Manners & to point out every deviation from the line of our Duty. Men never fail to compare the path of Duty which he points out & recommends with his own practice. And if any Discrepance is observed, this must greatly weaken the force of his Exhortations and Reproofs."[17]

Reid's explanation for this state of affairs is that an argument of insufficient strength to convince the arguer is unlikely to have sufficient strength to convince his audience. But this explanation is insufficient and we should recall that Reid has left us only a draught. A preacher might be fully convinced by his own arguments in favour of the virtuously lived life and yet have great difficulty living such a life. At the heart of the moral theology of the Kirk is the doctrine of the Fall and the attendant idea of the depravity of the children of Adam. For all of us "the well-lived life" is barely within reach and, for most of us, the phrase points to a life-long battle with our fallen nature. In this theological circumstance the preacher has at least the role of defining the virtues and duties that all people should seek to embody in their lives, and, if he fails to measure up to his own prescription, then the Kirk's theology offers an explanation, namely that its

---

17. Birkwood 2131/8/I/6. Broadie, *Thomas Reid,* p. 242.

preachers are no less children of Adam than are the rest of us. From which it follows that a preacher who sometimes does not practise what he preaches is not therefore a hypocrite. But he is a hypocrite if he does not at least try to live up to his prescriptions for others.

All this seems obvious, but Reid's insight into the psychology of church congregations is no doubt correct, as we may expect of a perceptive man who had been attending Kirk services for over half a century, and had spent more than a decade as a parish minister. Reid's judgment is this: ". . . little or no Indulgence will be given to him who takes upon him<self> to correct others for vices from which he himself is not free. There is therefore required in the Pulpit orator in Order to his Success an uncommon Degree of purity of Morals and Sanctity of Life. An unfeigned Concern for the honour of God and the Salvation of mens Souls. A Severity against Vice joyned with pity and compassion towards the Vicious."[18] For the sake of their flock, preachers must dedicate themselves to setting an example of virtuous living. People respond to the lived example as if it is a particularly persuasive premiss in an argument, far more persuasive than a set of propositions, however well proclaimed by a silver-tongued preacher.

Reid's reference to the preacher's "unfeigned" concern for the honor of God hints at a point that elsewhere he emphasizes, namely that the preacher must not pretend to be concerned for the honor of God and the salvation of men's souls. Congregations are not stupid or blind; if the preacher is pretending, his insincerity will be noticed, he will lose the confidence of his flock, and his power of persuasion over them will vanish. That the preacher must live a life of exemplary moral virtue is the first explanation that Reid presents in support of his claim that preachers have an exceptionally difficult task fulfilling their role.

As this first explanation concerns the nature of the preacher, so the second concerns the nature of his audience. Again a contrast is made with politicians and courtroom lawyers, for in the latter cases the speakers have a restricted class of audience. Reid has in mind an advocate addressing a judge or group of judges, members of the House of Commons addressing the Commons, and, even more so, members of the House of Lords addressing their peer group. Even in the popular assemblies of ancient Greece and Rome, Reid affirms, only free men participated, not women, children, and servants. In all these cases, like speaking unto like — people with similar values, similar education, often from the same level of society.

18. Birkwood 2131/8/I/6. Broadie, *Thomas Reid,* pp. 242-43.

In such circumstances it is exceptionally easy to make oneself understood. The preacher by contrast has to work hard. As Reid puts the point: "A Christian audience especially in a populous City is of all Audiences the most promiscuous. And therefore it requires the greatest Judgment and Art to suit what is said and the Manner of Saying it to the Audience."[19] The advocate knows the appropriate level for his discourse, as also does a peer in the House of Lords, but the preacher cannot speak at the level of the best-educated and best-informed members of his congregation without losing the attention of those with least attainment, nor aim specifically at those with least intellectual attainment without losing the attention of the others.

Reid is deploying here the thought that a congregation in a populous city represents society by being a microcosm of it, and the preacher must reflect this fact about the congregation. In a sense therefore the preacher is a principle of unity of society, by reflecting in his sermons a certain epistemic and evaluative common denominator, and also by being to his utmost power a repository of the values into which he wills society to rise. What is at issue here for Reid is not the exposition of a new set of values, but instead both an intensification of values which citizens will in any case possess and also a firmer will to live by those values.

As to the rhetorical means by which the preacher is to succeed with his flock Reid declares himself on the side of the newly-established rhetoric of "plainness." His model is natural science: "When a Botanist describes a New Plant, or a Writer in Agriculture directs the Operations of the Farm. When a Physician describes the case of his Patient, or prescribes him a Regimen. When a Philosopher [i.e. a natural philosopher] explains a natural Phenomenon. When a Prince or his Minister of State delivers Instructions to a General[,] an Admiral or an Ambassadour, the didactick Style is the onely one that is congruous to the Occasion. Perspicuity & precision are the onely Ornaments to be allowed."[20]

Of course, to describe perspicuity as an "ornament" is to push the rhetorical concept of "ornament" to breaking-point, as Reid would have appreciated. But the point is clear — perspicuity is analogically a kind of ornament, for as ornamentation is a virtue with regard to certain kinds of verbal communication, so perspicuity is a virtue with regard to scientific communication. Reid affirms: "There are certain occasions where truth

19. Birkwood 2131/8/I/6. Broadie, *Thomas Reid*, p. 243.
20. Birkwood 2131/8/I/3. Broadie, *Thomas Reid*, p. 214.

appears to most advantage Naked, where every Ornament but perspicuity and distinctness tends to disguise it. . . . . All that a good Speaker ought to aim at on such occasions is propriety in the choice of words<,> plainness & perspicuity in the Structure of his Sentences; so that there be nothing wanting to make his meaning distinct and determinate; nothing superfluous; nothing misplaced."[21] This is manifestly a requirement in the case of the exposition of science. Thus botany, agriculture, medicine, physics, and mathematics require the plain, perspicuous, precise style, and, it should be added, these sciences exclude almost all the rhetorical features and devices upon which the great classical rhetoricians focused.

Reid now adds that what is right for the scientist is also right for the preacher; perspicuity is the chief weapon for both. He affirms, "As in every Subject where the Didactick Style is used so particularly in Instruction from the Pulpit, Perspicuity ought carefully to be studied. There is no instruction where the Understanding of the hearer is not carried along. And the Preacher having, of all Audiences, the most promiscuous, ought to adapt his Style to the capacity of the greater part, which in all Congregations are the unlearned, & unimproved. There may <be> a want of Perspicuity even when Scripture Phrases are used, if they are not explained or so used as to make their meaning obvious. There are many Words and Phrases in use among the learned and among Persons in the higher Spheres of Life which are not understood by the Vulgar, which ought to be avoided in popular Discourses, in order to perspicuity. There are even Theological Terms of this Kind which ought to be kept within the Schools of Theology and ought not to be carried to the Pulpit."[22]

This is not to say that the preacher should never use metaphor, simile, and the thousand other types of rhetorical figure, but simply that the preacher must direct his words especially to the intellect of his audience. If they do not even understand him then how can they respond, as he wishes, in other more affective ways? In all this the sermon reflects society and unites its microcosm, the congregation, at an appropriate level of understanding. Reid hints that theological and even biblical language might have to be avoided — terms such as "apophasis," "kerygma," and "supersessionism" will mean nothing to many (or perhaps any) in the congregation. But that constraint does not make the preacher's task more difficult. Reid defines eloquence as "the Art of Speaking so as to answer the pur-

21. Birkwood 2131/8/I/3. Broadie, *Thomas Reid*, p. 213.
22. Birkwood 2131/8/I/6. Broadie, *Thomas Reid*, pp. 246-47.

pose intended by it."[23] The preacher's purpose is to secure the congregation's understanding of religious truths, truths that save, and the greater the perspicuity of the message the greater the prospect of the congregation grasping the meaning with due accuracy. This hardly needs supporting argument, and it means that perspicuity plays an immense role. By an infinite margin salvific truth is the most important truth, and of course perspicuity is the greatest rhetorical virtue in the exposition of such truth.

Without moving far from this point concerning the place of salvific truth in the scheme of things, Reid turns to the consideration of a third reason that may be adduced to explain why it is that, of those classes of people whose job it is to be persuasive, preachers have a harder task than politicians and courtroom lawyers. The point concerns the subject-matter of sermons. On the one hand, it might seem that the preacher has the advantage in respect of subject-matter since he deals with "the most Sublime and the most important of all Subjects of Discourse," namely the perfections and providence of God, the relations in which we stand to him and to our fellow-creatures, and the duties we have in consequence of these relations. Compared with these topics those within the brief of lawyers and politicians might seem less significant. Here one thinks of lawyers expounding the ambiguities of statutes and the apparent contradictions between laws or precedents, or arguing the relative weight to assign to conflicting testimony. But as against this it should be acknowledged that lawyers do sometimes have to speak on matters of life and death. And of course politicians sometimes have to speak on matters of immense moment, such as war and peace. Nevertheless, Reid insists, "The most important concerns of our present Life vanish when compared with those of the Life to come."

If the preacher has the great advantage of discoursing on the most sublime and important of all subjects, why is his task so difficult? Reid's reply is that the preacher is dealing with things, such as virtue and vice, that are objects of the intellect, not of the senses, and the majority of people, living mostly in the world of the senses, do not have the intellectual and spiritual ability needed to grasp abstract notions. Yet Reid immediately steps back from this line of thought, on the reasonable grounds that there are effective ways to expound abstract notions to the multitude. Thus even if the preacher should avoid abstract disquisitions on the virtues and vices,

23. Birkwood 2131/8/I/2. Broadie, *Thomas Reid*, p. 204.

he can and should speak about virtuous and vicious people. Sermons on saints and sinners can be understood by most or all congregations, and should hold their attention. In that sense the preacher's subject matter should not prove an obstacle to his success.

But there is another aspect to the subject matter that needs to be considered, one especially important in relation both to the civic discourse of the Scottish Enlightenment, and also to the concept of the preacher as a central figure of Scottish civic life. Let us therefore note that a fourth obstacle that the preacher has to overcome concerns the extent to which the Christian doctrine, or at least what Reid terms "the pure doctrine of Jesus Christ," is contrary to the principles, passions, and habits by which most people are governed. At the heart of this doctrine is the idea that our station in this life is that of pilgrims; we are wayfarers destined for a world which is not this one. But though our being is towards another life, it is in this life that we prepare for the later one. Since our nature is designed to enable us to live our present life, it is, therefore, on the here-and-now that we are for the most part focused. The necessities of our nature hold our attention, as also therefore do those things surrounding us that we naturally see as to hand, things out there that will enable us to survive and perhaps even to live well. This fact about our nature has implications for our intellectual powers. We live in this world, our experiences are of it, our language is formed as a means to enable us to communicate with like beings about this shared world. Hence, however much our being may be, by God's grace, towards another world and another life, that is not the direction in which our thoughts lie or in which they can easily be taught to lie. The preacher's problem seems clear. It is as if he has to work against the very grain of our nature, particularly the grain of our intellect, to persuade us to focus on the other-worldly message of Christ.

But, as with the preceding obstacle to the preacher's task, we realize on reflection that the preacher's problem is not so serious. For it is possible to overemphasize the other-worldliness of Christianity, and we do that if we do not also emphasize its this-worldliness. If the preacher cannot usefully preach a Christian message to his mixed audience about the next world, he can and should preach a Christian message about this one. Reid reminds his students that it is part of the divine dispensation that now we see through a glass darkly. The things that are wholly of faith are invisible to us and can, as he says, be assented to but not with that irresistible conviction which sense or memory produces. Here Reid helps himself to some phrases from a sermon preached by Hugh Blair that deserves to be far better known.[24] Paraphrasing Blair he declares: "Were we to discern the things of a future World with the same irresistible Evidence as we see those which occupy our thoughts & cares here, we should be rendered altogether unfit for the Occupations of our present State. Earthly concerns would not have the power of engaging our Attention for a single Moment. All human Objects would be annihilated in our Eye; and a total Stagnation in the Affairs of this world would be the Consequence. All the Studies and pursuits, the Arts and Labours which now employ the Activity of Man would be neglected and Abandoned. Man would no longer be a fit inhabitant of this World, nor be qualified for those exertions which are allotted to him in his present State of Being. His views being raised above the measure of humanity, he would regard the pursuits of Men with Scorn as Dreams and puerile Amusements."[25] On this account, to be granted now a vision of the future state would be a practical disaster. We would be so bewitched by what we saw as to be rendered incapable of recognizably human behavior, indeed of any behavior beyond that of gazing. But what has that to do with being a human being if that is all that there is to us?

Let the preacher therefore focus on our pilgrim state, and preach about what is most important that is also subject to our will, namely the mode of conduct that is appropriate for us in the course of our pilgrimage. It is in God's hands whether we are accepted for eternal life. But — and here we shift out of the long shadow that St Augustine had cast across earlier Protestant forms, including Scottish forms — it is in our hands whether we live a godly life, and it is the task of the preacher to give guidance. What are the qualities by which we may live our godly lives? Reid lists them: "The Virtues of Fortitude[,] Temperance & Self denial, of Moderation in prosperity, patience in Adversity, submission to the will of God, Charity and a forgiving disposition towards Men."[26] These, then, are the proper pursuits of us human beings here, and it is precisely these pursuits that would become impossible for us if now we could see "face to face," and not just "through a glass, darkly."

Most of the items in this list of virtuous qualities are no less Stoic than they are Christian — fortitude, temperance, self-denial, moderation in prosperity, patience in adversity: what Stoic could not assent to these? And

---

24. Hugh Blair, *Sermons* (Edinburgh 1824), vol. 1, sermon 4: "On our imperfect knowledge of a future state," pp. 40-53. The sermon is reproduced in A. Broadie, ed., *The Scottish Enlightenment: An Anthology* (Edinburgh: Canongate Books, 1997), pp. 333-43.

25. Birkwood 2131/8/I/6. Broadie, *Thomas Reid*, p. 245.

26. Birkwood 2131/8/I/6. Broadie, *Thomas Reid*, p. 245.

the list, being Stoic, has a conspicuously civic dimension. All these qualities are necessary if the state is to flourish; collectively they compose the virtue of citizenship. We pilgrims, as said earlier, cannot determine God to grant us eternal life, but we can at least be godly, and a major part of godliness is good citizenship, the promotion of the happiness of society, the promotion of the well-being of our neighbors and of our neighborhood no less than of ourselves and our own home. Good citizenship is a virtue that everybody can understand, and a preacher need face no great obstacle in seeking to enlighten his flock regarding its sovereign significance.

This is not to say that the preacher will easily secure compliance. Reid affirms, "There is no kind of Perswasion that has greater force of Argument to support it, yet there is none that is commonly attended with less Success than that which is employed to perswade Men to amend their Moral Conduct to correct their Vices to subdue their passions and to act the part which their own Minds dictate to them, they ought to act. This is the chief part of the bussiness of the Preacher and of all the most difficult. The difficulty . . . arises not from the want of Solid Arguments but from the strength of evil habits and of animal Passions and the Weakness of the governing Principles of Reason & Conscience."[27]

Though we do not possess sermons by Thomas Reid, we possess many by his fellow ministers among the moderates in the Kirk. A conspicuous feature of their message is that overwhelmingly it is this-worldly, not other-worldly, it emphasizes the imperative that we love our neighbor as ourselves, and this imperative is interpreted in civic terms. These men were not preachers of hell-fire, nor did they dwell long on the depravity that came into the world through the first sin. They rejected the enthusiasm that dictated attitudes of exclusivity and intolerance, for these were irrational things against which the Enlightenment placed the intellectual virtue of autonomous reason and the moral virtue of toleration.[28] Enthusiasm was a mode of spirituality that had to be rejected because it was neither mediated nor therefore moderated by reason, least of all by reason in the form of scientific enquiry. The moderate clergy insisted that reason, perhaps especially reason in the form of scientific enquiry, has by right an im-

27. Birkwood 2131/8/I/6. Broadie, *Thomas Reid*, pp. 249-50.
28. Reid contrasts enthusiasm with enlightened Christianity: "That fervour of Piety which is not grounded upon a Sound Understanding of the Principles of Religion, is commonly of short duration, and has but a small Influence upon the Conduct of Life when that fervour cools, and even while it lasts it borders more upon Enthusiasm than upon Rational Piety." Birkwood 2131/8/I/6. Broadie, *Thomas Reid*, p. 246.

mense role to play in relation to religion, for if a religion cannot defend itself effectively in cross-examination before the tribunal of reason then it is simply a failed religion.

To reach this position the Scottish enlightened Christians had to journey an immense distance from the concept, entertained by some Protestants, that reason was a corrupted faculty whose exercise in matters of religion was an obstacle to the flowering of faith. The moderate preachers preached Enlightenment values from the pulpit, and as they preached so they lived, embodying in their own lives those very values into which they encouraged their flock to grow. In this sense the moderate preachers of the Kirk were a principle of unity of Scottish society.

Trinity, Church, and Global Civil Society

Introduction to Part II

Peter J. Casarella and Paul Louis Metzger

Christianity, as Lamin Sanneh has cogently argued, is a translated religion without a revealed language.[1] In other words, the Gospels are accompanied and permeated by a process of translation from their inception. What is known as the apostolic witness to Jesus Christ, i.e. the inchoate church of the first century, is unrecognizable without the simultaneous recognition of the fact that Jesus did not write or dictate his own message and that no one language has ever received final authority as its authoritative form of transmission. The highlighting of a *process* of translation does not relativize the objective content of the message itself. To see the Gospel as translated is in fact not a rejection of pivotal concepts like a revealed Word, the inspiration of the Scriptures, or the canonicity of the final form. It is rather a frank admission of a global reality that was present at the original event and whose continued presence takes on a renewed relevance in the light of the considerations of this book.

The testing of a notion of global civil society by Christian theologians today thus parallels the desire for mutual translation and mutual transformation that appears in Part I in the essay by Kimberly Hutchings with thanks to Judith Butler. The frank exchange of ideas on the part of the theoreticians of civil society is met in Part II by a similar effort on the part of Christian theologians throughout the globe. The fear of an imposition

---

1. Lamin Sanneh, *Whose Religion Is Christianity? The Gospel beyond the West* (Grand Rapids: Eerdmans, 1993), p. 97. See also his *Disciples of all Nations: Pillars of World Christianity* (Oxford: Oxford University Press, 2008).

of a global ethic that is too hegemonic, too western, too modern, too white, and too tone deaf to the concerns of the global South and others remains in place here. But there is also the hope that by engaging the conversation the contemporary heirs of the translated Gospel of the first century can continue to engage in a process of inculturation. Sanneh has aptly called this founding search for fresh modes of communication the church's own birthmark.[2]

The present series of essays also make a contribution to the existing academic literature. Although much work is currently being done by scholars laboring at the intersection of public theology and civil society, there is a notable lack of reflection on the new global reality as a theme for *systematic* theology.[3] A notable exception is the recently published book edited by Jeanne Heffernan Schindler that touts a new collaboration between Roman Catholics working out of the tradition of Thomism and the modern papal teachings on subsidiarity and Neo-Kuyperian Calvinists attentive to the role that the Reformed tradition can play in the formation of U.S. public policy today.[4] The editors of Part II of this volume share with the noteworthy authors assembled by Heffernan a commitment to the challenging task of rebuilding structures of civil society in the public square of the United States, structures that can seem eclipsed both by society's own deep-rooted individualism and the state's functional ambiva-

---

2. Lamin Sanneh, *Whose Religion Is Christianity?* p. 97.

3. Representative works in the field include: John Keane, *Global Civil Society?* (Cambridge: Cambridge University Press, 2003); John Coleman and William Ryan, eds., *Globalization and Catholic Social Thought: Present Crisis, Future Hope* (Maryknoll, NY: Orbis, 2005); William F. Storrar and Andrew R. Morton, eds., *Public Theology for the 21st Century: Essays in Honour of Duncan B. Forrester* (London/New York: T&T Clark, 2004); Marlies Glasius, David Lewis, and Hakan Seckinelgin, eds., *Exploring Civil Society: Political and Cultural Contexts* (London/New York: Routledge, 2004); Pratt, ed., *Changing Expectations? The Concept and Practice of Civil Society in International Development* (INTRAC, 2003); and Salamon, Sokolowski, and List, *Global Civil Society: An Overview* (Baltimore: Johns Hopkins Center for Civil Society Studies, 2003); Max Stackhouse and Peter Paris, eds., *God and Globalization*, Volume I: *Religion and the Powers of the Common Life* (Harrisburg, PA: Trinity Press International, 2000); Max Stackhouse and Don S. Browning, eds., *God and Globalization*, Volume II: *The Spirit and the Modern Authorities* (Harrisburg, PA: Trinity Press International, 2000); Max Stackhouse, ed., *God and Globalization*, Volume III: *Christ and the Dominions of Civilization* (Harrisburg, PA: Trinity Press International, 2003); Max L. Stackhouse (with a foreword by Justo González), *God and Globalization*, Volume IV: *Globalization and Grace* (New York/London: Continuum, 2007).

4. Jeanne Heffernan Schinder, ed., *Christianity and Civil Society: Catholic and Neo-Calvinist Perspectives* (Lanham, MD: Lexington Books, 2008).

lence towards genuine subsidiarity. Like these Thomists and Neo-Kuyperians, we see collaboration between Catholicism and the churches of the Reformation (including, in our case, evangelical Protestants in the U.S.) as engaged in the sort of ongoing task outlined by Max Stackhouse in his essay in Part I of this volume. At the same time the new global discourse about Christianity and civil society cannot assume that the final terms of alliance between practicing Christians and today's builders of civil society have been negotiated once and for all. The conversation goes on, and new challenges to the discourse of civil society from across the globe — Christian and non-Christian — need to be faced.

In spite of the weakening of structures of civil society in many of the most developed parts of the globe, the editors of this volume remain convinced that the topic of civil society will continue to play a role in the public theological landscape for the foreseeable future and thus consider it both timely and necessary to bring theology into the conversation. Above all, we seek to guide the discussion of the emerging paradigm for a global ethic of civil society by gleaning insights from the contemporary renaissance in trinitarian thought. In the last few decades, theologians from many confessions and in diverse corners of the globe have all underscored the unique intimacy and love the three divine persons of the Trinity share and have suggested that there is a profound and provocative form of critical reflection imbedded within the ancient confession of faith. Some have argued that the creedal and liturgical affirmation of the Trinity must be imported into the social realm. More recently, there has been a justified backlash against the so-called "social analogy of the Trinity." The under standable critical response points reverently to a divine mystery disclosed only in a stammering fashion by the confession of the believer in one God who is Father, Son, and Holy Spirit. The social analogy's critics rightly caution against translating a central article of faith into a social program, for no such institutional program can replace or condition the praise for Father, Son, and Holy Spirit who as the one God constitutes the life of the church.[5] This volume represents a hitherto unexplored *via media* between the proponents of the social analogy and their recent critics. On the one hand, the authors of these essays affirm that the church is the true home and guardian of the trinitarian confession of faith. On the other hand, they resist the notion that the church's confession of triune faith is a silent witness. Deep within the ecclesial abode are treasures both old and new wait-

---

5. The literature on this topic is cited below in the essay by Peter Casarella.

ing to be proclaimed in the public square. The contributors to Part II of this volume seek to uncover these treasures.

The need to nurture and promote civil society is vital, not only in the western world, which is increasingly subject to the dehumanizing and to-talitarian forces of radical individualism and the market economy, but also in the non-western world, including emerging democracies and those cultures where Christianity has to be lived out in the context of multi-faith realities. The church is a participant in society not subject to the sphere of the market or the state. In this light, the church has a contribution to make to the civil society dialogue, especially in terms of its dogmatic reflections.

The authors recognize that the current interest in civil society makes it possible for the church to occupy a place at the table of democratic discourse and understand that such participation necessitates that the church make its theological discourse intelligible to a broader public. The contributors have no ambition of either desiring a restored Christendom or accommodating the church's vision of the good to the liberal model of a procedural republic. The mystery of God's kingdom allows for neither. Nonetheless, the divine love dwelling within the church propels its members forward to witness to and for civil society even while their gaze is fixed elsewhere. This volume is original in that it does not either follow or ignore recent attempts at a Christian political theology in a trinitarian key. A central thesis of *A World for All? Global Civil Society in Political Theory and Trinitarian Theology* is that the radical otherness of God is not sacrificed for the sake of promoting social progress. Rather, a radical giving that never cancels out difference is seen in the first instance as a revealed truth to which the church bears witness as it addresses social concerns in light of the ecclesial and eucharistic reception of the trinitarian gift of difference.

A Global, Ecumenical Conversation

It is no surprise that the editors faced new and sometimes unforeseen challenges in producing a volume of this scope. To the degree that we have met them, it is instructive to consider these issues, for they are precisely the ones that anyone will face today in attempting to undertake a conversation on a global, ecumenical level while maintaining a serious commitment to the particular convictions of one's local and ecclesial community.

The first challenge concerns how to negotiate concretely the complex reality of the Christian *oikumene* of the twenty-first century. The editors recognized that the catholicity of the volume had to extend beyond an earnest attempt to affirm geographically diverse voices. While the essays do emanate from local communities on the Asian, African, European, and American continents, there is even a more intriguing unity in diversity to be found in the various political, social, economic, and cultural realities that inform them. This catholicity extends the vision engendered by Stackhouse in Part I of a primarily western Catholic and European Reformed alliance onto a stage that highlights the contribution of the global South and includes as one of its most compelling proponents a Pentecostal drawing upon the Eastern Orthodox traditions of Bulgaria! From this vantage point new issues come to the fore. For example, contributors in Part II decry the problem of poverty in its global context and extol the need for ecclesial communities to contribute to existing networks within civil society that enhance interconnectedness and facilitate communication in such a way as to ameliorate such injustices. This volume does not proffer a single recipe for bringing this about. Nor do we have any illusions of supporting the artificial construction of a para-ecclesial global structure that somehow competes with existing religious or civil institutions. Instead we see our rootedness in particular local communities with fairly diverse Christian commitments as a necessary enrichment to the public conversation about civil society that now traverses the globe. There is in a real sense a "glocal" ecclesiology at work in this conversation whereby the deepening of one's particularity in a local community of faith was seen as a necessary prerequisite and thoroughly positive stimulus to the genuine catholicity of our collaboration. Moreover, each of the contributors faced a different set of questions regarding the conversation *ad extra* with non-Christian communities. The problem of interreligious dialogue is very different when considered from the perspective of Portland, Oregon or Bangalore, India. In each case, however, an immersion in the diverse richness of particular Christian narratives was no impediment to the all too timely and much needed dialogue with traditions other than Christianity. Particular narratives are also our point of entry to confronting the globalizing reality of the contemporary Areopagus.

Second, this project was conceived from the beginning as an experiment in ecclesial ecumenism. The contributors belong to Reformed, Anglican, Pentecostal, Lutheran, Roman Catholic, and Evangelical churches. Once again, one may reasonably ask in the absence of a single institutional framework what binds such diverse confessional standpoints into a common project. As a group the common viewpoints expressed are even different from that of a formal entity like the World Council of Churches. No one signed a common statement in order to participate in this project, and no one was even asked to recognize in a formal way the doctrinal congruences or divergences that evolved in the process. There are, however, common denominators. A unifying experience of the Lord's Supper during the struggle against apartheid in South Africa sheds considerable light on the approach to ecumenism that we adopted.[6] In his essay Dirkie Smit argues that Christian worship (a *lex orandi* that is simultaneously a *lex credendi*) creates its own uniquely Christian way of being in the world. We understand this form of life as integral to our identity as persons of faith. Christian worship, Smit further maintains, carries its own foundation and purpose, ecclesial ends that can never be made an instrument of any social program. For that reason, the editors see their ecumenical credentials, as it were, in the conjoining of a confession of faith, a personal and liturgical act of praise, and an actual being in communion that derives from the church's living witness to the triune God. Even without a signed statement, what Smit terms the common *lex convivendi* of Christian faith undergirds and strengthens our common purpose.

Third, the volume also offers a rich communion of theological perspectives. The trinitarian confession of faith as expounded in Scripture and the ecclesial nourishment handed down in the Christian tradition contribute a common idiom and firm, jointly held convictions for the collaborators. Beyond that, however, no theological litmus test was placed upon the individual authors. As a consequence, one notes significant differences of accentuation regarding the particular ways in which Trinity and even church function in the different essays. The authors are located in diverse theological traditions and inhabit unique perspectives within and on the one body of Christ. Likewise, the contributions contain highly particular narratives of struggle, liberation, identity, and recovery of tradition. They are also diverse in terms of sources, methods, and political orientations. However, the common aim was to test the new discourse of global civic participation and preserve what is good for the church and society.

Beyond Scripture and the recent trinitarian revival, the resources that have influenced the contributors to the present volume include Augustine's *City of God,* the Cappadocian Fathers' trinitarian theology, Richard of St. Victor's *On the Trinity,* the Reformers' theology of the proclaimed Word, Jonathan Edwards' trinitarian ethic, Karl Barth's theology

---

6. See the essay by Dirkie Smit below for this story and the analysis that follows.

of culture, Arnold A. Van Ruler's theocratic politics, and Hans Urs von Balthasar's theo-drama. The diverse essays recount struggles for democracy and social justice, concerns about expanding secularization and privatization of religious belief, prophetic cries against residual structures of colonialist hegemony, and fears of recurring inter-religious strife and violence inflicted in the name of God. Each contributor seeks to show the relevance of the trinitarian confession of faith for his or her ecclesial and social context.

The essays in Part II are further sub-divided into three sections: (1) Trinity and Church in a Global Civil Society, (2) Resources from the Christian Tradition for a Global Conversation, and (3) Contextual Approaches to a Global Civil Society. The first three essays set the stage for what follows and deal with the systematic starting points for a trinitarian view of dialogue.

The opening essay by Nico Koopman of the University of Stellenbosch in South Africa is entitled: "Global Civil Society, Church Unity, and World Unity." Koopman offers an overview of the history of the concept of global civil society and illustrates some of the dominant senses that the term has come to embody among political theorists and in global politics today. Koopman then turns to the tradition within Christianity of rooting the identity of the church in the biblical idea of a kingdom, but his political aim moves away whatever theocratic implications this image may have had in the Christian past. He argues rather that the unity embodied by the church can contribute positively to a vision of the world that supports and supplements the nascent ethic of a democratic civil society. More specifically, he says, the unity that the church proclaims and embodies in a provisional way is a sign of the eschatological salvation of the cosmos, specifically of *shalom.* The unity of the church as cosmic-eschatological sign entails that the local and global church, i.e. the glocal church, through its provisional embodiment of this *shalom,* and through its public involvement with other members of glocal civil society, serves the penultimate flourishing of *shalom* in the cosmos.

The second piece by Peter J. Casarella of DePaul University in Chicago examines "Thinking Out Loud about the Triune God: Problems and Prospects for a Trinitarian Social Ethic in a Procedural Republic." Casarella begins with the observation that a Christian social ethic based on God's self-revelation as triune faces serious problems in the United States. Defenders of "procedural liberalism" willy-nilly regard any thick description of the contents of faith as unsuited to public debate. They want the political discussion to focus on religiously neutral, individual rights rather than tradition-dependent visions of the good. More pointed objections derive from systematic theologians who find the "social analogy of the trinity" wanting because its defenders erroneously read attributes of the divinity into human relations. Increasingly in our world today the dogmatic privatization of faith that structures and even mars religious freedom in the U.S. is seen as a commodity for the global market of ideas. To that degree, even while the point of departure of this essay may be a current debate over the future of U.S. civic republicanism, the essay also aims to clear the ground for the conversation regarding Trinity, church, and global civil society in the essays that follow.

Kristin Deede Johnson of Hope College in Holland, Michigan considers "'Public' Re-Imagined: A Reconsideration of Church, State, and Civil Society." This essay examines one of the fundamental questions addressed by the entire volume and considers a path quite different from the main trajectory of Part I of this volume. She articulates a vision for a "post-secular political realm" in which the church is seen as an embodied social reality rather than as a mere voluntary association. She offers a criticism of Keane's concept of global civil society based upon the historical analysis of civil society by Adam Seligman and the retrieval of categories derived from Augustine's *City of God* by theologian Rowan Williams. Rather than treating Christianity as an essentially private discourse that needs to accommodate itself to the public realm now dominated by political liberalism, Johnson argues that the church is its own public, a claim that need not erase the distinction between public and private altogether. With a reinvigorated notion of the public as a post-secular communion of smaller solidarities, she maintains that "members of these publics still abide by the rule of law of a given political system, but their identities and conceptions of the good can be shaped more by the social realities of which they are a part than by that political system."

The recovery of an ecclesial memory is integral to the present task of reconstructing a wholly new approach to the social analogy of the Trinity and to a fundamental re-consideration of how Christian theology addresses its multiple publics. The second section of Part II thus offers three historical perspectives on the present situation in the church and the world. Petr Pokorný of Charles University in Prague in the Czech Republic contributes an essay on "Early Christianity and Politics: Its Real Role and Potential Contribution." He looks at the original meaning of *ekklesia* for the Christian community and underscores the special role of eschatological hope in the Christians' formation of a social strategy. While he emphasizes that the Christians formed no political party, he also sketches the way in which an impulse for social reform accompanied the idea of a fulfillment of history centered on Jesus' proclamation of the gospel and the empowering revelation of his resurrection from the dead.

J. Jayakiran Sebastian of the Lutheran Theological Seminary at Philadelphia (and United Theological College, Bangalore, India), contributes an essay entitled "Intertwined Interaction: Reading Gregory of Nazianzus Amidst Inter-religious Realities in India." Sebastian is writing from the intercultural and interreligious situation of contemporary India, and his essay looks simultaneously to the richness of trinitarian reflection by the Greek Father and to the complex negotiation of the politics of identity in a radically multi-religious country. He concludes: "Obviously our struggle at the beginning of the twenty-first century to understand the promise and peril of life together in a globalized world cannot conclude with the affirmation of a social reality beyond all conceptual understanding." On the other hand, he recognizes that the actualization of the *norm* of a global civil society can issue willy-nilly in a paradoxical tension between the absolute freedom of the individual and collective action pursued in the name of promoting justice and democracy. As such, the ancient Christian struggle to articulate the unfathomable mystery of a triune God, Sebastian argues, is a new paradigm for confronting such paradoxes and seeing beyond any possible foundationalism to the fruitful exchange of divergent perspectives.

The last historical contribution comes from William J. Danaher, Dean of Theology at Huron University College in Western Ontario. Danaher treats "Jonathan Edwards, Francis Hutcheson, and the Problems and Prospects of Civil Society." Danaher compares two alternative conceptions of civil society from the eighteenth century. Edwards and Hutcheson did not agree on their visions of either theology or society. Where Hutcheson grounded his social vision in a naturalized, if religious, account of beauty, benevolence, and virtue, Edwards insisted that these attributes properly emanate from the triune God, who communicates them directly to human beings. These diverging theological anthropologies generated divergent conceptions of civil society. For Hutcheson, the good society was one that allowed persons the freedom to express their naturally benevolent inclinations without the interference of overarching institutions or dogmatic structures. For Edwards, the good society was one in which every level of sociality — ecclesial, political, familial, associational — was transformed by the triune benevolence of God. Danaher further argues that the

theological contrasts between Edwards and Hutcheson indicate the difficult terrain over which contemporary theological evaluations of civil society must travel. Anyone interested in combining the best features of these
approaches must recognize the very real differences between their projects,
a recognition that can complicate any easy synthesis. In spite of that (or
perhaps even because of it), he concludes, all creation bears the marks of
the triune God, and such vestiges can also be found in contemporary civil
society.

The third section of Part II focuses on five contextual approaches and
explores global dialogue through the particularities of each situation.
Daniela Augustine of Lee University in Cleveland, Tennessee (and formerly a
professor of theology in Bulgaria) contributes "Pentecost as the Church's
Cosmopolitan Vision of Global Civil Society: A Post-Communist Eastern
European Theological Perspective." Augustine considers the fragile realities
of eastern Europe since the fall of communism and offers a paradigm for
civil society based upon the Pentecost experience. Whereas the Hegelian and
Marxist absolutization of historical ends were shattered with the end of
communism, the present eastern European task of reconstructing historical
ends within the new global setting beckons for new models. She argues that
due to its historical and cultural removal from the West, the eastern European context has maintained more distinctly communal dynamics. The current disillusionment of eastern Europeans with western capitalist democracy
could be seen as a consequence of the realities of communal disintegration,
alienation, and egocentrism that are the results of its new socio-economic
conditions. Eastern European countries could nonetheless contribute toward the recovery of the communal dimension in political economy and
democratic theory and enhance the process of developing a global moral
community. In this context, the event of Pentecost is both a reversal of Babel
and a welcome antidote to any reversion to a new imperialist consciousness.
The breathing of new life into the community by the Holy Spirit provides a
new language for affirming badly needed hospitality in a global civil society.
In the divine hospitality of Pentecost, she claims, "We find that we belong together, and this is a hopeful discovery for a world traumatized in its global
compression and exhausted political imagination." The global paradigm of
Pentecost issues in "a hope for a future of cosmopolitan hospitality — the
future of humanity in the likeness of God."

Christoffel Lombard of the University of the Western Cape in South
Africa (and formerly a professor of theology in Namibia) offers "Reflections on God, Church, and Civil Society in Namibia." This contribution

reflects on three related "entities": the new challenges for post-war and post-independence civil society in Namibia, the struggles of the ecumenical churches to generate a prophetic public theology and praxis within civil society, and the task of relating such initiatives in the public sphere to an empowering and encompassing theology (God-talk). Using the trinitarian and theocratic approach of the Dutch theologian, Arnold A. van Ruler, and reflecting upon a selection of social justice issues (including the test-case of the so-called "ex-detainee" crisis for the current SWAPO government and the churches), a theological way is sought for developing an adequate mode of public theology. The supposition is that only a fully-developed trinitarian theology can address issues such as dualistic tendencies ("two kingdoms"), real reconciliation in a divided nation, human rights abuses, poverty, marginalization, and ecological ethics, through developing a vision of justice, hope and peace — for church, state, and society at large.

Dirkie Smit of the University of Stellenbosch contributes an essay entitled "Worship — and Civil Society? Perspectives from a Reformed Tradition in South Africa." Christian worship played a crucial role in the struggle against apartheid. Common worship enabled the combatants in society to "see" the world in a different way. Through worship a new connection between a vision that arises from the spiritual depths of Christian piety and the renewal of public life is born. An even more precise connection between worship and the promotion of civil society can be seen in the overcoming of a false piety that degenerates into either a privatization of faith or the patriotic appropriation of the faith by a nation or the state. In other words, "the apartheid experience has made clear how important worship, and therefore ecclesiology and the life and practices of the church may be for public life and for civil society." This momentous experience left South African Christians with the awareness that questions regarding worship are extremely important for common life in civil society. The reason for this is not that Christian worship may ever be instrumentalized but rather, Smit concludes, that the question of social justice belongs to the very nature of Christian worship itself.

Rudolf von Sinner, who teaches at the Lutheran School of Theology in São Leopoldo, Rio Grande do Sul in Brazil addresses the topics of "Trinity, Church, and Society in Brazil." Von Sinner takes as his point of departure the seminal book of Leonardo Boff, *Trinity and Society* (1986). He offers an innovative reading of Boff's defense of the social analogy of the Trinity, showing how Boff conceives of the social analogy as a way of overcoming "monarchical" misinterpretations of the Trinity in Latin America. He also underscores how for Boff a cosmic dimension of ecological interrelatedness and awareness is an important by-product of the renewal of trinitarian theology. Most importantly, von Sinner illustrates how the model of Trinitarian *perichoresis* defended by Boff has promoted a pluralistic vision of society in Brazil today. For example, the issue of social participation and especially citizenship rights can be viewed as a constructive actualization of human *perichoresis* within an emerging Brazilian civil society.

Finally, Paul Louis Metzger of Multnomah Biblical Seminary in Portland, Oregon offers his reflections on "Beyond the Culture Wars: Contours of Authentic Dialogue." The fatal shooting in 2003 of an African American woman by a white police officer in the city of Portland led to an outcry from the African American community. The divergent responses from other communities exposed Portland's long-standing divisions and wounds. Metzger describes his involvement as an evangelical Christian in a dialogue with representatives from the Portland Police Department as well as religious leaders from Jewish, Buddhist, and other Christian backgrounds to address the racial and religious tensions present in Portland. He concludes with perspicacious insights regarding the nature of dialogue. Dialogue, he says, is not about changing someone's mind; nor is authentic dialogue simply about mutual understanding. Authentic dialogue involves mutual persuasion, whereby those of us from diverse perspectives persuade "one another to go more deeply into our respective traditions in view of what we learn from one another in search of sources that will advance further a compassionate form of shared existence." From this simple insight partners in a global dialogue on a local level begin with town-hall-like meetings involving the respective faith communities. They can then move toward the creation of more complex public spaces than simply the state or market to inhabit. These spaces for civil society provide an opportunity for individuals to resist the encroachment of the state and market. Not only will such intermediate communities mediate the individual to the state and market, but they also provide a safe haven so that those from the left and right can put down their arms to encounter one another beyond what they stereotypically hear of one another from the headline news. The Christian community, Metzger argues, has no corner on compassion, but his experiences as an American evangelical in ongoing dialogue with a Buddhist leader and his followers on the thorny cultural issues that divide their communities pointed him back to Jesus and towards a common path in search of a world for all.

Prospects for the Future

As editors we hope prospects for future work will deepen our own consideration of the church as an institution with a public voice and of the relationship of distinct ecclesial communities to other national, international, and transnational bodies. We are convinced that the on-going efforts toward the development of a global civil society can be enriched through the active engagement of Christian ecclesial communities and that this maturation of Christian public commitment can be realized without turning our common confession of faith in a triune God into a disjointed agenda for global politics.

No doubt, some "enlightened" critics of public religious bodies will be wary of the church playing such an overtly public role today. Their fears may stem from experiences of religious groups who aim to proselytize and win rights for their sects through civic involvement or from political parties who lobby for votes through faith-based initiatives. While abuses of this sort exist, it is vital to the well-being of a society that all parties — secular and religious — are invited to participate in the civil dialogue of the public square and that all work together to make this fragile world a more inhabitable place for all. The key, we think, is not to view the presence of the church in the public sphere as an intrusion but to clarify the identity, role, and relationship of the church to Christian and non-Christian groups who seek to build up structures of civil society and thereby contribute to a better world.

In his first encyclical letter, *Deus caritas est*, Pope Benedict XVI speaks to these matters. The pope's comments are instructive, for he represents a tradition that, according to Max Stackhouse, has played a historic role in the development of civil society in the modern world.[7] Although written as an official teaching of the office of the bishop of Rome, the document seems to have enjoyed a wider following. In fact, some remarks are a direct criticism of certain modern Protestant positions, e.g. the thesis of Lutheran ethicist Anders Nygren that *agape* as a Christian heritage of loving one's neighbor must be strictly separated from the Greek heritage of *eros* or love of God as an ascending fulfillment of one's own nature. In spite of that, scholars like the Luther scholar Mary D. Gaebler and the Methodist ecumenist Geoffrey Wainwright find much consolation and hope in the treatment of these themes by the theologian Joseph Ratzinger/Pope Benedict XVI.[8]

---

7. See Stackhouse's essay in Part I of this volume.

8. See Mary D. Gaebler, "Eros in Benedict and Luther," *Journal of Lutheran Ethics* 6,

In the encyclical Pope Benedict speaks "of the love which God lavishes upon us and which we in turn must share with others,"[9] given that God's name is often wrongly "associated with vengeance or even a duty of hatred and violence."[10] After addressing "the unity of love in creation and salvation history," the pope turns to discuss the church's practice of love. While our book has sought to guard against translating confession of the Trinity into a social program by rooting it in the church's life and witness in society, the pope seeks to guard against the church being reduced to a social program by rooting the church and its practices in the Trinity. The church practices charity, and this charitable activity is "a manifestation of Trinitarian love."[11] Charity is not something that the church should leave to others, for it "is a part of her nature, an indispensable expression of her very being" through her union with the triune God.[12] While engaging in a life of charity and concern for justice, the church's role is not "to bring about the most just society possible." This is the state's concern.[13] And while the church participates with other organizations through its own charitable ministries, the pontiff is careful to guard against reducing the church's charitable activity to "just another form of social assistance." He provides such safeguards by emphasizing that the church's love of neighbor is a "consequence deriving from" believers' "faith" and is "independent of parties and ideologies" or the attempt to impose the faith on others.[14] Benedict's remarks on the church's charitable activity being "a manifestation of Trinitarian love" offer clues to how the church of the triune God and its services are to participate in the public ordering of a more just and civil society.

---

no. 9 (September 2006). Accessed on-line at http://www.elca.org/What-We-Believe/Social-Issues/Journal-of-Lutheran-Ethics/Issues/September-2006/Eros-in-Benedict-and-Luther.aspx on March 16, 2009 and Geoffrey Wainwright, "A Remedy for Relativism: The Cosmic, Historical, and Eschatological Dimension of the Liturgy according to the Theologian Joseph Ratzinger," *Nova et Vetera* 5, no. 2 (2007): pp. 403-30. See also John Milbank, "The Future of Love. A Reading of Pope Benedict XVI's Encyclical *Deus caritas est*," *Communio: International Catholic Review*, Fall 2006: pp. 368-74.

9. *Deus Caritas Est*, #1. Accessed on-line at http://www.vatican.va/holy_father/benedict_xvi/encyclicals/documents/hf_ben-xvi_enc_20051225_deus-caritas-est_en.html on February 16, 2006.

10. *Deus Caritas Est*, #1.

11. *Deus Caritas Est*, #11.

12. *Deus Caritas Est*, #13.

13. *Deus Caritas Est*, #14-15.

14. *Deus Caritas Est*, #17-18.

In this volume we are not translating the trinitarian confession into a social program. Future systematic work pertaining to global civil society must guard against conceiving of the church itself as a social program. Just as it is important to root confession of the triune God in the church's life and witness, so too it is important to center the church in the triune God's life. The move to center the church in the life of the triune God will ward off the now globalizing urge to privatize Christian belief. There is ultimately nothing private about the triune God who creates and enters history in his Son through the Spirit to birth the church and redeem humanity. This conviction has led the church to play a public role in the development of a more civil society through the ages, and we hope through these modest contributions to refrain this respectful litany of the saints as a positive goad to the common global future of our fractured world.

Global Civil Society, Church Unity, and World Unity

Nico Koopman

In its first part this paper discusses the historical origins, definitions, and functions of civil society on national and international/global levels. In a second part a theological framework is offered which might be helpful for the very important discussions about the role of theology and churches in the context of a globalizing world and specifically in the context of the development of a global civil society. In outlining this framework, use is mainly made of the important work on ecclesiology by South African systematic theologian, Flip Theron. Theron's description of the church as cosmic-eschatological sign and pertinently his description of the unity of the church as sign of the eschatological unity of the cosmos are investigated.

Civil Society — An Inflated Concept

Civil society is not a homogeneous concept. It reflects diversity in terms of historical development, sociological traditions, uses, agendas, and reception in different regions of the world. Although the notion of civil society developed in the same historical situation of crisis in the late seventeenth and eighteenth centuries, sociologist Adam Seligman identifies two traditions or streams of development of this concept.[1] The first tradition is so-

---

1. Adam Seligman, *The Idea of Civil Society* (New York: The Free Press, 1992), pp. 10-11. Seligman describes the situation in which the idea of civil society developed as follows: "The general crises of the seventeenth century — the commercialization of land, labour and

cialistic, post-Hegelian and Marxist. The second tradition is Anglo-American and more capitalist in origin and consists of thinkers like John Locke and various thinkers of the Scottish Enlightenment. The modern revival of the term is associated with the resistance and freedom movements in East and Central Europe in the 1980s.[2]

The term civil society has various uses. Seligman identifies three such uses, namely the political, social scientific, and philosophical-prescriptive. The political use refers to different movements and parties, as well as individuals, who criticize government policies. The term is also used as a scientific tool to analyze and describe the social reality.[3] Former general secretary

---

capital; the growth of market economies; the age of discoveries; and the English and later North American and continental revolutions — all brought into question the existing models of social order and of authority. Whereas traditionally the foundation or matrix of social order was seen to reside in some entity external to the social world — God, King or even the givenness of traditional norms and behavior itself — these principles of order became increasingly questioned by the end of the seventeenth century" (p. 15). English scholar David Herbert also offers a helpful discussion about the origins of the concept of civil society. He points to the fact that before the modern development of this concept in the seventeenth century, it did function in classical cultures. The concept developed from Aristotle's *politike koinonia* (political community) through the Roman *societas civilis* to the medieval city-state. See his *Religion and Civil Society: Rethinking Public Religion in the Contemporary World* (Hampshire: Ashgate, 2003), p. 72.

2. Cf. John Keane, *Global Civil Society?* (Cambridge: Cambridge University Press, 2003), p. 1. In his helpful description of civil society the famous Latin American theologian Julio de Santa Ana focuses mainly on this socialist tradition. He explains that civil society is the product of modern nation-states and the emergence of citizens as new social and political actors. He refers to Jean-Jacques Rousseau's plea for the importance of the development of a general will, consensus, and some degree of hegemony which is expressed in a social contract without which modern societies cannot function. Although Rousseau, according to de Santa Ana, did not use the concept civil society, the idea of civil society was already present in his thinking. See Julio de Santa Ana, "The Concept of Civil Society," *The Ecumenical Review* 46, no. 1 (January 1994): 5.

The concept civil society, according to de Santa Ana, developed in the context of the Industrial Revolution which paved the way for the western bourgeois to take power in their societies, for a great influence of economic forces on social and cultural processes, and for massive pauperization. In this context of more complex societies Saint-Simon of France used the concept civil society to describe the so-called private sector, i.e. that part of reality which does not belong to the state, as organized political power. De Santa Ana also refers to Hegel who views civil society as the sector of society that mediates between the individual and family, on the one hand, and the state on the other hand. Later in the article it is indicated that civil society is not a private, but a public sphere. It is also shown that family is part of civil society. Cf. de Santa Ana, "The Concept of Civil Society," p. 6.

3. Seligman, *Idea of Civil Society*, pp. 201-204.

of the World Council of Churches, Konrad Raiser, uses the term as an analytical tool and not as a normative and prescriptive concept.[4] It is a heuristic
and analytical tool which enhances our understanding of contemporary social reality and which sheds light on some features of society that might
otherwise have remained obscure. The philosophical-prescriptive use of the
term refers to the fact that this term contains an ethical vision of a good society which guides policy and action and which implies the moral bonds of
citizens.[5] Those who reckon that civil society does have an ethical function
focus attention on the ambiguous nature of this ethical function. De Santa
Ana, for instance, uses Antonio Gramsci's distinction between traditional
and organic intellectuals in civil society to demonstrate this point. Although traditional intellectuals may be critical of the dominant system,
they do not break with what Gramsci calls the "common sense" of this system, i.e. the consciousness and ideology that protect the interests of the
powerful. The organic intellectuals, on the other hand, strengthen the so-
called "good sense," i.e. the consciousness about and commitment to the
plights and needs of the poor.[6]

The concept of civil society is used differently in different regions of
the world. In western societies it mainly focuses on individuals and on the
voluntary association of individuals. This is especially the case in the
United States. Societies in Eastern and Central Europe use the concept of
civil society with a communal connotation.[7] In the same vein South African political scientists Jannie Gagiano and Pierre du Toit distinguish between liberal societies (i.e. mainly western societies) that talk about civil
society in individualistic terms and liberationist societies (e.g. Latin
America and Africa) who emphasize notions like solidarity and community.[8] I am convinced that these differences should not be overempha-
sized. To varying degrees, all three functions of civil society are fulfilled in
different contexts. Moreover, in both western and nonwestern contexts

---

4. Konrad Raiser, "The World Council of Churches and International Civil Society,"
The Ecumenical Review 46, no. 1 (January 1994): 39.

5. Seligman, *Idea of Civil Society*, p. 204.

6. De Santa Ana, "The Concept of Civil Society," pp. 8-9.

7. Seligman, *Idea of Civil Society*, pp. 203-204. Seligman is even skeptical about the
prospects of the growth of civil society in non-western European societies like Hungary,
which do not accept the fundamental importance of the individual.

8. Jannie Gagiano and Pierre du Toit, "Consolidating Democracy in South Africa: The
Role of Civil Society," in *Consolidating Democracy: What Role for Civil Society in South Africa*,
ed. Hennie Kotze (Stellenbosch: University of Stellenbosch Press, 1996), pp. 47-48, 50-55.

communality and individuality receive attention, albeit with different emphases.[9]

Another point of diversity regarding the use of the notion of civil society has to do with its relationship to the political and economic spheres of society. Some thinkers like Hegel, Marx, and Lenin[10] are, according to de Santa Ana, limiting the autonomy of civil society. For Hegel it should be under the authority and management of the state, and for Marx and Lenin civil society should be under the authority of the proletariat. De Santa Ana, however, stresses the importance of the autonomy of civil society. He refers to a comparative study of Alexis de Tocqueville, who concludes that because of the greater freedom of so-called free associations in the United States, democracy late in the nineteenth century flourished more in the United States than in Europe where the roots of liberal democracies are. Democracy in the United States grew because of measures like the decentralization of power, the federative principle in the constitution, recognition of the autonomy of townships, and above all the commitment of people to associate and organize among themselves in order to address common plights and challenges.[11] Konrad Raiser is also concerned about the continuous threat to the autonomy of civil society from political and economic powers.[12]

In its development in the seventeenth and eighteenth century, civil society and the economic sector were closely related. With the increase of the power of the market, this relationship changed to such an extent that "some contemporary understandings of civil society view the economic sector as being not part of civil society." Raiser explains, "Civil society is usually defined over against the political and economic dimensions of society. . . . Civil society is as public as the state or the economy, and it has its own rationality and follows its own processes of institutionalization."[13]

---

9. South African scholar Mamphela Ramphele has rightly pointed out that the communality that is sought in African societies and that is expressed in the term *ubuntu* is not unique to African societies. The quest for community is present in all societies. The sociality of human personhood is expressed in classic political texts and mythologies. In Italy artist Carlo Levi describes personhood as the meeting place of relationships. In Japan communality is expressed in the term *amaeru*. See Ramphele, *Steering by the Stars: Being Young in South Africa* (Capetown: Tafelberg, 2002), p. 102.

10. For a helpful description of the development of the idea of civil society in the thought of John Locke, the Scottish Enlightenment, Immanuel Kant, Hegel, and Marx, see Seligman, *Idea of Civil Society*, pp. 15-58.

11. De Santa Ana, "The Concept of Civil Society," p. 6.

12. Raiser, "The World Council of Churches," p. 39.

13. Raiser, "The World Council of Churches," p. 39.

Here it needs to be noted that although many social theorists view the economic sector as not part of civil society, they would view trade unions specifically as indeed a crucial institution of civil society.

The diverse and conflicting understandings of the term civil society make somebody like Seligman become skeptical about the continuous use of this term.[14] Although I appreciate Seligman's description of the development of the concept of civil society, I do not share his skepticism about the continued use of the term. I rather reckon that the diversity and complexity of this term help us to appreciate the complexity and hybridity of current societies. Political scientist John Keane reasons in the same vein with reference to global civil society: "For its participants, rather, this society nurtures a culture of self-awareness about the hybridity and complexity of the world."[15] What Seligman views as a weakness is perhaps rather a strength. Israel Batista of the World Council of Churches also reckons that the variety of understandings of civil society need not inhibit the use of the term. "Not that the term should be reduced to a sort of 'action without reflection'; but it is preferable to use it as an open-ended, 'searching' concept, even if this means that we operate without clear definitions."[16]

While recognizing the complexity and diversity of the term "civil society," it might be possible to draw some points of convergence regarding the meaning of it. This can be done without running the risk of oversimplification with all its negative effects.

In this article, "civil society" will consequently be used with the following meaning. Civil society refers to the institutions, organizations, associations, and movements of society which, independently from the political and economic sectors, strive to enhance the quality of life, satisfy the needs and foster the interests of people, change the nature of society, and build the common good, that is, a life of quality for all. Families, schools, legal bodies, the media,[17] various types of clubs (cultural, arts, and sports),

14. Seligman, *Idea of Civil Society*, p. 206.
15. Keane, *Global Civil Society?* p. 15.
16. Israel Batista, "Civil Society: A Paradigm or a New Slogan?" *The Ecumenical Review* 46, no. 1 (January 1994): 16.
17. South African theologian Dirkie Smit pleads that the media even be viewed as a separate public sector in democratic societies, in the light of its unique role with regard to functions like dissemination of information to the public, quests for consensus, public opinion formation, and influencing of public policymaking which are all crucial elements of the building and strengthening of democracies. See Smit, "Oor die unieke openbare rol van die kerk (On the unique public role of the church)," *Tydskrif vir Geesteswetenskappe* 36, no. 3 (1996): 190-98.

as well as neighborhoods are all institutions of civil society. Sociologically speaking, churches are part of civil society, albeit institutions with a unique character.[18] Trade unions are also viewed as part of civil society since they do not form part of the political and economic systems of power. With regard to global civil society, it is interesting to note that Keane views international businesses and political movements that also advocate for justice as part of international civil society.[19]

This use of "civil society" coincides with Seligman's views sketched above that civil society constitutes a helpful instrument to describe contemporary societies and that civil society does have a moral function. In so far as civil society organizations do work of advocacy and campaign for the political and economic rights of people, this understanding of civil society also adheres to Seligman's proposals about the political function of civil society.

Global Civil Society — A Concept in Evolution

According to South African political scientist Rupert Taylor, the term "global civil society" has been in development over the last decade or two. It has been used increasingly within academia, the mass media, and broader society. The term "global civil society" is, like "civil society" on a national level, a diversified term. It needs much more development.[20]

18. For Raiser churches are natural partners in the spheres of both national and global civil society. "If national churches are typical actors in civil society at the level of the nation, may we not assume that the WCC [World Council of Churches], which understands itself as a fellowship of more than three hundred such churches in about one hundred countries, provides an important and ready-made space for promoting international civil society — particularly in view of the long heritage of ecumenical social thought and engagement?" ("World Council of Churches," pp. 41-42)

19. Keane, *Global Civil Society?* p. 9.

20. Taylor, "Interpreting Global Civil Society," in *Creating a Better World: Interpreting Global Civil Society*, ed. R. Taylor (Bloomfield: Kumarian Press, Inc., 2004), p. 1. He describes the search for clarity regarding the definition of this term as follows: ". . . the topic of global civil society is one of much confusion and contestation; among commentators there is a sense that this is a phenomenon which is less than fully understood and which defies conventional means of analysis. For example, Henry Milner has made the point that 'though much is written about GCS (Global Civil Society) both in academe and in the mainstream and alternative media, it remains very much under-researched, and, indeed, under-defined' (Milner 2003, 190); and Peter Waterman has remarked that the provenance of the term is not well grounded and that global civil society has not yet passed 'through the forge of theoretical clarification or the sieve of public debate' (Waterman 1996, 170). Similarly, writing in the

The idea of a global civil society developed in the context of political, cultural, and especially economic globalization. David Held gives a helpful description of the four major features of globalization: *Stretched social relations* refers to the existence and increasing importance of "cultural, economic and political networks of connection across the world." Regionalization, the "increased interconnection between states that border on each other," is an important form of this, but there are also many others. *Intensification of flows* refers to the increased density of interaction across the globe which implies that the impacts of events are elsewhere often felt much more strongly than before. *Interpenetration* refers to the extent to which "apparently distant cultures and societies [come] face to face with each other at [the] local level," creating increased (experience of real) diversity. *Global infrastructure* refers to the underlying formal and informal institutional arrangements that are required for globalized networks to operate.[21]

The world in which we live today is also described by the term "glocalization." In a *Festschrift* for Duncan Forrester, William Storrar borrows the term glocalization from the sociologist Roland Robertson to describe the interaction between the local and the global in the practice of public theology today:

> By "glocal," Robertson means exactly this interactive local-global dynamic at the core of globalization. Instead of seeing globalization as the conflict or polarization between the extremes of homogenizing global economic, cultural and informational systems and the anti-globalization resistance of heterogeneous local cultures, traditions and identities, Robertson has argued for another conceptual approach: one that recognizes their meeting and melding in "glocal" form around the world.[22]

---

journal *Contemporary Sociology,* Peter Evans has argued that 'analysis and theory have not caught up to practice when it comes to progress action at the global level' (Evans 2000, 231), and Paul Kingsnorth has observed that 'often the language and the methods are not yet available to describe what is happening' (Kingsnorth 2003, 233-34)."

21. Held, *A Globalizing World? Culture, Economics, Politics* (New York: Routledge, 2000), pp. 15-21.

22. Storrar, "Where the Local and the Global Meet: Duncan Forrester's Glocal Public Theology and Scottish Political Context," in *Public Theology for the Twenty-first Century. Essays in Honour of Duncan B. Forrester,* ed. W. Storrar and A. R. Morton (London: T&T Clark, 2004), p. 406.

The notion of glocalization is very helpful. This becomes clear when the local and global dimensions of civil society initiatives in various countries are analyzed.

Keane's definition of global civil society provides a good point of departure for discussing the meaning of global civil society. He writes,

> When the term global civil society is used in this way, as an ideal-type, it properly refers to a dynamic non-governmental system of interconnected socio-economic institutions that straddle the whole earth, and that have complex effects that are felt in its four corners. Global civil society is neither a static object nor a *fait accompli*. It is an unfinished project that consists of sometimes thick, sometimes thinly stretched networks, pyramids and the hub-and-spoke clusters of socio-economic institutions and actors who organize themselves across borders, with the deliberate aim of drawing the world together in new ways. These non-governmental institutions and actors tend to pluralise power and to problemise violence; consequently, their peaceful or civil effects are felt everywhere, here and there, afar and wide, to and from local areas, through wider regions, to the planetary level itself.[23]

Global civil society is constituted by institutions that transcend national borders. Japanese social thinker and practitioner Muto Ichiyo prefers the development of trans-border institutions of civil society, since national ones are compromised by their priority to national concerns.[24] To address global problems we indeed need these transnational bodies. However, I believe that there should also be room in global civil society discourses for the international cooperation of national institutions of civil society in different countries. In fact, civil society organizations in South Africa cooperated on an international level with civil societies in other countries to abolish apartheid. The same cooperation occurs currently in the endeavour to address the social challenges of post-apartheid South Africa. In the context of glocalization which calls for a focus on both the global and the local, this approach does also have merit.

Like national civil society, global civil society fulfills three functions. It fulfills a political function. Through various means, institutions of

---

23. Keane, *Global Civil Society?* p. 8.
24. Ichiyo, "Alliance of Hope and Challenges of Global Democracy," *The Ecumenical Review* 46, no. 1 (January 1994): 32.

global civil society have an impact on governmental decisions and policies. Keane describes this function as follows:

> Its social groups and organizations and movements lobby states, bargain with international organizations, pressure and bounce off other non-state bodies, invest in new forms of production, champion different ways of life and engage in charitable direct action in distant local communities, for instance through capacity-building programmes that supply jobs, clean running water, sporting facilities, hospitals and schools. In these various ways, the members of global civil society help to conserve or to alter the power relations embedded in the chains of interaction linking the local, regional and planetary orders. Their cross border links and networks help to define and redefine who gets what, when, and how in the world.[25]

Global civil society also serves as a social scientific tool to make sense of the current global society, especially with regard to the non-governmental spaces of global society.[26] Keane describes the socio-ethical

25. Keane, *Global Civil Society?* p. 17.

26. Keane refers to various civil society organizations: "To begin with, the term global civil society refers to non-governmental structures and activities. It comprises individuals, households, profit seeking businesses, not-for-profit non-governmental organizations, coalitions, social movements and linguistic communities and cultural identities. It feeds upon the work of media celebrities and the past or present public personalities — from Gandhi, Bill Gates, Primo Levi and Martin Luther King to Bono and Aung San Suu Kyi, Bishop Ximenes Belo, Naomi Klein and al-Waleed bin Talal. It includes charities, think tanks, prominent intellectuals, campaigning and lobby groups, citizens' protests responsible for 'clusters of performances', small and large corporate firms, independent media, internet groups and websites, employers federations, trade unions, international commissions, parallel summits and sporting organizations. It comprises bodies like Amnesty International, Sony, Falun Gong, Christian Aid, al Jazeera, the Catholic Relief Services, the Indigenous Peoples Bio-Diversity Network, FIFA, Transparency International, Sufi networks like Qadiriyya and Naqshabandiyya, the International Red Cross, the Global Coral Reef Monitoring Network, the Ford Foundation, Shack/Slum Dwellers International, Women Living Under Muslim Laws, News Corporation International, OpenDemocracy.net, and unnamed circles of Buddhist monks, dressed in crimson robes, keeping the mind mindful. Considered together, these institutions and actors constitute a vast, interconnected and multi-layered non-governmental space that comprises many hundreds of thousands of more-or-less self directing ways of life. All of these forms of life have at least one thing in common: across vast geographic distances and despite barriers of time, they deliberately organize themselves and conduct their cross-border social activities, business and politics outside the boundaries of governmental structures" (Keane, *Global Civil Society?* pp. 8-9).

function of global civil society as one of building civility, i.e. respect for others, even strangers, and of opposing incivility.[27] Batista's description of the ethical role of civil society is very helpful: "Civil society is not a panacea for intellectuals or an easy solution for social activists. Neither should it become an ecumenical slogan. Civil society is rather an ethical ideal, a dreaming of life-centered values in a world 'not standing like this.' It can energize utopias, strengthen people's aspirations for manageable societies, and elicit imagination and creativity in the search for alternatives."[28]

Global Civil Society in Ecclesiological Perspective

One of the outstanding features of globalization is the growing interdependence, interconnectedness, and unity of individuals and groups, as well as political, economic and cultural institutions all over the globe. The astronomic developments in the fields of science and technology, especially information, communication, and transportation technology, have intensified this interconnectedness and unity. Global civil society reflects this feature of interconnectedness, interdependence, and unity. Theologically, specifically ecclesiologically, this feature relates to the confession about the unity of the church. The Christian tradition is in the unity business, not only the unity of the church, but also the unity of the world!

In 1978, South African theologian Flip Theron wrote a very important doctoral dissertation about the cosmic and eschatological nature of the unity of the church. Specifically, he described the unity of the church as a sign of the eschatological unity of the cosmos.[29]

Theron argues strongly in favor of the continuity between church and cosmos. According to him the unity that applies to the church applies to the cosmos. He refers to the fact that the relationship of Christ to the world is expressed in the same concepts as the relationship of Christ to the church. Christ is the firstborn of all creation (Col. 1:15), and as firstborn

---

27. Keane warns against groups who might also by some be regarded as part of global civil society, but who pursue morally destructive aims and who carry out these aims in a non-civil way. In the ranks of these groups are international criminal gangs, organized international crime groups involved in drug and sex trafficking, war criminals, arms traders and terrorists. See Keane, *Global Civil Society?* p. 12.

28. Batista, "Civil Society," p. 20.

29. For Theron, cosmos refers to the *creatura*, the created reality which is the result of God's *creatio*, i.e., God's act of creation. See Theron, *Die ekklesia as kosmies-eskatologiese teken* (Pretoria: NG Kerkboekhandel, 1978), p. 3.

from the dead (Col. 1:18), he is also the firstborn in the church (Rom. 8:29). In him the whole cosmos was created (Col. 1:16), and in him the church is created for good works (Eph. 2:10). The cosmos has been created through him and for him (Col. 1:16), and the church exists through him (1 Cor. 8:6) and is focused upon him (Rom. 14:8; 2 Cor. 5:15).[30]

Theron bases the interrelatedness of church and cosmos pertinently in the fact that the church-mystery as Christ-mystery is also the creation-mystery. The Christ-mystery refers to God's intention to unify all things in heaven and on earth under the headship of Christ (Eph. 1:9-10). This unity is realized in the peace that Christ has made through the blood of his cross (Col. 1:20). This work of Christ is the foundation of the current and future existence of creation. The Christ-mystery (Eph. 3:4) was hidden in the council of God (Eph. 1:9) before the creation (Eph. 1:4) and is revealed to the apostles and prophets through the Spirit (Eph. 3:5). This mystery implies that believers and non-believers are now in Christ heirs, members of his body, and they share in God's promises in Christ (Eph. 3:6). Theron argues, with an appeal to the work of German theologian H. Schlier, that the book of Ephesians specifically portrays the Christ-mystery as ecclesia-mystery (Eph. 3:9). The ecclesia-mystery as Christ-mystery precedes the creation-mystery (cf. Eph. 1:4, 2 Tim. 1:9, 2 Thess. 2:13, Matt. 25:34). Theron states that the eternal intention of God in Christ Jesus our Lord (Eph. 3:11), which is brought to light through the life and proclamation of the congregation (Eph. 3:9), is the mystery which was hidden in God who created all things (Eph. 3:9). This mystery entails the unification of the whole creation through the cross and resurrection of Christ and the testifying to it by the church in word and preliminary embodiment.[31]

Theron writes in a very illuminating way about the sign-character of the church and of the unity of the church. The church is a sign of the kingdom. For Theron the kingdom does not only refer to a specific domain. It is also a dynamic concept that refers to the active reign of God, and also to the consequences of this reign. These consequences are justice, peace, and joy (cf. Rom. 14:17). He agrees with Dutch theologian Arnold Van Ruler who identifies the kingdom with the salvation in Jesus Christ.[32]

30. Theron, *Die ekklesia*, p. 71.
31. Theron, *Die ekklesia*, pp. 71-72. Since the ecclesial mystery precedes the creation-mystery, Theron observes that the church is not only a cosmic-eschatological sign, but that the creation also points to the church. In that sense the cosmos is also a sign of the church. The cosmos has some form of dependence on the church.
32. Theron, *Die ekklesia*, p. 89.

Theron provides evidence in support of the sign-character of the church. He is of the opinion that the woman, who is described as a sign in Revelation 12:1-6, refers to the church of the old and new covenants.[33] Theron, in line with Van Ruler, reckons that the church constitutes a manifold of signs of the kingdom. The sacraments are signs of the eschatological salvation in Christ (Rom. 4:11). Baptism refers to the new life in the kingdom (Rom. 6, Titus 3:5) and holy communion to the eschatological wedding of the Lamb (Rev. 19:7). More ecclesial signs of the kingdom are the people of Israel, the Bible, preaching, the offices of the church, the confession of the church, the communion of Christians in faith, hope and love as well as the pluriform activity of the church in the world.[34] Theron[35] emphasizes that the church is a cross-sign of the kingdom. As body of the Crucified the church shares in the suffering of Christ (Eph. 3:10, 1 Pet. 4:13, 2 Cor. 4:10). The church is also a sign of the resurrection, specifically the resurrection of the crucified One. Theron makes some important observations about the sign-character of the church: the church is not the kingdom. The church is only a sign of the kingdom. And since it is a cross-sign of the kingdom there is no room for triumphalism. The church as sign confirms the already and not yet character of the kingdom. The church is a sign of what it already has in the light of the reality of God's reign. It simultaneously is a sign of what it longs for. Namely it longs for that which it already has. The church desires what it already is. In this tension the church as sign functions. With regard to the world the church offers a critique of both the world and the worldly critique of the world, in light of the vision of the kingdom. This critique is an expression of the solidarity of the church with the world, since it seeks the salvation of the world. The church is a visible sign. It participates in that which it refers to as a sign, and it embodies what it refers to in a penultimate way.[36] Theron states that the same

33. Theron, *Die ekklesia*, p. 91.
34. Theron, *Die ekklesia*, p. 92.
35. Theron, *Die ekklesia*, pp. 95-96.
36. Theron, *Die ekklesia*, pp. 96-99. Theron does not opt for either a futuristic or realized eschatological approach. The unity of church and cosmos does not only lie in the future. Neither is this unity that is real in Christ perfectly actualized in the present. It is however proclaimed and embodied in provisional, penultimate ways in the present. Eschatology determines the present. Eschatological faith enables us to view time not only as *chronos* but also as *kairos*. Eschatological faith recognizes the *kairotic* nature of life. It acknowledges, is a witness to, and penultimately embodies the entrance of eschatological salvation and unity in this world.

observations and warnings apply to the unity of the church as cosmic-eschatological sign.[37]

According to Theron, the unity that the church proclaims and embodies in a provisional way is a sign of the eschatological salvation of the cosmos, specifically of *shalom*. Unity is not separated from the other *notae*, marks, of the church, namely holiness, apostolocity, and catholicity. All these features give expression to the *shalom*. They exist in a perichoretic relationship. They explain and determine each other. They represent different and complementing perspectives on the one cosmic-eschatological focus of the church. Where unity refers to the wholeness of the whole cosmos, catholicity refers to the fact that indeed the whole cosmos, including the nonhuman part of creation, will be unified and healed under the headship of Christ.[38]

The description of unity as *shalom* is important. Thereby Theron makes it clear that not only the idea of the unity of the world is important for Christian theology. The nature of this unity is also of importance. This unity is called *shalom*, peace. According to Theron, *shalom* refers to the healing and wholeness that stand in opposition to brokenness, division, and enmity. This unity does not do away with diversity. It only relativizes differences so that the diversity in this new community does not lead to division, brokenness, and enmity.[39]

Conclusion

The unity of the church as cosmic-eschatological sign entails that the local and global church, i.e. the glocal church, through its provisional embodiment of this *shalom*, and through its public involvement with other members of glocal civil society, serves the penultimate flourishing of *shalom* in the cosmos. Dutch theologian Hendrikus Berkhof, who also describes the church as cosmic-eschatological sign and whose views are supported by Theron, offers a strong plea for the renewal of the whole cosmos, for the

---

37. Theron, *Die ekklesia*, pp. 100-103.

38. Theron, *Die ekklesia*, pp. 99-102.

39. Theron, *Die ekklesia*, pp. 69-70. Nicholas Wolterstorff, *Until Justice and Peace Embrace* (Grand Rapids: Eerdmans, 1983), p. 70 gives a classic description of *shalom*: "But the peace which is *shalom* is not merely the absence of hostility, not merely being in right relationships. A nation may be at peace with all its neighbors and yet be miserable in its poverty. To dwell in *shalom* is to enjoy living before God, to enjoy living in one's physical surroundings, to enjoy living with one's fellows, to enjoy life with oneself."

flourishing of unity and peace in the whole world. Berkhof argues that the renewal of the whole cosmos has been neglected for a very long time in Christian theology, even though this theme is prominent in the Bible, namely in the Pentateuchal laws and Israel's theocracy that was based on it, in the prophetic messages and judgments concerning social problems, in Jesus' words and deeds regarding the plight of the poor, in Paul's thoughts on Christ's lordship over the powers, in the directives of the epistles regarding the relationship of Jew and Greek, the strong and weak, the rich and the poor, citizens and government, master and slave, husband and wife, parents and children. Against this background Berkhof states,

> . . . Christian conceptions of creation, of renewal, and of consummation, are bound to remain abstract, unless the world is included in the consideration. Particularly the doctrine of renewal has suffered from this neglect. On the one hand it reduces it to a study of man (sic) who is detached from his world and therefore is all too often unreal, not a real creature of real flesh and blood; on the other hand, by its silence about the world it suggests that this world is irrelevant for the faith, either because it is capable of saving itself or because it is unsaveably lost. Neither can be true. If it is God's desire to renew man, it must also be his desire to renew the world. Else he would renew only half a man.[40]

This urgent challenge of Berkhof makes it clear that Theron's analysis should not be used only as a tool that helps us to interpret the notion of a globalised world theologically. Neither should it only be viewed as a helpful theological rationale for our social involvement. It cannot be used only as a theological directive for the mode of our social involvement, as part of global civil society. No, this appeal makes it clear that what is also called for is the concrete obedience and active participation of the church,[41] on local, national, and global levels in the unification and dawn of *shalom* in the world.

40. Berkhof, *Christian Faith: An Introduction to the Study of Faith*, 2nd ed. (Grand Rapids: Eerdmans, 1986), pp. 503-504.

41. Dirkie Smit identifies six forms of the church, namely the church as worshipping community, local congregation, denomination, ecumenical church, individual Christians in their normal roles in the family, work and neighborhood and sixthly individual Christians in their roles as volunteers in various institutions of civil society, e.g. civil rights movements, advocacy groups, service groups. In all these forms the church is called to be a sign of *shalom*. See "Oor die kerk as 'n unieke samelewingsverband (On the uniqueness of the church)," *Tydskrif vir Geesteswetenskappe* 36, no. 2 (1996): 120-21.

Thinking Out Loud about the Triune God: Problems and Prospects for a Trinitarian Social Ethic in a Procedural Republic

Peter J. Casarella

Discourse regarding the Father, Son, and Holy Spirit is central to Christian self-understanding.[1] The question of whether such discourse should be proclaimed outside of the churches is a more vexing matter. The instinct to preserve trinitarian language within the abode of worship is not wrong-headed. Safeguarding Christian faith in this manner upholds the *qualified* sense in which God's revealed wisdom can properly be used to illuminate contemporary social ills. But the issue of drawing out social implications from Christian doctrine is not simply a matter of how to situate religious discourse in either the Church or contemporary society, for the question of a social trinity has accompanied the Church's proclamation of a trinitarian faith virtually from the outset. Throughout the *longue durée* of Christian theology, the question of whether the harmony of Father, Son, and Holy Spirit is of any direct and intelligible consequence for those who stand outside of the Christian community remains a matter of significant debate.[2]

In this presentation, I argue that the society of the trinity is relevant to how U.S. citizens might think about society at large. The burden of my argument, however, is not so much to advocate this view as either an ecclesial or political platform. In order to be cogent, a public argument

1. See, for example, Karl Rahner, "*Theos* in the New Testament," *Theological Investigations,* Volume I, trans. Cornelius Ernst (Baltimore: Helicon Press, 1961), pp. 79-148.

2. See Trevor Hart, "Person and Prerogative in Perichoretic Perspective — an Ongoing Dispute in Trinitarian Ontology Observed," *Irish Theological Quarterly* 58, no. 1 (1992): pp. 46-57.

for a trinitarian social ethic requires a different form of rhetoric than the analysis that will be undertaken here.[3] More significantly, it seems that the trinitarian claim, if it is to be at all convincing, also requires a social setting radically different from the one that now dominates U.S. society. Rather than advocating a trinitarian overhaul of public life, the burden of this essay is to show how the proposal of a trinitarian social ethic is likely to be misconstrued in the political and theological discourse of the contemporary United States. This is not to say that the gift of a trinitarian faith will never contribute to the reform of social ills, only that these pressing preliminary questions need to be met and answered if a trinitarian approach to social renewal is to be considered on its own terms.

The application of the trinitarian vision shared by Christian believers to society at large is not easy. The potential misunderstandings of the trinitarian social analogy are essentially twofold — political and theological. The current philosophy of social life in the United States, or more precisely the lack thereof, actually impedes the trinitarian view from being voiced, even by believers who are truly tolerant, non-ideological, and politically savvy. The problem lies with neither democracy nor pluralism. The problem is the particular form of political liberalism that dominates public life in the U.S. Michael Sandel and others have argued that the republican tradition of tolerance and local deliberation based on shared democratic values has been eclipsed and is in desperate need of revival.[4] In Sandel's estimation there is no public philosophy or vision of the good undergirding the policy decisions of most public officials, and most reasonable efforts to interject such a perspective into the debate is ruled out by the restriction of new initiatives to mechanisms for extending "the dialogue" within a procedural republic. Communitarians like Sandel want to restore the priority of the good over individual rights and allow for a less utilitarian and individualistic account of what constitutes human happiness to influence social life today. Sandel is no religious proselytizer trying to undo the disestablishment of the churches. In fact, he does not speak from within a specific religious tradition and rightly castigates the vices of those whose passion for renewal involves shoring up the borders and hard-

3. See, for example, Amelia J. Uelmen, "Toward a Trinitarian Theory of Products Liability," *Journal of Catholic Social Thought* 1, no. 2 (2004): 603-45.

4. Cf. Michael Sandel, *Democracy's Discontent: America in Search of a Public Philosophy* (Cambridge, MA: Belknap Press of Harvard University Press, 1996). See also Kenneth R. Craycraft, *The American Myth of Religious Freedom* (Spence Publishing Company).

ening the distinction between insiders and outsiders.[5] He is well aware of the rejoinder that the republican tradition in American culture has sometimes advocated a political philosophy that is either exclusive or coercive. To counter this charge, he disassociates his democratic and pluralist reading of the republican tradition from the elitist past of American republicanism. He also vehemently rejects the view that the pressure for globalizing homogeneity renders republicanism obsolete or impractical. If anything, the social pressure to force power upward that emanates from a globalizing economy makes the communitarian's respect for difference on the local level all the more timely. Sandel acknowledges that his version of republicanism shares with the new cosmopolitan ethic a concern that the nation-state as an exclusive form of political identity is losing its relevance. The emergence of new transnational political institutes constitutes in his view "the moment of truth in the cosmopolitan vision."[6] But he sees an equal danger that the transnational entities may mimic the nation-state in their usurpation of democratic forms of participation as they develop in diverse regional cultures such as those of the Catalans, the Kurds, the Scots, and the Québecois. "The hope for self-government," he states, "lies not in relocating sovereignty but in dispersing it."[7] The primary lesson to be taken from his analysis is that a particular narrative regarding the good life as understood and practiced by specific religious communities can continue to contribute to a shared vision of the common good. "The formative aspect of republican politics requires public spaces that gather citizens together, enable them to interpret their condition, and cultivate solidarity and civic engagement."[8] These narratives can play a public role only if citizens revive a democratic way of thinking about the common good that is less procedural and more in the spirit of civic republicanism.[9]

Although far removed from his own agenda, Sandel's analysis helps to explain the difference between trinitarian thinking and the now dominant form of liberalism in the United States. From the standpoint of contemporary theological discourse, the difference is hardly self-evident. At first blush the ideas of harmony and the promoting the conditions for

5. Sandel, *Democracy's Discontent*, p. 350. In this instance, he quotes the former candidate for President of the United States and pundit Patrick Buchanan.

6. Sandel, *Democracy's Discontent*, p. 345.

7. Sandel, *Democracy's Discontent*, p. 345.

8. Sandel, *Democracy's Discontent*, p. 349.

9. Cf. Robert W. Jenson, "How the World Lost Its Story," *First Things* 36 (October 1993): 19-24.

open, transparent discourse seem to marry trinitarian ontology with procedural liberalism. In both visions the proponents aim to promote concord and mutual dialogue. In fact, however, the trinitarian model goes far deeper than the virtues of tolerance and respect advocated in political liberalism. Promoting formal, religiously neutral ideals of tolerance and respect, as when the Supreme Court upholds the right of a city to pay for a nativity scene on the grounds that it serves a legitimate secular purpose, serves the ends of a civil religion, but this least common denominator approach to a national faith neither hinders nor promotes genuine forms of social communion.[10] The problem here is more political than theological. In other words, it is not the office of the Court to pay proper respect to the triune God, but its *de jure* indifference with respect to the substantive visions of the good shared by religious communities represents a curious brand of tolerance. The difference between trinitarianism and political liberalism lies partly in the nature of the communion. In political liberalism communion is seen as a subjective quality of an isolated individual unbound by traditions that norm communal social existence. Political liberalism poses a grave danger to anyone who attempts to ground rights to liberal, unconstrained freedom in the Christian vision of reality. For one thing, believers have *no monopoly* on tolerance and respect. The false pretense to understand the origins of subjective freedom in a religious worldview can lead only to a more subtle form of persecution than the outright suppression of legal rights.[11] Whether undertaken on Christian or secular terms, the legitimation of a complete freedom from external constraint has great difficulty in acknowledging the destructive will to power (Augustine's *libido dominandi*) built into real human choices. By contrast, the trinitarian *revelation* of communion points to a trace of harmonious order in God's creation frequently obscured by personal and structural sin and highlights the need for a deeply personal, spiritual conversion as a prerequisite for social reform. In the Christian account of such conversion, baptism is offered to those who freely wish to receive the gift of faith or in the case of infants to those whose parents freely choose to raise the children as Christians. If the freedom of faith is a prerequisite for the life of faith in the Church, then the public call to conversion and repen-

10. Jenson, "How the World," p. 60.

11. Cf. Adrian J. Walker, "Dialogue, Communion, and Martyrdom: Thoughts on the Relation between Intra-ecclesial and Inter-religious Dialogue," *Communio: International Catholic Review* 27, no. 4 (2000): 816-24.

tance must respect as a bare minimum the strict prohibition against coercion or the implicit promotion of a sectarian divisiveness. In witnessing in a public way to a trinitarian faith, Christians need not mandate adherence to any particular faith as a prerequisite for political participation; however, openness to religion as a source of communal self-identity seems like a real necessity for the renewal of civic life.

An example of a civic republican ethic based upon a modern understanding of the Christian claim can be found in the nineteenth-century anti-slavery advocate, philosopher, and social reformer Félix Varela. The uniqueness of the Varelian proposal is best epitomized in the *Letters to Elpidio* published in New York City between 1835 and 1838.[12] Although the name of the recipient could refer to the pseudonym of a real friend or student, it seems more likely that "Elpidio" is a neologism based on the Greek term *elpis* or "hope." The situation of Catholics in New York City was grim, and Varela's initial words of address to his "beloved Elpidio" sound like those of an Old Testament prophet. Varela isolated three social ills that were destroying the lives of his fellow Catholics — insensitive irreligiosity, somber superstition, and cruel fanaticism.[13] "Irreligiosity" for Varela is "insensitive" because it fails to grasp the religious constitution of the human person. This unswervingly theistic claim may seem to be at odds with Varela's free-thinking style and probably appears by today's relativistic standards as itself "insensitive." But the defense of belief in God for Varela is not just an abstract postulate of cold, hard reason; it is essential to understanding our "well-being." Varela's argument in favor of a living God serves both as a philosophical foundation of Varela's letters and a pointed political lesson to the Cuban intellectuals of his day who were inclined towards French Deism.

Varela's opposition to "somber superstition" needs to be viewed within his own social climate. Varela was a vocal opponent of the Spanish crown, which he considered to be an unjust aberration from genuine Christian governance. But his more visible opponent in this battle is the expanding polemics of Protestant revivalism. Because of the construction of the Erie Canal, New York State had been inundated with Irish Catholic immigrants in the first half of the nineteenth century. Nativist Americanism took hold of many Protestant Churches and fueled an antagonism aimed directly at working class "Papists." As a consequence, "superstition" for Varela does not arise from an overly pious attraction to Marian appari-

12. Félix Varela, *Letters to Elpidio*, ed. Felipe Estévez (New York: Paulist, 1989).
13. Varela, *Letters*, p. 6.

tions or reports of demonic beings. It is a philosophical error that stems from the equation of genuine religious belief with a false or idolatrous system of belief. Ministers of God who spread calumny regarding the beliefs of fellow Christians in the name of the gospel are as superstitious as despotic monarchs. Varela defended the reasonableness of the beliefs of the people of God and noted that his strong rhetoric against the purported patriots should not be confused with anti-Americanism. The prophetic Cuban attempted in vain to show New Yorkers that a priest could embody the ideals of Thomas Jefferson better than a zealously anti-Catholic minister. Although his confessional invectives could be sharp, Varela's rational defense of religious tolerance was still well ahead of its time. Writing over a century before the historic decree on religious liberty at Vatican II, Varela paved a *religious* path to a modern notion of political freedom. He discovered a modern concept that would find a nurturing home in the Catholic Church only in the second half of the twentieth century. Even without explicitly invoking trinitarianism, Varela's conception of human freedom derives from the Christian understanding of the human person as created in the image and likeness of God. As a Catholic intellectual and as a social progressive shaped by the second Enlightenment of the American continent, he defended this vision of universal dignity with eloquence and wit.

Varela forged for the nineteenth century a model of the Christian public intellectual on the American continent who engages in a public philosophy. He sided with European liberal Catholicism without wavering about the distinctiveness of a Catholic identity in his own context. Trinitarian thinking today likewise needs to be seen more as an ecclesial stance than a political strategy. The social impact of trinitarian communion is actually diminished if one obscures this point.[14] But even as a reality nurtured by the Church, it has an objective form that can be communicated in a public forum. To understand trinitarian communion as an objective reality, one must explore the meta-anthropological dimensions of the divine revelation.[15] This task extends beyond Christian theology, and the idea of

14. Some of the proposals regarding the postmodern politics of the Church made by Stanley Hauerwas and his followers seem to have this weakness. The trinitarian theology espoused in this essay nonetheless shares with both Hauerwas and Alisdair McIntyre a critique of secular liberalism and the modern idea of politics as statecraft in the name of the narratives and traditions of particular communities of belief.

15. The term "meta-anthropological" derives from von Balthasar. See Martin Bieler, "Meta-anthropology and Christology: On the Philosophy of Hans Urs von Balthasar," *Communio: International Catholic Review* 20, no. 1 (1993): 129-46.

interreligious solidarity poses a particular challenge to the trinitarian approach.[16] Emmanuel Levinas' ethics of alterity, which derives in part from the Talmud, is enormously helpful in identifying the shortcomings of a view of the person solely tied to individualistic freedom.[17]

The warrants for rejecting procedural freedom on the grounds of the Christian trinitarian claim can be summarized as follows. For Christians the God of Jesus Christ took on flesh and dwelled among us. Christians who maintain the traditional confession of faith affirm Jesus Christ as one person of two natures. Within the *unio hypostatica* of the Word made flesh, Christians encounter real unity "without confusion, without change, without division, without separation." Jesus Christ discloses God as the one who preserves an infinite depth of unity within a genuine embrace of otherness. The Spirit of Jesus Christ bridges the Church and the world by pouring forth this reality into our midst. The pledge of God's Spirit conforms to no known social program. Trinitarian Christian realism demands a prophetic naming of the vacuity of the reigning liberal model for social amelioration as well as a spiritual deepening of the meaning of human freedom espoused by liberalism's communitarian critics. St. Augustine was correct to counsel that the kingdom of God cannot be extrapolated from the virtues of any society, and his admonition pertains to the most profound incarnations of social harmony in a utopian republic. The rejection of procedural liberalism does not involve training the sights of the Christian community on a purely otherworldly goal. While those who hunger for the spiritual bread of God's kingdom may yearn for an even more concordant vision than that of civil society or a harmonious republic of virtuous citizens, there still is no reason why the realistic hope for a coming reign of peace and reconciliation cannot permeate the present order of social life. The articulation of this social vision requires, however, a properly theological orientation.

The social analogy has far too long a history to recount in this venue. Adherents to the trinitarian reading of the created order include Richard

16. Cf. Kathryn Tanner, "Trinity" in *The Blackwell Companion to Political Theology*, ed. Peter Scott and William T. Cavanaugh (Oxford: Blackwell, 2004), p. 323.

17. See E. Levinas, *Difficile liberté: Essais sur Judaïsme* (2nd ed., Paris: Albin Michel, 1976); idem, *Totality and Infinity: An Essay on Exteriority* (The Hague: Martinus Nijhoff, 1969); and idem, "Un Dieu homme? Qui est Jesu-Christ?" in *Recherches et Débat*, n. 62, 1968, pp. 186-192, reprinted in idem, *Entre nous, Essais sur le penser-à-l'autre*, Grasset, 1991, pp. 69-76. Cf. Adriaan Theodoor Peperzak, *Beyond: The Philosophy of Emmanuel Levinas* (Evanston, IL: Northwestern University Press, 1997), pp. 121-30.

of St. Victor,[18] St. Bonaventure,[19] Jonathan Edwards,[20] Hans Urs von Balthasar,[21] Gustav Siewerth,[22] Klaus Hemmerle,[23] Piero Coda and his circle,[24] David Schindler,[25] Robert W. Jenson,[26] Colin Gunton,[27] and Richard Swinburne.[28] In the realm of systematic theology some have argued that the trinitarian view of creation involves a new path to the social analogy of

18. Richard of St. Victor, *De trinitate*, book III.

19. See, for example, Luc Mathieu, *La Trinité Créatrice d'après Saint Bonaventure* (Paris: Les Editions Franciscaines, 1992) and Gilles Emery, *La Trinité Créatrice* (Paris: Librairie Vrin, 1995). Paul Tillich claimed to be influenced by Bonaventure's thinking on this issue. See John P. Dourley, *Paul Tillich and Bonaventure* (Leiden: E. J. Brill, 1975).

20. See William Danaher, "'The Society or Family of the Three': Trinitarian and Moral Reflection in Edwards's Social Analogy," in *The Trinitarian Ethics of Jonathan Edwards* (Louisville: Westminster John Knox Press, 2004), and Stephen H. Daniel, "Postmodern Concepts of God and Edwards's Trinitarian Ontology," in *Edwards in Our Time*, ed. Sang Hyun Lee and Allen C. Guelzo (Grand Rapids: Eerdmans, 1999), pp. 45-64.

21. Angela Franz Franks, "Trinitarian Analogia Entis in Hans Urs von Balthasar," *The Thomist* 62 (1998): 533-59.

22. Michael Schulz, "Being, World, and Man: Images of the Triune God in Gustav Siewerth's Trinitarian Ontology," *Communio: International Catholic Review* 29, no. 2 (2002).

23. Klaus Hemmerle, *Thesen zu einer trinitarischen Ontologie* (Einsiedeln: Johannes Verlag, 1996). Hemmerle's published theses were originally composed in the form of a letter to Hans Urs von Balthasar. They are discussed in the latter's *Theodramatik, IV: Das Endspiel* (Einsiedeln: Johannes Verlag, 1983), pp. 64-65.

24. Piero Coda, "Perspectives on Theological Knowledge from the Perspective of the Charism of Unity," in *An Introduction to the Abba School: Conversations from the Focolare's Interdisciplinary Study Center*, ed. David L. Schindler (Hyde Park, N.Y.: New City Press, 2002), pp. 38-55; Piero Coda and Andreas Tapken, eds., *La Trinità e il pensare: figuri percorsi prospettive* (Rome: Città Nuova, 1997); Piero Coda and L'ubomír Žák, eds., *Abitando la Trinità. Per un rinnovamento dell'ontologia* (Rome: Città Nuova, 1998). The article by Andreas Frick in *La Trinità e il pensare* deals with Hemmerle's theses. The articles by Antonio Maria Baggio and Adriano Fabris in the last volume treat trinitarian thinking and politics.

25. David Schindler, *Heart of the World, Center of the Church: Communio Ecclesiology, Liberalism, and Liberation* (Grand Rapids: Eerdmans, 1996); idem, "Communio Ecclesiology and Liberalism," *Review of Politics* 60 (1998): 775-786. See also his contribution to the volume *Wealth, Poverty, and Human Destiny*, ed. Douglas Bandow and David Schindler (Wilmington, DE: ISI Books, 2003).

26. Robert W. Jenson, *Systematic Theology*, I-II (Oxford: Oxford University Press, 1997, 2001).

27. Colin E. Gunton, *The One, the Three, and the Many* (Bampton Lectures) (Cambridge: Cambridge University Press, 1993).

28. Richard Swinburne, *The Christian God* (Oxford: Oxford University Press, 1994), pp. 17-191. For criticisms of Swinburne's argument, see David Brown, "Trinity" in *A Companion to the Philosophy of Religion*, ed. Philip L. Quinn and Charles Taliaferro (Oxford: Blackwell Publishers, 1997).

the trinity, one that appreciates but moves beyond the trinitarian proposals put forward by advocates of liberation and political theology.[29]

Recently, the trinitarian social analogy has been attacked by theologians who are concerned that what is propounded as a traditional defense of Christian faith is really a projection of worldly social agendas into the Trinity.[30] These critics of the social analogy are generally not opposed to the progressive political slant of those who defend the analogy. Their concerns have more to do with the departure from a traditional form of trinitarian belief that is tacitly presupposed in the social analogies that dominate current academic theology. The critics generally believe that the social analogy involves the erroneous projection of an idealized form of the body politic onto the divine. Rowan Williams, for example, questions the christological underpinnings of a "'social' doctrine of the Trinity."[31]

The articulation of a full-scale social ethic rooted in a trinitarian view of the created order is beyond the scope of this presentation. Two pivotal issues, however, need to be addressed as starting points: the relationship between God and the world and the question of the end of the world. The relationship between God and the world is properly analogical, which means that the mystery of the triune God must be safeguarded even with the introduction of a social analogy.[32] A properly analogical account of the social Trinity will restrain the attempt by some current social trinitarians to project metaphors of idealized social existence or interpersonal relations onto the divinity. While metaphorical speech about God can serve its own purposes,

29. Cf. Jürgen Moltmann, *Trinity and the Kingdom* (Minneapolis: Fortress Press, 1993). The difference between the analogical ontology of social harmony and the social trinity of Jürgen Moltmann is found in a Christian understanding of analogical predication instead of panentheism and a Bonaventurian notion of eternally fecund divine simultaneity as the ground of history as opposed to the quasi-cyclical revolutions of process thought. See also von Balthasar's critique of Moltmann in *Das Endspiel*, pp. 148-59.

30. See Kathryn Tanner, *Jesus, Humanity, and the Trinity: A Brief Systematic Theology* (Edinburgh: T&T Clark, 2001) and "Trinity" in *The Blackwell Companion to Political Theology*, ed. Peter Scott and William T. Cavanaugh (Oxford: Blackwell, 2004), pp. 319-32; Karen Kilby, "Perichoresis and Projection: Problems with Social Doctrines of the Trinity," *New Blackfriars* 81 (Oct. 2000): 432-45; Sarah Coakley, "'Persons' in the 'Social' Doctrine of the Trinity: Current Analytic Discussion and 'Cappadocian' Theology," in Sarah Coakley, *Powers and Submissions: Spirituality, Philosophy, and Gender* (Oxford: Blackwell, 2002), pp. 109-30.

31. Rowan Williams, *On Christian Theology* (Oxford: Blackwell Publishers, 2000), pp. 225-38, here at p. 226.

32. Cf. Kenneth Schmitz, "Naming God: Analogical Negation," in *Christian Spirituality and the Culture of Modernity*, ed. Peter Casarella and George Schner, S.J. (Grand Rapids: Eerdmans, 1998), pp. 159-75.

the idea of an analogy between the triune creator and what the Creator has wrought in the finite order derives from the order of things. Analogy differs from metaphor in that it takes as its point of departure a reality or highest good that can never be constructed through human imaging or intellection. Signifying that which cannot be signified is of course a problem. Aquinas settles on a pure act of self-subsistent being. Robert W. Jenson speaks of an event of pure music.[33] Analogies to the final "tranquility of order" (Augustine) in creation are thus not the product of our social imagination. Poetic geniuses like St. Bonaventure, Jonathan Edwards, and Gerard Manley Hopkins are still needed to give fitting expression to these sublime realities. Analogy unlike equivocity points to an ontological relationship between God and the world, albeit an asymmetrical one. All of these qualifications simply indicate that whatever triune attributes one selects, e.g., a kingdom of love, mutual self-giving, or perichoresis, the existence of its likeness in the creaturely realm is *not* one of comparative proportion. Between the infinite Creator and the finite creature there can be no comparative proportion. Analogy bridges the span that a logic of more or less can never cross.

A more strictly analogical account of the relationship between God and the world will highlight that the prime analogate, namely, God as Father, Son, and Holy Spirit, is a revealed datum of faith. This move puts the renewal of social trinitarianism back into the living stream of the tradition that spawned it, which could pose a problem for revisionist trinitarian theologians. Sarah Coakley argues that the authoritative givenness of *revealed* trinitarian language freed theologians such as Gregory of Nyssa to radicalize the unknownness of God the Father and treat *human* fatherhood as strictly derivative and secondary.[34] Gregory was more interested in the fulfillment of human *eros* in the wholly transcendent goodness of the divine being than in trinitarian politics. His apophatic erotics of creaturely participation in the triune God serves as an instructive counterweight to any modern attempts to read trinitarian social analogies in an overly innerworldly fashion. Participation in the divine life and engendering a greater sense of participation in democratic institutions need not be viewed as antitheses. Thinking about their convergence, however, begets new ways of conceiving of the inner unity of contemplative prayer and apostolic activity. The dialectical opposition between theory and practice must thereby be abandoned.

33. *Systematic Theology,* I.
34. Sarah Coakley, "'Persons' in the 'Social' Doctrine of the Trinity," p. 126.

The Catholic theologian Karl Rahner rejected as false apocalypticism the view that one could legitimately interpolate events from the present historical sequence into the Biblical unveiling of the world's end.[35] As it goes, Rahner was correct. In fact, all attempts to conflate the Scriptural vision of the end with linear history need to be viewed with critical scrutiny. In other words, the form of personal and communal existence disclosed through the social analogy is only a proleptic anticipation of the love that will be shared by God's people in the kingdom. Accordingly, God's relationship to the temporal dimension of social existence (e.g., the week of work and rest) is neither that of evolutionary progress nor that of timeless cycles. The God of Jesus Christ becomes incarnate in time, and time takes on a new meaning in light of God's self-disclosure in Christ. Repeated invocations of the tension between the already realized and not yet fulfilled temporality of God's kingdom tend to obscure what Robert Jenson citing Augustine calls "an inner contradiction" that destabilizes every polity of this age.[36] Jenson summarizes Augustine's still relevant doctrine as follows:

> The one triune God can be "enjoyed" and so is immune to exploitation by our love of self; there is nothing we can use this God for. But partial goods can indeed be used for our antecedent purposes, in fact they invite such use, and so they can be manipulated by self-love. . . . The self-destructive inner dynamic of every polity of this age is self-love in its political form, the passion to dominate: *libido dominandi*, as Augustine calls it.[37]

The end of the world is the final enjoyment of God as our *eschatos*, our personal and communal end. There is little that politics can do to bring about this end since it is wholly of God's making. Yet there is a distinctively ecclesial form of communion that witnesses in the present to the final encounter of God and the world in the eschaton, namely, the eucharist. In the eucharist, Jenson continues, the Church of the present age experiences "a parliament of common and mutual prayer," which is also "a perfect participatory democracy."[38] But here at least we have a visible sign of how the enjoyment of God can be directed to an ever new social communion.

35. Karl Rahner, "The Hermeneutics of Eschatological Assertions," *Theological Investigations,* IV (New York: Herder/Crossroad, 1960), pp. 323-46.

36. Robert W. Jenson, "Eschatology," in *The Blackwell Companion to Political Theology,* p. 412.

37. Jenson, "Eschatology," p. 412.

38. Jenson, "Eschatology," p. 413.

Sandel's analysis is helpful to a trinitarian social ethics because it illustrates the possibility for adherents to this view to gain a foothold in the naked public square. The above theological analysis shows that the analogy of concord can be pursued without projecting attributes that apply in the first instance to God into the body politic and without immanentizing the eschaton. If this political and theological analysis is correct, then it is reasonable to espouse a view that favors the possibility of a trinitarian social ethic. Let me conclude with a few concrete examples. Pope John Paul II's notion in the post-synodal apostolic exhortation *Ecclesia in America* that social solidarity is the fruit of trinitarian communion inspires an ecumenical vision for a social reform extending from Alaska to Tierra del Fuego.[39] The document is still only beginning to be heeded and contains concrete directives regarding the canceling of foreign debts, immigration policies, ending the violence from narcotics trafficking, and many other pressing social concerns that affect North and South America. The Christian call for solidarity cannot be separated, the Pope argues, from the task of *metanoia*, of a personal encounter with the redeemer. The linkage of participation in the divine life with the creation of urgently needed social bonds is instructive. A second example is the economy of communion initiated in 1991 by Chiara Lubich to counter the degradation of the poor in São Paulo, Brazil.[40] Here a highly developed trinitarian model for thought and action was applied to economic and social structures. The model proved to be a successful and empowering enterprise and has been replicated elsewhere. In terms of concrete models of democratic participation, I would follow Sandel in highlighting the Industrial Areas Foundation Network model for community organizing, especially as that was realized in the COPS program in San Antonio, Texas.[41] This highly effective model of bringing self-empowerment to urban neighborhoods of poor Hispanics

39. Peter Casarella, "Solidarity as the Fruit of Communio: Ecclesia in America, 'Post-Liberation Theology,' and the Earth," *Communio: International Catholic Review* 27 (Spring 2000): 98-123.

40. Jim Gallagher, *A Woman's Work: Chiara Lubich* (Hyde Park, N.Y.: New City Press, 1997), and Dr. Lorna Gold, "The Roots of the Focolare Movement's Economic Ethic," available on-line at http://www.edc-online.org/testi/gold-lorna-e.pdf.

41. On this last point see Ernesto Cortes, Jr., "Reweaving the Fabric: The Iron Rule and the IAF Strategy for Power and Politics," in *Interwoven Destinies: Cities and the Nation,* ed. Henry Cisneros (New York: W. W. Norton, 1993), and Mark R. Warren, *Dry Bones Rattling: Community Building to Revitalize American Democracy* (Princeton: Princeton University Press, 2001). Cf. Michael Sandel, *Democracy's Discontent*, pp. 336-38.

enlisted the aid of many Catholic parishes and served to advance a sense of dignity and social communion in ways that many people had previously thought impossible. Sandel cites the effort in San Antonio as one paradigm of overcoming the discontent that arises in a democratic society when the only venues for participation are channeled through overly abstract and often divisive procedures of state policies, partisan politics, and the tendency of the media to falsely dichotomize all social realities through paper-thin constructions of progressivism and conservatism.

I have highlighted some of the exigencies that a trinitarian social ethic faces within the context of public life in the United States. Given my emphasis on the particularity of the Christian worldview, it may seem that the proposal under consideration will utterly lack universal appeal or is merely utopian, a position that has been openly espoused by some prominent trinitarian theologians. On the contrary, I would by way of conclusion highlight that trinitarian communion as a social reality must *embody* the highest sense of ecumenicity. In other words, through the particularity of a concrete vision of the good there arises the surprisingly hopeful sense that diverse groups can share in a dialogue regarding the embodiment of commonly desired goods in their concrete circumstances of life. Christian theology is certainly not needed in order to grasp the importance of the task of dialogue on the level of both local and global civil societies. But hopefully the theological account given here will at least promote this pressing goal.

"Public" Re-imagined: A Reconsideration of Church, State, and Civil Society

Kristen Deede Johnson

The language of "civil society" has been undergoing something of a re-naissance in the fields of sociology and political theory in recent decades. More and more thinkers have looked to the concept of civil society on both national and global levels for a variety of reasons: some use the con-cept to point out the problems facing liberal democracies based on de-clining involvement in the types of organizations that have typically been associated with civil society; some propose civil society as a crucial aspect of our common life together in which we need to invest in order to rein-vigorate our political culture; others are positing that the globalization that marks our time has been accompanied by the development of a vi-brant global civil society. Some Christian thinkers have tried to join the conversation occurring around civil society by offering Christianity as a crucial contributor to civil society and political citizenship; these efforts have a concomitant goal of legitimizing Christianity's place in contempo-rary political society. These proponents of Christianity, many of whom are continuing the project begun by John Courtney Murray, tend to ac-cept the basic language and assumptions of the liberal nation-state as they try to find space for the church within the public square and look to Christianity as a resource for reinvigorating the culture's public philoso-phy.[1] Other political theorists and theologians, however, are questioning

---

1. Daniel M. Bell, "State and Civil Society," *Blackwell Companion to Political Theol-ogy*, ed. Peter Scott and William T. Cavanaugh (Malden, MA: Blackwell Publishing, 2004), p. 431.

the very language involved in conversations about "church," "state," and "civil society," wondering how adequate traditional (Rawlsian) political liberalism is for an increasingly post-secular and globalizing western world. In an effort to recover democracy, post-Nietzschean political theorists and proponents of radical democracy articulate a vision for a post-secular political realm; with the hope of revitalizing the western church, theologians such as William Cavanaugh and Stanley Hauerwas offer a vision of the church as an embodied social reality rather than a mere voluntary association.

In light of the resurgence of interest in civil society and the differing Christian responses to the idea, it seems important both to think through the background of the concept of civil society and to evaluate it in terms of its compatibility with a Christian understanding of the church. This paper provides a brief historical overview of the idea of civil society, and in so doing shows that civil society has had conceptual difficulties since its inception. This means that no mere retrieval or easy reinvigoration of civil society is possible. Furthermore, when we look at the space allotted to the church within contemporary conceptions of civil society, we have reason to question the adequacy of civil society and its concomitant components, for Christianity, and other faith traditions, are more identity-constitutive and intrinsically social than many of the other associations placed within the realm of civil society. Based on this diagnosis, I conclude that we need to enter into the more rigorous task of reimagining our current configurations of church, state, and civil society and the main ideas that accompany these configurations, particularly the ideas of public and private. The goal here, then, is not to provide legitimacy for theological and ecclesiastical contributions to the public square but to re-think the very conceptions of public and private that have come to be taken-for-granted within contemporary liberal society.

Civil Society Defined and Explored

The term "civil society," as used today with reference to the national level, is usually thought to refer to that section of society that mediates between the political and personal realms. It consists of the cluster of associations, organizations, and activities that bring individuals together and, without being political *per se*, strengthen the social good. This realm also protects individuals from a potentially overreaching state or potentially overpowering economic organizations.[2] When we look at the concept historically, we see that civil society was not always considered a realm separate from the state; when the concept first arose it referred more broadly to the area of social interdependence within a given society.[3] Civil society as used today, however, most often refers to "that aspect of social existence which exists beyond the realm of the State."[4] To be more concrete, such "social existence" is thought to include parent-teacher associations, service organizations, bowling leagues, and neighborhood associations. It is important to this conception of civil society that participation in these groups is voluntary and that the groups themselves are not directly linked to the political realm.

Whence comes the concept of civil society? The idea first emerged in the later seventeenth and eighteenth centuries, in response to a new but important problem facing political societies. Changing times, theories, philosophies, and practices resulted in an increased sense of the person as a private individual distinct from a communal whole. Questions related to how to reconcile the private and the public, and the individual and the social, had to be addressed for the first time.[5] The seventeenth and eighteenth centuries were witness to significant changes in European social thought and practice that broke with previous traditions and forged new ground in efforts to find moral and political unity. As Seligman writes,

> By the middle of the eighteenth century it became increasingly difficult to square the traditional image of the individual as bounded by and validated within the network of social relations with that of the autonomous social actor pursuing his (not yet her) individual interests in the public realm. The very grounding of new forms of social action and motivation based on self-interest (indeed, on the very concept of the self) made it imperative to posit a new moral order that would accommodate and in a sense "hold" the development of interpersonal relations based not on a shared vision of cosmic order but on the principle of rational self-interest.[6]

2. See Steven M. DeLue, *Political Thinking, Political Theory, and Civil Society*, 2nd ed. (New York: Longman Publishers, 2002), p. 346.

3. Adam Seligman, *The Idea of Civil Society* (Princeton: Princeton University Press, 1992), p. 3.

4. Seligman, *Civil Society*, p. 3.

5. Seligman, *Civil Society*, p. 5.

6. Seligman, *Civil Society*, p. 26; see also pp. 15-16.

In other words, traditional understandings of the foundation of social order, based in a sense of shared cosmic order or an external entity such as
God or King, were being questioned; at the same time as the foundation of
social order was increasingly thought to lie within humans, philosophical
and economic developments were increasing the sense that humans could
act as individuals within the public realm. As the human and the this-
worldly came to be viewed as more important than the transcendent and
other-worldly, syntheses once taken for granted were no longer considered
viable, and distinctions between morality and theology, between the individual and the social, and between the public and the private had to be addressed. This is what brought forth the idea of civil society.[7] To quote
Seligman again,

> To a great extent the developing idea of civil society is — within the
> Scottish Enlightenment — an attempt to find, or rather posit, a syn-
> thesis between a number of developing oppositions that were increas-
> ingly being felt in social life. These oppositions, between the individual
> and the social, the private and the public, egoism and altruism, as well
> as between a life governed by reason and one governed by the passions,
> have in fact become constitutive of our existence in the modern world.
> Not surprisingly the attempt to return to the eighteenth-century idea
> of civil society is today an attempt to readmit that synthesis of private
> and public, individual and social, egoistic and altruistic sources of ac-
> tion that such an ideal represents.[8]

How did the original idea of civil society seek to hold together these
different components? The individual and the social were held together by
a philosophical anthropology that defined the individual in terms of the
social, so that a single human was considered to be but one part of a communal whole. The real innovation, at least according to Seligman, came in
the effort to reconcile the public and the private. The public realm, which
could have been treated as a neutral space of exchange, was instead invested with moral significance, and this moral significance was not derived
from or connected to a transcendent reality but came solely from an innerworldly logic, from the nature of humanity. It was thought that we would
find within ourselves a natural benevolence that would provide the moral

7. See Seligman, *Civil Society,* pp. 26-30.
8. Seligman, *Civil Society,* p. 25. When referring to the Scottish Enlightenment, he
seems to have in mind primarily Francis Hutcheson, Adam Ferguson, and Adam Smith.

basis for our public life, so moral sentiment and natural sympathy came to be viewed as the source of the moral order. The bond that would hold the individuals of a society together was found in moral sentiment, or the innate instinct found in humans to act with kindness and friendship towards others in society.[9] These natural affections combined with reason were thought to lead individuals to put the good of the social order above private goods. Unfortunately, Seligman notes, the synthesis between public and private that the Scottish Enlightenment thinkers located in moral sentiment and reason was a fragile one that could not and did not support the expansion of capitalism and the growth of rationality.[10] Indeed, it was not to survive the questioning of David Hume.

We do not have the space here to go step by step through the history of the idea of civil society. It is, however, important to acknowledge that the effort to find in civil society the means to hold public and private together while allowing them to be differentiated has been marked by difficulty from the start. It is also important to identify what some of these difficulties have been so that today's efforts to reinvigorate civil society are not naively undertaken. Indeed, Seligman argues that we can only understand the development of liberalism if we take time to consider the disintegration of the original idea of civil society, for the challenges posed to the idea of civil society in the thought of Hume deeply informed the thinking of Immanuel Kant and those who followed and continue to follow in Kant's footsteps (not that all forms of contemporary liberalism are Kantian, but they are at least influenced by Kant's thought). Hume's main critique came from his questioning of the connection between moral sentiment and reason. Whereas the original conception of civil society was predicated upon an understanding of natural human benevolence that was complemented by the use of reason, Hume posited that reason and morality were two distinct, unconnected notions; neither morals nor actions were derived from the use of reason, while moral thinking did not lead to universal truths. Motives for human action come from sentiment, according to Hume, which is distinct from that which can be determined by reason. Likewise, the universal truths uncovered by reason are distinct from the realm of morality. How, then, does society have a moral or normative dimension? It does not. Hume, unlike his predecessors, envisioned the social order without a morally substantive good. The public good was not

9. Seligman, *Civil Society,* p. 27.
10. Seligman, *Civil Society,* p. 31.

upheld by moral sentiment or human benevolence, as in the original conception of civil society, or by a notion of transcendence, but by self-interest, which would lead individuals to follow common rules of justice in order to have their own interests maximized. As Seligman puts it, "With Hume (and after him Smith) the distinction between justice and virtue, between a public sphere based on the workings of self-interest (in conformity to law) and a strictly private sphere of morality, is present in its starkest form. It was this distinction and its attendant dilemmas that the Scottish Enlightenment and the whole civil society tradition had attempted to avoid. The ensuring [sic] dilemma, of how to posit a prescriptive and not just descriptive model of the social order . . . has defined the modern period from Hume onward."[11]

Kant attempted to respond to the problems raised by Hume, but in so doing he retained and solidified the distinctions that Hume first articulated, linking the political realm to reason and the private realm to morality. Reason was deemed to be universal enough in scope to link the public and private realms, and it was thought to be substantive enough to provide a vision of individual rights that were connected to the moral law. In Kant's thought the natural moral sentiment upon which the original conception of civil society relied is replaced by the dictates of reason. Crucial to Kant's conception was the existence of a shared public realm in which the workings of reason could be validated, and this shared public arena, distinct from the state, came to be viewed as civil society. Indeed, it was in the thought of Kant that civil society was first separated from the state. According to Kant the state embodies political society, while civil society is the realm in which public rational debate and critique occur. Defining the public in terms of reason is Kant's way of trying to overcome the distinction between individual interests and the public good that had led to the concept of civil society in the first place. But as he makes this move, he perpetuates the distinction first wrought by Hume between the public and the moral. In Kant's thought the public realm is the sphere of the juridical, in which primary importance is placed upon the idea that all citizens are equal, while the private realm is the sphere of the ethical, which has to do with the inner motives and workings of the individual. While it provided a working solution to the question of how to reconcile public and private, it did not ultimately resolve this tension. As Seligman notes, "This solution (and distinction) to the dilemma of how to represent the public good, still

11. Seligman, *Civil Society,* p. 41.

critical to the discourse of liberal political theory, perpetrated rather than resolved the tension between public and private realms. By distinguishing right or duty from ethics and reserving the latter for the private realm, Kantian theory left unresolved the critical issue of ethical representation — of the status of the public sphere."[12]

To summarize, the original concept of civil society maintained that the public realm was a realm of moral significance, even if its significance was not connected to a transcendent source; with Kant, and those who have built upon his thought, this moral importance is no longer attached to the public realm. This means that one of the foundational building blocks of civil society is no longer present to support the idea. That is to say, "Within this tradition, civil society as an ethical space has no intrinsic meaning, and its regulative and attendant values are there for the protection and preservation of individual liberties. Here ethical value is the province of the particular individual and not of society as such."[13] No longer do we find moral reasons to engage in the public realm; the purpose of the public realm is primarily to protect our own liberties. Perhaps one of the significant reasons that we have such a diminished civil society today is the loss of this ethical dimension of the public realm. This is not to say that the original conception of civil society was unproblematic; history alone, never mind a healthy doctrine of sin, prevents us from thinking that we can rely on the natural benevolence and moral sentiment of humanity. (On a side note, Seligman points out that Hegel and Marx sought alternative solutions to the problem raised by Hume as they attempted, in different ways, to preserve the ethical quality of the public space; Hegel collapsed civil society into the state while Marx envisioned the eradication of the differences between them in the society that would begin after the Revolution.)[14]

We have been tracing the rise of the idea of civil society and the inherent links between civil society and the questions of the relationship between the public and private realms and the moral basis of the public realm. Seligman believes that the renaissance occurring today around the concept of civil society is a response to very similar circumstances that brought forth the original idea of civil society, in the sense that we are again looking for answers to the question of how to hold together the public and the private, and the individual and the social. Other scholars have

12. Seligman, *Civil Society*, p. 44.
13. Seligman, *Civil Society*, p. 51.
14. See Seligman, *Civil Society*, pp. 51-52.

noticed a rise in the use of the term civil society to refer to phenomena happening globally. John Keane has written extensively about global civil society, calling it "a big but modest idea with fresh potency" and noting that global civil society "is today on the rise."[15] It goes hand in hand with the rise of globalization, so that while its foundations rest upon the original conceptions of civil society we have been discussing, its existence is dependent upon the international trade, commerce, travel, media, and social movements that are a part of today's global world. That is to say, as the original conception of civil society and its recent resurgence on the national level were responses to changing political and economic circumstances, so is the rise of global civil society a response to, as Keane writes, "rising concerns about the need for a new social and economic and political deal at the global level."[16] While global civil society, similar to national civil society, has a responsive nature, in that its emergence can be understood as a response to new and changing circumstances on the global scale, it has some distinct characteristics.

A concise definition of global civil society is offered by Keane as "a dynamic non-governmental system of interconnected socio-economic institutions that straddle the whole earth, and that have complex effects that are felt in its four corners."[17] Included in global civil society, according to Keane, are "individuals, households, profit-seeking businesses, not-for-profit non-governmental organizations, coalitions, social movements and linguistic communities and cultural identities."[18] The organizations and movements typically associated with global civil society are marked by an aversion to violence and a sense that treating others with non-violent respect takes priority over treating people on the basis of ethnicity, culture, national identity, sex, or religion.[19] They also help to limit the influence of political rule by acting as a brake upon different forms of government.[20] This is all while operating in the absence of an overarching political society. This is one significant difference from older conceptions of civil society, which usually understand or define the role of civil society in relation to a particular political society or structure. Today's world is

15. John Keane, *Global Civil Society?* (Cambridge: Cambridge University Press, 2003), p. xi.

16. Keane, *Global Civil Society?* p. 2.

17. Keane, *Global Civil Society?* p. 8.

18. Keane, *Global Civil Society?* p. 8.

19. Keane, *Global Civil Society?* p. 13.

20. Keane, *Global Civil Society?* p. 15.

marked by global interactions that happen in a variety of realms, from the economy to the media to large-scale humanitarian efforts, yet these international interactions do not happen within the framework provided by one global political system. "Our situation is different," as Keane writes, "and without historical precedent."[21] The global civil society about which Keane writes is also distinct, inasmuch as it "has emerged and today operates in the absence of a global state, a world empire, or comprehensive regulatory structures that are describable in the state-centered terms of political 'realism.'"[22]

Although global civil society has some differences from classic conceptions of civil society, it nevertheless remains connected to many of the original concerns of civil society. For example, civil society from its inception has been thought to help protect individuals from being overly dominated by either the political realm or economic organizations. Global civil society likewise is concerned with providing protection from political, economic, and cultural infringements, although it has a wider purview in that it is concerned with providing this protection for all people regardless of their national identity. According to Keane, "Within a world otherwise riddled by violence, great imbalances of wealth, and nasty prejudice, global civil society is a safe haven that guarantees the right to asylum for many different and potentially or actually conflicting morals."[23] Keane acknowledges that it also extends the original purposes of civil society in that it seeks to provide permanent rather than temporary sanctuary for people: "In respect of this permanency, it goes beyond what Kant had in mind when he spoke of civil society . . . as a place where universal peace can reign because strangers . . . can enter and reside there temporarily."[24] And yet the protective element on behalf of the individual is the same. This is the same protective element that seems to have caused the public realm some trouble, insofar as strong moral reasons to be involved in the public square have been eclipsed by a sense that the public realm exists primarily to protect our liberties. Keane, while attempting to make conceptual sense of the global phenomenon that can be classified as global civil society, acknowledges that global civil society is in need of normative justification. The idea of global civil society is not yet sup-

21. Keane, *Global Civil Society?* p. 94.
22. Keane, *Global Civil Society?* p. 94.
23. Keane, *Global Civil Society?* p. 197.
24. Keane, *Global Civil Society?* p. 197.

ported by an articulated sense of its goodness or an ethical basis that underlies our investment in it.[25] Keane tries to develop this ethical basis by positing global civil society as a universal ethical ideal that is "the universal precondition of the open acceptance of difference."[26] He writes of global civil society as "a universal ethical principle that guarantees respect for . . . moral differences"[27] and "a haven of difference and identity."[28] In other words, Keane acknowledges that global civil society needs a moral basis just as civil society on the national level needs one. He describes different efforts to provide these moral bases and ultimately tries to posit an ethical principle that he thinks can underlie global civil society. Yet he seems to derive the need for this moral basis from the newness of global civil society and from the desire to answer critics of global civil society, rather than undertaking a deeper investigation of the moral foundations of the concept of civil society as it has been inherited from its classic origins. He dismisses Seligman's analysis of civil society in a footnote, rather than pausing to seriously engage with the concerns that Seligman brings to the fore.[29]

According to Seligman's diagnosis, we cannot retrieve former conceptions of civil society without understanding and reckoning with the difficulties that have plagued civil society since its inception. Seligman's less-than-optimistic observation is that the synthesis between public and private that the original conceivers of civil society posited did not hold long even in the eighteenth century, and subsequent efforts did not provide more sustainable support for the synthesis. This means that we cannot merely retrieve former conceptions of civil society and hope that they will help us make sense of or reinvigorate our public culture today, whether that be on a national or a global scale. On the contrary, Seligman believes that a collapse in the public realm was inevitable, given both the contradictory premises of what he calls "modern, liberal-individualist society"[30] and the lack of a moral basis for the public realm. Because the public realm lacks moral value in and of itself, its value is often derived from those who are involved in it. In Seligman's diagnosis, the American

25. Keane, *Global Civil Society?* pp. 174-175. Keane dedicates a large portion of this book to an exploration of the ethical basis of global civil society; see pp. 175-209.

26. Keane, *Global Civil Society?* p. 203.

27. Keane, *Global Civil Society?* p. 202.

28. Keane, *Global Civil Society?* p. 208.

29. Keane, *Global Civil Society?* p. 3.

30. Seligman, *Civil Society,* p. 132.

phenomenon of publicly disclosing matters that have traditionally been considered private is an attempt to give the public realm meaning and value. The private is projected into the public in order to give the public realm an ethical significance that it does not have under liberal democracy operating in the legacy of Kant.

Ethical significance is also needed for the realm of civil society on a global scale. We have seen how Keane has offered such an ethical basis by positing global civil society as a haven for moral differences. While Keane is attempting to use theoretical imagination to reconsider civil society as a global concept, rather than trying to draw it into our current situation as is, he does not seriously engage with its conceptual history or address how today's usage links to the concern over public and private that originally brought forth the concept. Neither does he articulate how the ethical basis of global civil society he puts forward will help to motivate involvement in it or provide enough of a moral basis to help us reclaim the moral significance of the public realm. Whether on a global or a national scale, we still have many reasons to question whether we today have a *meaningful* public realm.

The Need to Reconsider the Public

Many people today are questioning the health and even the existence of the public realm in contemporary western, and often more specifically American, society. Some scholars are drawing attention to the disappearance of public spaces and involvement within our current political arrangements. One thinks here, of course, of Robert Putnam's analysis in *Bowling Alone,* in which he attempts to empirically trace the decline of civil society.[31] More drastic perhaps is the diagnosis of the neo-Marxists Michael Hardt and Antonio Negri. Hardt and Negri argue that under the conditions of post-modernity, public space has been privatized to such a large degree (they cite the transition from common squares and public encounter to gated communities and the closed space of shopping malls) that the spaces of modern liberal politics no longer exist. With the loss of the clear distinction between the private world of the household and the public world outside the home, they maintain that not only has the place

---

31. Robert D. Putnam, *Bowling Alone: The Collapse and Revival of American Community* (New York: Simon & Schuster, 2000).

of politics been de-actualized, but a deficit of the political has arisen.[32] Another concern arises from Charles Taylor, who believes that the rise of individualism and the primacy of instrumental reason have led to decreased levels of political involvement and have therefore increased the power of the political realm itself. We are now faced with "an immense tutelary power" that runs everything; this political enterprise that acts as our protector is difficult for us to identify with as a community or as *our* community, so we feel powerless rather than empowered to be involved in the political realm.[33] Whereas Hardt and Negri helpfully point out the privatization of certain public spaces and realms, Taylor draws our attention to the other side of the coin: the politicization of the public realm. That is to say, today "public" most often means "political." Between the different diagnoses offered by these thinkers, we have reason to be concerned about the status and the existence of a public realm that attracts involvement from individuals and acts as a mediator between individuals and the state. Hence the resurgence of interest in the idea of civil society and the hope that, by drawing upon the classical concept of civil society, we can help to remedy the challenges facing us today.

As we have seen, one Christian response to these concerns has been to offer Christianity as a helpful contributor to civil society. On both theoretical and empirical levels, arguments are made that Christians are significant participants in the public realm and that Christianity can, therefore, serve to strengthen the public square. Some argue that a significant reason that the current public square is diminished is that religious voices have been excluded from it.[34] Even John Courtney Murray, who was more influential than any other thinker in demonstrating the compatibility of democracy with Catholicism and endorsing the separation of church and state, acknowledged that America's public philosophy was in crisis and in need of refurbishment.[35] Murray believes that America at one time had a strong and rich public consensus that it drew from Catholic political

---

32. See Michael Hardt and Antonio Negri, *Empire* (Cambridge, MA: Harvard University Press, 2000), pp. 186-190, esp. 188.

33. Charles Taylor, *The Ethics of Authenticity* (Cambridge, MA: Harvard University Press, 1991), pp. 9-10, 117.

34. One thinks most obviously of Richard John Neuhaus, *The Naked Public Square: Religion and Democracy in America* (Grand Rapids: Eerdmans, 1986).

35. See Michael J. Baxter, "John Courtney Murray," in *The Blackwell Companion to Political Theology*, ed. Peter Scott and William T. Cavanaugh (Malden, MA: Blackwell Publishing, 2004), pp. 159-163.

thought and its natural law tradition, and he believes that we ought to renew this tradition in order to reinvigorate our public life. But what if the
issues go deeper than Murray acknowledges? What if we cannot just look
back to one tradition or another in order to help our public life today because the very concepts of public and private that we inherited from the
language surrounding civil society are problematic? Seligman acknowledges that the idea of civil society, particularly as it took root in America,
was deeply influenced by natural law doctrines and what he calls
Protestant-individualism.[36] But this does not lead him to believe that our
current public realm can be reinvigorated by a mere retrieval of traditions
surrounding either natural law or civil society. Instead, a review of the history of the concept of civil society has revealed that tensions have always
existed in this attempt to reconcile the public and the private, whether the
public is thought to be equivalent to the political realm or whether it is
viewed as a mediating realm between the state and the individual. Perhaps
what is needed now is a deeper questioning of the categories and the concepts which we have inherited, particularly our conceptions of public and
private.

Public Reimagined

We turn now to begin to explore what might be involved in reimagining
our current conception of public. As a Christian theologian, I do not undertake this exploration with a sense that Christianity directly translates
into a political theory or that there is one political arrangement that is
sanctioned by God more than others. I follow my understanding of Augustine on this point, namely that Christianity can co-exist with a variety of
political arrangements so long as these arrangements do not inhibit worship of God. That is to say, my primary measure of evaluation for our current conceptions of public, private, and civil society is whether they allow
for the church to exist and to worship God as it is called to by God. On
both conceptual and practical levels, I find reason to question whether
civil society provides adequate space for the church to be faithful to its
calling. Even if we did have a thriving civil society, as defined today, we
would still need to reconsider our categories, for Christianity properly understood is not the same thing as a voluntary association like the PTO or

36. Seligman, *Civil Society,* p. 59.

PTA. Since we are in need of a renewed public space that will not be swept into either the private or the political realms, we have all the more reason to reconsider these categories.

In contemporary usage, "public" is most often equated with the political realm. Not only do we, in actuality, face a troubling increase in bowling alone, but in our vernacular we scarcely make room for a public realm that is distinct from the political realm, for that mediating space in which public debate and critique occur while the social good is strengthened. The public has been eclipsed by the political. By definition, "public" need not refer only to a nation or a state, or to the explicitly political realm of nations and states. It can also refer to a community or a group of people united by a common interest or good, say, for example, worship of God, the highest and most unchanging good. A people united together through worship of God can be considered a public just as much as a people united together through a common national allegiance. According to a verse like Ephesians 2:19, to be a Christian is to be a citizen of the Kingdom of God and a member of God's family. This identity is a matter of truth and belief, but this truth and belief call forth a response and an ethic that are visible and tangible, embodied in the collective life and practices of the church. Christianity is at heart a communal and public enterprise: the church is comprised of a group of people sharing the common interest of worship of God and love of neighbor. Augustine reminds us that through participation in the church and its sacraments, citizens of the heavenly city are united around the communal and unchanging good of God, their collective *summum bonum*.

Indeed, Rowan Williams argues that Augustine's main purpose in *City of God,* and particularly in Book 19, is not only to show that the church is its own public but to redefine the very understanding of what is truly public and political: "he is engaged in a *redefinition* of the public itself, designed to show that it is life outside the Christian community which fails to be truly public, authentically political."[37] On this reading, for something to be truly public it must provide common ends around which people can be united, common purposes around which shared life can take shape, a common good that is unchanging; such ends and purposes, such a common good cannot be found outside of Jesus Christ and his body, the church. It must, furthermore, address the truest human needs, which according to Augustine are, of course, related to God. Human beings, who

37. Rowan Williams, "Politics and the Soul: A Reading of the City of God," *Milltown Studies* no. 19/20 (1987): 58.

148

were created for communion with and enjoyment of God, cannot have their deepest needs addressed outside of a restored relationship with God or the community of those who have been similarly restored. While a social or political unit united around certain aims that do not include enjoyment of God "may be empirically an intelligibly unified body, it is constantly undermining its own communal character, since its common goals are not and cannot be those abiding values which answer to the truest human needs."[38] Such societies cannot, ultimately, cohere, because they fail to be united around the only true source of coherence; "their character and structure are inimical to the very nature of an ordered unity in plurality, a genuine *res publica*."[39]

Of course many people today consider Christianity to properly be a private matter, a matter of private belief that is subject primarily to individual choice and conscience. This is quite a different picture of Christianity than the one that emerges from Augustine, for whom Christian faith is necessarily concomitant with a different identity, loyalty, allegiance, and practice. For Augustine, a Christian is primarily a citizen of the heavenly city, and only secondarily a pilgrim in the political society in which she or he happens to live. It would have been inconceivable for Augustine to divorce Christianity from the life of the church or to view it as anything but a public, social ethic. Indeed, the very categories of public and private that go hand in hand with liberalism are foreign to Augustine. As Jean Bethke Elshtain notes, Augustine does not bifurcate "the earthly sphere into rigidly demarcated public and private realms";[40] instead, Augustine sees a continuum in which the peace of a person, of the household, and of the city are all connected.

So how did we get from this Augustinian picture of Christianity to that depicted in Seligman's thought? In the traditional story, Christianity had to become private and learn to tolerate differing interpretations of its key doctrines to avoid the bloodshed and conflict that inevitably arise when Christianity, or one strand of it, attempts to lay claim to being public. According to many versions of the story, liberalism emerged out of the religious diversity of post-Reformation Europe and the religious wars of the sixteenth and seventeenth century, which raised the question of how

38. Williams, "Politics and the Soul," p. 60.
39. Williams, "Politics and the Soul," p. 60.
40. Jean Bethke Elshtain, *Public Man, Private Woman: Women in Social and Political Thought* (Oxford: Martin Robertson, 1981), p. 70.

the relationship between groups with different interpretations of Christianity should be configured and negotiated. Toleration was offered as the answer, understood as the best way to move beyond the antagonism and bloodshed that were afflicting the differing strands of Christianity. Recently, however, some scholarship has emerged to challenge the story that presents the rise of liberalism as the solution to religious conflict.[41]

Regardless of how we think about the wars of religion and the rise of liberalism, there is no disputing that Christianity is now almost automatically considered a private matter of beliefs and values in ways that are not consistent with a historical, orthodox conception of Christianity. I am not arguing that Christianity played no role in this transformation. Rather, I would suggest that along the way Christians have accepted reigning paradigms of thought in order to be included in political society. But I would also argue that such inclusion should not need to come at the expense of Christianity's identity as communal and public; it should not need to require Christianity to compromise its integrity by distancing itself from its social, public, and institutionalized home so that it becomes a privatized system of beliefs with relevance only for the "life of the soul." In short, a way should exist for Christianity to be public without taking over what we commonly understand as the public square or ceasing to abide by the rule of law established by the larger political society (that is to say, public does not need to mean political). Christianity, at least Christianity in an Augustinian vein, cannot remain content with the way it has let itself be positioned by contemporary political liberalism. Nor can other communal constituencies currently residing in western societies.[42]

This discussion is not meant to deny a place or a role for the political realm, but it is supposed to raise questions about how we understand what is meant by "public" and what is allowed to be public and enter the so-called public square in contemporary liberalism. We are not disputing the claim ably represented by Elshtain that some distinction between public and private is necessary for politics to exist, nor are we disagreeing with the idea that important and significant areas of life can best flourish when left outside of the direct purview of an all-embracing public (as in political)

41. Pierre Manent, *An Intellectual History of Liberalism*, trans. Rebecca Balinski (Princeton: Princeton University Press, 1994), esp. pp. viii, xvii, 114, 116; William T. Cavanaugh, "'A Fire Strong Enough to Consume the House': The Wars of Religion and the Rise of the State," *Modern Theology* 11, no. 4 (October 1995).

42. William E. Connolly begins to discuss this in relation to Islam in *Pluralism* (Durham, NC: Duke University Press, 2005), pp. 55-59.

imperative.[43] We are, however, like Elshtain, wondering how different conceptions of public and private and, here differently than Elshtain, an expanded space for overlapping "publics," might help expand our current political and theological imagination. From a theological perspective, we must be wary of accepting definitions that undermine the essence of Christianity as an embodied, social public, united around the common interest of love of God. We must be careful to prevent the church from grafting into its self-understanding ways of thinking that do not allow it to be seen as the site of the true common good around which people can be united in shared purpose, as the commonwealth in which justice and peace are actual possibilities, through the mediating and redeeming work of Jesus Christ.

To look at this from another perspective, let us briefly follow the argument of Reinhard Hütter as he considers the concept of public. Whereas our contemporary understanding of public legitimizes only the public of liberal political society, Hütter offers a vision of "a structural concept of public" that allows for "a whole multiplicity of different publics that overlap and complement one another and yet also are able to relate to one another from within positions of serious, fundamental tension."[44] Why is this important? Because if the church is not understood fundamentally and explicitly as its own public, then it is defined and positioned "from the perspective of the normative public of modern, differentiated liberal society that promptly effects the church's eclipse *as* a public."[45] When the church loses its sense of itself as public, it begins to be defined and to define itself by an alien logic, by the logic of, for example, contemporary liberalism, thereby losing its ability to stand alongside, apart from, or in critical relationship to the public of modern society.[46] This could, in fact, be what so often leads the (Protestant) church to align itself with the purposes of the nation-state: "this eclipse of the Protestant church as public might be one reason it is susceptible to becoming the bearer of national and other identities and projects, securing for itself thus as a national or civil religion a measure of public relevance within the framework of the public arena of society at large."[47] This eclipse of the church as a public,

---

43. See Elshtain, *Public Man, Private Woman,* pp. 201, 351. On the importance of the private sphere, see also Duncan B. Forrester, *Beliefs, Values, and Policies: Conviction Politics in a Secular Age* (Oxford: Clarendon Press, 1998), pp. 7-8.

44. Reinhard Hütter, *Suffering Divine Things* (Grand Rapids: Eerdmans, 2000), p. 159.

45. Hütter, *Suffering Divine Things,* p. 169.

46. See Hütter, *Suffering Divine Things,* p. 171.

47. Hütter, *Suffering Divine Things,* p. 11.

then, affects not only the church's self-understanding, but also its ability to stand as a critical or prophetic voice in the larger society.

That is to say, one of the dangers of allowing "public" to remain synonymous with the political realm as defined by contemporary political theory and practice is that it limits the critical abilities of other constituencies within political society. By creating space for multiple publics, overlapping yet each marked by its own telos, doctrine, and practices, we open the possibility of critical interaction between these publics, and between these publics and the political society of the time. Such intercourse between publics would, furthermore, avoid the prioritization of the individual that is concomitant with much liberal theory. Those who view themselves primarily as individuals and who place their identity first and foremost in the public of political liberal society continue to be welcome to do so, but those who find in other publics their more formative identities and allegiances can be given the space to operate from within those publics in interaction with the public of political society, which will continue to supply the overarching rule of law. This does not mean that it will always be easy to negotiate the different identities and allegiances that may come from the different publics and the political society of which citizens are a part, but it does mean that it is worth allowing space for these tensions to arise. Michael J. Sandel's effort to articulate a renewed version of republicanism for our time similarly seeks to allow such space. Recognizing that "most of us organize our lives around smaller solidarities," Sandel writes that whatever political vision we adopt "will have to enable us to live with multiple, overlapping, sometimes contending moral and political loyalties. It must equip us to live — this is the difficult part — with the tensions to which multiply-situated and multiply-encumbered selves are prone."[48]

A Brief Conclusion

This chapter clearly represents but a first effort to begin to rethink our conception of "public." Our brief look at the history of the idea of civil society revealed that civil society is intrinsically connected to the need to hold public and private together and furthermore that we have always

48. Michael J. Sandel, "The Politics of Public Identity," *The Hedgehog Review* 2, no. 1 (Spring 2000): 87.

struggled to find an adequate basis for this synthesis. This revelation helps us to see the need to probe more deeply as we think about our contemporary public and political life and to question the very concepts that have been handed down to us. We undertook this questioning with the church in mind, in an effort to imagine what conception of public would enable our current political structures to allow Christianity to exist as it was intended to be, that is to say not as a privatized set of beliefs but as a social, embodied reality. As we reimagine our current conception of public, we begin to see a picture of a society with truly reinvigorated publics — not a public realm that has been collapsed into the political, nor a public realm that only has space for organizations that do not lay claim to the allegiances and identities of its members, but publics that consists of groups of people united by substantive and identity-forming common interests and goods. Members of these publics still abide by the rule of law of a given political system, but their identities and conceptions of the good can be shaped more by the social realities of which they are a part than by that political system.

Early Christianity and Politics:
Its Real Role and Potential Contribution

Petr Pokorný

Analyzing the social and political bias of early Christianity may help us to understand the cultural and political development of the Mediterranean and Europe from Late Antiquity up to the formation of modern democracies. Scripture provided early Christians with only a few concrete instructions for orientation in Jewish or pagan society. Complex political projects originated in the post-Constantinian period only (e.g. Augustine's *De civitate Dei*) and represented a new period of Christian theology. At first, the followers of Jesus belonged to synagogues, but surprisingly soon (in the thirties), society recognized them as a special group known as "Christ-people" (*christianoi;* Acts 11:26), and, before the end of the first century, it also became one of their self-designations (Acts 26:28; 1 Pet. 4:16). The political influence of these *christianoi* was an indirect one. It had its specific features anchored in the public activity of Jesus of Nazareth, in the post-Easter experience of his followers, and in their ability for theological reflection. The influence of Christians in the first two centuries was indirect because it was mostly the influence of a model that had been shaped within the Christian groups themselves. The church formed a society within society and thereby provoked and inspired its surroundings.

The Value of History

A special feature of Christian worship was its concentration on the person of Jesus Christ. He was adored as Messiah (Christ) and considered to be

God: the Greek *kyrios* (Lord) was a substitute for God's name (tetragram) and he became the addressee of prayers (*maranatha* — Come oh Lord!; 1 Cor. 16:22). Even so, the Christians knew that he was a human being, and Paul was able to visit his brother James in Jerusalem (Gal. 1:19). The significance of Jesus was expressed in various ways: his death as a sacrifice, his identification with the apocalyptic Son of Man, and especially his resurrection as an anticipation of the Age to Come which would arrive after the Last Judgment (1 Thess. 1:10). A concrete piece of history thus became a "revelation" of the eschatological future. The theological concept of revelation was formulated by Ignatius of Antioch (*Magn* 8:2; the verb *phaneroun*). The concept did not entail the idea that all of history was God's sole form of revelation but that it was its concrete piece and that witnesses to it had an obligation to point towards this revelatory aspect of history so that the addressees of their witness might make responsible decisions in the world. Under such a concept history acquired a special value. In fact, this concept of history as revelation merely took to the extreme the revelatory narratives of the Jewish Bible (the Law and Prophets). There history had a similar function: the narrated history enabled the hearers to orient themselves in history.

The knowledge of revelatory history did not point to some special qualification which made some people worthy of knowing the "myth" about the founder. Admittedly, the feeling of an election and a special mission is a dangerous dimension of the whole Judeo-Christian tradition. But the biblical heritage also contained a kind of remedy against a feeling of superiority on the part of the elect: in the Law and the Prophets some stories reflected the failure of God's people (the deuteronomist tradition) and the Gospels spoke about the failure of Jesus' disciples as well. The self-critical dimension of the sacred texts enabled Christians to think realistically about themselves and to communicate with their surroundings.

Jesus' Teaching and Preaching: A Promise and a Vision

The self-critical, deuteronomist tradition of the biblical view of history culminated in Jesus' teaching in his definite rejection of the idea of a sacred kingdom on earth. His Kingdom of God (or the Reign of God) was eschatological, albeit near (Luke 10:11), coming into history from outside. It would approach the people not by historical development, but as an *adventus,* and in Jesus' activities it "has come upon" his contemporaries

155

(Matt. 12:28 par /Q/). He interpreted the kingdom as the eschatological future which was already working in history and at the end would dominate all creation (Mark 4:30-32 par). For Jesus, to believe meant to take this power seriously which does not lean upon violence (he wished his enemies to also have a part in God's kingdom; Luke 6:27 par /Q/) yet cannot be exterminated from history. His own firm belief, which he proclaimed as a promise, was linked to a general vision expressed by a set of metaphors (parables) — such an eschatological vision is a necessary prerequisite of any far-reaching activity in the history.

The political power of his teaching is indirectly confirmed by the fact that he was designated as a potential Messiah (Mark 15:26), even if he did not accept the messianic role himself (Mark 8:29, 33). Nevertheless in his teaching he put into question some prescriptions of the Law (Mark 7:14-23 par) as well as the temple (Mark 14:58; 15:29). He probably had in mind the eschatological temple (Ezek. 40–47) or the vision of God's presence among humans (Rev. 22:21). One of his controversial points was undoubtedly his extension of the Kingdom to all peoples (". . . many will come from the east and from the west and sit at the table with Abraham . . . in the kingdom of heaven, while the sons of the kingdom will be thrown outside into the darkness" [Matt. 8:11-12]). This inclusive character of Christianity was one of the most effective prerequisites for its impact in history, and now it is being opposed by all kinds of conservatives.

The most traumatic background to Jesus's death was his miscalculation about the coming of the Kingdom. He expected its coming during his life (Matt. 10:23), and only his deep relation to God as his father ("My God . . .") saved him from total despair ("why have you forsaken me?" [Mark 15:34 par]). We have to analyze this crisis as deeply as possible so that we may understand why, in spite of it, he became so influential in history. Such a thing is difficult to understand; the deepest, existential level of testing social projects is, however, the analysis of why they survive a crisis or failure.

Easter: The Gospel as Political Power

Jesus' first followers were Jews and their program, like the program of Jesus, was the reform of Israel. However, unlike Jesus himself, they proclaimed him the Messiah, the King of the Age to Come. It was an audacious innovation. The Proclaimer became the Proclaimed One. The eschatological expectation split into two poles ("telescopic" eschatology); the story of Jesus became a "revelation" of God's intention. The Messiah was already known, the Messianic Age was still a matter of an eschatological future. The reason for such an innovation was Easter as event: they experienced a new kind of his personal presence and assistance and, as a result, unlike other people after their deaths, after the cross his impact increased immensely.

"Resurrection" cannot be interpreted as a mere miracle. Rather, it was a "revelation," i.e. a demonstration of the very reason for the impact of any person, idea, or project that seems to be an outsider in history but after some time shows itself to influence history more than any economic or even military power. Therefore the resurrection of Jesus was a revelation indeed. Christian theology understood the resurrection of Jesus as the principal demonstration of God as the guarantor for the power of all good ideas and movements in history. For example, baptism anticipates for any human being his or her future life with Jesus Christ (Rom. 6); any harvest is in fact a resurrection of a seed and an event guaranteed by God's creative power, etc. In some cases the category of cause and effect explains only the surface of an event while the very guarantor of the impact of martyrs, teachers, poets, and other powerless people is God himself. The story of Jesus is the key which brings understanding to this specific and immensely important phenomenon. This is the reason why Jesus really "survived" his death. By no means is this an exhaustive interpretation of Christian soteriology, but it is an attempt to understand it for our contemporaries. It is from here that we must start our analysis of Christian activity in history.

It is impossible to reflect on history as a whole since we are a part of it. Nevertheless, Hebrew and early Christian texts try to grasp the problem of history by reflecting on stories that anticipate history's fulfilment and include God's judgment (2 Cor. 5:10). In this view history ceases to be an area dominated by various fatal powers and becomes a realm of struggle against alienation — a struggle with only one winner. That is why Paul was able to interpret the sufferings of his time as a childbirth pain of the Age to Come (Rom 8:18). This is the theological background of the general political dimension of the Gospel.

The main contribution of early Christianity for politics was not in any new tactics for political activity (e.g. a new model for a political party). Most of the political elements of early Christianity correspond to the model of a movement which could use more tactics but which still manages to unite different groups in support of its aims. Nevertheless, the main horizon which motivated Christian activity transcended history, consisted in a more or less convergent attitude towards life, and was open to reinterpretation. The possibility of dynamic reinterpretations and innovations is, of course, only a possibility inherent in the gospel *(euangelion)*. Throughout history the church has often neglected it. This possibility has, however, inspired reforms and reformations and enabled the church to survive many crises.

Social Structures and Their Theological Meaning

We have already mentioned that Christians originally lived within the synagogue as a special faction. They were often punished as heretics (2 Cor. 11:24), and so they also gathered in "houses" *(oikos)*, in households including at least three generations of the family, the servants and slaves, clients, and guests. Usually the lord (in Latin *paterfamiliae*) was a Christian himself (Rom. 16:3-4), but in some cases he tolerated a Christian group in his house, even if he did not adhere to Christianity himself (Rom. 16:10b, 11b). In this way Christianity spread at the grass-roots level. The basic group, however, was a gathering of several families, the local congregation (church, *ekklēsia;* 1 Cor. 14:23). In such a gathering they celebrated the Eucharist and baptized neophytes. These gatherings were held in larger houses of wealthier patrons.

Since the Jews, the "children of Abraham," considered themselves to be the people of the Messiah, the way to Christianity led through Judaism, including circumcision. After some partial solutions to this problem (the so-called apostolic decree), Paul of Tarsus proposed a radical solution by declaring that all who believed in God as Abraham did were the very descendants of Abraham (Rom. 4). This interpretation enabled him to integrate the former pagans and, at the same time, to preserve the biblical heritage, the long-time experience of the Jewish past, for the church. His role was appreciated only after the fall of Jerusalem in A.D. 70, when the Christians were expelled from the synagogue. Traditionally we suppose a concentric development of Christianity from the center in Jerusalem, but in fact the post-Easter followers of Jesus appeared in various places, particularly in Galilee. And the Pauline theological concept of God's people enabled them to integrate. The rooting in basic social cells, the opening towards non-Jews, and the decision to accept a tradition which reached far into the past (the adoption of the Jewish Bible) were the important marks of the successful development of the church as a body inspiring the life of society as whole.

Political Elements of Theological Projects

The central role of Jesus in Christian belief led practically to a subordination of all other relationships to the relationship between Jesus and Christians and between the values represented by his teaching about the Kingdom of God and the daily responsibility of believers. The model of God as teacher and all disciples of Jesus as brothers (and sisters) evoked a strong tendency toward the compensation of social differences, toward attempts at the community of goods in Jerusalem (Acts 2:41-47; 4:32-35), and toward a feeling of solidarity with the church's poor members (2 Cor. 8:1–9:15). It also supported an openness toward pagans: "There is neither Jew nor Greek, slave nor free, male nor female, for you are all one in Christ Jesus" (Gal. 3:28); "For God does not show partiality" (Rom. 2:11); "My brethren, show no partiality" (James 2:1). These are the motives which can be transferred to the present in the form of Christian support for democracy.

Unlike Jesus' expectation of a pilgrimage of pagans to Zion (a centripetal mission; Matt. 8:11-12 par; cf. Zech 8:20-23), the practice of early Christians (especially after the destruction of the temple) was to proclaim Jesus Christ in new areas. However their centrifugal mission (see Matt. 28:19) was not any attempt at agitation or propaganda; it was anchored in an attractive life at the foundation of which were Christian cells (household groups, congregations), where newcomers could find their real home (1 Cor. 14:23-25).

The postponing of the *parousia,* the coming of the Age to Come, and the prolongation of the expected period of history were balanced by exhortations to perseverance *(hypomonē)* and coping with the problem of Roman political power. Rejected was the escapist strategy of spiritual anticipation of the Kingdom of God (1 Cor. 4:6-13). The Christians realized the positive functions of political power such as security, communication, and commerce, and Paul initiated the strategy of submission to the governing authorities (Rom. 13:1-7; cf. 1 Pet. 2:13-17). For him such submission was an active, missionary strategy — a sign that the new movement did not intend to destroy society but was truly good news *(euangelion).* That his advocating submission was not motivated by political opportunism only can be deduced from the parallel exhortations for Christians not to divorce their pagan partners (1 Cor. 7:13-16); Christian wives were even to obey their pagan husbands, since in this way the husbands might have been won without words by the behaviour of their wives (1 Pet. 3:1). With his idea of submission Paul continued the tradition reaching back to Jesus himself with his "Render to Caesar what is Caesar's and to God what is God's" (i.e. taxes and civil subordination; Mark 12:17 par; ThomEv 100; cf. PapEgert 2:2r). The Christian strategy was not to oppose pagan political power, but to build up cells with an alternative social structure that could strengthen basic human relations. Christians created their own social world (a counterculture), but the inner tendency of the gospel prevented them from violent opposition (a contraculture).[1] In Acts 5:38-39, the author offers the pagan authorities a strategy of dealing with Christians: "Leave these men alone, for if this plan or activity is of human origin, it will fail; but if it is of God, you will not be able to stop them." Christians prayed *for* kings (1 Tim. 2:1-4), but they did not pray *to* the deified rulers as was expected in the empire. The Johannine Jesus says to Pilate: "You would have no power over me if it were not given to you from above" (John 19:11).

The eschatological hope of Christians played a special role in the formation of their social strategy. This has often been interpreted as an escape from history. But this escapism does not belong to the substance of Christian faith. Paul had to explain to the Christians in Thessalonica that their faith includes also hope in death (1 Thess. 4:13-18), and, on the other hand, in Philippians he had to suppress his desire for death by realizing his responsibility for the addressees (Phil. 1:21-26). Eternal life does not mean a never-ending post-mortal life. Time is a category of temporality, not of eternity. Eternity entails a new dimension of life, a life in an intensive social interrelation. Practically speaking, the promise of eternity means that humans can never be used as instruments for reaching other aims: for the survival of empires, for building up a new society, or for union with God. The human being himself holds the ultimate value in the mind of God. Unity with God is not the aim, but communion. The metaphors of meeting face to face (1 Cor. 13:12) or of the names in the Book of Life (Rev. 21:27; Heb. 12:23) demonstrate the specific role of the individual in the Christian tradition. (These two images correspond to a modern identity card with the name of the holder and a photograph of his face.)

The choice of the term of self-designation by Christians is instructive, namely *ekklēsia*, in the Septuagint the translation of the Hebrew

---

1. The terminology is that of K. A. Roberts, reinterpreted by V. K. Robbins.

qahal, a gathering of the people (of Israel). However, in Greek society, *ekklēsia* was the name for a gathering of free citizens of a city-state *(polis).* This was a surprising decision, since religious groups of the time called themselves *thiasos* ("Bacchic revel," "confraternity"), *eranos* ("feast," "permanent association"), or *teletē* ("mystic rites of initiation"). *Ekklēsia* as the Christian self-designation expressed the public claim of the new movement. The church did not build upon hidden mysteries like the Hellenistic religions (Acts 20:27).

I have presented several typical features of the church in its earliest period. Due to the limited space, I could not elaborate on their theological interrelation. Later, many of the original features and principles of Christianity were pushed to the background, but once they were canonized, the church was not able to get rid of them, and they have become fundamental to a sound theology. They also speak to the inner power of ideas that can be operative in political situations today.

Intertwined Interaction: Reading Gregory of Nazianzus amidst Inter-religious Realities in India

J. Jayakiran Sebastian

Trinity of love and peace,
Father, Son and Spirit,
God treats his children all the same,
Offers them his fellowship.
Father God, Spirit God:
make us one as you are one,
God in Jesus,
Word made flesh,
Come, adopt us as your own;
Sisters, brothers, all are yours;
If forgiveness fills our hearts,
You will vindicate our cause.[1]

The heart in misery
Has turned
upside down.
The blowing gentle breeze
is on fire.
O friend, moonlight burns
like the sun.

1. Verse 2 from the Burmese hymn, "Gracious Father, Love Divine" (Words: George Kya Bing, Myanmar, trans. Sang Maung; para. Roland S. Tinio), found as Hymn 196 in *Sound the Bamboo: CCA Hymnal 2000* (Tainan: Taiwan Presbyterian Church Press, 2000).

Like a tax-collector in a town
I go restlessly here and there.
Dear girl go tell Him
bring Him to His senses.
Bring Him back.
My lord white as jasmine
is angry
that we are two.[2]

Introduction: Pertinent Praise and Pressing Predicaments

I come from the city of Bangalore,[3] a city that is increasingly playing a dominant role in the new economic realities of the world, especially in terms of attracting business process "outsourcing" from all over the world, the way companies offer a variety of services to their clients through "call centers," and the reality of the availability of a huge force of highly trained professionals at the cutting edge of global information technology inventiveness. Near the heart of the city, Mahatma Gandhi Road, I was passing by a pile of books and magazines of a "pavement" book shop when my eyes chanced upon a magazine called *Civil Society*. Bangalore never fails to surprise! It turned out to be an Indian magazine, newly started, and the issue I bought had several articles on what the editors considered matters of pressing urgency, including saving the tiger, problems with access to drinking water, poll reforms, educational restructuring, and a very interesting article on a new initiative of Vandana Shiva (an experimental restaurant recently opened in Delhi called the Navdanya Café) attempting to show-

---

2. Mahadeviyakka (12th century), Vachana 321, translated from Kannada by A. K. Ramanujan in A. K. Ramanujan, trans. and ed., *Speaking of Siva* (Harmondsworth: Penguin Books, 1987), p. 139. Used by permission.

3. See the new book by Janaki Nair, *The Promise of the Metropolis: Bangalore's Twentieth Century* (Delhi: Oxford University Press, 2005), for a detailed analysis of the growth and development of the city. Nair also analyzes the discourse on civil society and citizenship and writes that "the city of Bangalore has, over the past forty years, been swiftly remapped as a territory for accumulation of economic power on an unprecedented scale. It has also served as a site for newly defined notions of citizenship. Only in some instances do these notions of citizenship conform to the liberal desire for peaceful and orderly development. Cities are increasingly the site for the assertion of new and empowering identities, which, in striking contrast to the forms of collective action in the past, re-territorialize urban space in ways that challenge the functional logic of the market or the economic uses of time" (p. 345).

case and serve "the rich diversity of agricultural produce grown organically in India by small farmers."[4]

India is a country that is almost frightening in its multiplicity. Responding to the richness of the God-experience in this multi-religious country evokes a great deal of emotions. In this context singing hymns is never a neutral enterprise, just as the Indian debate on secularism has pointed out that all talk of secularism cannot be a "neutral" possibility, where the secular is understood "as a self-contained sphere of neutral reason, from which religion is thinned out by definition."[5] One sings to express joy or sorrow, contentment or commitment, lament or protest. Even a hymn in praise of the Trinity contains these elements. As sung by Christian believers in a country that neighbors India, like Myanmar, with all its attendant problems — political, social, and religious — such sentiments can even be subversive, whether this is acknowledged or not.[6] In the Indian bhakti tradition, the anguished outpourings of the devotee, lamenting the reality of separation from the divine Lord, has given rise to stunningly evocative and hauntingly beautiful poetry. Given this, I believe that an investigation into how discourse on the Trinity impacts inter-religious relationships is not only very important but a pressing need. In coming to terms with how we are seen by others,[7] we need to understand how we see ourselves, and to do this, what better metaphor than our understanding of the Trinity? However, such a task is not a simple exercise in self-understanding; rather it functions to orient us to be true and honest to ourselves in recog-

---

4. Vidya Viswanathan, "Catch Up with Slow Food in Delhi," *Civil Society* 2, no. 8 (June 2005): 19.

5. See the analysis and interaction with contemporary writing on this subject in Sasheej Hegde, "Always Already Secular? Afterthoughts on the Secular-Communal Question," in *Economic and Political Weekly* 40, no. 4 (January 22, 2005): 322-34, with quotation on p. 332. On what the secularism debate means for Christians in India, see my article, J. Jayakiran Sebastian, "Believing and Belonging: Secularism and Religion in India," *International Review of Mission* 92, no. 365 (April 2003): 204-11.

6. For an analysis of contemporary Myanmarese society, along with important historical background, see Christina Fink, *Living Silence: Burma Under the Military Rule* (London: Zed Books, 2001). Fink writes: "Burma's military regimes attempted to erase the humiliation of colonialism and shore up their own legitimacy by linking their political and religious activities to the accomplishment of great Burmese kings in the past" (p. 14).

7. See Robert Louis Wilken, *The Christians as the Romans Saw Them*, 2nd ed. (New Haven: Yale University Press, 2003), for a very important analysis of how the early Christians were "seen" and "interpreted" by various people in the early years of the existence of the church. Much can be drawn from this fine analysis for the understanding of the "images" of Christians in minority situations today.

nizing how we function in the wider society. One of India's most prominent historians, who has thrown herself into the struggle against fundamentalist tendencies attempting to engulf historiography, writes, "The fight is not only against the dominance of Hindu communalism asserting itself amidst a range of minority communities, but also the need within each community to marginalize the communal elements. This would be imperative if there is to be an alternative to the politics of religious communities."[8] In an inter-religious context it is important not only to look without, but also within. Writing on biblical interpretation and context, R. S. Sugirtharajah writes,

> Our job is not simply to critique the prevailing systems outside our little biblical world but to critique the very world we inhabit and function in. It is one thing to promote values like liberation, justice and equality in the outside world, but it is of no value unless we work to promote these same values within the disciplines and institutions in which we work.[9]

In a chapter of his book on the global face of public faith, David Hollenbach writes, "religious contributions to policy debates need not always wait until a larger cultural consensus is achieved."[10] While we recognize that the wider context on which he comments is the church in American public life; nevertheless, such comments offer much food for thought for those of us reflecting on the role of religion, religious symbols, and religious discourse in public life in India. One of the issues that continues to be a source of strife, deliberate misunderstanding, and division is that regarding the identity of various religious minority communities in India and the constitutionally guaranteed right (Article 25) to citizens of India to "profess, practice, and propagate" their own religion. A recent important book problematizes this issue and analyzes in great historical detail the vexing question regarding the relationship between mission, conversion, and proselytizing. How does one distinguish between these? Are

---

8. Romila Thapar, *Cultural Pasts: Essays in Early Indian History* (New Delhi: Oxford University Press, 2000), p. 1107.

9. R. S. Sugirtharajah, *Postcolonial Criticism and Biblical Interpretation* (Oxford: Oxford University Press, 2002), p. 203.

10. In the chapter, "The Context of Civil Society and Culture," in David Hollenbach, *The Global Face of Public Faith: Politics, Human Rights, and Christian Ethics* (Washington, DC: Georgetown University Press, 2003), p. 170.

they absolutely inter-related? Can there be mission without conversion or proselytizing without mission? How does one evaluate the educational, medical, and social activities of the church? Can there be conversion without discontent? How does one interpret the mass movements which were a feature of religious conversion at the turn of the nineteenth and beginning of the twentieth centuries, not to say anything about the mass conversions to Buddhism under Ambedkar in the middle of the twentieth century? Can conversion be seen as the quest for identity?[11]

Biblical scholars, too, are recognizing the reality of identity-formation in terms of how orienting symbols shape our identity. Writing about biblical theology, Brevard Childs notes that "those biblical commentators who laid claim to an objective, scientific explanation of what the text really meant, often appear as uninteresting museum pieces to the next generation." He goes on to say that "part of the task of modern Biblical Theology is to provide a proper context for understanding various usages of the Bible for shaping Christian identity that is of a very different order from modern historical critical exegesis."[12]

Regarding the complex of issues raised by attempting to problematize identity in relation to the question of "otherness," Timothy Beal, in interaction with the feminist cultural commentators Luce Irigaray and Judith Butler, asks, "To what extent is otherness posited and enforced by a particular system of identity politics in ways that are logically impossible? What are the inherent problematics of such identities of excluded not-selves within the logic of the system itself?"[13]

11. Sebastian C. H. Kim, *In Search of Identity: Debates on Religious Conversion in India* (New Delhi: Oxford University Press, 2003), passim. Also see my articles "Conversion and Its Discontents," *Bangalore Theological Forum* 32, no. 1 (June 2000): 165-72; and "A Strange Mission Among Strangers: The Joy of Conversion," in *Vom Geheimnis des Unterschieds: Die Wahrnehmung des Fremden in Ökumene-, Missions- und Religionswissenschaft*, ed. Andrea Schultze, Rudolf von Sinner, and Wolfram Stierle (Münster: LIT Verlag, 2002), pp. 200-210.

12. Brevard S. Childs, *Biblical Theology — A Proposal* (Minneapolis: Fortress Press, 2002), p. 72. For a comprehensive and thorough analysis of the issue see Eric Lott, *Religious Faith, Human Identity: Dangerous Dynamics in Global and Indian Life* (Bangalore: Asian Trading Corporation/ United Theological College, 2005).

13. Timothy K. Beal, *The Book of Hiding: Gender, Ethnicity, Annihilation, and Esther* (London: Routledge, 1997), p. 92. In another book, *Religion and Its Monsters* (New York: Routledge, 2002), building on the work of Homi Bhabha, Beal writes:

> Translation of cultural, especially *religious* differences encountered by European travelers in India into biblical apocalyptic terms of monstrosity achieves precisely this end: it projects an image of *familiar otherness,* and thereby orients and stabilizes the

At this point, it would be good to remind ourselves of important theological voices and contributions to inter-religious dialogue, especially from those coming from the Indian context. The first director of the department for Dialogue with People of Living Faiths and Ideologies at the World Council of Churches, the Indian theologian Stanley J. Samartha, captured the essence of what was needed in the collection of his essays, written during his time at Geneva, entitled *Courage for Dialogue*.[14] He writes that religions "have a dismal record in the history of community relations. They have disrupted existing groups, divided people, sometimes intensified conflicts. Plurality of religions within certain countries has not helped national integration. . . . Thus there is considerable justification for secular disappointment with religions as bearers of peace."[15] Nevertheless the imperative of dialogue demands that, even though many experiences of dialogue could be a rough experience, the "growing in truth will demand rejection of distortions of truth about each other, distortions which may even be close to untruth and which may sometimes amount to giving false witness against one's neighbor."[16] Much of what Samartha writes resonates very well with the following point by Hollenbach:

> Serious dialogue is risky business. At least some religious believers have been willing to take it. The future of public life in our society could be considerably enhanced by the willingness of a considerably larger number of people to take this risk of cultural dialogue, whether they begin as fundamentalists convinced of their certitudes or agnostics convinced of their doubts. Our society needs more imagination about how to deal creatively with the problems it faces than instrumental rationality can provide.[17]

---

identity of western *otherness,* and thereby orients and stabilizes the identity of western, European, Christian, modern, civilized (non-primitive, non-ritualistic) society against that projected image — at the expense, of course, of other people's gods and their vital religious practices. (p. 116)

14. S. J. Samartha, *Courage for Dialogue: Ecumenical Issues in Inter-religious Relationships* (Geneva: World Council of Churches, 1981).

15. In his "World Religions: Barriers to Community or Bearers of Peace?" in *Courage for Dialogue,* p. 124.

16. In his "Ganga and Galilee: Two Responses to Truth," in *Courage for Dialogue,* p. 154.

17. Hollenbach, *The Global Face of Public Faith,* pp. 164-165. In this connection see the probing analysis of Max L. Stackhouse regarding the "ecclesiological character of the corpo-

This "imagination,"[18] at least for the Christian partners in the dialogical enterprise, can be provided by interpreting the reality of the Trinity as the orienting symbol for Christian faith, life, and practice, in interaction with the faith claims of other participants, without avoiding the difficult questions regarding "absoluteness," colonial realities, and the fear of conversion. For Samartha,

> the particularity and distinctiveness of Christian mission needs to be restated in such a way that co-operation with neighbors of other faiths for common purposes in society is not seen as a betrayal of mission but as the context in which the Christian witness to God's saving work in Jesus Christ becomes transparently clear. No one demands that the Church should abandon this mission. Mission is integral to the gospel. . . . The distinctiveness of Christian mission lies precisely in its being *Christian*, that is, in its being rooted in God through Jesus Christ and in being active in the world in the power of the Spirit, without denying, however, that neighbors of other faiths too have *their* "missions" in the global community.[19]

"Early Christian interpretation, grounded in its strong sense of God's long involvement with humanity, can offer us at least parallels and models for reviving our exegetical imagination."[20] Today, theological imagination leading to acknowledgement and respect are concepts that need to be

---

ration," and how the understanding of vocation today needs to recapture "a moral and spiritual vision" of why people do what they do, in his "The Moral Roots of the Common Life in a Global Era," in *Loving God with Our Minds — The Pastor as Theologian: Essays in Honor of Wallace M. Alston,* ed. Michael Welker and Cynthia A. Jarvis (Grand Rapids: Eerdmans, 2004), pp. 50-61.

18. In "*Gloriosus Obitus:* The End of the Ancient Other World," in *The Limits of Ancient Christianity: Essays on Late Antique Thought and Culture in Honor of R. A. Markus,* ed. William E. Klingshirn and Mark Vessey (Ann Arbor: University of Michigan Press, 1999), p. 314, Peter Brown writes: "A new style of Christianity, preoccupied with different problems and so in need of a different imaginative world, did not wish to appropriate the rich imaginative structures of its own, more ancient past. As a result, they have remained either opaque to us, or strangely out of focus."

19. S. J. Samartha, *One Christ — Many Religions: Toward a Revised Christology* (Maryknoll, NY: Orbis, 1991; third Indian edition, Bangalore: South Asia Theological Research Institute, 2000), p. 171.

20. Brian E. Daley, "Is Patristic Exegesis Still Usable? Some Reflections on Early Christian Interpretation of the Psalms," in *The Art of Reading Scripture,* ed. Ellen F. Davis and Richard B. Hays (Grand Rapids: Eerdmans, 2003), p. 88.

integrated into the multi-faith context of India. The level of political discourse is becoming increasingly shriller, and deep-held prejudices are spilling out into the open. For the Christian partners in the dialogical enterprise, what is needed is "imagination" in interpreting the reality of the Trinity as the orienting symbol for Christian faith, life, and practice, interacting with the faith claims of other participants, without avoiding the difficult questions regarding "absoluteness," residual colonial realities, and the deep-rooted fear of conversion as a tactic. The fractured multiplicity of India and the way in which the living reality of plurality has been addressed should lead us to the understanding of a non-vicious, non-violent, and non-vociferous way of dialogue,[21] whereby ecumenical perspectives in understanding civil society and the dynamics of the Trinity are brought into fruitful interaction.

Societal Realities in India Intertwined with the Trinitarian Theologizing of Gregory of Nazianzus in His Theological Orations

In an earlier programmatic article entitled "Why Should Asian Theologians Read Texts of the Early Teachers of Faith?,"[22] I interrogated the writings of several of the early teachers of faith. I used Gregory of Nazianzus, "the mellifluous bishop from Asia Minor who lived in the late fourth century,"[23] to raise several issues regarding the way theology had to be done, taking the sermon that he preached in the year 380 in Constantinople in the first of his five "theological" orations as the basis of my analysis.[24] Gregory said,

21. See my "Towards a Christological Missiology Today with the Guide-Who-Stands-Aside," *Theology Today* 62, no. 1 (April 2005): 18-28.
22. In Samson Prabhakar, ed., *Inter-Cultural Asian Theological Methodologies: An Exploration* (Bangalore: South Asia Theological Research Institute, 2002), pp. 46-61.
23. The phrase is used by Robert Louis Wilken in his *The Spirit of Early Christian Thought: Seeking the Face of God* (New Haven: Yale University Press, 2003), p. 122. Also see Rosemary Radford Ruether, *Gregory of Nazianzus: Rhetor and Philosopher* (Oxford: Clarendon Press, 1969), esp. pp. 42-48, for a description of his time in Constantinople.
24. For these orations see Frederick W. Norris, intro. and commentary, trans. Lionel Wickham and Frederick Williams, *Faith Gives Fullness to Reasoning: The Five Theological Orations of Gregory Nazianzen* (Leiden: E. J. Brill, 1991). Original Greek text (with French translation) in Grégoire de Nazianze, *Discours 27-31 (Discours Théologiques)*, intro., texte critique, trans. and notes, Paul Gallay, Sources Chrétiennes No. 250 (Paris: Les Éditions du Cerf, 1978).

Discussion of theology is not for everyone. I tell you, not for everyone
— it is no such inexpensive or effortless pursuit. Nor, I would add, is it
for every occasion, or every audience; neither are all its aspects open to
inquiry. It must be reserved for certain occasions, for certain audiences, and certain limits must be observed. It is not for all . . . , but only
for those who have been tested and have found a sound footing in
study, and, more importantly, have undergone, or at the very least are
undergoing, purification of body and soul. For one who is not pure to
lay hold of pure things is dangerous, just as it is for weak eyes to look at
the sun's brightness.

What is the right time? Whenever we are free from the mire and
noise without, and our commanding faculty is not confused by illu-
sory, wandering images, leading us, as it were, to mix fine script with
ugly scrawling, or sweet-smelling scent with slime. We need actually
"to be still" in order to know God. . . .

Who should listen to discussions of theology? Those for whom it
is a serious undertaking, not just another subject like any other for en-
tertaining small-talk, after the races, the theatre, songs, food, and sex:
for there are people who count chatter on theology and clever deploy-
ment of arguments as one of their amusements.

What aspects of theology should be investigated, and to what
limit? Only aspects within our grasp, and only to the limit of the experience and capacity of our audience.[25]

I went on to say that I suspected that most professional theologians
would be in sneaking agreement with some of the sentiments expressed
here but would go on to ask as to whether the writer was not going a bit
too far in drastically limiting the scope and ambience of theologizing. In
his desire to be pragmatic and reasonable, was Gregory looking for an
ideal audience, an ideal situation, an ideal topic, and an ideal theologian?
What about doing theology in the context of ongoing life and real struggles? What about the theologizing of ordinary people, who cannot "be
still" or achieve a state of detached equanimity or calm, undisturbed leisure, but have to carry out reflection within the hermeneutical circle of
action-reflection-action? Indeed, even the task of reflection could be an
unattainable prospect for some of those caught in the spiral of violent ex-

25. Gregory of Nazianzus, Oration 27: "Against the Eunomians" (Oration 27:3), trans.
in *Faith Gives Fullness to Reasoning*, pp. 218-219. Original in Grégoire de Nazianze, *Discours
27-31*, p. 76 and p. 78.

ploitation. The question is important: has theology anything to do with the reality of life in all its complexity? Can theologizing be something that is detached from the hustle and bustle or the messiness of real life?

Take for example the quest for a "uniform civil code" in India. While different religious groups have their own personal laws deriving from a long colonial-historical process, a neglected aspect of any attempt to bring about some kind of "standardization," according to Nalini Rajan, is the complicity between religion and patriarchy.[26] How can we theologize in India without taking into consideration the reality of caste distinctions, exclusion, inequalities, privilege, and opportunity?[27] The emergence and insistent interrogation of Dalit theology with regard to the "classical," "Brahmanical" modes of theologizing has brought about both ferment and renewal in the Indian church,[28] not to say anything about the persistent questions raised by "tribal" theology.[29] Theologizing in India is a "sweaty" business. It cannot be a matter detached from the life and struggles of the people. While Gregory is clearly drawing lines between those who are using the Trinity to further their own interests and those who are

---

26. Nalini Rajan, "Personal Laws and Public Memory," *Economic and Political Weekly* 40, no. 26 (June 25, 2005): 2653-55. This aspect is also mentioned by Kumkum Sangari who analyses the relationship between the community, state, religion and patriarchy, as well as the question regarding personal laws and homogenization, in her article, "Politics of Diversity: Religious Communities and Multiple Patriarchies," in *Communal Identity in India: Its Construction and Articulation in the Twentieth Century,* ed. Bidyut Chakraborty (New Delhi: Oxford University Press, 2003), pp. 181-213.

27. See the chapter on "Caste Inequalities in India Today," in Satish Deshpande, *Contemporary India: A Sociological View* (New Delhi: Viking, 2003), pp. 98-124.

28. From the vast literature see Arvind P. Nirmal, "Towards a Christian Dalit Theology," in *Frontiers in Asian Christian Theology: Emerging Trends,* ed. R. S. Sugirtharajah (Maryknoll, NY: Orbis, 1994), pp. 27-40; Sathianathan Clarke, Chapter 1: "Indian Christian Theology and the Dalits," in *Dalits and Christianity: Subaltern Religion and Liberation Theology in India* (Delhi: Oxford University Press, 1998), pp. 17-57; and John C. B. Webster, "Dalits and Religion after Ambedkar," Chapter 5 in *Religion and Dalit Liberation. An Examination of Perspectives,* 2nd ed. (New Delhi: Manohar, 2002), pp. 74-100.

29. On aspects of this see Nirmal Minz, "A Theological Interpretation of Tribal Reality in India," in *Frontiers in Asian Christian Theology,* pp. 41-51; Lalsangkima Pachuau, "In Search of a Context for a Contextual Theology: The Socio-Political Realities of 'Tribal' Christians in Northeast India," in *National Council of Churches Review* 107, no. 11 (December 1997): 760-72; Lalsangkima Pachuau, "'Tribal' Identity and Ethnic Conflicts in Northeast India: A 'Tribal' Christian Response," *Bangalore Theological Forum* 30, no. 1 (July 1999): 157-67; and A. Wati Longchar, *An Emerging Asian Theology: Tribal Theology — Issue, Method and Perspective* (Jorhat: Tribal Study Centre, 2000).

indeed capable of offering informed and nuanced interpretations of the Trinity, he would certainly acknowledge the reality of the involvement of the Trinity in the life of the people. Discourse on religious realities in India, which so often has been oriented toward polemics, scoring points, "proving" something over against the "other," and justifying certain deeply-held ideological arguments, hardly offers "space" for dialogue.[30] In this sense the seriousness of the commitment to the discourse on God stressed by Gregory is something which needs to be underlined and fostered, without however pushing this discourse beyond those whose lives are most impacted by, and who constantly live with, the problematic of communities in dialogue and communities in tension.

While this is not the place to go through all the orations of Gregory and recapitulate what they say about Trinitarian "orthodoxy," what can be done in the scope of this article is to highlight some aspects of his rich, complex, yet lively, thinking[31] in order that they may accompany us in our attempt to offer an intertwined reading and reflection.

In order to arrive at his conviction that "no one has yet discovered or ever shall discover what God is in his nature and essence" (Oration 28:17), Gregory goes through the gamut of those who created for themselves "counterfeit" gods, and goes on to describe those who "made gods of their emotions," to whom they "put up statues whose very costliness made them bait, and periodically saw fit to honor them with reeking blood and with vile acts of frenzied human slaughter," and in so doing "they took God's glory and attached it to monstrous animals, four-footed beasts and reptiles" (Oration 28:15). Having done this, he goes on to point out that "reason took us up in our desire for God" and commends the "non-Christian" who asked "what set these elements in motion and leads their ceaseless, unimpeded flow?" (Oration 28:16)[32] What we have here is not some kind

30. See, for instance, Ashok V. Chowgule, *Christianity in India: The Hindutva Perspective* (Mumbai: Hindu Vivek Kendra, 1999), one of the more "sophisticated" treatments of the subject by the President of the Maharashtra Pranth of the Vishwa Hindu Parishad, which is frighteningly self-righteous in its convictions.

31. Norris writes that "Gregory's attractiveness is in his complexity and liveliness." See Fredrick W. Norris, "Of Thorns and Roses: The Logic of Belief in Gregory Nazianzen," *Church History* 53 (1984): 455-64, quotation on p. 464.

32. Gregory of Nazianzus, Oration 28: "On the Doctrine of God" (28:15-17), trans. in *Faith Gives Fullness to Reasoning*, pp. 232-34. Original in Grégoire de Nazianze, *Discours 27-31*, pp. 130, 132, and 134. *Tēn physin* and *tēn ousian* are the words translated "nature" and "essence" in Oration 28:17.

of Christian triumphalism. While convinced of the truth of his own commitment, Gregory gives room to those who have desired and sought God in the past. Commenting on this, Norris writes that "although he has not found the exact question anywhere, the important feature is Nazianzen's positive reference to a pagan writer after his attack on paganism in the preceding two paragraphs. In this way Gregory again recognizes his debt to certain non-Christian philosophers and thus refuses to view all Greeks as an idolatrous lot. Given the larger context of pagan society, distinguishing between wise and foolish pagans is important."[33]

Those of us living in postcolonial "third-world" contexts have been represented and interpreted for far too long by those who have claimed the privilege of knowledge and power. India proved to be a fertile hunting ground for those who were simultaneously fascinated and repelled by the lush, intoxicating variety of life on offer. "The Bible and the medieval patristic literature offered another interpretation of the culture and religions of India for the European travelers: this was the home of the traditional enemies of Christianity, Satan and his devils. . . . To have found the devil and Satan in India was not strange and unusual to the Europeans, as they knew they were there all along. . . . When traveling in a strange land, even meeting an old enemy, the devil, is something of a comfort."[34] This observation reminds us of Samartha's retort to the charge that in dialoguing with "advaita" he "indirectly affirms the Brahmanical system," that "to reject, or not to admit *anyone* to dialogue, is against my life-long commitment to the dialogical principle. I am prepared to dialogue even with the devil as long as the language of discourse is Indian English."[35] How can the voices of sanity be heard amidst the din of those who claim to be working for the renewal of society? Is Neera Chandhoke right in claiming that what we see in discourse about civil society today is nothing but "the politics of narcissism"?[36]

33. In *Faith Gives Fullness to Reasoning*, p. 119. Ruether gives a list — "by no means definitive" — of the huge range of classical poets, orators, philosophers, and prose writers referred to by Gregory in "Appendix I: References and Allusions to Classical Literature in Gregory of Nazianzus' Letters and Orations," in her *Gregory of Nazianzus,* pp. 176-77.

34. In Bernard S. Cohn, *Colonialism and Its Forms of Knowledge: The British in India* (New Delhi: Oxford University Press, 2002/ orig. Princeton, 1996), p. 78.

35. S. J. Samartha, "In Search of a Revised Christology: A Response to Paul Knitter," *Current Dialogue* 21 (December 1991): 35.

36. Neera Chandhoke, *The Conceits of Civil Society* (New Delhi: Oxford University Press, 2003), p. 25.

What, then, can the person who is immersed in the reality of God claim? Gregory writes that "our noblest theologian is not one who has discovered the whole — our earthly shackles do not permit us the whole — but one whose mental image is by comparison fuller, who has gathered in his mind a richer picture, outline, or whatever we call it, of the truth" (Oration 30:17).[37] Truth has to be put at the service of trying to untangle the complexity of the relationship between God and Christ, in whom "Man and God blended" (Oration 29:19).[38]

How can one hold on to "truth" in the midst of "truths"? Because of his bold exploration of theocentric Christology, Samartha has been accused of diluting the centrality and finality of Christ. However, one needs to take into account his unambiguous certainty and conviction that "to those who have responded to the Mystery of Truth, and so have received the Truth through a particular relative, that *relative* becomes true, *becomes* the norm. *For us as Christians* the meaning of this Mystery is revealed through Jesus Christ and the Spirit. *For us as Christians* Jesus Christ, and no other is the norm. . . . Plurality does not relativize *Truth;* it relativizes different *responses* to Truth."[39] Given this, the plurality of the Trinity and a sensitive and committed ecumenical response to religious plurality[40] offers much for those concerned persons who are committed to fostering the deepening and strengthening of the dynamic flowering of relationships in multicultural and multireligious India and a "revival of the encounter between sociology and theology at new levels."[41]

37. Gregory of Nazianzus, Oration 30: "On the Son" (30:17), trans. in *Faith Gives Fullness to Reasoning*, p. 274. Original in Grégoire de Nazianze, *Discours 27-31*, p. 262.

38. Gregory of Nazianzus, Oration 29: "On the Son" (29:19), trans. in *Faith Gives Fullness to Reasoning*, p. 257. Original in Grégoire de Nazianze, *Discours 27-31*, p. 218.

39. S. J. Samartha, *Between Two Cultures: Ecumenical Ministry in a Pluralistic World* (Geneva: WCC Publications, 1996), p. 157.

40. See, for example, Raimundo Panikkar, *The Trinity and the Religious Experience of Man: Icon-Person-Mystery* (Maryknoll, NY: Orbis Books, 1973), and Geevarghese Mar Osthathios, *Theology of a Classless Society* (Maryknoll, NY: Orbis Books, 1980). Panikkar, talking about the quest for a "universal master key," makes a provocatively creative comment regarding the Trinity and globalization when he writes: "The Trinity is neither One nor Many (nor Three). There are winds of globalization in our times which are nothing but a continuation of the predominantly western syndrome which, explicitly since Kant, takes universalization as a criterion for truth." In his "Preface" to Steven L. Chase, ed., *Doors of Understanding: Conversations in Global Spirituality in Honor of Ewert Cousins* (Quincy, IL: Franciscan Press, 1997), p. x.

41. This is a call of Max L. Stackhouse in an article entitled "Social Theory and Christian Public Morality for the Common Life," in *Christianity and Civil Society: Theological Ed-*

One important thing to be noted regarding Gregory's understanding of God is that our ingress into the richness of the mystery of God is through a process, and in this process we need to recognize our own limitedness: "It is better to have a meager idea of the union [of the Father and the Son and the Spirit] than to venture on total blasphemy" (Oration 31:12).[42] Going on to talk about the Holy Spirit, he comments: "You see how light shines on us bit by bit, you see in the doctrine of God an order, which we had better observe, neither revealing it suddenly nor concealing it to the last. To reveal it suddenly would be clumsy, would shock outsiders. Ultimately to conceal it would be a denial of God, would make outsiders of our own people" (Oration 31:27).[43] The intra-Trinitarian relationship[44] is such that "the Godhead exists undivided in separate beings. It is as if there were a single intermingling of light, which existed in three mutually connected Suns" (Oration 31:14).[45]

The cultural critic Gayatri Spivak points out that, even though the claim is made that the world today has been "transnationalized or globalized," the reality remains that "the boundaries of a civil society still mark out the individual state and are still nationally defined." She goes on to problematize this reality for the praxis of gender justice, where the ambiguity of upholding certain structures of civil society in a particular location to foster justice fails to take into consideration the implicit role played by those very same structures in promoting things like the "financialization of the globe" in other locations, a process that impacts the "continuing calculus of gender justice *everywhere*."[46] The mutually interconnected

---

ucation for Public Life, ed. Rodney L. Petersen, The Boston Theological Institute 4 (Maryknoll, NY: Orbis Books, 1995), pp. 26-41, quotation on p. 40.

42. Gregory of Nazianzus, Oration 31: "On the Holy Spirit" (31:12), trans. in *Faith Gives Fullness to Reasoning,* p. 286. Original in Grégoire de Nazianze, *Discours 27-31,* p. 300.

43. Gregory of Nazianzus, Oration 31: "On the Holy Spirit" (31:14), trans. in *Faith Gives Fullness to Reasoning,* p. 286. Original in Grégoire de Nazianze, *Discours 27-31,* p. 302.

44. Regarding intra-trinitarian relationships, Robert Jenson writes that "only in their mutuality *is* there God at all. God . . . is what happens between Jesus and the one he called Father, as they are freed for each other by their Spirit." Robert W. Jenson, "With No Qualifications: The Christological Maximalism of the Christian East," in *Ancient and Postmodern Christianity — Paleo-Orthodoxy in the 21st Century: Essays in Honor of Thomas C. Oden,* ed. Kenneth Tanner and Christopher A. Hall (Downers Grove, IL; InterVarsity Press, 2002), pp. 13-22, quotation on p. 17.

45. Gregory of Nazianzus, Oration 31: "On the Holy Spirit" (31:27), trans. in *Faith Gives Fullness to Reasoning,* p. 294. Original in Grégoire de Nazianze, *Discours 27-31,* p. 328.

46. Gayatri Chakravorty Spivak, *A Critique of Postcolonial Reason: Toward a History of*

nature of much of the discourse on civil society by those committed to a vision of peace without injustice, of progress without discrimination, of equality without stratification, of commitment without artificiality, of respect without arrogance, resonates with the mutual interconnectedness of the Trinity, moving away from insensitive alienation and indifferent accommodation to informed acceptance.

Conclusion: Tangled Trinitarianism or Timely Trajectories?

Reporting from long years of experience in inter-religious and inter-cultural interaction in India, Sister Sara Grant, originally Scottish, recollected an incident where at the end of a Hindu-Christian retreat-seminar the question regarding the need to "discard the Trinitarian terminology" was respectfully raised since "in the eyes of many Hindus [this doctrine] seems to obscure the absolute simplicity of the One-without-a-second." After a pause for reflection and consideration, Sara Grant responded, pointing out that this would not be possible since Jesus himself expressed

> his own unfathomable experience of his relationship to the Mystery beyond all name using the terms "Father," "Son," and "Spirit." Taking into consideration the fact that the great Indian philosopher Sankara, whose teachings she had studied in depth over a lifetime of patient scholarship and committed praxis, had used the terms "Atman" and "Brahman," terms "which also point beyond themselves to a Reality only dimly apprehended in faith," she said that this dilemma, of knowing how to "name" the Mystery, could be resolved if the terms used to describe the persons of the Trinity "can be pointers to a reality beyond all conceptual understanding."[47]

---

the Vanishing Present (Calcutta: Seagull Books, 1999), p. 399. On aspects of feminist thinking and praxis in the Indian context see Evangeline Anderson-Rajkumar, "Towards Theologizing in the Indian Context — A Woman's Perspective," *Religion and Society* 44, no. 4 (December 1997): 122-41; Monica J. Melanchthon, "Indian Women and the Bible: Some Hermeneutical Issues," in *Feminist Theology: Perspectives and Praxis*, ed. Prasanna Kumari, Gurukul Summer Institute 1998 (Chennai: Gurukul Lutheran Theological College and Research Institute, 1999), pp. 273-91; and Mrinalini Sebastian, "Implications of Postcolonial Thinking for Feminist Praxis in India," in *Feminist Theology: Perspectives and Praxis*, pp. 82-99.

    47. Sara Grant, "The Contemporary Relevance of the Advaita of Sankaracarya," in *New Perspectives on Advaita Vedanta: Essays in Commemoration of Professor Richard De Smet, S.J.*, ed. Bradley J. Malinovsky (Leiden: Brill, 2000), p. 162.

Obviously our struggle at the beginning of the twenty-first century to understand the promise and peril of life together in a globalized world cannot conclude with the affirmation of a social reality beyond all conceptual understanding. However, the plurality of the Trinity and the plurality of voices within the discourse on civil society should lead us to take seriously the conclusion to which Neera Chandhoke comes at the end of her detailed and sustained interrogation of the conceits of civil society:

> Though the fact that civil society is plural, consisting as it does of a variety of agents, is important, it is not as important as saying that certain values have to be privileged over other values, the values that represent democracy, freedom, equality, rights, and above all justice and dignity. At some point, collective action has to be measured against norms, which we privilege in democratic theory as democratic. If this is taken as a slip into foundationalism, so be it. For if we are foundationalist inasmuch as we privilege Constitutions as embodiments of normative projects in our political life, civil society cannot be left to itself. It requires determined intervention, for it may require the taming of undemocratic instincts. This, perhaps, is the ultimate paradox of civil society.[48]

Faced with paradoxes, we should perhaps recognize that there is much to celebrate, even as we struggle with ways of articulating our commitment to the doctrine of the Trinity within the bewildering predicaments of the present. We began this article by quoting a hymn and it is appropriate to end with what Gregory says about the "hymn" that he has written through the orations: "If our hymn has been worthy of its theme, it is the grace of the Trinity, of the Godhead one in three" (Oration 28:31).[49]

---

48. Neera Chandhoke, *The Conceits of Civil Society,* p. 251.

49. Gregory of Nazianzus, Oration 28: "On the Doctrine of God" (28:31), trans. in *Faith Gives Fullness to Reasoning,* pp. 244. Original in Grégoire de Nazianze, *Discours 27-31,* p. 174.

Jonathan Edwards, Francis Hutcheson, and the Problems and Prospects of Civil Society

William J. Danaher

Generally speaking, historical surveys of civil society treat the Christian tradition in a chapter that stands between one on antiquity and one on the Enlightenment.[1] As such, the impression is left that the transition from Christian conceptions of civil society to those of the Enlightenment was an orderly evolution over time, an impression that I plan to disrupt by comparing two alternative conceptions of civil society from the eighteenth century. In the process, I hope to add further nuance and background to contemporary theological discussions.

Though overlooked or treated cursorily, Jonathan Edwards (1703-1758) and Francis Hutcheson (1694-1746) believed that benevolence is innate in human nature and that the good society was comprised of the social relations these affections generate. As such, both stand at the head of the tradition of civic humanism in the Scottish Enlightenment, with Hutcheson directly influencing later eighteenth-century civil society theorists, such as Adam Ferguson (1723-1816), Adam Smith (1723-1790), and David Hume (1711-1776). Unlike later theorists, however, Edwards and Hutcheson offered explicit theological justifications to argue that beauty, benevolence, and virtue should reign in the good society. Consequently, they considered problematic what later accounts presupposed: that the claims of civil society rested on theological conceptions of the person. Thus, the divisions between Christian and Enlightenment accounts of

---

1. For an example of this treatment, see John Ehrenberg, *Civil Society: The Critical History of an Idea* (New York: New York University Press, 1999).

civil society are not so clear-cut as the chapter divisions in historical surveys suggest.

Examining Edwards and Hutcheson together also recovers the contours of their theological differences. Where Hutcheson grounded his social vision in a naturalized, if religious, account of beauty, benevolence, and virtue, Edwards insisted that these attributes properly emanate from the triune God, who communicates them directly to human beings. These diverging theological anthropologies generated divergent conceptions of civil society. For Hutcheson, the good society was one that allowed persons the freedom to express their naturally benevolent inclinations without the interference of overarching institutions or dogmatic structures. For Edwards, the good society was one in which every level of sociality — ecclesial, political, familial, associational — was transformed by the triune benevolence of God.

Hutcheson and Edwards on Beauty, Benevolence, and Virtue

In *An Inquiry into the Original of our Ideas of Beauty and Virtue* (1725) Hutcheson defined virtue in terms of benevolence rather than free decisions, prudential considerations, or the practical intellect.[2] Like the affections that attend the apprehension of beauty, harmony, and proportion, humans have a moral sense that inclines to sociality and the public good. Virtue therefore has "one general foundation" in benevolence, defined as the disinterested "desire of the happiness of another," but benevolence has three levels of extensiveness. In its most universal sense, it is a "good-will towards all beings capable of happiness or misery." In a more restricted sense, it is the desire for the "happiness of certain smaller systems," in the form of "patriotism," "friendship," and "parental affection." Finally, benevolence issues in "particular passions of love, pity, sympathy," and "congratulation." Every sense of benevolence is commendable, but only the universal desires the "good of the whole." We should therefore cultivate "universal benevolence" and work for the "most extensive happiness of all the rational agents to whom our influ-

2. Hutcheson's full title is *An Inquiry into the Original of our Ideas of Beauty and Virtue in Two Treatises.* Edwards used the fourth edition (London, 1738; reprint, Charlottesville, VA: Lincoln-Rembrant, 1993). In writing this essay, I also used the first edition (London, 1725) reprinted in the *Collected Works of Francis Hutcheson: Volume 1,* facsimile edition prepared by B. Fabian (Hildesheim: Georg Olms, 1971).

ence can reach."[3] Hutcheson thus views perceptions of beauty, expressions of benevolence, and the possession of virtue as interconnected.

Although he drew from Anthony Ashley Cooper, third Earl of Shaftesbury (1671-1713), who preferred the Stoics as moral and religious guides, Hutcheson argued that this philosophy was compatible with Christianity.[4] Granted, it was impossible to prove the necessity of a benevolent deity from the mere experience of benevolence, and God could have created humans differently, so that we do not take pleasure in benevolence.[5] But the existence of benevolence provides evidence that God is a benevolent being. Further, God's "universal benevolence" is evident in that God freely made benevolent creatures such as ourselves. The "obvious frame of the world" therefore makes probable the existence of "the Deity *benevolent* in the most *universal impartial manner.*"[6]

If these reflections appear lukewarm by Christian standards, in his *System of Moral Philosophy* (1755), Hutcheson argued that being conscious of God provided a supervening motive to live virtuously:[7]

3. Hutcheson, *Inquiry*, 2.2.1, p. 127 (1725 ed.); 2.3.1-9, pp. 150-165 (1725 ed.). For more on Hutcheson's relationship to Aristotle, see Alasdair MacIntyre's *Whose Justice? Which Rationality?* (Notre Dame: University of Notre Dame Press, 1988), pp. 260-280.

4. Hutcheson, *Inquiry*, Preface, xvii (1738 ed.). For more on Shaftesbury's idiosyncratic religious and moral reflections, see Isabel Rivers, *Reason, Grace, and Sentiment: A Study of the Language of Religion and Ethics in England 1660-1780: Vol. II* (Cambridge: Cambridge University Press, 2000), pp. 86-114.

5. Hutcheson, *Inquiry*, 1.8.4-5, pp. 94-97 (1725 ed.); 2.7.10-11, p. 274 (1725 ed.). In other words, Hutcheson rejected "first cause" arguments and considered "design" arguments probable, but not necessary. Further, God's will towards us is contingent rather than necessary. See M. A. Stewart, "Religion and Rational Theology," in The *Cambridge Companion to the Scottish Enlightenment,* ed. Alexander Broadie (Cambridge: Cambridge University Press, 2003), pp. 39-40, 56. See also J. B. Schneewind, *Invention of Autonomy* (Cambridge: Cambridge University Press, 1998), p. 339.

6. Hutcheson, *Inquiry*, 2.7.10-11, pp. 274-76.

7. Admittedly, the connection I draw between Hutcheson's earlier and later writings on God is perhaps contestable. Among commentators on Hutcheson are those who argue that his thought lacks coherence and progressed through different stages of development, depending on the audience for whom he was writing. I do not believe, however, that the connection I am making here is controversial or commits one to the thesis that all of Hutcheson's writings necessarily cohere. For a recent example of this interpretation, see James Moore, "The Two Systems of Francis Hutcheson: On the Origins of the Scottish Enlightenment," in *Studies in the Philosophy of the Scottish Enlightenment,* ed. M. A. Stewart (Oxford: Clarendon Press, 1990), pp. 37-59. The edition of *A System of Moral Philosophy* I use in this essay is from the *Collected Works of Francis Hutcheson: Volume V and Volume VI,* facsimile edition prepared by B. Fabian (Hildesheim: Georg Olms, 1969).

A constant regard to God in all our actions and enjoyments, will give a new beauty to every virtue, by making it an act of gratitude and love to him; and increase our pleasure in every enjoyment, as it will appear an evidence of his goodness: it will give a diviner purity and simplicity of heart, to conceive all our virtuous dispositions as implanted by God in our hearts . . . our minds shall be called off from the lower views of honors, or returns of men, and from all contempt or pride toward our fellows who share not equally this goodness . . . our hearts will chiefly regard his approbation, our aims shall be obtained when we act the part assigned us faithfully and gratefully to our great creator, let others act as they please toward us.[8]

Despite this theocentrism, Hutcheson departed from the Reformed orthodoxy that preceded him. He refrained from discussing doctrines like the Trinity, and the metaphysical distinctions he drew from his predecessors were sifted through the deliverances of the moral sense. Thus, he accepted the traditional distinction between incommunicable and communicable divine attributes: the former, like infinity or immutability, humans cannot share or receive; the latter, like knowledge or beneficence, are reflected in human nature imperfectly and analogously.[9] But he drew the line between Creator and creature more sharply than his forbearers. Transposed into the grammar of benevolence, this entails that while a benevolent God created benevolent creatures, the benevolence in each is distinct. Although divine and human benevolence are analogous, the expression of the latter represents merely the realization of unaided human nature. Hutcheson minimized, in other words, the sense of participation or subsistence in God that the traditional distinction had identified. For Hutcheson, divine and human benevolence correspond to each other, but there is no participation of God's love in human nature through the indwelling of the Holy Spirit.[10]

Further, Hutcheson rejected unitary approaches to love, in particular the Augustinian doctrine that all love is the diffusion of God's love and

---

8. Hutcheson, *System of Moral Philosophy*, 1.10, p. 216.

9. See Hutcheson, *Synopsis Metaphysicae* (1744), in *Collected Works of Francis Hutcheson: Volume VII*, facsimile edition prepared by B. Fabian (Hildesheim: Georg Olms, 1971), 3.2-5, pp. 97-123.

10. For an example of how the traditional distinction operated in Reformed scholasticism to develop a participatory doctrine of the Spirit's indwelling, while avoiding metaphysical merger, see Francis Turretin (1623-1687), *Principles of Elenctic Theology*, 3 vols., trans. G. M. Giger, ed. James T. Dennison, Jr. (Phillipsburg, NJ: P. & R. Publishing, 1992) 1:190; 2:182.

that we must love all things as they are in God and God in all things. Such a view, Hutcheson argued in *Illustrations upon the Moral Sense* (1728), overlooks the particular love for creatures viewed as "good beings distinct from God." It is therefore necessary to differentiate expressions of benevolence. Hutcheson asked, "Does the parental affection direct a man to love the Deity, or his children?" Though "we must approve the highest affections toward the Deity," our "affections towards creatures, if they be distinct natures, must be approved" as well.[11] Hutcheson adopted, then, a pluralist position with regard to benevolence. The ethical life does not hinge on whether or not all our loves can be resolved into the love of God, but on whether or not we honor each love appropriately.

Finally, Hutcheson did not believe that the soul's affections changed as a result of the fall. Where the traditional doctrine of original sin asserted that the fall caused disharmony and corruption in the affections, Hutcheson argued that the deliverances of the moral sense were misled only by artifice, treachery, bad education, custom, and inappropriate associations of ideas.[12] Instead of blaming our sinfulness, we should learn to prioritize our loves through self-reflection. Hutcheson also had no use for the correlative belief that through grace we regain spiritual affections lost in the fall that alone can quiet inordinate desires.

Like Hutcheson, Edwards located moral agency in the affections and construed virtue in terms of beauty and benevolence. In *Religious Affections*, Edwards argued that human nature is a fountain of affections — the mind is never an "indifferent, unaffected spectator," but is either "liking or disliking," "pleased or displeased."[13] Edwards defined the moral life not in terms of making the right decisions, or cultivating the character through habituation, but in terms of the change of affections through the reception of a "new sense" of the love of God.[14] Edwards conceived of the love born

---

11. Francis Hutcheson, *Illustrations upon the Moral Sense* (1728) in *Collected Works of Francis Hutcheson: Volume II*, facsimile edition prepared by B. Fabian (Hildesheim: Georg Olms, 1971), Sec. VI, pp. 329-33.

12. Hutcheson, *Inquiry*, 1.7.1-5, pp. 79-87. See Moore, "The Two Systems of Francis Hutcheson," pp. 52-53.

13. Jonathan Edwards, *A Treatise Concerning Religious Affections*, in *The Works of Jonathan Edwards: Volume 2*, ed. John E. Smith (New Haven: Yale University Press, 1959), p. 96. For the sake of economy, I have chosen *Religious Affections* to illustrate the differences between Hutcheson and Edwards. There are many other writings, as the rest of this essay will illustrate, where Edwards specks of the topics of beauty, benevolence, and virtue.

14. Edwards, *Religious Affections*, p. 253.

of this change as a participation in the "beauty" or "excellency" that flows from God.[15]

Nonetheless, where Hutcheson viewed the moral sense as the work of unaided human nature, Edwards viewed the new sense as the work of the indwelling Spirit. The new sense is "spiritual" and "supernatural," altering the "present exercise, sensation, and frame of the soul" through "God's communicating himself and his Holy Spirit."[16] Consequently, it differs from "natural" affections and "natural principles" such as "honesty, justice, generosity, good nature, and public spirit." If the former is the communication of the "moral image of God," the latter are merely the "natural" image of God represented in human "reason and understanding." Further, where Hutcheson held a pluralist view of benevolence, Edwards held a unitary view centered on God's love. God's own love, modeled on Christ's redemption and given through the Spirit's indwelling, gives definitive shape to disinterested benevolence. Truly "gracious affections" are ecstatic — they have "their foundation out of the self, in God and Jesus Christ."[17]

Edwards's most sustained engagement with Hutcheson occurred in his *Two Dissertations* (1765). In the first dissertation, *The End for Which God Created the World*, Edwards argued that God alone is the proper end for God's creation of the world and the source of all benevolence.[18] To argue this point, Edwards deployed a Neoplatonic vision of the analogy of being that appropriated Hutcheson's conception of benevolence. This is clearest in an early analogy Edwards used: out of the simple love for "society," a person desires a family. But once he or she has a family, other values become desirable, such as "peace, good order, and mutual justice and friendship." All of these desires are ultimate desires, and yet the "justice and peace of a family" are consequential ends in comparison to the original end of desiring a family.[19] In the same way, just as no one starts a family simply to be wise and just, so the divine attributes of wisdom and justice

---

15. Edwards, *Religious Affections*, pp. 262-63.

16. Edwards, *Religious Affections*, p. 340.

17. Edwards, *Religious Affections*, pp. 254, 253.

18. Edwards, *God's End*, in *The Works of Jonathan Edwards: Volume 8*, p. 535. At points, my analysis of *God's End* and *True Virtue* follows what I have written previously in *The Trinitarian Ethics of Jonathan Edwards* (Louisville: Westminster John Knox Press, 2004), pp. 205-220. Nonetheless, what I write here revises and expands my previous interpretation significantly, particularly with regard to the discussion of apologetics and civil society.

19. Edwards, *God's End*, p. 412.

did not serve as God's original end in creation. Rather, God's original, supreme end was "to communicate of his own infinite fullness of good."[20]
This disposition "to communicate of his own fullness" is "benevolence or
love, because it is the same disposition that is exercised in love: 'tis the very
fountain from whence love originally proceeds, when taken in its most
proper sense."[21] Therefore, what "excited" God to "create the world" was
the simple desire to express benevolence so that "God's glory should be
known by a glorious society of created beings."[22]

In the second dissertation, *The Nature of True Virtue,* Edwards explored what truly qualifies as "disinterested benevolence" in humans, arguing that it is the love, or "consent," to God as "being in general." Edwards
interweaved two arguments: The first is aesthetic. All agree that virtue is a
moral "beauty or excellency" that has its seat in the *"disposition* and *will,"*
or the "heart." The question, however, is what comprises this beauty. Like
intrinsic beauty, virtue is beautiful viewed from the most comprehensive
standpoint possible. Virtue is not a "particular beauty" that is viewed
within a limited "private sphere," but a "general beauty," or something that
appears beautiful when viewed "universally, with regard to all its tendencies and its connections."[23] Further, the beauty of virtue is not "secondary
beauty," or the mere delight in harmony, order, or proportion. Rather, it is
"primary beauty," or the relation of "consent, agreement, or union of being" that attends "spiritual or moral beings."[24] Therefore, true virtue must
consist in "benevolence" to God as "being in general." For if virtue is a *general* beauty, and general beauty refers to that which is beautiful in all its relations, then true virtue must be a "union of heart" and "consent with the
great whole," which is "immediately exercised in a general good will."[25]
And if true virtue is a *primary* beauty, and primary beauty is exercised only
in spiritual relations, then as the sum of all spiritual relations, God is the
proper object of true virtue.

The second argument concerns benevolence. If virtue is an instance
of beauty, then something other than beauty must be its source and object.
To maintain otherwise would be to fall into circular reasoning, arguing
that "the beauty of intelligent beings primarily consists in love to beauty,

20. Edwards, *God's End,* p. 433.
21. Edwards, *God's End,* p. 439.
22. Edwards, *God's End,* pp. 435, 431.
23. Edwards, *True Virtue,* pp. 239-40.
24. Edwards, *True Virtue,* p. 561.
25. Edwards, *True Virtue,* p. 540.

or that their virtue first of all consists in their love to virtue." But if beauty is not the object of virtue, then the love of true virtue cannot be "complacence," or the love that "presupposes beauty" in the "beloved." Nor can it be a benevolence motivated by complacence or gratitude, for in either case the cause of benevolence does not originate in the agent's nature. Ironically, the only love that can be the source of virtue's beauty is that which does not recognize "beauty" in "particular beings." True virtue therefore embodies God's "absolute benevolence" described in *God's End*.[26] The "benevolence or goodness in the divine Being" is the "ground" of creaturely "existence" and "beauty." Similarly, the benevolence of true virtue is the love of "those that are not considered as beautiful; unless mere existence be accounted a beauty."[27]

Edwards and Hutcheson on Civil Society

From these two theological accounts of the moral life, Hutcheson and Edwards developed divergent social visions. For Hutcheson, the good society integrates the different loves of benevolence. In his "Inaugural Lecture on the Social Nature of Man" (1730), Hutcheson addressed the "probable causes and origins of civil society," arguing that the good society enables the free expression of the "entire structure of human nature." By "civil society," Hutcheson meant "society under no human authority," or the inherent human sociality, rather than imposed by law or prudential considerations.[28] By "nature," he meant those "solid or durable" dispositions that "God has given" as "appetites" that constitute human flourishing; these are identified by asking what distinguishes the "cultivated" from the "uncultivated." The former follow "God as a father and guide" and engage in society in order to express "mutual affection" and "trust." The latter engage in "external force" and "cunning schemes" to outwit the "generality of people."[29]

In distinguishing "cultivated" and "uncultivated," Hutcheson employed a longstanding category in civil society discussions originating in the division between civilized *(hellēnes)* and barbarian *(barbaros)*. Further,

26. Edwards, *True Virtue,* pp. 543-44.

27. Edwards, *True Virtue,* pp. 540-42.

28. "Inaugural Lecture on the Social Nature of Man" in Francis Hutcheson, *On Human Nature,* ed. T. Mautner (Cambridge: Cambridge University Press, 1993), pp. 127-29.

29. Hutcheson, "Social Nature," pp. 132-33.

Hutcheson drew from Cicero's doctrine of *hēgemonikon* or the belief that right reason is consonant with nature, exists independently of human history, and orders the universe. This doctrine, he reasoned, is consonant with what "Protestant theologians" argued concerning the "original contrivance and structure of our nature," and "clear signs of this design and art are preserved even in the ruins" of postlapsarian humanity.[30] Thus, Hutcheson contrasted his understanding of the natural with the "state of nature" of Thomas Hobbes (1588-1679) and John Locke (1632-1704), who asserted that persons are originally independent beings that enter society voluntarily and artificially, only after considering their private interest.[31] Hutcheson also distinguished his view from natural law advocates such as Hugo Grotius (1583-1645) and Samuel Pufendorf (1632-1694), who argued that the move to sociality is a natural extension of self-interest and therefore is only natural in a "secondary sense."[32] Rather, Hutcheson argued that the desire for sociality was an inherent human good, which delights in the communication of happiness to another. While other, self-interested desires exist alongside benevolence, these do not express that which is "virtuous, praiseworthy, beautiful, and becoming."[33]

Clearly, standing behind Hutcheson's definition of "natural" and "cultivated" sensibilities is his theological vision of the interconnection of beauty, benevolence, and virtue. "God has given us a sense of what is becoming and beautiful," which "leads to a kind and social life, and gives rise to virtuous actions which benefit others and which are most useful and most pleasant to the agent."[34] Hutcheson argued that the apprehension of beauty is not achieved empirically through the senses, nor is it the product of rational deduction, but it is a sense of what is "whole and perfect" that is possessed *a priori* like an "innate" idea.[35]

Particularly in his *System of Moral Philosophy,* Hutcheson expanded further on his theory of civil society. Throughout every sphere or "state" in society, senses of benevolence limit the rights and obligations of superiors over subordinates. In "domestic" relations "of married persons, of parents and children," and "of masters and servants," the well-being of the whole confers upon subordinates the right to resist or reject the authority of

---

30. Hutcheson, "Social Nature," p. 132.
31. Hutcheson, "Social Nature," p. 133.
32. Hutcheson, "Social Nature," p. 135.
33. Hutcheson, "Social Nature," p. 143.
34. Hutcheson, "Social Nature," p. 141.
35. Hutcheson, "Social Nature," p. 144.

those who disregard it.[36] Thus, while men generally act as head of the family, this does not mean that women have no rights within the family, especially when it comes to the education of children or the disposal of common property. Similarly, children also have rights that the heads of family must respect, given that their "consent" is required for family unity. Finally, concerning slavery, Hutcheson accepted it but argued that the reason for enslavement should be specific to the individual, on account of misfortune or as a punishment, rather than extended to a whole race of persons. Further, slaves only lose the right to their labor and retain all other "rights of mankind."[37]

In "civil or political relations," Hutcheson argued for a mixed state comprised of monarch, aristocracy, and a representative body drawn from property owners. This arrangement, however, was merely the best way to promote prosperity. Despite his belief that sociality is grounded in nature and not artifice, Hutcheson conceived of civil power as the product of three voluntary acts of a "whole people" — a contract between each citizen and the society, a designation of the "plan of power," and a "mutual agreement between governors and people."[38]

Finally, in the ecclesial sphere, Hutcheson did not offer much commentary, except to deplore the way "religious controversies" could undermine the stability and goodwill of the common good. Anyone with sufficient detachment, he argued, could see that "Calvinists," "Arminians," "Socinians," and the "orthodox" leveled allegations against each other that were "groundless," and these recriminations were the cause of "the highest contentions and mutual persecutions." As such, doctrinal debates among "Christian sects" always had the potential to undermine "true piety" and the "social virtues."[39]

A very different social vision flows from Edwards's account. As we have seen, Edwards tried to recast Hutcheson's moral anthropology within a Neoplatonic metaphysics in order to offer a participatory and unitive vision of divine and human benevolence. Consistent with this Neoplatonism, Edwards viewed the world as hierarchically ordered from greater to lesser beings, with the lower levels of existence bearing an analogous relation to that which is higher. "It pleases God to observe analogy in his

36. Hutcheson, *System*, 3.1, p. 149.
37. Hutcheson, *System*, 3.3, p. 200.
38. Hutcheson, *System*, 3.5, p. 227.
39. Hutcheson, *System*, 3.9, p. 316.

works, as is manifest in innumerable instances; and especially to establish inferior things in an analogy to superior," he wrote in *True Virtue*.[40] Analogous relations exist from plants to animals, from animals to humans, and from humans to the divine, as well as the natural to the spiritual. Unlike other articulations of Neoplatonism, Edwards argued that a kind of sociality existed at each level, which is evident in the experience of "beauty" and "excellency," he argued in his notebook, "The Mind." In the "beauty of figures," beautiful "notes in music," or "the beauty of the body" there is a "shadow of love" that is like a "society united by sweet consent and charity of heart."[41] Here as well, Edwards drew from Hutcheson's definition of beauty as "uniformity in the midst of variety," an aesthetic that defined beauty in terms of comprehensiveness rather than simplicity.[42] But Edwards appropriated this aesthetic in order to place God's triune relations at the apex of what is beautiful. Thus, in the "mutual love of the Father and the Son" and the "personal Holy Spirit," there is "infinite beauty" and "infinite consent." The beauty of creatures hinges on whether they "partake of more or less" of God's own "excellence and beauty" through receiving the "communication" of God's self in the "Holy Spirit."[43]

As these reflections demonstrate, Edwards turned to trinitarian grammar when no other language would convey his point adequately. In *God's End*, to describe how the saints' love of God is a spiritual relationship of deepening intimacy, Edwards introduced the doctrine of *perichoresis*, or that between the divine persons there is mutual indwelling without loss of distinction. The culmination of the spiritual life is one where "we will forever come nearer and nearer to that strictness and perfection of union there is between the Father and the Son."[44] As the end for which God created the world, these trinitarian relations generate the infinite fullness of benevolence from which all things came to be. In *True Virtue*, Edwards appropriated the doctrine of the *vestigium trinitatis* to describe how social relations throughout the chain of being are vestiges of the "love and friendship which subsist eternally and necessarily between the several persons of the Godhead, or that infinite propensity there is in these three persons one to another." Thus, all benevolence bears the image of God's tri-

---

40. Edwards, *True Virtue*, p. 564.
41. Edwards, "The Mind" in *The Works of Jonathan Edwards: Volume 6, Scientific and Philosophical Writings*, ed. W. Anderson (New Haven: Yale University Press, 1980), p. 380.
42. Edwards, *True Virtue*, p. 562. Here Edwards quoted Hutcheson directly.
43. Edwards, "The Mind," p. 364.
44. Edwards, *God's End*, p. 443.

unity, for the love expressed between the divine persons is the source of
"God's goodness and love to created beings." But only that love that spiritually participates in God's own triune love comprises the absolute "benevolent affection, or propensity of heart towards being in general," or
true virtue.[45]

Though these references are brief, they make clear that Edwards believed that God's triune relations condition the social implications that his
metaphysics entails. God is not properly understood as solitary being but a
community of persons from which flows a love that seeks to include others
in its circle of friendship. As distinctly spiritual, the benevolence that is
communicated from God to humanity draws them into a relationship in
which they are forever progressing towards greater intimacy with God.
While this does not mean metaphysical merger with the deity, it does mean
that the indwelling of the Spirit incorporates persons into the mutual love
of the Father and the Son. In his "Miscellanies Notebooks," Edwards offered the following image in a commentary on the Christ calling his disciples "friends" in John 15:15:

> Christ has brought it so pass, that those that the Father has given him
> should be brought into the household of God, that he and his Father
> and they should be as one society, one family; that his people should
> be in a sort admitted to that society of the three persons of the God-
> head. . . . In this family or household, God is the Father, Jesus Christ
> his own natural and eternally begotten Son. The saints, they are also
> the children of the family; the church is the daughter of God, being the
> spouse of his Son. They all have communion in the same Holy Spirit.[46]

As this passage demonstrates, Edwards drew from the deep well of
Scriptural images to explain the polyvalence of God's triune love, viewing
it from the vantage point of every type of social relationship — friendly,
marital, paternal, among others. Each of these social relationships could be
grounded in God's love in a way that rendered it a seminary. At other
points in his "Miscellanies" notebooks, Edwards engaged the classical conception of civic friendship — which defined friendship as a bond between
two persons united in a common good — to elaborate on the social impli-

---

45. Edwards, *True Virtue*, p. 557.

46. Edwards, "Miscellanies" entry 569 in *The Works of Jonathan Edwards:* Volume 18,
The "Miscellanies" 833-1152, ed. A. Chamberline (New Haven: Yale University Press, 2000),
p. 110.

cations of his theology. In and of itself, all social relations where benevolence is expressed can be described as a kind of "communion," which he
defined as "a common partaking of benefits, or of good, in union or society."[47] The potential motives underlying social relations are manifold and,
in many cases, less than godly. A person "may come to love another person" from an interest in "profit," "pleasure," the "love of justice," or the
"love of generosity."[48] But in relationships where true virtue is expressed,
the common good is founded in God's Spirit and benevolence. "Communion, we know, is nothing else but the common partaking with others of
good: communion with God is nothing else but a partaking with him of
his excellency, his holiness, and happiness."[49] To be in communion with
God is to receive, within the context of any given relationship, the blessing
of God's triune presence through the indwelling of the "Holy Ghost,"
which is a "communication of himself."[50]

Although every particular relationship has the capacity to express
spiritual communion with God, Edwards considered the church the highest form of community humans can embody. Not only did he refer to the
church in hypostatic terms as the "daughter of God" and "spouse" of
Christ, as observed above, but in his sermon series *Charity and Its Fruits*
(1738), he invoked the Augustinian doctrine of church as an *altera civitas,* a
city founded on a heavenly *ethos* centered in God's triune love and reconciliation. Properly understood, the church's reception of the Spirit is the
primary end of God's triune redemption: "God the Father is the person of
whom the purchase is made; God the Son is the person who makes the
purchase, and the Holy Spirit is the gift purchased." Therefore, the "sum"
of all "good things in this life, and the life to come, which are purchased for
the church is the Holy Spirit."[51] Of course, this side of the *eschaton,* the
church struggles in its "imperfection" on account of its failure to receive
and express fully the Spirit's "love and charity." Therefore, congregation
members must develop characters that resist the sins of "selfishness," "jeal-
ousy," "contention," "schism," "revenge," and "deceit." When the love of
God is absent, the church is no different from communities in which "all

47. Jonathan Edwards, "Miscellanies" entry 404 in *The Works of Jonathan Edwards:
Volume 13, The "Miscellanies," a-500,* ed. T. Schafer (New Haven: Yale University Press, 1994),
p. 468.
48. Edwards, "Miscellanies" entry 473 in *Works,* vol. 13, p. 515.
49. Edwards, "Miscellanies" entry 330 in *Works,* vol. 13, p. 409.
50. Edwards, "Miscellanies" entry 314, in *Works,* vol. 13, p. 415.
51. Edwards, *Charity and Its Fruits,* in *Works,* vol. 8, pp. 353, 358.

are for themselves, and self-interest governs, and all are striving to set themselves up" with no regard for "what becomes of others." The world, then, is a "wilderness" with two radically different "countries" on either side — one where the love of God reigns, the other where "self-interest" governs. Those who choose the former have chosen the "better country."[52]

In spite of this dialectic, Edwards appropriated the traditional Gelasian distinction between church *(sacerdotium)* and the kingdom *(regnum)*, which he reworked along Reformed lines, arguing that church and state were distinct institutions united in a common purpose and that God directly authorized the civil government to maintain order and natural justice. In his "Miscellanies" notebooks, Edwards wrote that God's general revelation made possible human governments with "beauty," "proportion," and "harmony." God established that "a good moral government should be maintained over man, that his intelligent, voluntary acts should be subject to rules" and that "he should be the subject of a judicial proceeding." The form of this government is revealed to the "conscience" and exists "in nations, provinces, towns or families," without which "the world of mankind could not exist." But it is concentrated in those called to be rulers of a given society. Like the rule of parents over children, "God hath set those to be moral rulers that are the wiser and the stronger" as well as those that are "to be in subjection," who are "less knowing," "weaker," and "dependent" on these rulers to protect and provide for them.[53] Implicit here is the classical doctrine of the body politic, the belief that the ideal political society is one where its members are like a body, of one heart and mind. Indeed, Edwards utilized this imagery: "we see that in other parts of the creation, wherein many particulars are dependent and united into one body, there is an excellent harmony and mutual subserviency throughout the whole." In the same way, "God has so made and constituted the world" that it is "natural and necessary" that persons "be concerned one with another, and linked together in society" in the "manner of their propagation," their "descending one from another," their "need for one another, and their inclination to society."[54]

Edwards did not explore models of political organization, but he did reflect on the role of government, particularly to prescribe the worship of

52. Edwards, *Charity and Its Fruits*, pp. 392-94.

53. Edwards, "Miscellanies" entry 864 in *The Works of Jonathan Edwards:* Volume 20, *The "Miscellanies" 833-1152*, ed. A. Pauw (New Haven: Yale University Press, 2002), pp. 97-100.

54. Edwards, "Miscellanies" entry 864, in *Works*, vol. 20, p. 99.

God. The argument that "more hurt" than "good" would be done if the "power of the civil magistrate" were exercised "in matters of religion" was "overstrained and too much concluded by it." By the same argument, "it would be best that mankind should be without a power of reason, because commonly this power" did "more hurt than good." As with "all other powers and abilities God has given," there is always the potential for abuse, and just as it is desirable for "the ruling faculties" of "understanding and will" to preside over "particular persons," so it is "with regard to councils and rulers in society."[55]

Nonetheless, Edwards maintained that clear boundaries should exist between the jurisdictions of magistrate and minister — the former maintained the natural order of justice and the latter taught doctrine and administered the ordinances of the church. Further, Christ ultimately reigns over "all things visible and invisible, whether they be thrones and dominions, principalities or powers."[56] For as the *Logos* of the Father, Christ is the agent of creation — the Word though whom all things were made. Finally, within a theological vision that placed spirit over nature, the church's political life stood over civil government as the source of its legitimacy and intelligibility. That is to say, the church represented the fulfillment of humanity's vocation to embody God's triune love and thus the paradigm of sociality.

Theological Constructions of Civil Society

Edwards and Hutcheson, then, held alternative visions of civil society. Of the two, Hutcheson's vision was more prominent. Hutcheson was a major influence in the Moderate party in the Church of Scotland, an important minority comprised of well-placed clergy and academics that sought to bring the church in line with the new political climate resulting from the Act of Union (1707) and Patronage Act (1712). Thus, Hutcheson's support of the state, his avoidance of Christian doctrines, his aversion to theological controversy, and his use of non-Christian sources resonated with those who were trying to chart a more moderate course. Nonetheless, as David

---

55. Edwards, "Miscellanies" entry 1163 in *The Works of Jonathan Edwards:* Volume 23, *The "Miscellanies" 1153-1360*, ed. D. Sweeney (New Haven: Yale University Press, 2004), pp. 85-86.
56. Edwards, "Miscellanies" entry 1174 in *Works,* vol. 23, pp. 89-90.

Allen has noted, this cosmopolitan turn legitimized the state's usurpation of the church, which undermined the Moderate party's sensitivity to the poverty created by rapid urbanization and its conception of the church's distinctive mission within the good society.[57]

Hutcheson also influenced the later civil society theorists such as Adam Ferguson, Adam Smith, and David Hume, but this influence belies the viability of his theory. As we have seen, Hutcheson derived his vision of civil society from a theological anthropology that synthesized beauty, benevolence, and virtue. Those who came after him, however, established a different foundation in a natural law based on self-evident, universalizable norms. Hutcheson initiated this transition when he placed human benevolence in an entirely separate, if analogous, arena from divine benevolence. Further, in his pluralist account of benevolence, Hutcheson rendered divine benevolence powerless except as an exemplar. Finally, he avoided philosophical and theological unifying frameworks that might challenge the sovereignty of the moral sense. Those who followed him, then, merely rendered his account more consistent.

But once based in natural law, later civil society theorists could not retain Hutcheson's doctrine of innate human sociability. For the transition to a natural law foundation raised the question: which desires are truly reflective of human nature and social relations? The answer to this question forced later theorists to abandon benevolence in favor of self-love and self-interest. As Adam Smith remarked in the *Wealth of Nations* (1776), it is "not from the benevolence of the butcher, the brewer, or the baker, that we expect our dinner, but from their regard to their own interest." Thus "we address ourselves, not to their humanity, but to their self love, and never talk to them of our own necessities but of their advantages."[58]

While grounded in the affections and benevolence, Edwards's theory of civil society revolved around a trinitarian vision that provided its unifying structure. Edwards also utilized traditional political categories, emphasizing in particular the church. Not only was his vision less influential than Hutcheson's, but it was soon displaced by one in which the church was disestablished. Indeed, Edwards's career as pastor signaled the demise of his social vision. In 1750, Edwards was dismissed as minister of the church in

---

57. David Allen, *Scotland in the Eighteenth Century: Union and Enlightenment* (New York: Longman, 2002), pp. 65-68.

58. Adam Smith, *The Wealth of Nations*, ed. E. Cannan (New York: Random House, 2003), pp. 23-24.

Northampton after a much-publicized dispute over his policy for admission to the Lord's Supper. Where his predecessor and grandfather, Solomon Stoddard (1643-1729), admitted those who professed the faith outwardly but could not demonstrate the inward dwelling of the Holy Spirit, Edwards wanted to restrict the Lord's Supper to those who were "in profession, and in the eye of the church's judgment, godly or gracious persons."[59] Historians have surmised that this dispute was merely the presenting issue in a pastoral relationship long gone sour. Nonetheless, the issue of communion stood at the center of Edwards's political theology. If the earthly church's embodiment of the love of the Trinity is the paradigm of sociality, nothing could be more crucial than the sacrament that celebrated the saints' communion in the body of Christ. Consequently, the Lord's Supper was the most important political act of his congregation, not only as the means to assert Edwards's authority as minister, but also in terms of reinforcing the *ethos* his congregation was to demonstrate as Spirit-filled Christians to the wider society.[60]

In addition, internal problems are evident in Edwards's account. While Neoplatonism enabled him to articulate his unitive and participatory account of love, it also drew a tight correlation between the divine life and human life, so that human social arrangements reflected some of the immutability of the divine relations. As a result, Edwards did not appreciate God's power to change social structures for the better over time, as well as God's transcendence beyond all creaturely concepts and doctrines. Ironically, given the notoriety of *Sinners in the Hands of an Angry God* (1741), Edwards failed to recognize how his own context, commitments, and circumstances were conditioned by finitude and sinfulness, which further complicates the retrieval of his social vision by later generations. Throughout his social thought, one can find justifications of the status quo, in particular relations of subordination between genders, in the family, in the church, and in every level of political society.[61] The most egre-

---

59. Edwards, *An Humble Inquiry . . .* (1749) in *The Works of Jonathan Edwards:* Volume 12, *Ecclesiastical Writings* (New Haven: Yale University Press, 1994), p. 174.

60. For much more on Edwards's understanding of the Lord's Supper, see William Danaher, Jr., "By Sensible Signs Represented: Jonathan Edwards' Sermons on the Lord's Supper," *Pro Ecclesia* 7, no. 3 (1998): 261-87.

61. For example, to argue for patriarchy, Edwards wrote the following in a sermon on John 15:10: "[T]hough there be no difference of degree or Glory or excellency [among the divine persons], yet there is order in the Trinity. The three persons of the Trinity may be looked upon as a kind of family, so there is an Oeconomical order. Thus the Father, though

gious example is Edwards's defense of slavery. As Ken Minkema has shown, Edwards believed that African-Americans could experience the "liberty" of being "children of God," but theirs was only a liberation of spirit, not a social liberty on par with whites. Not only did Edwards own slaves, but he defended the institution of slavery.[62]

What, then, do Hutcheson and Edwards offer to contemporary theological discussions of civil society? The focus of most contemporary discussions is on intelligibility, that is, on how to articulate religious accounts in a pluralistic context in which there are competing overarching visions of the good society. The question, then, most often asked is more or less the following: given the particularity of our religious beliefs, how do we articulate our values and norms in a way that is accessible to non-Christians, on one hand, and yet not robbed of their transformative power, on the other? Underlying this question is the epistemological concern to develop a common moral vocabulary that can sustain substantive discourse between discrete religious traditions that possess distinctive, internally coherent faith-claims. While these concerns are discernable in the discussion between Edwards and Hutcheson, their discussion differs from ours: both shared a common moral vocabulary and even general assumptions about the moral life, thus displacing the problem of intelligibility.

The differences between Edwards and Hutcheson were more explicitly theological and anthropological. Where Hutcheson saw doctrines such as the Trinity as secondary, Edwards saw them as essential and irreplaceable. Where Hutcheson naturalized the religious life, such that human affections are resolutely natural and plural, Edwards maintained that truly godly affections are spiritual and subordinate to the love of God. Where Hutcheson developed a theory of civil society that leaves little room for the distinctive role of the church, Edwards saw the church as the paradigm of all sociality and therefore the fundamental instance of civil society. Where Hutcheson used his theory of civil society to ameliorate social hierarchies, Edwards used his to justify them.

These theological contrasts between Edwards and Hutcheson indicate the difficult terrain over which contemporary theological evaluations

---

he be no greater than the Son and the Holy Ghost, yet he is first in order, the Son is next, and the Holy Ghost last." Cited from Amy Plantinga Pauw, *"The Supreme Harmony of All": The Trinitarian Theology of Jonathan Edwards* (Grand Rapids: Eerdmans, 2002), p. 106.

62. Ken Minkema, "Jonathan Edwards's Defense of Slavery," *The Massachusetts Historical Review* 4 (2002) http://www.historycooperative.org/journals/mhr/4/minkema.html.

of civil society must travel. While discussions of intelligibility are certainly legitimate, these occupy a small part of what is required for an adequately theological construal of civil society. Those interested in retrieving Hutcheson's account must struggle with his naturalism and ponder the eclipse of the church in his social vision. Those interested in retrieving Edwards's account must struggle with the viability of his vision in contexts where the church is disestablished, as well as his unwitting accommodation of the injustices of the status quo. And those interested in combining the best features of each of these approaches must recognize the very real differences between their projects, which complicate any straightforward synthesis. To be sure, all creation bears the marks of the triune God, and this includes civil society in every definition it currently has in contemporary thought. But how to treat these different definitions of civil society remains an enduring problem, one that demands a deeper theology than contemporary accounts have yet developed.

Pentecost as the Church's Cosmopolitan Vision of Global Civil Society: A Post-Communist Eastern European Theological Perspective

Daniela C. Augustine

At its current historical location, over 2000 years after the biblical event of Pentecost, humanity finds itself compressed by globalization and faced once again with the immediacy of the language of the other. There is an escalating sense of urgency that our survival as a human race depends on our ability to transform the multicultural polyphony of the globe into a purposeful dialogue motivated by a cosmopolitan vision of a just future. Our striking cultural diversity, situated among the pressing trans-national realities of poverty, genocide, ethnic and religious hatred, and terrorism, shows that institutionalized multiculturalism is central to any viable global transformation. Yet, as we struggle to translate and expand the ideas of democracy from the dimensions of the nation-state to those of the global village, we again encounter the discrepancies between ideals and their institutionalization and witness the inabilities of international institutions to achieve their inaugural visions.[1]

Among the remnants of trivialized utopias, broken societal dreams, and the escalating pressure of the continual demand for re-spacing under the influx of the other, it is often difficult to maintain a hopeful and creative outlook toward the future. Our hope-depleted geopolitical terrain thirsts for prophetic dreaming and political imagination, for the discovery

1. Mayda Yegenoglou, "Liberal Multiculturalism and the Ethics of Hospitality in the Age of Globalization," *Postmodern Culture* (http://www3.iath.virginia.edu/pmc/issue.103/13.2yegenoglu.html); David Loyed in "Race under Representation," *Oxford Literary Review* 13. 1-2 (1991): 70; Slavoj Žižek, "Multiculturalism, Or, the Cultural Logic of Multinational Capitalism," I/225 *New Left Review* (September/October 1997): 28-51.

of an oasis — an oasis that opens time and space for the construction of alternative socio-political realities and extends hospitality to the other, embracing them as part of one's own present and future.

After all, any transition to building a viable democracy (as well as attaining social emancipation and redemption) is impossible without the other. Such a transition requires a cosmopolitan vision of an inclusive, emancipated global community. In the words of Desmond Tutu, such a vision demands a spirituality of transformation that takes seriously the well-being of all members of society, including that of our political opponents, our former oppressors, our present economic exploiters, our abusers and torturers, and our enemies.[2] Tutu points to the spirituality needed to incarnate a covenantal moral society. Such a spirituality would contribute to what Vaclav Havel has termed "the moral state"[3] (outside of which democracy remains an impossible project)[4] and assure the existence of "politics as the practice of morality."[5] Contrary to the traditional capitalist priority of economic self-interest and benefit,[6] the spirituality of transformation needed in the larger global village upholds covenantal institutions of civil society[7] by prioritizing the other as an indispensable part of a just future. This spirituality draws courage from the presence of the other and speaks the language of hope on their behalf. It involves civil responsibility for the other that in turn demands "internal restraints,"[8] e.g., a form of responsible and reverent consumption committed to economic and ecological justice.[9] Persons who adopted such an attitude would be characterized by the

2. Desmond Tutu, *The Rainbow People of God* (New York: Doubleday, 1994), esp. chapter 6.

3. Vaclav Havel, "Politics, Morality and Civility," in *The Essential Civil Society Reader: Classic Essays in the American Civil Society Debate*, ed. Don E. Eberly (New York: Rowman & Littlefield Publishers, Inc., 2000), p. 396.

4. Havel, "Politics, Morality and Civility," p. 401.

5. Havel, "Politics, Morality and Civility," p. 397.

6. For a more detailed political and economic exposition on the wealth-accumulating and consumption reflex of capitalism, see Alex Callinicos, *An Anti-Capitalist Manifesto* (Cambridge: Polity Press, 2003), pp. 35-39.

7. Jonathan Sacks, *The Politics of Hope* (London: Vintage, 2000). The author describes the so-called "third-sector institutions," those sustaining the civil society, in the conditions of late capitalism. He calls the relationships they form covenantal (vs. contractual) and sees them as foundational for just society. Jean Bethke Elshtain also highlights the need for a "new social covenant" in "Democracy on Trial," in *The Essential Civil Society Reader*, pp. 101-22, esp. pp. 117-20.

8. Sacks, *Politics of Hope*, p. 268.

9. Timothy Gorringe, "The Principalities and Powers: A Framework for Thinking

civic virtue of fasting from oneself on behalf of the fellow human and the rest of nature. In this spiritual discipline one is committed to sharing possessions with one's neighbor and redistributing wealth according to human needs rather than political and economic benefits. As thinkers both on the left and on the right have observed, the development of this type of consciousness requires our personal transformation. "We can change the world if we can change ourselves."[10]

Civil society and any economic and socio-politically just governance are matters of moral relationships.[11] In view of that, Gertrude Himmelfarb has suggested that perhaps the contemporary global crisis of democracy and capitalist production should be viewed as being the consequence of "the moral bankruptcy that comes with the depletion of both religious and quasi-religious moral capital."[12] According to Himmelfarb, the central question that confronts us today is whether there are "prospects for a moral reformation of society."[13] This question is obviously linked to a different one — that of secularization and the development of secular politics of social salvation.[14]

The ideas of human rights, equality, and justice have their origins in the Judeo-Christian tradition and its capacity to nurture a covenantal communal consciousness.[15] According to Gordon Graham, the world after Darwin and Nietzsche was marked by a shift from covenantal (divinely ordained) to contractual (humanly ordered) liberalism, democracy, and guardianship of human rights.[16] If Hegel and Marx were right that self-consciousness is a product of one's cultural and historical circumstances, then it is legitimate to ask whether democracy and human rights can be

---

about Globalization," in *Globalization and the Good,* ed. Peter Heslam (London: SPCK, 2004), pp. 79-91.

10. Sacks, *Politics of Hope,* p. 269.

11. Michale Woolcock, in *Globalization and the Good,* ed. Peter Heslam (London: SPCK, 2004), pp. 48-49. Also Sacks, *Politics of Hope,* p. 269.

12. Gertrude Himmelfarb, "The Renewal of Civil Society," in *Culture in Crisis and the Renewal of Civil Life,* ed. T. William Boxx and Gary M. Quinlivan (Lanham, MD: Rowman and Littlefield, 1996), p. 72.

13. Himmelfarb, "The Renewal of Civil Society," p. 72.

14. Gordon Graham, *The Case Against the Democratic State* (Charlottesville, VA: Imprint Academics, 2002), pp. 64-68.

15. Max Stackhouse, "Sources and Prospects for Human Rights Ideas: A Christian Perspective," in *The Idea of Human Rights: Traditions and Presence,* ed. Jindøich Halama (Prague, Czech Republic: UK ETF, 2003), pp. 183-84.

16. Graham, *Case Against the Democratic State,* pp. 66-67.

authentically sustained if the historic cultural foundation on which they have been built has lost its plausibility. Reflecting on this question, Gordon Graham suggests that Locke and Habakkuk "have more in common than do Locke and contemporary liberal democracy. They both believed that the ultimate source of moral and political authority is God."[17]

Today many would agree that the commodification of life has robbed us of dreams and trivialized the diversity of the global village, reducing the world to an exchange-value at the omnipresent free marketplace. Yet, for over 2000 years, Christianity has sustained — through the rise and fall of empires — the vision that the world's ultimate destiny is to become a house of prayer, worship, and healing in which all nations are bonded in a covenantal global community (Revelation 7:9-10). This cosmopolitan vision is sustained by a spirituality incarnated in the community of faith that lives out the reality of the kingdom as a faith-praxis of the body of Christ on behalf of the world. This vision and its incarnation are the threefold work of the Holy Spirit as the giver of dreams and visions. The creator Spirit inspires prophetic speech-acts. The transformer Spirit induces change in human beings and communities towards Christ-likeness. The liberator Spirit sets us free to be and to become. All in all, the Spirit is the giver and sustainer of life and hope in the face of despair. The Holy Spirit deconstructs imperial historical ends, overwhelming them from beyond their boundaries and opening an exodus out of exile and displacement, marginalization, and suffering. The Spirit guides us ultimately towards the cosmic Christ as the One who is the Truth that sets us free and makes us whole as human beings, as communities and as a world. As Max Stackhouse states, Christ can renew the covenant between God and humanity while pointing souls and societies toward a New Jerusalem.[18]

This paper addresses the need for a prophetic revisioning of historical ends and a hopeful political imagination within the global context. In it we look at the event of Pentecost as offering a transformational vision for the cosmopolitan future of the world. This vision highlights the radical hospitality of God towards the other, incarnated in the community of faith via the agency of the Holy Spirit.

17. Graham, *Case Against the Democratic State*, p. 68.
18. Max Stackhouse, "Public Theology and Political Economy in a Global Era," in *Public Theology for the 21st Century*, ed. William F. Storrar and Andrew R. Morton (London: T&T Clark, 2004), p. 191.

Images of Babel and Pentecost in the Global Village
in Search of an Antidote to Imperial Consciousness

Christian theology has a long-standing tradition of viewing the event of Pentecost as an overcoming or a reversal of Babel.[19] The connection between the two events, however, can also be seen in the continuity of God's prophetic deconstruction of every imperial consciousness that is inherently homogenizing and violently marginalizing those who are other and different.[20]

The account in Genesis 11 describes the architectonic of an empire suppressing all differences that attempt to destabilize its own grand project for self-immortalization. The text contrasts the speech and action of the empire (vv. 2-4) with the speech-act of God (vv. 5-8). The imperial project looks for shortcuts to its goal of totalizing uniformity. Substituting "brick for stone and tar for mortar" (v. 3), the architects of empire hurry to mark a territory and establish dominion. In order to assume superiority over the "plain of Shinar," they use imperial propaganda that cultivates in the populace a fear of the future and of the other. The boundaries of empire are presented as the demarcations of safety (v. 4). Beyond them is "the face of the whole world" (v. 4), which is a special designation for the location of *the face of the other*.[21] "Heaven" (v. 4) is the ultimate goal of the project; the empire has identified itself with the final, undisputed authority. With that move nothing remains beyond its scope. Sacred space collapses in its grip and leaves humanity with no exodus from the totalitarian order.

As God comes down in the plurality of personhood expressed by the divine speech ("let us" — v. 7), he acts in conformity with his nature of creating and affirming diversity. He extends self-giving by opening space and time for the other and thereby creates the possibility of an authentic human community, one in which life can be shared together in a multiplicity of forms and locations. In view of that, the destruction of the em-

19. On the view of Pentecost as a reversal of Babel see Avery Dulles, *The Catholicity of the Church* (Oxford: Oxford University Press, 1987), p. 173.

20. Miroslav Volf, *Exclusion and Embrace: A Theological Exploration of Identity, Otherness, and Reconciliation* (Nashville: Abingdon Press, 1996), pp. 226ff.

21. The immediate association of this phrase is with the work of Emmanuel Levinas and his emphasis on the other as the focal point of ethics, and on ethics as being the first philosophy. The face of the other, as an expression of their presence, summons us to responsibility, and justice becomes defined as our relationship to the other.

pire's project is an act of deconstructing a world order that has eliminated the possibility of the other. God induces this imperial collapse by bringing the language of the other forth within the homogeneity of human space. The monotone superiority of imperial culture is challenged by the polyphony of human speech as the inaugural address of a multicultural human reality (vv. 7, 9). The demanding immediacy of the other's presence brings about the demolition of the empire's boundaries, as the formerly homogenized population overflows and spreads "abroad over the face of the whole earth" (v. 9). The new accomplishment of human community after Babel demands accepting the other and making the effort to learn his or her language. This is God's response to the self-perpetuation of imperial consciousness and is inseparable from his providential plan for the salvation of humanity.

The confusion following the eruption of the other (v. 9) will accompany humanity in its journey after Babel. Fallen human nature continues to gravitate to the homogenizing shortcuts of empire, offering its dehumanizing patterns of association as a substitute for the need of sociality in the diversity of authentic human community. God's alternative, designed to bring the restoration of his communion with humanity (and of authentic human sociality as a reflection of the restoration of his image in human beings) situates salvation within the relationship to the other (Exod. 20:12-17). From the midst of "the thunder and lightning flashes and the sound of the trumpet and the mountain smoking" at Sinai (Exodus 20:18), God establishes in a creative speech-act a covenant with his people. The divine utterance unites the aural and visual dimensions of human communication, and his flaming words become visible to the multitude (similar to the burning bush experience of Moses in Exodus 3:2-5 and later to the flames of Pentecost in Acts 2:3).[22] He brings the other into the center of personal and corporate social redemption (Deut. 5:16-21; Exod. 20:12-17). The appropriation of the covenant bond with God demands the establishment of covenantal bonds with the other —

22. In his commentary on Acts, Luke Timothy Johnson points to the symbolism utilized by Philo Judaeus, "who explicitly attaches the giving of the Law by God to the communication of speech by flame." Johnson offers the following quotation of his work (On the Decalogue): "Then from the midst of the fire that streamed from heaven there sounded forth to their utter amazement a voice, for the flame became articulated speech in the language familiar to the audience, and so clearly and distinctly were the words formed by it that they seemed to see rather than hear them." The Acts of the Apostles (Collegeville, MN: A Michael Glazier Book, The Liturgical Press, 1992), p. 46.

the immediate other (one's mother, father, neighbor) as well as the distant other (the stranger, the foreigner, the gentile). God remains in our midst as the omnipresent Other in whom we move and live and have our being (Acts 17:28). Therefore, we see in the Sinai event the establishment of a communal covenant as an immediate embodiment and extension of the salvific covenant with God.

God's words have the unique quality of embodying a creative force that bespeaks reality. As such, they stand before the people not only as a covenantal demand (or a command) but also as a promise. The hearers of the words can love God and neighbor as the Holy Spirit engraves the law on their hearts, and they are thereby transformed into his likeness.[23] The fulfillment of the promise is already initiated in the moment of its impartation, for God and his Word already inhabit the future. In the immutability of the divine presence, the proclamation of the promise becomes an articulated preview of its fulfillment.

The event of Pentecost could also be understood in relation to the promised fulfillment of a renewed covenant with God and neighbor that is brought about through God's transformational self-giving.[24] Therefore, as outlined in Peter's sermon (Acts 2:14-39), the incarnation, crucifixion, resurrection, and ascension of Christ are central to the Pentecost theophany

23. Leonid Ouspensky, "The Meaning of and Content of the Icon," pp. 33-63 in *Eastern Orthodox Theology,* ed. D. B. Clendenin (Grand Rapids: Baker Books, 1995), pp. 37-38.

24. Reflecting on the connection between the giving of the Torah and the celebration of Pentecost, Luke T. Johnson states that: "After the destruction of the temple in C.E. 70, it is clear that Pentecost was universally understood by the Jews to be the celebration of the giving of the Torah on Mt. Sinai." *The Acts of the Apostles,* p. 46. Roger Stronstad points out that the feast of Pentecost was historically celebrated as "the second of three pilgrim festivals in Israel's liturgical calendar." *The Prophethood of All Believers: A Study in Luke's Charismatic Theology* (Sheffield: Sheffield Academic Press, 1999), p. 54. Regarding the possibility of Luke's account on Pentecost to be influenced by the rabbinic tradition equating the feast of Pentecost with the giving of the Law, Stronstad suggests that it is unlikely, since this rabbinic tradition developed later than the Pentecost narrative in Acts. *The Charismatic Theology of St. Luke* (Peabody, MA: Hendrickson, 1984), p. 58. The rabbinic tradition eventually developed the belief that when the law was given, it was heard not only by Israel but by the 72 nations listed in Genesis 10:2-31. In his commentary on Acts, F. F. Bruce cites the Midrash Tanchuma 26 C, that at Sinai the voice of God divided into "seven voices and then went into seventy tongues." *Commentary on the Book of Acts,* The New International Commentary on the New Testament, ed. F. F. Bruce (Grand Rapids: Eerdmans, 1979), p. 60. In opposition to Stronstad, Johnson points out that "Luke certainly could have made the connection" between the Pentecost feast and the giving of the Torah on his own, in spite of the existence or not of such a tradition prior to his account of Pentecost in Acts.

of the Spirit. Pentecost authenticates the redemption accomplished by God on behalf of humanity in Christ Jesus. Christ is the new Adam (1 Cor. 15:45), the perfect icon and representation of God (Col. 1:15, 2 Cor. 4:4). Humanity is thus restored to its proper position in relation to the divine and the rest of creation. Human sociality is redeemed in communion with the other as a reflection and extension through the Holy Spirit of the trinitarian life of God.[25]

The event of Pentecost could also be viewed as the incarnation of Christ in the community of faith, a moment brought about through the agency of the Holy Spirit. As the third person of the Trinity pours himself over the hundred-and-twenty in the upper room, they become both Christ-bearers and a living extension of his resurrected body on earth. Sergius Bulgakov has given us the image of Jesus' conception as being "the Pentecost of the Virgin."[26] As the Holy Spirit descends on Mary in response to her willingness and readiness for service (Luke 1:38), she is transformed into an instrument of God's Word becoming flesh in our midst (John 1:14). For Bulgakov, it takes a willing human instrument to authenticate the humanness of Christ in the incarnation.[27]

In a similar manner, as the Spirit descends upon the disciples, Christ is conceived in them and they are empowered (Acts 1:8). Individually and corporately, they become Christ-bearers and bear forth an embodied gospel as a hope realized in the midst of a destitute humanity. The proclamation of the good news is an announcement of God's providential presence with the hearers of the Word. It is an invitation to partake in the life of God and ultimately in the future of the world. The witness of the disciples on the day of Pentecost, "speaking of the mighty deeds of God" (Acts 2:11), reminds us of Mary's Magnificat (Luke 1:46-55). In both cases, it is the voice of the socially marginalized, ostracized, and persecuted. They announce the just socio-political reality of God's kingdom, adventing among humanity in Jesus Christ, in whom the fulfillment of the divine covenantal

---

25. For an in-depth discussion on the Trinitarian sociality as expressed in the human socium, see: Miroslav Volf, *After Our Likeness: The Church in the Image of the Trinity* (Grand Rapids: Eerdmans, 1998). Also see Vladimir Soloviev, Трочное и его Обществнно Приложение, pp. 243-334 in Чтения о Богочеловечество (St. Petersburg: Азбука, 2000), esp. in chapter 10, Soloviov's passage on the Social Trinity.

26. Sergius Bulgakov, "The Virgin and the Saints in Orthodoxy," in *Eastern Orthodox Theology: A Contemporary Reader,* ed. Daniel B. Clendenin (Grand Rapids: Baker Books, 1995), p. 67.

27. Bulgakov, "The Virgin and the Saints in Orthodoxy," p. 67.

promises of salvation (Luke 1:54-55; Acts 2:33, 38-40) has been extended to all, even "to the ends of the earth" (Acts 1:8).[28]

The Christocentrism of this event is associated further with the transference of the messianic anointing from Christ to the community of faith. The community is his body present in the world; they are thereby called and empowered to continue his mission and ministry outlined in the programmatic citation of Isaiah in Luke 4:18-19.[29] In a manner similar to that in the narrative of Jesus' inauguration (Luke 3:21-22), the Spirit of Pentecost descends upon his own — the incarnated Christ empowering the body for the fulfillment of the messianic task. Therefore, the prophetic, royal, and priestly dimensions of Christ's ministry become a part of the charismatic reality of his body, and the community of disciples is transformed into a royal priesthood and prophethood of all believers.[30] As such, the body represents a new Christ-like consciousness. This global and cosmic consciousness of the kingdom is expressed in a redemptive relationship with the other — as love for God and neighbor (Matt. 25:37-40). Since Christ's messianic mission is fulfilled in self-giving to the other, the consciousness formed by the Spirit in his body is an antidote to that of empire. While the imperial consciousness commodifies, consumes, marginalizes, and even eliminates the other for its own benefit, the messianic consciousness of Christ's body prioritizes the other and the other's well-being.

This incarnationalist view of the Pentecost also allows us to consider the possibility of looking at the remainder of Acts as rooted in Christ's extended presence on earth in his body. Therefore, if the Gospel of Luke represents the first volume of "all that Jesus began to do and teach" (Acts 1:1), the book of Acts can be seen as the second volume outlining "the continuation and fulfillment of what Jesus did and thought."[31] Being a living exten-

28. Beverly Roberts Gaventa, *The Acts of the Apostles*, Abingdon New Testament Commentaries (Nashville: Abingdon Press, 2003), p. 80.

29. Roger Stronstad (in *The Charismatic Theology of St. Luke* [Peabody, MA: Hendrickson, 1984]) draws the parallel between Pentecost and the transfer of the Spirit from Moses to the seventy elders (Numbers 11:10-30). As Stronstad notes: "Both narratives record the transfer of a leadership from a single individual to a group. . . . In both cases the transfer of the Spirit results in an outburst of prophecy" (p. 59).

30. On the prophethood of the Pentecost Community see Stronstad, *The Prophethood of All Believers*, pp. 65-70.

31. Matthias Wenk, *Community-Forming Power: The Socio-Ethical Role of the Spirit in Luke-Acts* (Sheffield: Sheffield Academic Press, 2000), p. 242. The author points to the outpouring of the Spirit at Pentecost as a clear example that the ministry of Christ (the Baptizer

sion of the risen Lord and continuation of his ministry in this world, the body follows the extroverted orientation of Christ's mission, namely, from oneself towards the other. Therefore, for the community of faith, Pentecost is also a literal crossing of the bridge from the private to the public. As the church moves beyond the enclosure of the upper room into the public space of the city and begins to participate in the public discourse about the welfare of its citizens, it becomes a distinct factor of social change. This movement is also a crossing from the zone of meditation on the incarnated Christ to an incarnation of his presence. It is a transition from reflection (prayer) to interaction (witness) to action (transformation). It is a movement from "the innermost being" (John 7:38) to the "ends of the world." Incarnation is the mode of this extroverted movement, and the Spirit is its agent, engine, and navigator. The Spirit's mission (in continuity with the character and nature of God) is realized through self-sharing — God pours himself upon all flesh. In sharing his life, he becomes the source of life that sustains the spiritual ecology of the faith community.

The fact that Christ is the Truth (John 14:6) that sets people free (John 8:32) brings into view the image of the prophetic Pentecost community as a truth-embodying and truth-proclaiming social reality that unites the story of the kingdom with its praxis. The community's voice in the life of the city calls all civic dimensions to moral responsibility and discernment between good and evil. Once again, the incarnation is essential for exercising discernment, for each spirit is known by its fruit (Matt. 7:16; 1 John 4:2), and the fruit of the Holy Spirit is revealed within the human *socium* through the prioritization of the other in one's social interactions (Gal. 5:22-23).

This aspect of the kingdom is an outcome of the Spirit's dialectic of liberation. This new human consciousness is not a result of social evolution (Hegel) or revolution (Marx). Rather, as Nikolai Berdyaev has stated, the Kingdom of God is an outcome of a "marvelous transfiguration."[32] Marx's saint and hero was Prometheus. He stole fire from the gods in order to give it to humanity and meet the human need of light, illumination, and the free-

---

with the Holy Spirit) continues in Acts (p. 243) He mentions also the passages of Acts 7:55-56; 9:5, 10; 13:39; 17:7; 18:10; 19:15 and 25:19 as indicative of Jesus' acting upon the disciples. Another example is the healing of the beggar in Acts 3:1-16 "presented as a continuation of Jesus' healing ministry (Acts 4:30)" (p. 245). Beverly Gaventa's work also supports the view of the book of Acts as presenting a continuation of the ministry of Jesus. See her commentary *The Acts of the Apostles,* pp. 34, 62-63.

32. Nikolai Berdyaev, *Philosophy of Inequality* (Sofia: Prozoretz, 1923), p. 220.

dom to chart one's own journey. In contrast, the fire of the Spirit is a divine act of self-giving, an expression of divine hospitality. In this fire a self-pouring God meets all human needs. God's Spirit invites humans into his light, gives them dreams and visions, and empowers them to prophesy a just socio-political reality beyond the order of empires. Herein lies a true actualization of human freedom in covenantal community with the Trinity and with one another. The light of the Spirit illuminates and initiates the dialectic of true human freedom beginning with a clarity of vision — "you shall know the truth and the truth shall set you free" (John 8:32). This is a different kind of knowing than that of the Marxist revolutionary consciousness emphasizing one's self-interest as a representative of the proletarian class. Illuminated by the Spirit, the liberating epistemology is that of knowing Christ in the other (Matt. 25:31-46) — or knowing otherwise.[33] First of all, knowing the truth is being in a covenant with the one who is the Truth and then seeing him in the other even in their "most distressful disguise" (Mother Teresa). Knowing the Truth gives us his perspective towards the other, informing and constructing our actions. The other is known otherwise than in the imperial consciousness. We come to know the other as Christ knows him or her, a knowing in which human dignity and wholeness are restored. It is the knowing of love in flesh — knowing in Christ-likeness.

It is no accident that the language of the other stands at the center of the Pentecost event as an expression of the prioritization of the other in the kingdom of a new humanity. In the words of Mikhail Bakhtin, "language, for the individual consciousness, lies on the borderline between oneself and the other."[34] Language participates in the composition of one's personal and corporate identity and therefore could be viewed as being "constitutive to reality and not just a reflection of it."[35] Jean-François Lyotard reminds us that the translatability of language points to the fact that all human beings are called to a speech community and that the silencing of the speech of the other is a violation of a basic right.[36] Human

---

33. James H. Olthuis, ed., *Knowing Other-Wise: Philosophy at the Threshold of Spirituality* (New York: Fordham University Press, 1997), p. 8.

34. Mikhail Bakhtin, "Discourse in the Novel," in *The Dialogic Imagination*, ed. Michael Holquist (Austin, TX: The University of Texas Press, 1981), p. 293.

35. Maria Teresa Morgan, "Tongues as of Fire: The Spirit as Paradigm for Ministry in a Multicultural Setting," in *The Spirit in the Church and the World*, ed. Bradford E. Hinze (Maryknoll, NY: Orbis Books, 2004), p. 107.

36. J.-F. Lyotard, "The Other's Rights," in *On Human Rights*, ed. S. Shute and S. Hurley (New York: Basic Books, 1993), pp. 140-141.

speech is therefore inseparable from the notion of justice as "the relationship to the other," and knowing the language of the other is integral to knowing the other's reality. In light of this, it is necessary to address the demand for cosmopolitan hospitality, for such hospitality will be indispensable to the future of a viable global civil society.

The Language of the Other and the Demand for Cosmopolitan Hospitality

The seemingly uncontested superiority claims of global capitalism and western democratic theory, in their certainty of victory over the world's cosmopolitan future, have highlighted the problems of institutionalized multiculturalism within the current debates over globalization.[37] Multiculturalism is suspect in its evasion of the need to cultivate authentically dialogical spaces and has been perceived as a vehicle for the ideological propaganda of western capitalism. Seeing institutionalized multiculturalism as the universalizing force of global capitalism, Slavoj Žižek suggests that its current position in the world entails *Eurocentric* (or perhaps North-Atlantic) *distance*.[38] This distance displays outwardly an attitude of respect and tolerance toward the local cultures, yet it insists on its cultural superiority among them and self-justifies its privileged status in the world.[39] Its position of cultural relativism recognizes the voice of the other yet makes the other irrelevant to the economic and political mechanisms of global governance. The voice of the other is reduced to just one more parallel voice among many. The other has the right to exist as long as he or she does not dominate the development of the global political space. Therefore, western multiculturalism assumes the position of a superior

37. The tension between western liberal democracy and multiculturalism is not new. For example, it is evident in the work of John Stuart Mill. While writing passionately in defense of individual freedom, Mill wholeheartedly supports the colonization policy of the British Empire. He believes that "despotism is a legitimate mode of government in dealing with barbarians, provided the end be their improvement and the means justified by actually effecting the ends." *On Liberty* (New York: Penguin Books, 1985), p. 11.

38. Slavoj Žižek, "Multiculturalism, Or, the Cultural Logic of Multinational Capitalism," I/225 *New Left Review* (September/October 1997): 44.

39. Yegenoglou, "Liberal Multiculturalism and the Ethics of Hospitality in the Age of Globalization," *Postmodern Culture* (http://www3.iath.virginia.edu/pmc/issue.103/13 .2yegenoglu.html).

subject who, due to its neutrality, can be a universal representative and can exercise an uncontested global rule.[40] While accommodating polyphony within the boundaries of its convenience, institutionalized western multiculturalism, through its insistence on relativity, effectively eliminates the need of a dialogue with the other. In a Bakhtinian sense, it asserts monological utterance over against the development of dialogical *heteroglossia*.

Bakhtin points out that words are not neutral and impersonal.[41] Language is also historically and ideologically specific.[42] Yet, his view of the dialogization of languages reaches further than the Socratic debate or the Hegelian dialectic. Dialogical *heteroglossia* creates a multi-dimensional unity of oneself with the other while preserving the distinctiveness of each one. On the one hand, the word we speak is always "half someone else's."[43] On the other hand, the words we speak become populated with the intentions of the other (as well as with our own), for language is always directed towards understanding the other.[44] Since language is a historically charged reality, dialogical unity with the other involves our participation in the story of the other. However, this co-habitation of the story of the other gives us, at the same time, an-other perspective on our own language and story.[45] We are able to see ourselves through the eye of the other.

By relativizing the voice of the other, we eliminate the need for dialogical participation in and with the other. In this manner, institutionalized multiculturalism effectively obscures and belittles the significance of alternative voices. The elimination of the need for a dialogue compro-

40. David Loyed in "Race under Representation," has articulated the concept of "the subject with ultimate properties." "Its universality is attained by virtue of Literal indifference: this subject becomes representative in consequence of being able to take anonymous place, of occupying any place, of pure exchangeability. Universal where all others are particular, partial, this Subject is perfect, disinterested judge formed for and by the public sphere." *Oxford Literary Review* 13, no. 1-2 (1991): 70.

41. Bakhtin, *The Dialogic Imagination*, p. 294.

42. Bakhtin, *The Dialogic Imagination*, p. 294.

43. Bakhtin, *The Dialogic Imagination*, p. 293.

44. Bakhtin, *The Dialogic Imagination*, p. 282.

45. Bakhtin, "Response to a Question from Novy Mir Editorial Staff," in *Speech Genres and Other Late Essays*, trans. Vern W. McGee, ed. Caryl Emerson and Michael Holquist (Austin, TX: The University of Texas, 1986), pp. 1-7. See also James P. Zappen, "Mikhail Bakhtin, in *Twentieth-Century Rhetoric and Rhetoricians: Critical Studies and Sources*, ed. Michael G. Morgan and Michelle Ballif (Westport: Greenwood Press, 2000), pp. 7-20.

mises human sociality, connectivity, and community. It trivializes the covenantal social relationships that create authentically democratic space and secure the participation of the other in the formation of a cosmopolitan civil society. The absence of dialogue eliminates the inconvenience of the need to learn the language of the other. Consequently, it relieves us from the burden to recognize the other *de facto* even when we are required to recognize them *de jure*. This discrepancy in the recognition of the other is evident in the chasm between institutionalized and actualized multiculturalism and between institutionalized and realized democracy on a national, regional, and global scale.

Engaging Žižek's reflection on western multiculturalism, Mayda Yegenoglu poses the following critical question: "If the institutionalized pluralism that characterizes the post-national global order implies a foreclosure of politics proper [a term utilized by Žižek] and is far from offering a potential for democratic politization, then where do we locate the possibility of politics that interrupt this foreclosure?"[46] In search of an answer to this question, Yegenoglu turns to Jacques Derrida's argument concerning conditional and unconditional hospitality as a "useful philosophical and theoretical apparatus for deconstructing the ideology imbedded in liberal multiculturalism"[47] and thus creating conditions for a "democratic possibility" on a cosmopolitan scale.

Derrida develops his ideas of conditional and unconditional hospitality in a dialogue with the thought of Emmanuel Levinas, a textual form of offering a tribute to his late colleague's work.[48] Derrida contrasts Kant's cosmopolitical law as "law or politics of hospitality" with Levinas' "ethics of hospitality" while addressing the question of the possibility of both within the global human existence.[49]

According to Derrida, rethinking Levinas' ethical discourse on hospitality invites us "to think law and politics otherwise." Such rethinking could open "both the mouth and the possibility of another speech, of decision and a responsibility . . . taken without the assurance of ontological

46. Yegenoglou, "Liberal Multiculturalism," p. 6.

47. Yegenoglou, "Liberal Multiculturalism," p. 16.

48. Derrida's work on hospitality has occupied the text of various volumes; however, the immediate association with this topic brings us to the following two titles: *Adieu to Emmanuel Levinas* (Stanford: Stanford University Press, 1990) and *Of Hospitality*, with parallel text by Anne Dufourmantelle (Stanford: Stanford University Press, 2000).

49. Derrida, *Adieu*, pp. 19-20. On the contrast between Kant and Levinas see also pp. 48-51.

foundation."[50] Derrida sees the relationship between conditional and unconditional hospitality in a manner similar to that between law and justice. The law could be deconstructed — it could be analyzed, critiqued and changed. The history of legal systems is "a history of the transformation of law."[51] On the other hand, justice is not the law.

> Justice is what gives us the impulse, the drive, or the movement to improve the law, that is to deconstruct the law. This is why . . . the condition of the possibility of deconstruction is a call for justice. Justice is not reducible to the law, to a given system of legal structures. That means that justice is always unequal to itself. It is non-coincidental with itself.[52]

Derrida embraces Levinas' definition of justice as being "the relation to the other"[53] and points out the fact that in accordance with such an understanding, justice continually questions the law since it is always "incalculable" and "unequal to the other."[54] The face of the other in its unique singularity remains irreducible to categorizing or "thematization."[55] In view of that, Derrida invites us "to think of another way of interpreting politics" as "the place for hospitality, the place for the gift,"[56] and to rethink "the concepts of the political and of democracy" in a way that would be compatible and articulated with "these impossible notions of the gift and justice."[57]

Derrida points out that legislated hospitality is conditional. It is a giving gesture, for it subjugates the guest (the stranger, the foreigner) to the law of one's home. Therefore, it allows the stranger to enter the hosts'

50. Derrida, *Adieu*, p. 21.

51. Derrida, *Deconstruction in a Nutshell: A Conversation with Jacques Derrida*, ed. John D. Caputo (New York: Fordham University Press, 1997), p. 16. The first chapter of the book records the Villanova Roundtable conversation with Derrida.

52. Derrida, *Deconstruction in a Nutshell*, p. 16. See also Derrida, "The Force of Law: 'The Mystical Foundation of Authority,'" trans. Mary Quaintance, in *Deconstruction and the Possibility of Justice*, ed. Drucilla Cornell et al. (New York: Routledge, 1992), pp. 14-15.

53. Levinas, *Totality and Infinity*, trans. Alphonso Lingis (Pittsburgh: Duquesne University Press, 1969), p. 89.

54. Derrida, *Deconstruction in a Nutshell*, p. 17. In understanding Derrida's idea of *justice* it is helpful to also look at the idea of *the gift*. See *The Gift of Death*, trans. David Wills (Chicago: The University of Chicago Press, 1995) and *Given Time*, vol. 1, *Counterfeit Money*, trans. Peggy Kamuf (Chicago: The University of Chicago Press, 1991).

55. Levinas, *Totality and Infinity*, p. 229.

56. Derrida, *Deconstruction in a Nutshell*, p. 18.

57. Derrida, *Deconstruction in a Nutshell*, p. 19.

space under the hosts' conditions and regulations.[58] Reflecting on Kant's *categorical imperative,* Derrida suggests that

> to be what it "must" be, hospitality must not pay a debt, or be governed by a duty: it is gracious, and "must" not open itself to the guest . . . either "confirming to duty" or even to use the Kantian diction again, "out of duty." This unconditional law of hospitality, if such thing is thinkable, would then be a law without imperative, without order and without duty. A law without law in short. For if I practice hospitality "out of duty" . . . this hospitality of paying up is no longer an absolute hospitality, it is no longer graciously offered beyond debt and economy, offered to the other, a hospitality invented for singularity of the new arrival, of the unexpected visitor.[59]

The language of the other is of great significance in Derrida's and Levinas' understanding of hospitality. According to Levinas, "the essence of language is goodness . . . is friendship and hospitality."[60] Hospitality is "interrupting oneself" in opening space for the other,[61] or welcoming the other. Therefore, hospitality is "intentionality, consciousness of, attention to speech or welcome of the face" of the other.[62]

In his discourse on hospitality, Derrida makes the important observation that "language resists all mobilities because it moves about" with us. "It is the least immovable thing, the most mobile of personal bodies which remains the stable but portable condition of all mobilities."[63] Therefore, displaced people — "exiles, the deported, the expelled, the rootless, the stateless, lawless nomads, absolute foreigners, often continue to recognize the language, what is called the mother tongue, as their ultimate homeland, and even their last resting place."[64]

If the mother-tongue is our mobile habitat, our home away from home, then it is essential to the act of welcoming the other in unconditional hospitality. When the other encounters their mother-tongue in us, they enter their homeland. Our space becomes their space, and they are fi-

---

58. Derrida, *Of Hospitality,* pp. 75-85.
59. Derrida, *Of Hospitality,* p. 83.
60. Levinas, *Totality and Infinity,* p. 305.
61. Derrida, *Adieu,* pp. 52-53.
62. Levinas, *Totality and Infinity,* p. 299.
63. Derrida, *Of Hospitality,* p. 91.
64. Derrida, *Of Hospitality,* pp. 87, 89.

nally at home. Therefore, unconditional hospitality could be understood as an act of taking the place of the stranger in our own home, handing the keys to the other, and letting him or her abide in it on their own terms and conditions.

Derrida has mixed feelings toward this willingness to make the other "the host of the host."[65] While commenting on Levinas' statement that language is hospitality, he questions "whether absolute, hyperbolical, unconditional hospitality doesn't consist in suspending language, a particular determinate language, and even the address to the other."[66] Yet, discussing the possibility and impossibility of unconditional hospitality, Derrida gives the final word to Levinas and his Torah-inspired stand for the other as the focal point of all ethics. Levinas states:

> The Torah is transcendent and from heaven by its demands that clash, in the final analysis, with the pure ontology of the world. The Torah demands, in opposition to the natural perseverance of each being in his or her own being (a fundamental ontological law), concern for the stranger, the widow and the orphan, a preoccupation with the other person.[67]

Derrida ends his *Adieu to Emmanuel Levinas* with this passage, fulfilling the mandate of the very subject of the book. He fittingly adopts the language of Levinas in a final gesture of farewell and parting gift of hospitality.

The Hospitality of God and the Event of Pentecost

In his book *The Trinity and the Kingdom,* Jürgen Moltmann gives us a compelling image of God as Creator epitomizing the essence of divine love. This is the image of God's "withdrawal of himself," his "self-limitation," in opening space for the existence of creation.[68] Perhaps we could think of this profound expression of the Trinity (itself an act of love)

---

65. Derrida, *Of Hospitality,* pp. 124-127.

66. Derrida, *Of Hospitality,* p. 135.

67. Levinas, *In the Time of the Nations,* trans. Michael B. Smith (London: The Atholone Press, 1994), p. 61. Derrida ends with this passage his book *Adieu to Emmanuel Levinas.*

68. Jürgen Moltmann, *The Trinity and the Kingdom* (Minneapolis: Fortress Press, 1993), p. 59.

as the *motherhood* of God and therefore as hospitality *par excellence*. The reflexive re-spacing of the Creator as a cosmic womb that conceives, tabernacles, nurtures, and sustains the other (and protects the possibility of their otherness) is consistent with God's continual self-giving in his relation to humanity and the rest of creation. A womb symbolizes sanctuary and self-sacrifice. A womb embraces one's irreversible transfiguring, for it is motivated by love that is committed to birth forth life — the life of the other. It is a gift of unconditional hospitality.

God's love "bears all things, believes all things, hopes all things, endures all things" (1 Cor. 13:7). God establishes his self-limitation on behalf of the other. This is an act of fasting from oneself in order to nurture the other and serves as the model of striving towards God-likeness (in Christ-likeness). Therefore, being holy as God is holy (1 Pet. 1:15-16) includes unconditional covenantal love towards the other as one's neighbor (Eph. 1:4).

In light of this, hospitality as law can be contrasted with hospitality as a gift from the Spirit (Rom. 12:13). Practicing hospitality as an extension of God's welcome (in us) for the other becomes an outcome of bearing forth the fruit of the Spirit (Gal. 5:22-23). This fruit is produced in inter-sociality for the sake of the other and the different, as an act of Christ-like self-giving in love. As the other comes and feasts on it, he or she "tastes the Lord and finds that he is good" (Psalm 34:8). This is a type of production that differs in kind from the production of social capital invested on behalf of the other in response to their needs. It implies a different political economy, one that builds its forms and relationships of production as an extension and result of the covenant relations necessary for bearing forth this new social capital. Christ-like productivity bears forth a consciousness that prioritizes the needs of the other and meets them in hospitality through self-limiting and in faith, hope, and love through self-fasting. This hospitality demands the re-spacing of the self and the redistribution of one's resources. It creates new conditions for the host in which the supplying of his or her personal needs becomes a function of supplying the needs of the other. Their own nurture becomes indispensable from "doing the will of the Father" and accomplishing "his work" as an extension of Christ on earth (John 4:34). The host is welcomed, in reverse, into what was once his or her space and makes himself or herself available to the other in and through God's welcoming encounter (Matt. 25:31-46). Ultimately, it is the hospitality of God that is offered and received by the other through the agency of the Spirit.

The response to the other as an act of economic and social justice is not an outcome of socio-political persuasion but of a spirituality that extends one's participation in the life of God and his presence on earth in the community of faith. This self-limiting ascetic spirituality stands in a clear contrast to the motives of the secular gestures of one's re-spacing under the legislated and institutionalized forms of redistribution of wealth associated with the capitalist and socialist arrangements. Nikolai Berdyaev asserts that both capitalism and socialism are ultimately motivated by individualism, and their displays of concern for the common good cannot be separated from this prioritizing of self-interest.[69] Both capitalism and socialism have substituted the spiritual goals of life with material means and are therefore unable to sustain authentic human rights and freedom (since they represent high spiritual goals and have spiritual origin).[70] Berdyaev points out that "the historical material force is a part of the spiritual historical reality," and that "the entire economic life of humanity has a spiritual base, a spiritual foundation."[71] Therefore, the individualist inversion of social vision, as well as the secularization and fetishism of materialism and economism is, according to him, "a violation of the natural hierarchism of human society."[72] Economic individualism substituted truth with Mammonism by presenting itself as superior in the pursuit of truth and attaining freedom from illusions.[73] "Economic Materialism," in turn, "has formulated this in a most perfect way by declaring the entire spiritual life of the human as being an illusion and a fraud."[74] In view of this, "socialism is only a further development of the industrial capitalist system; it is the final celebration of its beginnings and a triumph of their universal spread."[75] Berdayev concludes that both "Capitalism and Socialism are accompanied by decline and deflaming of spiritual creativity, as a result of the recession of spirituality in human society."[76] Therefore, any expectation of social transformation that facilitates authentic human freedom and justice would demand a "revolution of the Spirit."[77] Only the

---

69. N. Berdyaev, *The New Middle Ages,* vol. 2 of *Collected Works* (Sofia: Zachari Stoyanov, 2003), pp. 526, 530-31.

70. Berdyaev, *Philosophy of Inequality,* pp. 110, 116.

71. Berdyaev, *The Meaning of History,* vol. 2 of *Collected Works* (Sofia: Zachari Stoyanov, 2003), p. 313.

72. Berdyaev, *The New Middle Ages,* p. 531.

73. Berdyaev, *The New Middle Ages,* p. 531.

74. Berdyaev, *The New Middle Ages,* p. 531.

75. Berdyaev, *The New Middle Ages,* p. 531.

76. Berdyaev, *The New Middle Ages,* p. 532.

77. Berdyaev, *The New Middle Ages,* p. 522.

Spirit creates a brotherhood and sisterhood that are a realization of true freedom — as freedom in Christ. In the Christ-centered spiritual togetherness *(sobornost)* there is no "mechanical equality." There is also no contradiction and difference between "a right and an obligation."[78] The personal freedom in the Spirit's *sobornost* does not contradict the freedom of the other, for it is not based on competition for the limited resources of the material reality. It is based rather on the eternal and infinite reality of divine love and grace.[79] In this divinely initiated and infused *sobornost,* the hospitality of God is incarnated in the community of Christ as a gift of the Spirit, a gift of freedom to the other to be and to become.

The event of Pentecost offers a paradigmatic vision of the incarnation of God's self-giving hospitality in the community of the believers as an extension of Christ's body on earth. The outpouring of the Spirit upon the body manifests God's self-sharing in welcoming all nations under heaven (Acts 2:5), through submitting his Word to the form and sound of their ethnic tongues (v. 6). Therefore, the proclamation speech of the faith community on the day of Pentecost embraces the language of the other. The divine embrace is no mere rhetorical strategy. It is a gift of divine hospitality. The Spirit invites all humanity to make its habitat in the intersociality of the Trinity. This invitation implies the host's self-giving (or surrender) to the other and not their colonization. It is an initiation of dialogue by re-spacing oneself and creating conditions for conversational inclusion of the other. It is a gesture of welcoming all foreigners, aliens, strangers literally in their own terms.

The all-inclusive multiplicity of languages employed by the Spirit in sharing the good news about "the mighty deeds of God" (v. 11) on behalf of all humanity brings together two significant dimensions of the divine hospitality. On the one hand, it demonstrates a differentiation among the ethnic groups within the multitude and pays attention to the unique singularities present within such diversity. On the other hand, the multiplicity of languages also expresses an affirmation of each separate ethnic identity and establishes the equality of each one before and in the presence of the Creator. Therefore, the self-expression of God's Word in all ethnic tongues could also be viewed as their consecration. The Word fills the words of the nations with the story of God. The languages of the people become the vocal embodiment of God's active, creative presence. The

78. Berdyaev, *Philosophy of Inequality,* p. 115.
79. Berdyaev, *Philosophy of Inequality,* p. 115.

Word translates itself into all languages while sustaining their unique distinctions. The invitation to the people to embrace a common spiritual genesis and destiny does not eliminate but sustains ethnic diversity. The divine Word reminds us (in the words of Desmond Tutu) that among humanity "God has no enemies, only family."[80]

On the day of Pentecost, the diverse multitude within the empire hear the Word of God each in their own tongue. The hearers are aware of the transitionality of empires, of their sudden rise and fall, and of their succession by other empires competing for time and space in the global history. Among the hearers are those who themselves have become displaced and dislocated as a result of the rise and fall of empires. They have become strangers in new lands, refugees and exiles under the commodifying rule of the empire. As the Spirit brings the Word of God to them in the form and sound of their mother-tongue, the one non-transitional and immutable eternal reality that "will never pass away" (Matt. 24:35) visits them in their mutability and displacement. As it indwells the mother-tongue — the single ethnic identity dimension that accompanies the listeners in their journey from the cradle to the grave — the Word of God welcomes them as a motherland in which they can find rest from their wandering and uncertainty of belonging. God becomes their eternal home, an act consistent with who he is in his self-giving from before the foundations of the world (1 Pet. 1:20).

The radical hospitality of God is further articulated in the vision of the prophesying community of faith (Acts 2:17-18). It is a vision of the future of the world as God's future. He invites and empowers humanity to speak forth its reality and content. The voices of the Spirit-saturated believers shape and form God's future for humanity by calling forth in prophetic utterance. The speakers and the Word become one incarnated creative force. This is a striking vision of the democratization of society, one in which radical emancipation and inclusivity permeate all socioeconomic strata. Sons and daughters, old and young, bound slaves and free persons join their voices in speaking forth the just future of God. They all participate in the envisioning, articulation, and realization of that future. In a self-consistent act of hospitality, God grants them ownership of his future where he is all in all. In the Spirit, they extend the hospitality of God to the other and the different (to the class-opponent, to the demographi-

---

80. Desmond Tutu, *God Has a Dream: A Vision of Hope for Our Time* (New York: Doubleday, 2004), p. 47.

cally opposite) by embracing them as a part of their own destiny. Because the Spirit mandates the body with the ministry of reconciliation (2 Cor. 5:18-19), the future becomes impossible without the voice of the other, even without the enemy.[81] Therefore, global democracy becomes an outcome of divine hospitality taking residence in a Spirit-infused humanity.

The Pentecost community, as an outcome of the socio-transformative work of the Spirit, becomes the embodiment of God's hospitality to the other within the present (Acts 2:43-47). This divine hospitality is an all-inclusive justice. It reunites economics with their spiritual foundations in the new Christ-like consciousness of the believers. The consequence is a new form of economic relationships, i.e. relationships that embrace the other and provide for the needs of the other out of one's own resources. The result is "having all things in common" (v. 44) and sharing possessions. These new economic relations set the Pentecost community apart from the economics of empire. Thus, one encounters in the midst of empire the doing of the Spirit[82] who has birthed the believers into the socio-political reality of God's kingdom and has transformed them into an extension of that reality on earth. The Spirit is the one who initiates and sustains the conditions that make this radical economic justice possible, for such justice is an outcome of one's act of worship in spirit and truth. Therefore, as was proven by the Eastern-European Marxist experiment, the secularization of this vision is destined to failure.

Breaking bread together daily (v. 46) becomes a symbolic centerpiece of living out the just socio-political reality of the kingdom. As Brian Blount points out, "The first-century, Palestinian table symbolized much more than a meal; it was a representation of community."[83] Jesus had already extended the hospitality of God to the gentiles, inviting them around

81. In his book, *No Future without Forgiveness* (New York: Doubleday, 1999), pp. 257-263, Desmond Tutu offers a reflection out of the African context of tribal conflicts, genocide and apartheid. He points to the impossibility of societal future apart from forgiveness to the ones identified as enemies.

82. Miroslav Volf, *Exclusion and Embrace: A Theological Exploration of Identity, Otherness, and Reconciliation* (Nashville: Abingdon Press, 1996), pp. 228-229. For an extensive study on the spiritual mandate of sharing possessions, see Luke T. Johnson, *Sharing Possessions: Mandate and Symbol of Faith* (Philadelphia: Fortress Press, 1981). The author discusses the topic also in relation to the event of Pentecost (p. 21).

83. Brian K. Blount, "The Apocalypse of Worship: A House of Prayer for all Nations," in *Making Room at the Table: An Invitation to Multicultural Worship*, ed. Brian K. Blount and Leonora Tubbs Tisdale (Louisville: Westminster John Knox Press, 2001), p. 20.

the table of God in the feeding of the four thousand in the region of Decapolis (Mark 8:1-10). Reflecting on this event, Blount states:

> This time loaves are multiplied for four thousand Gentiles; it is they who eat, with the table language of the Lord's Supper rippling through the story, until they are satisfied. The future, turning back on the present, has altered the entire narrative of life in the kingdom community. Jesus has offered the bread on God's table to people of all the nations.[84]

Likewise, the Pentecost community as the body of the risen Christ continues his ministry of hospitality to a starved and destitute humanity. Under the messianic anointing of the Spirit, the community of Christ is empowered daily to follow the Lord who gives his broken body so that others may live. Through the incarnational agency of the Spirit, the Pentecost community becomes an extension of this Messianic self-giving and lays down its bruised and broken body as a table where the nations can come and feast freely. After they have tasted the Lord, nothing else may satisfy their hunger. From the beginning, "it was God's intention to bring all things in heaven and on earth to a unity in Christ, and each of us participates in this great movement."[85] This process of transformation of all reality has its ultimate goal in Christ, the "omega" of all existence. The process is one of "the 'Christification' of the whole cosmos."[86] Beyond the historical horizon stands the cosmic Christ. His immanent presence calls into question the consciousness and arrangements of empire, exposing their conflict with the ultimate destiny of humanity and deconstructing their claims of ownership over its historical ends. The Spirit — the great giver of dreams and visions — empowers us to prophesy together (in spite of our differences) and to imagine God's just future. It is the very nature of a tri-une God to welcome the stranger, the wanderer, the marginalized, and the displaced in an embrace of divine hospitality. This future is not a matter of speculation. It is incarnated by the Spirit in the Pentecost community in that community's identification with Christ as the *telos* of all creation. Therefore, the community of Pentecost enters the present from the future

---

84. Blount, "The Apocalypse of Worship," p. 21.

85. Desmond Tutu, *No Future without Forgiveness,* p. 265.

86. Jürgen Moltmann, *Jesus Christ for Today's World* (Minneapolis: Fortress Press, 1994), p. 101. Moltmann picks up the idea of cosmic evolving towards Christ from Pierre Teilhard de Chardin's "Christ the Evolver" in *Christianity and Evolution,* trans. René Hague, 1st American ed. (New York: Harcourt, 1971).

of the world as the realization of its social destiny and embraces it in the hospitality of God, transfiguring the human village into the City of God. In divine hospitality we find we belong together, and this is a hopeful discovery for a world traumatized in its global compression and exhausted political imagination. It is a hope for a future of cosmopolitan hospitality — the future of humanity in the likeness of God.

Church, God, and Civil Society —
A Namibian Case Study

Christoffel Lombard

Introduction

Namibia presents an interesting case study for the role of religion in civil society. Against the background of international support, *inter alia* by the United Nations (UN), the Lutheran World Federation (LWF), and the World Council of Churches (WCC), Namibia's struggle for liberation was "globalized." The churches in Namibia, cooperating with various NGOs, supported the liberation struggle, using the Christian religion to provide moral identity, resources of resistance, and an ethical framework to deal with issues of war, racism, and liberation. After successful implementation of an international peace plan in 1989, Namibia faces new challenges. The new situation calls for a "public theology" that can deal with such issues as national reconciliation, human rights, education, and economic justice.

In assessing the role of religion and civil society in the ongoing process of liberation, it is impossible to ignore the impact of the so-called SWAPO detainee issue on the shaping of a just and democratic culture in post-apartheid Namibia.[1] The ecumenical churches stood firm in the struggle for justice and liberation in Namibia, but in the process allowed SWAPO, now the ruling party, to cover up abuses of human rights perpetrated against

---

1. "SWAPO" stands for the "South West Africa People's Organization," the major liberation movement that originated in the struggle for Namibian independence. SWAPO was formed in the 1950s and, after a 23-year guerilla war with South Africa, returned peacefully to Namibia in 1989 to win the UN-supervised elections for a Constituent Assembly.

large numbers of Namibians. Many Namibians are deeply disappointed with the churches, since they were expected to act as trustworthy custodians of truth and reconciliation but have instead displayed a lapse of integrity in the face of serious human rights problems within the national liberation movement. Even though it is common knowledge that South African hegemony, torture, murder, and abuse were running rampant in beleaguered Namibia during the 23 years of war, at least since Independence (1990), SWAPO's own culture of authoritarianism and the churches' complicity in silencing voices of critique have been systematically exposed. The time has come to face up to the shameful truth of "an international scandal."[2]

The detainee issue has become a test-case, not only for the churches' integrity and witness, but also for civil society as such. The overall Namibian handling of detainees and missing persons may become the acid test determining the nation's future.[3] The central role of civil society in solving this national dilemma is therefore the focus of this essay. The first section deals with the test case of church and civil society in Namibia. In the second part, the question about religion and civil society, specifically the theological question about God's involvement in and through civil society, is explored.

A Test Case: Religion and Civil Society in Namibia

The Namibian churches have been hailed for their strong stance against the apartheid regime.[4] Since the famous "Open Letter" of 1971, the churches fulfilled the typical role of "the voice of the voiceless," and the ec-

---

2. See P. Trewhela, "SWAPO and the Churches: An International Scandal," *Searchlight South Africa* 2, no. 3 (1991): 65.

3. The detainee issue is a result of SWAPO's unfortunate history of detaining hundreds of its own members since the late 1960s, but especially during the extremely bitter phases of the war, in the late 1970s and in the 1980s, and accusing them of being dissidents, rebels, traitors, and spies. Not only were these people detained and tortured in the most inhumane fashion, but many are still considered to be "missing persons," unaccounted for by SWAPO. After protracted investigations by the International Committee of the Red Cross into this issue, the ICRC report, issued after its search deadline of April 30, 1993, still considered 1605 out of 2161 tracing requests as unaccounted for by SWAPO, while the previous South African government still had to account for 34 persons.

4. This was especially true since the Open Letter, addressed to Prime Minister John Vorster, and signed by two Lutheran bishops of the indigenous Lutheran churches, on June 21, 1971, a letter in which these leaders clearly spelled out the churches' concern for social justice vis-à-vis the colonial masters.

umenical movement in Namibia became the carrier of an influential message of hope, justice, and freedom for Namibians. The words of the "Epistle to the Namibians," explaining to congregations all over Namibia why the churches simply had to speak out, receive increased prophetic significance in the post-independence Namibian "culture of silence,"[5] which in effect covers up the grave human rights abuses that took place under the SWAPO leadership in exile and ensures the continued firm political grip of the authoritarian leadership elite.[6] In this "Epistle," sent out by the Lutheran church leaders on June 30, 1971, the message was clear: "We are concerned about the future of this country and about the future of the various peoples who live here. . . . We feel that if we, as the church, remain silent any longer, we will become liable for the life and future of our country and its people."[7] After the Open Letter to Premier John Vorster, the mainline churches, representing more than 80% of the Namibian population, consolidated their cooperation and jointly launched an impressive ecumenical program supporting liberation and independence.[8]

In 1974 an ecumenical Christian Centre was founded in Windhoek to provide a forum for strategies for the churches' participation in the struggle for independence.[9] The Lutheran and Anglican Bishops, Auala and

5. Cf. M. Parlevliet, "Truth Commissions in Africa: the Non-Case of Namibia and the Emerging Case of Sierra Leone," in: *International Law FORUM du droit international* 2 (2000), 98-111.

6. This is also the overall drive of the analysis given in the authoritative publication of Leys and Saul on the legacy of Namibia's liberation struggle: that the same authoritarian leadership style of the "Old Guard" may be allowed to continue unabated, within the rhetoric of democracy. See C. Leys and J. S. Saul, *Namibia's Liberation Struggle. The Two-edged Sword* (London: James Currey, 1995), pp. 1-8, 196-203. Cf. also C. Leys and J. S. Saul, "Liberation without Democracy? The SWAPO Crisis of 1976," *Journal of Southern African Studies* 20, no. 1 (March 1994): 123-147.

7. "Epistle to the Namibians," quoted in P. Katjavivi, P. Frostin and K. Mbuende (editors), *Church and Liberation in Namibia* (London: Pluto Press, 1989), pp. 136-138. It is interesting to note how prominent church leaders were speaking out against "neutrality" and "silence"; cf. Z. Kameeta, "South African Illegal Presence in Namibia and the Confessing Church," in *Namibia in Perspective*, ed. G. Tötemeyer with V. Kandetu and W. Werner (Windhoek: CCN, 1987), p. 53: "A prophetic voice can never be neutral in a situation of conflict. Neutrality has in fact no place in the vocabulary of God."

8. For a detailed analysis, cf. C. Lombard, "The Role of Religion in the Reconstruction of Namibian Society: The Churches, the New Kairos and Visions of Despair and Hope," in *Reconstruction. The WCC Assembly Harare 1998 and Churches in Southern Africa*, ed. Leny Lagerwerf (Zoetermeer: Meinema, 1998), pp. 162-197.

9. See Trewhela, "SWAPO and the Churches," p. 71.

Wood, successfully took legal action against the new practice of public floggings of suspected SWAPO members and sympathizers implemented since 1974. In 1975 the Catholic Vicar General, H. Henning, issued a Statement on "Conditions for Reconciliation in SWA," which included an end to the use of violence in keeping the majority down, equal human rights for all, a fair trial for all political prisoners, and free and fair elections of the true leaders.[10] Father Heinz Hunke and Justin Ellis (of the Christian Centre) published a booklet, *Torture: A Cancer in Our Society.*[11] What is striking about all these early examples of "church action," or what today would be called "public theology," is that they were actually part of what would now be seen as "civil society action" by individual Christians or small groups of concerned Christians.

After the establishment of the Council of Churches in Namibia (CCN) in 1978, various statements were sent to the South African Prime Minister.[12] After the failure of the 1978 initiatives to implement UN Security Council Resolution 435 and the South African answer of "internal" elections and an "interim" government, the CCN suffered in-house division, sparked by the escalating violence of the struggle for liberation and the ghosts of Marxist ideology observed within SWAPO.[13] Against many odds, the successful implementation of the UN Resolution 435 in 1989 supported by the ecumenical churches and various civil society groups brought independence to Namibia. Such prophetic support for initiatives, of which numerous originated "outside of the church," became crucial for

10. See G. Tötemeyer, *South West Africa/Namibia* (Randburg: Fokus Suid Publishers, 1977), pp. 245-248. Cf. *The Green and the Dry Wood. Documentation on the Roman Catholic Church, Vicariate of Windhoek, and the Namibian Socio-Political Situation, 1971-1981* (Windhoek: The Oblates of Mary Immaculate, 1983), for an overview of the contributions of the Roman Catholic Church towards the ecumenical agenda of liberation.

11. Cf. H. Hunke, ed., *LWF Documentation, The Church and the Namibian Quest for Independence*, no. 22/23 (July 1987): 75-79.

12. Cf. the declaration of October 4, 1978 (in H. Hunke, *LWF Documentation*, pp. 35-45), after SWAPO's acceptance of the Western peace plan for Namibia: "At this decisive time and mindful of the ongoing suffering of our people, we call upon you, Mr. Prime Minister, to accept this opportunity for peace under the guarantees provided by the United Nations. We feel compelled to caution that should your government not make use of this opportunity, you will be held responsible worldwide for the escalation of an unavoidable, terrible and tragic war in this country." Ecumenical solidarity was strengthened through the Southern African Catholic Bishops' Conference's *Report on Namibia* (published in May 1982), containing details of South African atrocities.

13. See P. Steenkamp, "The Churches," in: Leys & Saul, *Namibia's Liberation Struggle*, pp. 97-120.

what many Christians saw as part of God's ongoing agenda of justice and peace. Both the churches and civil society paid a heavy price for these courageous involvements.[14]

The Namibian churches questioned the legitimacy of South Africa's actions, came to the aid of victims of state action, and courageously took the ultimate step as well: "not just to bandage the victims under the wheel, but to put a spoke in the wheel itself through direct political action."[15] They broke the silence with a prophetic voice, serving as an avant-garde movement for social justice and political liberation. Through their contacts in the LWF and the WCC, the ecumenical churches in Namibia created an international platform for the Namibian cause, even though, influenced by the authoritarian culture of SWAPO, the churches, unfortunately, developed the same top-down leadership patterns.[16]

Would the churches keep up the same agendas of pursuing justice and human rights after independence?[17] In their testimony during hearings on racism, the Namibian church leaders testified as follows: "The churches do not believe naively that SWAPO will bring a utopia to Namibia. They hope to continue the positive relationships which have been developed. However, there is also a realization that, as the churches in other parts of Africa have shown, the churches may also have a prophetic role to play in opposition to any new tyranny that may emerge."[18] In view of the story that has to be told here, we must state that similar challenges to the churches remain largely unanswered. Are the churches who, in the

14. See Colin Winter's description of the harassment, including arson, in: *The Breaking Process* (London: SCM, 1981), pp. 48-50; cf. also the privately published press clippings by the BWS Movement (Windhoek: BWS, 1996-1998).

15. Kameeta, as quoted in *Namibia in Perspective,* p. 212. Steenkamp, "The Churches," p. 94, also presents a useful typification: "There were three distinct facets of the church's role in opposition to the authoritarian regime: institutional, ideological and operational."

16. See Steenkamp, "The Churches," pp. 107-111; also Trewhela, "SWAPO and the Churches," pp. 67-72.

17. The Namibian church historian, Nambala, makes interesting remarks on this challenge: "The ministry of the church . . . is not caged. It is directed to all people of God, irrespective of their political affiliation. Moreover, the church is a 'thorn in the flesh' to those who love injustice and violate human rights. The church . . . indicates how SWAPO is 'godless' or 'godly.'" . . . "It is important for the church to be constant and faithful. . . . The hope is that the church in Namibia will in all situations continue to be a voice of the voiceless and the oppressed." Cf. S. Nambala, *History of the Church in Namibia,* published by *The Lutheran Quarterly* (editor K. Olson, 1994), pp. 159, 169.

18. As documented in Katjavivi, *Church and Liberation in Namibia,* p. 190.

words of Katjavivi, "shared the suffering and the guilt of spilt blood in defeating the previous system of injustice" now "judging the revolution fearlessly as to its outcome," taking the further steps towards nation-building, and "reconciling the aggressor and the aggressed under the scrutiny of truth and justice?"[19]

Indeed, during those struggle years, the churches and "organized religion" played a major role as part of a vibrant civil society, which included non-government organizations such as the Namibian Peace Plan 435 Study and Contact Group, the Ai-Gams initiative for peace, the National Society for Human Rights, and NANGOV, the umbrella organisation for all Namibian NGOs. However, after the joint victory, the CCN was not only immediately saddled with the challenging task of "Repatriation, Resettlement, and Reconstruction" of almost 50,000 returnees (delegated to the "RRR Committee");[20] it also had to face the severe challenges of a new role and status in a liberated society. After five years of painful reorientation, the year 1996 saw the inevitable implementation of drastic pruning, resulting in a CCN with a core staffing of 10 (instead of more than 70) full-time members, and only a handful of "facilitating" clusters remaining. In spite of several praiseworthy initiatives, e.g. on democracy, a human rights culture, and national reconciliation,[21] and addressing issues such as children's rights, drug abuse, AIDS, disabled persons, and the ideological abuse of religion by right-wing political groups,[22] the churches after independence could hardly manage to move beyond fruitful debate at conferences, with scarce effective implementation of good recommendations. The need for urgent clarification of the highly ambiguous relationship with the SWAPO government also became more than evident.[23] This trend of moving away from rather than developing a public theology has simply continued.

To add to the woes of the CCN, the year 1996 squarely placed the ne-

19. These are some of the conditions set by Katjavivi himself. Cf. *Church and Liberation in Namibia*, p. 24.

20. Cf. the article on the work of the RRR Committee in *CCN Messenger*, Windhoek, August 1991, p. 16.

21. Cf. the contributions in *Together in Jesus Christ* (Report of CCN Conference, March 27-31, 1990); "Proceedings of the CCN-Roundtable Consultation," in *CCN Documentation* (Windhoek, 1990), pp. 20-32, as well as *CCN Messenger*, September and October 1991, the focus of which was "national reconciliation."

22. *CCN Documentation*, March 1991: "Focus on Right-wing Religion in Southern Africa."

23. Cf. Proceedings of the Ninth Ordinary General Meeting of the CCN, July 12-14, 1994, pp. 30-45.

glected detainee issue once again on the churches' agenda, exposing cracks in the edifice of "independent Namibia." The policy of national reconciliation came under pressure of the tests of truthfulness and consistency. Indecisiveness and uncertainty, even blatant differences about the way forward, seem to have replaced the conviction and courage of yesteryear. With the evidence that has become available since independence, it simply cannot be denied that the Namibian churches and their ecumenical allies such as the LWF and the WCC received details of disappearances, detentions, and torture within SWAPO from impeccable sources, already in the mid-seventies.

Remarkable, for example, is the very clear language of Rev. Salatiel Ailonga, the first Namibian pastor-in-exile, who had to flee Zambia after taking up the detention issue with the SWAPO leadership, as addressed to Bishop Leonard Auala, in a letter dated May 24, 1977: "As you know, since 1976 there was a conflict among the Namibians in Zambia. This led to many members in SWAPO and my Chaplaincy being imprisoned on the request of SWAPO's leadership. First, eleven leading members of the Party and Youth League, then forty-eight from the front, talking on behalf of the soldiers, and later on over one thousand Namibians disappeared. In the wake of this I had to leave Zambia and since June 1976 I have been staying in Finland." After giving Bishop Auala many details, especially about who were involved and where they were imprisoned, Rev. Ailonga urgently requested his Bishop to find a way of addressing these issues in the ecumenical world. The rest of Ailonga's letter proved to be visionary in its prophetic clarity:

> According to the proofs and my knowledge, this is not a purely political case or internal SWAPO affair. It is a case concerning the wellbeing of the Namibians and their human rights, which touches the church and its responsibility to a great extent. The imprisoned in Tanzania and Zambia are members of all churches, including Lutherans, Anglicans, and Roman Catholics. The reason for the imprisonment is not yet known to the world, and there is no legal ground to hold people without trial. . . . There is a reliable report that at Mboroma camp in August last year many people were shot at, many were wounded and some died. . . . In matters like these, which may have the most serious effect for the future, the church should not be silent. All these thousand may be lost within a short time and never to return to Namibia. But there are thousands of families, friends and relatives of these peo-

ple, and their voice will be demanding an explanation. What will the answer of the church be? I would say that in every leadership, church or state, the leaders have to be led and shown the truth without fear or partiality. That shows not enmity, but love for the leaders you correct, because you care about what he is doing. If you as leaders of the church in Namibia will fail to go with love into the question in SWAPO, which is a small group, how will you be able to cope with the problems which will arise on a much larger basis within a free Namibia, be it under the leadership of SWAPO or someone else? I request you in all humility to take this matter seriously and prevent more vain bloodshed.[24]

Parallel to Rev. Ailonga's letter (which was also sent to the President of the Evangelical Lutheran Church in Namibia, and top functionaries of the LWF) are the many occasions on which another well-known pastor-in-exile, Pastor Siegfried Groth, gave even more detailed accounts of such events to church leaders from Namibia and abroad.[25] Confidential documents of Pastor Groth were included in the shock publication by Erica, Attie, and Hewat Beukes, *Namibia, a Struggle Betrayed*,[26] in which the ruthless suppression of the attempts by some SWAPO Youth League and PLAN[27] cadres towards democratic reform and consolidation of the struggle, by the "Old Guard" SWAPO leadership, is revealed. The publication of these documents in 1986 broke the silence on the open secret of SWAPO's scandalous handling of criticism and dissent once and for all.[28]

During the late 1980s a civil society action group, the Committee of Parents, was formed to act on behalf of the parents and relatives of "missing persons," and to seriously challenge SWAPO, the churches, and the international allies of Namibia's liberation struggle to address the human rights abuses within SWAPO. This shameful truth, however, could simply not be faced at that stage. It was underplayed, ignored, and even opposed

24. This letter (now in safe-keeping, with many similar documents of Rev. Ailonga, in the National Archives in Windhoek) is an excellent example of the Divine prophetic spirit at work in an individual who understands the structural impact of the Gospel in the world.

25. For details of Groth's "revelations" in the seventies and eighties, see Trewhela, "SWAPO and the Churches," and Steenkamp, "The Churches."

26. A. Beukes et al., *Namibia. A Struggle Betrayed* (Rehoboth: own publication, 1986).

27. The People's Liberation Army of Namibia.

28. Steenkamp gives a useful summary of the "detainee crisis," and the attempts by Erica and Attie Beukes, as employees of the CCN, to get the churches and ecumenical world to react effectively ("The Churches," pp. 104-107).

energetically in lieu of another "truth": "Some church leaders, while aware of SWAPO's abuses, believed that only SWAPO was capable of bringing peace, and that any public action by them on the detainees issue would have weakened the movement fatally, leaving the South African supported Party, the DTA, to win any UN-sponsored elections. They were not prepared to allow this to happen for the sake of exposing a few 'bad apples' in SWAPO. Their conviction that SWAPO and liberation were inseparable led them to sacrifice their religious principles on the altar of political expediency."[29] Once this political agenda was endorsed by the churches and other international partners, it became more and more difficult for them to admit and to confess their complicity and to raise a new, critical voice. That is why the same pattern of discrediting efforts such as those of the Committee of Parents has befallen similar critical voices and movements up to this day.[30]

Fortunately, due to a convergence of important factors,[31] the quick turn of events leading to the implementation of the UN Peace Plan in 1989 also saw the return of at least 200 of the so-called detained "spies" who publicly verified the allegations of human rights abuses in SWAPO with gruesome details of their fate at the hand of the SWAPO security system.[32] After meeting with a group of detainees and SWAPO leaders (on August 23-24, 1989), the CCN Executive issued a cautious statement, conceding on the one hand that many of the victims of the vicious cycle of wars were innocent, but on the other hand also blaming apartheid for the suspicion and distrust that led to the destruction of the unity within the liberation movement. While stressing the need for forgiveness as the basis of nation-

29. Cf. Steenkamp, "The Churches," p. 107. (DTA is the abbreviation for the "Democratic Thurnhalle Alliance.")

30. A telling example of this was the way in which Mr. Samson Ndeikwila, first chairperson of the Breaking the Wall of Silence (BWS) Movement, was asked to choose between his involvement in BWS and keeping his job as Coordinator of the CCN Cluster for Faith and Justice. Ironically, Mr. Ndeikwila became chairperson of an effective civil society organization promoting democracy at the grass roots level: Forum for the Future.

31. For background, see the analysis in *Namibia Peace Plan 435 or Society under Siege*, published by the NPP 435 Group (editors: C. Lombard and B. O'Linn, Windhoek: NPP 435, 1987).

32. SWAPO was forced to release more than 200 detainees from the "dungeons" of Lubango in Angola, on April 19, 1989. Their testimonies sent shock waves through pro-SWAPO circles, but it was the press conference of the first group of 153 on July 6, 1989 in Windhoek, where some of them showed their torture scars, that forced the churches, and other SWAPO allies, to break their silence.

building, the CCN leaders "failed to acknowledge their own failure to respond earlier,"[33] thus endorsing a policy of reconciliation in which confession of guilt seemed unnecessary.

These double standards by the churches and international partners of SWAPO made it possible for a deadly pattern of actively allowing the "silent complicity agenda" to develop, preventing public scrutiny of SWAPO's own human rights abuses and avoiding a true confrontation with the darker side of the Namibian struggle for liberation.[34] The detainee issue became a hotly debated election campaign topic. The Parents Committee and the newly formed Political Consultative Council (PCC) pursued the demands of justice as civil society action groups and put tremendous pressure on SWAPO and the churches.[35] All these efforts, combined with the public outrage in the Namibian press, resulted in statements from *inter alia* the Green Party in Germany, the UN and the German Churches (EKD), condemning the human rights abuses of SWAPO in exile. Here again, the almost spontaneous formation of civil society action groups, leading society to a raised level of moral and political consciousness, played a major role to break the plot of silence.

Typically, however, a publication of Pastor Groth, as part of a German church documentation series,[36] giving a clear picture of the complicity of the churches in promoting the deadly "culture of silence," was imme-

33. Steenkamp, "The Churches," p. 107.

34. This deadly pattern was revealed when SWAPO vehemently denied the shock revelations by ex-detainees who were rescued by the Red Cross from Angola, but left the uncomfortable task to Mr. Gurirab (soon to become Minister of Foreign Affairs) to admit publicly that "the issue of the former detainees was a painful subject affecting virtually every family in Namibia," that it would not go away and could not be ignored, that the time for dialogue on this painful issue had arrived. "At the end of the day we will have to sit around the fire and take inventories: who is alive, who is dead, how did it all happen? As a SWAPO leader, I will never defend the humiliation and suffering of torture. If the allegations are true, I apologize to the victims and to their parents and pledge to you now that the SWAPO leadership will take the necessary steps to bring those involved to book." Unfortunately, this promise was never fulfilled.

35. Ex-detainees, working together in the PCC, issued detailed statements and documents, giving grim details of torture, lists of missing persons, and names of torturers and high-ranking SWAPO officials who knew about or were actively engaged in torture practices. Cf. *A Report to the Namibian People*, Windhoek, 1989; also D. Niddrie, "The Detentions," *Work in Progress*, September/October 1989, pp. 21-23.

36. *Menschenrechtsverletzungen in der namibischen Exil — SWAPO, die Verantwortung der Kirchen*, published by the Vereinigte Evangelische Mission in Wuppertal, September 1989, just before the elections in Namibia.

diately attacked by church colleagues from Germany: "Groth's statements did not support reconciliation, but division, suspicion and non-peace. With this publication he does not only discredit the party that, for decades, has carried the main burden of the liberation struggle, but also the churches in Namibia, who expect definite signs of solidarity from us."[37] Looking at such a statement from the perspective of the trinitarian God's work in history, one cannot avoid asking: what about the other kind of solidarity that forms the heart of the gospel, the solidarity with the victims of the power games of the powerful, the solidarity with the marginalized?[38] What about respect for the truth? Whatever the motivations and rationalizations at the time, SWAPO was let off the hook, and allowed to continue its authoritarian and uncompromising culture and to take over the governing responsibility without having accounted for its own human rights abuses.[39] For reasons still unknown, the church leaders decided at independence to leave the arena of public theology and civil society involvement and to revert to a model of church and state "separation" and, at most, "cooperation" in terms of which the church deals primarily with the so-called spiritual aspects of life and the state runs the practical-political side of things.

After winning the elections comfortably, the detainee issue was buried by SWAPO, and the notorious "Butcher of Lubango," the person in charge of the torture and disappearances of SWAPO members, Jesus Solo-

---

37. "Siegfried Groth Taken to Task," *Namibian,* October 20, 1989. The Green Party in Germany, however, criticized SWAPO's statement of July 7, 1989, saying, "It does not contain a single word of self-criticism," and asked for immediate action on four crucial points: (1) that SWAPO provide reliable official information on whether — and if so, how many — prisoners were still being detained in SWAPO camps, and that these should immediately be released, (2) that an independent commission of investigation be set up, as promised, without delay, (3) that the responsible persons be identified and called to account as soon as possible (including the security chief, Jesus Hauala), and (4) that the victims of torture and the members of their families be rehabilitated and given adequate compensation. See the *Namibian,* August 21, 1989.

38. Cf. W. Wink, *Violence and Non-violence in South Africa: Jesus' Third Way* (Philadelphia: New Society Publishers, 1987).

39. It is this culture that made it possible for Mr. Nujoma, who under pressure of "Constitutionalism" had to step down after his third term in office as President, to keep control of the appointments made by SWAPO, and to currently launch a renewed campaign to return to the Presidency, after the term of President Pohamba is over. In spite of formal structures of "democracy," Namibia is tightly controlled by a small band of loyalists orchestrated by Nujoma, similar to the rule of Mugabe in Zimbabwe. Cf. the *Mail and Guardian,* 16-22 March 2007 ("Play it again, Sam").

mon Hauala, was appointed as Commander of the Namibian Army in October 1990, as part of "national reconciliation." At that stage the protests of the CCN fell on deaf ears: the established style of "discussing" such issues with the SWAPO leadership had no effect.[40] The churches were part and parcel of an international scandal which cannot be rationalized.[41]

Just when it seemed as if Namibians had accepted to live cynically with all the skeletons of war in the national cupboard, another book by pastor Siegfried Groth stirred up emotions, memories, and discussions. In *Namibia — the Wall of Silence* (1995) Groth simply told the stories of approximately one hundred SWAPO detainees or dissidents, their struggles to survive the SWAPO security system, and the desperation of people seemingly forgotten by the outside world.[42] My review of the German edition of the book in the *Windhoek Observer* of June 24, 1995 was given a provocative caption by the editor: "Shattering SWAPO's Wall of Silence," which inspired the English title of the book and sparked intense public interest. When the English translation became available towards the end of 1995, bookstores could not cope with the demand, and ex-detainees discussed the idea that the CCN should be approached to launch the book, using the opportunity to publicly confess the churches' guilt in this sad chapter and simultaneously initiate a process of national reconciliation and healing.[43]

At the Annual General Meeting of the CCN, early in December 1995, high-ranking officials of the CCN openly admitted that they had been misled through the SWAPO propaganda, such as enforced videotaped "spy confessions." In mid-January 1996 the CCN received a formal request, signed by forty-two ex-detainees, to launch the Groth book, which was described as "just the tip of an iceberg." The book's revelations could be sup-

40. As with the Dutch Reformed Church's support of apartheid, the official version of a new "civil religion" could not break through an ideology of self-interest, and could not liberate people to a culture of truth and justice.

41. Trewhela, "SWAPO and the Churches."

42. S. Groth, *Namibia. The Wall of Silence* (Wuppertal: Peter Hammer, 1995), translation of *Namibische Passion*, same publisher, 1995; also translated into Afrikaans by J. H. and J. Hunter, as: *Namibië. Die muur van swye* (Windhoek: EIN Publications, 1996).

43. At that stage I personally thought and propagated the idea that it could be as straightforward as having a big symbolic meeting (presided over by the President of SWAPO and e.g. Bishop Kleopas Dumeni), where honest admissions about the atrocities of the war were made by SWAPO and the churches' complicity was confessed openly and publicly; a meeting where the victims were offered apologies at a national ritual of forgiveness and reconciliation.

plemented with many living testimonies as to the hell experienced in Lubango and other SWAPO detention centres. They also asked for an audience with the CCN Executive, to ensure that these church leaders were in a position to make a well-informed decision. On February 19, 1996 the CCN Executive issued a statement, explaining that the CCN had decided not to launch the book but to organize a national conference "somewhere between May and July 1996" to address "the serious issues raised by the author of the book . . . more fully." Ordinary members of churches and the public at large were advised to read the book for themselves. Sadly, however, the CCN Executive never met those who requested a hearing. The promised conference also never took place.

In the meantime a new civil society movement, the Breaking the Wall of Silence Movement (BWS), was growing rapidly. BWS actively engaged in the ensuing public debate through the media. It pledged to contribute towards the success of the proposed church conference and challenged the negative utterances by some Bishops about the Groth book.[44]

Suddenly the nation realized that Namibia was confronted with important unfinished agendas. A nationally transmitted TV programme which included a very frank interview with members of our BWS Committee and the General Secretary of the CCN at the time (Rev. Ngeno Nakamhela) resulted in a surprise appearance on TV the next evening by the President of Namibia, Dr. Sam Nujoma. He attacked the Groth book as "false history," speaking forcefully as "the President of SWAPO and the Commander-in-Chief of the Namibia Defence armed force." His long speech was characterized by a scathing personal attack on the person of Pastor Groth and the assessment that "Pastor Groth's agenda will only lead to bloodshed in our country," something that would not be tolerated.[45] He also construed "Mr. Lombard" as someone "assigned to work as an apostle of apartheid to ensure that Bantu education and white domination were perpetuated in Namibia," who "dutifully served that apartheid system" and had to remember that it was because of the policy of national reconcilia-

44. BWS media release, February 29, 1996. Bishop Dumeni, for example, stated that the Groth book was "one-sided," "not written on the assignment of the CCN," "even written by an outsider," and was "disturbing the policy of reconciliation in the country." It soon transpired that selected church leaders were summoned for "talks" with President Sam Nujoma, the content of which remains unknown.

45. This ignores the fact that Groth was banned from Namibia by South Africa for almost seventeen years exactly because of his involvement with SWAPO and Namibia's liberation struggle.

tion that he was not dismissed from his work at the university.[46] When I reacted in the media with a personal letter to the president, asking whether he had no respect for the truth and pointing out that he had also not addressed the real issue at stake: the truth about SWAPO atrocities against Namibian compatriots, a heated debate was sparked in the media.[47] When the SWAPO general secretary reacted with even stronger language than his president, again playing the politics of fear-mongering against "irresponsible, unpatriotic elements and foreign remnants of fascism, and apartheid," an enormous reaction broke loose in the media. It was evident that SWAPO had miscalculated the national mood on these issues and that the personal attacks were counter-productive. In a show of civil courage, people simply spoke their minds. Even the SWAPO-affiliated umbrella body for NGOs, NANGOV, responded critically.[48] The National Society for Human Rights (NSHR) energetically took up the agenda, responding with various to-the-point media statements, such as "Civil war against the truth?"[49] A debate on the merits of the Groth book was also sparked in German church circles.[50]

Amid these hectic debates the BWS Movement organized a very successful launch of the Groth book. The book was translated into Afrikaans

46. These words came as quite a shock and surprise for many, since Namibians know that I was one of the few Namibian whites who travelled to Lusaka and Stockholm to discuss the implementation of UN Resolution 435 with the SWAPO leadership (including the president), and who helped launch Namibia Peace Plan (NPP) 435, a group that campaigned successfully, nationally and internationally, for the scrupulous implementation of the "Namibia Peace Plan 435."

47. In an "Open Letter to the President," of March 9, 1996, published in all the Namibian papers, I pleaded for truthfulness for the sake of true reconciliation: "I urge you to have SWAPO participate in the CCN conference and to trust God and 'the way of truth' to help us clear this serious hurdle to real reconciliation. If we fail here, the tradition of fear and authoritarianism will simply continue in our beloved Namibia. Then all SWAPO's good work would have been in vain."

48. For selected documents reflecting the enormous national debate, see the two documents prepared by BWS: *BWS Statements and Clippings: February-April 1996* and *BWS Statements and Clippings: August-November 1996*.

49. See the following releases of the NSHR: *Namibia: Human Rights Report 1995* (February 12, 1996), "Breaking the Wall of Silence: Reaction to Bishop Dumeni's Remarks" (February 28, 2006), and "SWAPO'S Book of the Dead" (September 1996).

50. See M. Braun, "Siegfried Groth: Namibische Passion," *Junge Kirche* 4 (1996): 251; R. Kössler, "Bricht die Mauer des Schweigens?" *Afrika Süd* 2 (1996): 23-25. H. Weiland, "'Namibische Passion.' Anmerkungen zu einem Buch über die Menschenrechtsverletzungen der SWAPO während des Befreiungskampfs," *Afrika Süd* 4 (1995): 28-29.

in record time, and all English copies were time and again sold out almost immediately upon arrival. An Oshivambo translation was published by the Ecumenical Institute for Namibia, which was also responsible for the Afrikaans one.[51] After the book launch, the detainee issue also attracted international attention: the BBC made several in-depth broadcasts, and German, British, South African, and American papers and church magazines published critical articles, covering the developing debate.[52] Without the initial, small group of determined people who first met to stand by the victims of detention and torture, there would have been no "Breaking the Wall of Silence movement," or any media attention to the plight of these victims of history.

A new twist to the detainee saga became apparent: that the CCN itself was divided on the viability of its own proposed conference. Instead of the conference, 1997 would be dedicated as "A Year of God's Grace" in Namibia. An interesting development also came on Heroes Day (August 26, 1996), when SWAPO launched a book, *Their Blood Waters Our Freedom,* containing the names of almost 8000 "heroes of the liberation struggle" who paid the ultimate price. Unfortunately, however, the book is controversial because of glaring omissions and repetitions, obvious mistakes, inclusion of the names of people who were previously branded as spies and traitors, and failure to shed light on the statistics of the Red Cross.[53]

In spite of some sympathetic utterances, even in Parliament, by leading figures in government, SWAPO never followed up on any suggestions to participate in any national initiative to address the detainee issue, and the churches never held their promised conference on reconciliation.[54] Directly

51. Initially critical questions were asked at the University of Namibia, where the Ecumenical Institute for Namibia (EIN), of which I was the director, took responsibility for the publication of the book in Afrikaans (and later also in Oshivambo). Academic freedom was restored after the EIN Board re-affirmed its endorsement of the project.

52. Particularly influential was the in-depth article by David Miller in *The Lutheran,* a church magazine with a circulation of a quarter million: "Tortured by the Past: Can Namibian Lutherans Free Themselves from Their Liberators?" (July, 1996).

53. See especially the media statements of the NSHR, dated September 4, 1996, and calling the "Book of the Dead" a massive cover-up, and of the BWS, dated October 29, 1996, in which they called on SWAPO to apologize to the victims of their human rights abuses and to meet such victims under the auspices of neutral mediators. On October 11, 1996 the Prime Minister admitted that the SWAPO book contained mistakes and also regretted that some innocent people might have been branded as spies. For the "statistics," cf. note 3.

54. There was, for example, a suggestion by the Deputy Speaker of Parliament, Dr. Zephaniah Kameeta, a well-known church leader during the struggle, that the SWAPO book

after a call for dialogue rather than confrontation by the CCN president, however, SWAPO officially called for a boycott of any conferences organized by the CCN. When the new general secretary of the CCN, Rev. Nangula Kathindi, from the smaller but politically active Anglican Church, agreed to meet a delegation from the BWS, renewed hope sprang up that eventually the CCN would honor its undertaking of directly dealing with the detainee issue, especially when the CCN officially asked BWS to prepare a document stating what its expectations were from the churches regarding this issue. However, when the BWS asked a committee consisting of Mr. Samson Ndeikwila and myself in 1997 to draw up the document: *What do you want from us? CCN asks BWS*, we never received any official response from the CCN to the detailed twelve-page document. It became quite clear that the ecumenical body of churches in Namibia had to deal with too many different voices and agendas, and that it would not easily develop the same kind of prophetic involvement it previously showed in the struggle for liberation.

Whether Namibia will eventually go through a formal Truth and Reconciliation process, as South Africa did, remains to be seen. Since the debate was sparked in 1996 through a book by a theologian and a civil society group started by Christians who drew together critical voices from civil society, not much has changed in the positions of the two traditional poles of "a Christian society": "the state" (in this case: embodied by the SWAPO government) and "the church" (embodied by the Council of Churches in Namibia). Within civil society, however, the spirits of change have been working tirelessly and courageously. The BWS has kept its course, pushing for a meeting between SWAPO and the detainees, and for a just and honorable solution to the dilemma. The CCN pursued 1997 as "the Year of God's Grace" but without the promised conference on reconciliation. Towards the end of the year, African church leaders met in Windhoek for a pre-assembly meeting in preparation for the Harare WCC Meeting in 1998. A strong delegation saw Pres. Nujoma and spoke with him about the detainee issue. He took offence, and they offered help, but, again, nothing came from this initiative.

---

be corrected where necessary and supplemented with a "Book Two," supplied by South Africa and the opposition parties. He proposed that the "revised book" should be supervised and published by a government body and should be "launched at a solemn occasion of forgiveness and reconciliation and the brave people of Namibia will close this chapter of our liberation history in unity" (cf. the *Namibian,* October 16, 1996). Mr. Nahas Angula (currently serving as Prime Minister) made a similar suggestion for a solution to the present impasse. Cf. the *Windhoek Observer,* October 12, 1996.

Some politicians and human rights activists have been toying with the idea of an International Tribunal; others have promoted the idea of forcing the opposition parties and South Africa to deliver a "Volume Two" of "missing persons." The second chairperson of the BWS Movement, Mr. Reinhardt Gertze, was also elected to the post of general secretary of the break-away party from SWAPO, the Congress of Democrats, in 1999 and since then has spoken on the detainee issue quite frequently and forcefully in Parliament, trying to solicit support for a political solution to the self-inflicted wound of SWAPO. In recent times, the BWS Movement has dwindled, due to a lack of funding, but is still keeping the issue on the national agenda through its sheer existence, meetings, publications, and a public display each year on Human Rights Day.

A significant development parallel to, but quite independent from, the work done in the ecumenical circles or the BWS Movement, was the establishment of a Project for the Study of Violence and Reconciliation, another civil society project. It was designed initially to counsel victims and their relatives and to prepare sworn legal statements. Since 2000, this initiative developed into the PEACE Center, with a focus on trauma counselling but also peace education and empowerment of people traumatized by, *inter alia,* the Namibian war. Thus, again, instead of the churches, who have the infrastructures and the mandate to deal with these critical issues, it was left to committed Christians and other people of goodwill to develop structures within civil society to handle these problems.[55]

People who deal with the painful and ironical details of prolonged struggles for reconciliation and justice frequently revert to the well-known slogan "aluta continua," the struggle continues! In the second, more reflective part of this article I wish to reflect on the kind of public theology that may contain ingredients to sustain such continuing struggles. What is needed is a kind of theology that is not content with being too "private," church-bound, heaven-oriented, priestly, or overawed by sin and evil, but is directed towards the future and the kingdom of God, and thus prophetically also towards the state and power and society at large, a theology that fully includes the initiative of human beings in God's work for reconciliation, peace, and justice. To indicate the availability of such a brand of theology, I shall give a very brief sketch of one such

---

55. I am thankful for the information provided to me by the current Director of the PEACE Center, Dr. Gudrun Kober, on the new emphasis on peace education and empowerment of all traumatized people in the aftermath of the war.

"theology of hope," the trinitarian-eschatological theology of A. A. van Ruler (1908-1970).[56]

Trinity and Civil Society — A Few Theological Pointers

In this reflective part I wish to link two perspectives: first, a brief reflection on the role of *religion* in contemporary society, specifically civil society, and, second, the *theological* question about God and civil society. It is interesting to discover how much has been written in recent times about the link between religious conviction and civil society action. In this regard we can even speak of civil society initiatives, many of them religiously inspired, as new global news-breaking phenomena, such as the Jubilee 2000 campaign and the mass protests at G8 meetings on ecological issues and the world economy. To cover the first perspective, I shall briefly test the religious language and motivation evident in the make-up and work of the BWS as a typical civil society action group against *contemporary theories of religion and civil society.* Then I wish to go a step further, by exploring a Christian understanding of history *theologically,* specifically from the perspective of the trinitarian God. Such an approach believes that it is indeed the trinitarian God who works historically in and through his creatures and who binds together and consummates "all these initiatives" (of church and state, of individual and civil society) in what is metaphorically called "the kingdom of God." Within such a framework a new sort of public theology becomes not only possible, but also necessary and viable: a theology re-energizing and applying biblical concepts in the public square.

Our first perspective thus deals with *religion* and civil society. Let us revisit the Namibian case under the caption of the role of religion in the motivation and message of the BWS. In working towards *reconciliation* after an atrocious war, concepts such as *truth* and *justice* are obviously of paramount importance, as was also evident in the South African example of the Truth and Reconciliation Commission. As we have learned from Desmond Tutu, *forgiveness,* seen in a Christian context, is not dependent on *confession* or apology, but *reconciliation* is incomplete without both. A process of reconciliation cannot seek revenge and cannot endlessly be opening cans of worms. It also cannot tolerate easy solutions, such as

---

56. For his very extensive oeuvre, cf. *Inventaris van het archief van Prof. Dr. Arnold Albert van Ruler (1908-1970)*, ed. E. M. L. Kempers (Utrecht Universiteitsbiblioteek, 1997).

sweeping the truth about atrocities under the carpet of history. It will look for a long-term solution, a permanent *healing* of the wounds, and lasting *peace*.[57] However, as also emphasised repeatedly by Tutu, wounds can not be healed if their existence is not acknowledged, confessed.[58]

In the case of extreme human rights abuses, like in South Africa and Namibia, the truth of Richard Neuhaus's insistence on the impossibility of the modern dream of "neutrality," of a "naked public square," becomes quite evident.[59] In Namibia, after independence, the SWAPO movement did not tolerate any other "truth" than their own version of "reconciliation," which meant nothing less than a cheap policy of "forgive and forget." The mediation efforts by the CCN, after the return of 150-plus detainees, in July 1989, were swept aside and replaced by the rhetoric of what had in fact become a new "civil religion." The truth of the new policymakers was duly blessed by the bishops of the mainline churches (who could easily be called in for "consultations" by the powers to be in State House — very much like the comfortable state-church arrangement between the National Party and the Dutch Reformed Church in the days of Apartheid

57. Daan Bronkhorst of Amnesty International has illustrated, in his analysis of similar problems elsewhere in the world (in Chile, Argentina, Peru, Philippines, Guatemala, etc.), that all conciliation processes have four crucial elements that need to be addressed: *investigation* (through which the truth is established), *mediation* (which needs grace, preparedness to reconcile, apologize, and forgive), *adjudication* (which could mean legal action, to let justice be done to victims), and *settlement* (which seeks redress, retribution, and restoration of peace). It is not difficult to link these "secular" concepts to profound Biblical and theological parallel concepts. It is interesting to see how the four elements of Psalm 85:11 are all part and parcel of a truthful process of reconciliation, as depicted by Bronkhorst: "Love and truthfulness meet together, justice and peace kiss each other." Cf. D. Bronkhorst, *Truth and Reconciliation. Obstacles and Opportunities for Human Rights* (Amsterdam: Amnesty International, 1995), chapter 6, "The model of reconciliation."

58. This article does not deal with the intricacies of a "theology of reconciliation," but in the Southern African context many valuable lessons have been learnt (of which a few are merely summarized here), and a sizeable body of literature has grown out of the trauma of apartheid and civil war. Cf. the publications of Desmond Tutu, John de Gruchy, Charles Villa-Vicencio, and colleagues of the Institute for Justice and Reconciliation in Cape Town, and many others.

59. Richard J. Neuhaus, *The Naked Public Square*, 2nd ed. (Grand Rapids: Eerdmans, 1984), p. 80: "Such a religious evacuation of the public square cannot be sustained, either in concept or in practice. When religion in any traditional or recognizable form is excluded from the public square, it does not mean that the public square is in fact naked. . . . When recognizable religion is excluded, the vacuum will be filled by *ersatz* religion, by religion bootlegged into public space under other names."

South Africa). This is the new truth that filled the public square with a new state theology, supported by a new church theology, as famously analyzed in the South African context by the Kairos Document.[60]

Namibia was Christianized by Lutheran missionaries from the Wuppertal Mission in Germany (in the central and southern parts) and the Finnish mission (in the northern regions). During the struggle for liberation, the mainline churches united in the Council of Churches in Namibia, where Lutherans, Catholics, and Anglicans took the lead. However, after independence the prophetic voice demanding real *reconciliation* "here and now" fell silent, as though someone had suddenly remembered that the Lutherans were supposed to have a two-kingdom model of society, that the Catholics distinguished nature and grace, and that the Anglicans came from a state-church tradition in which the church was responsible for the spiritual sphere of life and the state took care of the mundane spheres.[61] Whatever the complex factors involved in this sudden and strict "division of labor" between church and state, it is important for a realistic approach to contemporary public theology to acknowledge that these traditions within the ecumenical movement represent quite distinct ways of standing and being in the world, of experiencing history, of exercising agency, and of defining "spiritual life."[62] They represent different paradigms of religion in the public square.

Indeed, such a specific approach is also discernable in the small group of Christians who started the Breaking the Wall of Silence movement in Namibia. They were inspired by a vision of God's kingdom coming in this world, a kingdom in which *reconciliation* was to become a reality, which would mean that the *truth* about violence and atrocities

60. Cf. the analysis of "state theology," "church theology," and "prophetic theology" in the *Kairos Document,* rev. 2nd ed. (Braamfontein: Skotaville Publishers, 1986).

61. In the Southern African Reformed circles the Calvinistic notion of church and state both serving one Lord and one kingdom was also drawn into a much more dualistic frame of mind via the Kuyperian distinction of common and special grace, and the Dutch Reformed Church was functioning much more like a "priestly" (officiating) state church than an independent prophetic "servant of the Lord." Cf. the insightful analysis of these very different paradigms for public theology by J. J. F. Durand, "Kontemporêre modelle vir die verhouding van kerk en samelewing," in *Teks binne Konteks. Versamelde opstelle oor kerk en politiek* (Bellville: University of the Western Cape, 1986), pp. 13-37.

62. Cf. A. A. van Ruler, "The Kingdom of God and History" (originally 1947), pp. 89-103, and "Christ Taking Form in the World: The Relation between Church and Culture" (originally 1956), in *Calvinist Trinitarianism and Theocentric Politics,* trans. and ed. by J. Bolt (Lewiston: The Edwin Mellen Press, 1989), pp. 105-148.

committed during war would be admitted, *forgiveness* would be asked and given, and a process of reconciliation would be started which would mean quite concretely the working out of viable ways and means to make good, to effect *restitution* for wrongs.[63] This would definitely not only entail priestly and pastoral mending of wounds, or prophetic pronouncements about guilt and restitution; it would proceed to the level of practical politics in which structural legislation and procedures would be agreed upon to handle past differences and to find a way towards a shared future, not just "spiritually" but quite concretely in terms of "materiality": employment, compensation, accommodation, inclusive structures of community — in brief, "kingly" aspects of life.[64]

In our Namibian case study, the small civil society action group who first sought to get the churches intimately involved with the plight of fellow-Namibians who were detained and tortured mercilessly by their own liberation movement and who saw many of their friends simply disappearing, like Chileans under Pinochet, stuck to the agenda of justice prophetically, even when the church leaders failed them. The churches who in effect used the (neo-liberal!) excuse of religion post-independence being "a private matter," seem simply to fall prey to a new totalitarian "civil religion" which cannot bear the message of "the kingdom of God and its righteousness" in and into the world. They are in dire need of a biblically inspired vision of God's work in the world and through history. In biblical imagery the church is called to be the salt and the light of the world: influ-

---

63. Such a vision of concrete reconciliation is worked out by Robert Schreiter. According to him the legitimacy of Christianity is and has often been compromised by its silence and complicity with victimizers in the interests of *Realpolitik*. Cf. Robert Schreiter, *Reconciliation, Mission and Ministry in a Changing Social Order* (Maryknoll, NY: Orbis Books, 1993). In an article on "Reconciliation and Ministry in Civil Society," Rodney Petersen draws attention to an interesting aspect: ". . . Schreiter's remarks about the reality (perhaps prophetic necessity) for communities of Christians to distance themselves (for a while) from the larger church in their search for and discovery of reconciliation — particularly if that larger church is implicated in the very violence it seeks to overcome. . . . This is not the absence of faith but rather a prophetic distancing from faiths and churches and creeds that appear to have taken on the appearance, despite themselves, of idolatries." Cf. Rodney L. Petersen, *Religion in a Secular City: Essays in Honor of Harvey Cox,* edited by Arvind Sharma (Harrisburg, PA: Trinity Press International, 2001), p. 41.

64. Reformed thinking has always tried to balance these three theological perspectives, and I believe this is a wonderful and worthwhile theological "game" to play. Indeed, Jesus, the spiritual prophet of justice, became God's priestly gift of atonement, so that the world may participate in God's enthronement as king.

encing and guiding the world in the direction of God's kingdom of righ-teousness. This kingdom is one of peace, *shalom.* Here "love and truth em-brace" and "justice and peace kiss" (Psalm 85). The testimony and work of the church, and God's Spirit, towards this "reign of God" are both hidden (like the work of salt) and public and open, for all to see (like the light shining forth from on high).

At this point it is tempting to link our analysis of church and civil so-ciety to similar debates that are currently consuming much energy in the United States of America.[65] However, in the context of this contribution I shall merely refer to Jeffrey Stout's recent intervention in the debates about religion in the public square in order to quickly move to the second per-spective: to explore a few steps in the direction of a viable *theological ap-proach* to public theology.

Stout's analysis of the place and role of religion in civil society has taken the debate further than merely a critique of "private religion" (as promoted by the influential contractarian theories of Rawls and Rorty). His conclusions hit hard at exactly the same kind of cynicism hovering be-hind the totalitarian new civil religion fabricated by the powers to be in Namibia. This negative view regarding the possibilities of a "kingdom of justice" is directly due to the absence of a vibrant, prophetic witness that could give public meaning to the key words by which we live as a *res publica,* a living community of people seeking the common good for our common humanity. "The sticking point, the issue that reveals the implau-sibility of the contractarian premises, is the question of what role religious reasons are allowed to play in political argument."[66] In Namibia there de-veloped a similar credibility gap in the deeper levels of understanding of a human rights culture, which was supposed to be supported by the new Namibian Constitution, with its liberal Bill of Rights, but which clearly did not seem capable of protecting citizens of the new Namibia against past

---

65. I hope to do this in a separate article, dealing with the contemporary debate on civil society and religion (in conversation with *inter alios* Jeffrey Stout, Stanley Hauerwas, Richard Rorty, John Rawls, Jim Wallis, David Hollenbach, and Cornel West).

66. Jeffrey Stout, *Democracy and Tradition* (Princeton: Princeton University Press, 2004), pp. 294-298. According to Stout, both these proponents of an aggressive liberalism are ironically caught in the inexplicable intolerance of the so-called enlightened "culture of tol-erance," violating "what his fellow citizens recognize as common sense." For a very similar assessment of Rawls and Rorty, cf. David Hollenbach, *The Global Face of Public Faith* (Wash-ington DC: Georgetown University Press, 2003), pp. 148-165, where he argues against Rorty's "instrumental rationality" and Rawls's "method of avoidance" of religion.

atrocities and new threats of hegemony — a development that could clearly be seen as contrary to the key words of the gospel, but that was also not addressed by the churches on religious or moral grounds, not to speak of theological grounds.

Against anti-democratic theocratic theologies and radical forms of separatism which also bedevils real citizen participation in civil discourse, Stout encourages acknowledgement of the indispensable public role played by "small dedicated groups," civil society groups who can also voice religious concerns and religious premises within the broader democratic dialogue and debate.[67] Thus, this important intervention in social theory by the former president of the American Academy of Religion concludes pretty close to the need for the kind of civil society action of a group such as Breaking the Wall of Silence in the Namibian context.

After De Tocqueville's affirmation of the dynamics of civil society (comparing it to, and even seeing its origins in, the fresh local engagements of Congregationalism), Marx associated the concept civil society "with the play of egotistical, purely private interests," but also saw it as a "superstructure . . . produced as camouflage for the domination of commodities and the capitalist class."[68] After the democratizing interventions of Antonio Gramsci into Marxist discourse, however, civil society was redefined during the two last decades of the twentieth century as the space between society and the state where the state could secure *authority by consent* rather than coercion, and where the *most effective resistance against abuse of state power* could be staged.[69] Herbert links his discussion of civil society and religion to the following definition: "Civil society is that part of social life which lies beyond the immediate reach of the state and which . . . must exist for a democratic state to flower. It is the society of households, family networks, civic and religious organizations and communities that are bound to each other primarily by shared histories, collective memories and cultural norms of reciprocity."[70]

This new focus of civil society as a democratizing and empowering force within society at large is also underlined by the important contribu-

---

67. Stout, *Democracy and Tradition*, p. 305.

68. David Herbert, *Religion and Civil Society* (Burlington, VT: Ashgate, 2003), pp. 72-73.

69. Herbert, *Religion and Civil Society*, p. 74.

70. Herbert, *Religion and Civil Society*, p. 61. Cf. C. Douglass and J. Friedmann, *Cities for Citizens: Planning and the Rise of Civil Society in a Global Age* (Chichester: Wiley, 1982), p. 2, from whom Herbert borrows this definition.

CHRISTOFFEL LOMBARD

tions by David Hollenbach on the role of religion in civil society: "The *res publica* is much larger than the sphere of government. It includes all those communities and institutions that form the rich fabric of civil society. It also includes all those public forms of discourse, conversation, and argument that constitute culture."[71]

Such a focus on the empowerment of the "small people" ties in closely with Walter Wink's now famous analysis of the Jesus movement. Jesus' new religious movement functions like a civil society movement within the power relations of the Roman Empire, and within that empire, of the Jewish authorities. Interestingly enough, Jesus agitates against the abuse of power by Roman soldiers (cf. the story about the voluntary "second mile," which could only have the military background of hegemony, where people could be forced to carry a soldier's baggage for the first mile), against the authority of the Pharisees and Scribes, and the status quo attitudes of the Sadducees. He also shunned the privatism and "flight" of the Essenes and the violence of the Zealots. So, what was his strategy, his alternative? He was empowering people to think in terms of God's inclusive love and care for all, to question all shackles of bondage and injustice, to believe in the power of God's Spirit in and through joint human action.[72] This kind of Christian vision of society can inspire and did inspire people who were tortured and marginalized during Namibia's struggle with "the powers." Unfortunately, this vision was lost on the ecumenical churches that could have and should have acted as a major people's force within civil society, so that the task of empowering the "small people" was left to small groups in civil society itself, groups that felt empowered by God's Spirit to also empower the powerless.

Let us now move to our second perspective: looking at religion and civil society from a *theological perspective*. The concept of civil society, its link with the public role of religion, and its strong development as an empowering and democratizing force in society at large all seem to ask

71. Hollenbach, *The Global Face of Public Faith*, p. 148. On the basis of this inclusive approach, Hollenbach proceeds to develop what can be called an empowering model of civil society, arguing against what he calls the "privatization of thick versions of the good" (as favored by Rawls and Rorty). He quotes Alan Wolfe who also protests strongly against this trend: "We need civil society — families, communities, friendship networks, solidarity workplace ties, voluntarism, spontaneous groups and movements — not to reject, but to complete the project of modernity."

72. Cf. Wink, *Violence and Non-violence in South Africa*, and his well-known Trilogy on "the powers."

244

for a new understanding of God and God's involvement in history and society. What is needed is an understanding of God as the God of history, the God who is fully engaged in human affairs, in culture, in politics, in economies, in work, and in play. In all the grand social theories of Christianity (such as the nature-grace model of the Catholic faith, the two kingdoms of Lutheranism, the cooperation of church and state in the service of the coming kingdom of God of the Reformed tradition, and the historical-eschatological model of liberation theology), God's involvement in human history and the concrete affairs of humanity has been traced and portrayed.[73] One of the most interesting and challenging views of the trinitarian God and this God's concrete involvement in our human and earthly affairs comes from the imaginative pen of Arnold A. van Ruler. Of his extensive oeuvre of 800 titles only a handful of selected articles, all dealing with his notion of "theocentric politics," are available in the English language.[74] From this work I shall string together a few core references to give the reader some idea of Van Ruler's dynamic view of God and humanity as partners and hopefully stimulate further study on the intricate and intimate relationship of God (Trinity) and civil society.

In the first article from 1956 (reworked in 1967) on "The Necessity of a Trinitarian Theology,"[75] Van Ruler draws up a list of reasons why a trinitarian theology is the only viable approach to God and humanity: the Reformation has discovered the insight "that in Christ, God mirrors himself, mirrors himself in my self-consciousness, in my heart, and in my existence. The point of evangelical love *(agapē)* is that it touches human beings. God's revelation only reaches its goal in my faith." For Van Ruler the implications of such *iustificatio Dei activa* is that it results in a *iustificatio Dei passiva,* in our own acceptance of God's work done in Christ as our own. The internal testimony of the Holy Spirit, God's wrestling with us, results in our reciprocal wrestling with God. Van Ruler then proceeds to link this insight to "the needs of modern consciousness" (an affirmation of humanity's active agency), "the ecumenical future" (the church as part of God's eschatological movement towards the kingdom of God), and the

---

73. Cf. Jaap Durand, "Kontemporêre modelle vir die verhouding van kerk en samelewing," in *Versamelde opstelle oor kerk en politiek,* Universiteit van Wes-Kaapland, s.d., pp. 13-37.

74. A. A. van Ruler, *Calvinist Trinitarianism and Theocentric Politics,* trans. and ed. John Bolt (Lewiston: The Edwin Mellen Press, 1989).

75. Van Ruler, *Calvinist Trinitarianism,* pp. 1-25.

"role of the church in the world" (affirming God's involvement as creator, savior and fulfiller of God's plan in and for the concrete world). For Van Ruler, it is of extreme importance that Christian theology does not stay enclosed in Christology but moves on to Pneumatology, so that Christ can gain contemporary form in the world through his people, through "the body of Christ," which is a dynamic, human, pneumatological reality: "Ontology is not closed up in soteriology, nor the world in the church, the creation in Christ, the kingdom of glory in the atonement, philosophy in theology. We always end up in a duality and thus, in the overall scheme of things, in a plurality."[76] "God is Trinitarian. Therefore, his kingdom is catholic. In that kingdom no knots are cut through; rather a game is played, the game of being, the game of love and glory."[77] The point of this playful, trinitarian view of history is nothing less than that we as humans are full, participating partners in God's work.

In the next two articles, in which Van Ruler develops his emphasis on the work of God the Spirit in and through us in order to bring the full orchestra of the Trinity into play theologically, he focuses on the structural differences between Christology (the work of Christ, *extra nos*) and Pneumatology (the work of the Spirit in and through us, *in nobis*),[78] arguing for the "necessity of a relative independent Pneumatology."[79] Central to Van Ruler's understanding of Christian life is the fact that in and through the Spirit God's work in Christ becomes *our own work*; it is being affirmed in and by us willingly. There is thus a rational and a deeply existential element in our participation in God's work in and through history and in society and all its forms and structures. Crucial for a Christian anthropology, according to Van Ruler, is that God's incarnation which takes place through the *unio naturarum* in Christ (i.e. God assuming human *nature*), now, in the dispensation of the Spirit, happens in and through the "second wonder" of the outpouring and indwelling of the Spirit *in us*, through God's indwelling in the human *person*. For Van Ruler this means that God deeply wishes the individual person to be, to be an independent God-serving and God-praising entity. God wishes this, respects this, and

---

76. Van Ruler, *Calvinist Trinitarianism*, p. 23.

77. Van Ruler, *Calvinist Trinitarianism*, p. 25.

78. Van Ruler, "Structural Differences between the Christological and Pneumatological Perspectives" (originally from 1964), in *Calvinist Trinitarianism*, pp. 27-46.

79. Van Ruler, "Grammar of a Pneumatology" (originally delivered on German radio in 1957), in *Calvinist Trinitarianism*, pp. 47-87.

makes this possible by indwelling spiritually: in the individual, in the church, in the human structures and realities.[80]

Already in his inaugural lecture in 1947 on "The Kingdom of God and History,"[81] Van Ruler combined insights of Troeltsch and Cullmann, and Kierkegaard and Hegel, to develop a fully human understanding of God's work in history. Against Barth and Berkhof *(Christ the Meaning of History),* he claims: *Humanity the meaning of history!* However, Van Ruler makes it very clear that he is not on a neo-liberal trip of self-gratifying humanism. Christ takes form in the world, through the work of the Spirit in the individual *(corpus Christiani),* in and through the church as the *corpus Christi,* and in and through society at large, which in the "Christian west" will always still be, to some extent, a *"corpus christianum,"* a culture stamped by the image of God, in Christ, through the Spirit.

It is within this framework of God's work in and through humanity that Van Ruler develops his "prophetic-evangelical vision of social justice": "Our notion of culture should not be restricted to science and art. Social and economic aspects of life are at least as significant. What in fact is the concern of the Bible is a vision of human community that is structured by the fundamental concerns of justice and love. It is for this life in community and society that Jesus Christ came and gave his life as a sacrifice. Only if this is kept in mind, are we kept from a gnostic understanding of the gospel. Only in this way do we understand it properly, that is to say, in an Israelitish way."[82] Behind Van Ruler's concrete, earthly vision of God's kingdom lies his full acceptance of the "real" Bible, the Old Testament, as the vehicle of God's revelation of his purposes and intentions for humanity and the world, with the message that God needs a people to live out the universal law of love in community, in concrete justice and peace — a people participating in God's triune love and compassion, and giving form and extension in the world to that love. In Van Ruler's trinitarian theology the love of God, incarnate in Christ, is applied in and through us, as God's human partners, in the forms of the world. In the process both state and church, and even the work of Christ and the Spirit, are "means," as is civil

---

80. Van Ruler worked out the implications of this necessary "switch" between Christology and Pneumatology in a brilliant monograph, first published in German in 1956 as *Gestaltwerdung Christi in der Welt, über das Verhältnis von Kirche und Kultur,* and deeply influencing the theology of Moltmann and to some extent that of Pannenberg. Cf. *Calvinist Trinitarianism,* pp. 105-148.

81. Van Ruler, *Calvinist Trinitarianism,* pp. 89-103.

82. Van Ruler, *Calvinist Trinitarianism,* p. 115.

society, but civil society aiming at "the brotherhood of all" is closer to the "end" or eschaton: a society of justice, peace and love, which is the real *form* of God's kingdom.

On the problem of community, Van Ruler writes: "The communal existence of humanity is as significant before God as is individual existence. This must not be understood in a purely personalistic way, or from the perspective of individual persons. In the life of a community, structures (institutions, establishments, organizations) play as significant a role as persons." Already in his dissertation, on the fulfilment of the Law, Van Ruler developed the view of human history as the ongoing syntaxis, the reconciliation, of "guilt and grace" in ever new circumstances and contexts, until the final revelation, the full eschatological revelation of the cosmic relevance of Christ's work of reconciliation:

> History is thus to be understood as God ascending his throne. Undoubtedly this has something festive about it. It is also an essential aspect of the Christian-European sense of life that one summons up the courage to enter history from out of the expectation of the kingdom of God. Yet it is perhaps too much to speak here of 'festive'. God ascending his throne is not so much a feast as it is a struggle. It is a matter of reigning in the midst of adversity (Psalm 110; I Cor. 15). . . . The other side of this divine ascension is to be found in the atonement for guilt. God's throne is the cross. In these two aspects — guilt and atonement — the puzzle of history is not resolved but summarized. History is to be understood as a permanent syntaxis of guilt and atonement, and the cross as the most essential form of the kingdom of God in history.[83]

The world seems to be in dire need of such a versatile view of God as Trinity, working in and through individuals, through the church structures, but also outside of the church, in the wide world of God's kingdom. Such a vision can even turn the bitter struggles within civil society, for "atonement" of the guilt of personal, national, colonial, and neo-imperial histories, into a participation in God's own struggle, through the *Gestaltwerdung Christi in der Welt,* to stamp our very life with God's own life.

---

83. A. A. van Ruler, *De vervulling van de wet* (Nijkerk: G. F. Callenbach, 1947), p. 535. The quote is from *Calvinist Trinitarianism*, p. 103.

Worship — and Civil Society? Perspectives from a Reformed Tradition in South Africa

Dirkie Smit

Apartheid and Christian Worship

It is tragic but true that the twentieth-century story of apartheid in South Africa in a way originated in the Lord's Supper, in the heart of the Christian worship. In 1855 white worshippers in a rural Dutch Reformed congregation refused to share the Lord's Supper with Colored believers. In 1857 the Dutch Reformed Synod decided that it was indeed "preferable and Scriptural" that all believers shared the same worship and the same congregation, but granted that, where these measures obstructed the Christian cause "as a result of the weakness of some" — clearly the requests from those white members who were not willing to share the same table and cup with black believers, often from slave origins — there Christian privileges could be enjoyed "in separate buildings and even separate institutions," in other words worship could be organized separately, based on descent, race, and social status.

   Over many years, this historical concession — not-preferable and un-Scriptural! — gradually became the common practice in these churches, and still later even the norm for the order and structure of the church. In 1881 a separate "church" or denomination, the Dutch Reformed Mission Church, was established for Colored people, and during the twentieth century several others would follow, all divided according to race or ethnicity. Although they all belonged to the so-called "Dutch Reformed Church family," almost without any structural or visible unity, white believers in the (white) Dutch Reformed Church (DRC) were gradually made to believe that having separate churches for each nation *(volkskirke)* was the norm, according to Scripture and the explicit will of God. This church policy of separate churches would later form the religious roots of the ideology and since 1948 the official political policy of apartheid. Since 1960, the few (white) theologians, ministers, and believers in the DRC who opposed this ecclesiology and pleaded for the unity of the church were rejected as traitors of the *volk,* the people.

The story is, obviously, much longer and much more complicated than this. The history of racial tension, discrimination, and segregation reaches back to the beginning of colonization. Many philosophical, cultural, social, legal, and economic factors contributed to what became apartheid. However, there is no denying that Christian faith also formed an integral part of that process. The Dutch Reformed church and mission policy of separate churches played a pivotal role. The DRC increasingly appealed to government to introduce apartheid laws. "Scriptural proofs" legitimated the ideology — and in a way it all began, sadly, in the Lord's Supper, in the heart of Christian worship.

In the struggle against apartheid, Christian worship would again play a crucial role, in many and complex ways — but perhaps reaching a dramatic highlight again in the Lord's Supper. The decades after 1948 saw increasing opposition against the apartheid policy, ideology, and theology in church circles, both inside South Africa and in the ecumenical movement. In 1982, at the Ottawa meeting of the World Alliance of Reformed Churches (WARC), eight representatives from the so-called "daughter churches" in the DRC-family refused to participate in the official Eucharist, claiming that it would be false to do so in an ecumenical context, while they were excluded from the Eucharist in the DRC, back in South Africa.[1] After a long debate, the WARC declared a *status confessionis.*

1. The full text, available online at http://www.warc.ch/where/21gc/safrica reads: "There are some South Africans who have participated with pain up to this point in the service, and who now feel constrained not to take part in the Lord's Supper, which is the essence of Christian fellowship. . . . The reasons for this refusal are threefold. (1) In our country, by custom and by church decision which are defended theologically, black people are not permitted to partake of the Lord's supper in the NGK and the NHK [the main white Dutch Reformed denominations]. (2) The theological heresy which undergirds apartheid racism finds its origin in separate communion. Our refusal to participate is a choice for righteousness and a refusal to reinforce the Christian roots of our oppression. These churches, which are members of WARC, have consistently refused to have genuine reconciliation with us black Christians, through a confrontation with the evil of apartheid and by participating in the search for justice and peace and true humanity. To share communion

Back in South Africa, receiving the report from their delegates, the Dutch Reformed Mission Church also declared a *status confessionis* regarding the theological legitimation of apartheid. According to them, the issues were no longer adiaphora. A moment of truth had arrived. The truth of the gospel itself was at stake.

Synod decided that they owed it to their own members and everyone interested to explain why they now claimed — after decades of theological controversy and debate — that the truth of the gospel itself was at stake. The *Confession of Belhar* was born, and four years later, in 1986, officially accepted as confession. Synod also published an official *Accompanying Letter* in which they described their attitude, the authority, the purpose, and the expectations of *Belhar*. They declared solemnly that this was not a political act but something done for the sake of the church and the gospel it proclaims. Their prayer was that "the act of confession would not place false stumbling-blocks in the way, but would be reconciling and uniting, in spite of the pain and sadness, the repentance, remorse and confession needed on such a way of individual and collective renewal." They knew that this called for "the dismantling of structures of thought, of church, and of society which had developed over many years," but they prayed that "our brothers and sisters will want to make this new beginning with us, so that we can be free together and together may walk the road of reconciliation and justice." Their prayer was "that the pain and sadness will be a pain and sadness that lead to salvation." The hope was obviously that such "dismantling of structures of thought, of church and of society" would be based on renewed Christian worship, would proceed from shared celebration of the Lord's Supper, the heart of Christian worship — but this way ahead would prove even more difficult and painful than envisaged.[2]

---

with those who represent this disobedience to the gospel would mean eating and drinking judgement upon ourselves. 'For if he does not recognize the meaning of the Lord's body when he eats the bread and drinks from the cup, he brings judgment upon himself as he eats and drinks' (1 Cor. 11:29). (3) Our refusal to participate anticipates the day of our freedom when we shall all — black and white — drink from one cup and eat from one loaf." It is immediately clear how the denial of Christian fellowship at the Lord's Supper is related to public and political issues, including righteousness and justice, genuine reconciliation and peace, humanity, freedom instead of oppression, in short, to "the evil of apartheid."

2. The text of *Belhar* is available online at http://www.vgksa.org.za/confessions/ belhar_confession.htm. For discussion of the Accompanying Letter, see D. J. Smit, "'No other motives would give us the right': Reflections on Contextuality from a Reformed Perspective," *Studies in Reformed Theology 8. Christian Identity in Cross-Cultural Perspective*, ed. M. E. Brinkman and D. van Keulen (Zoetermeer: Meinema, 2003), pp. 130-59.

Apartheid theology, in its fully developed form, was based on the theological premise that "creation structures re-creation." For apartheid theologians, this was their interpretation of the age-old adage of the tradition that grace does not destroy nature but perfects it.

Concretely, this implied — according to apartheid theology — that the New Testament church of Jesus Christ should therefore be structured and organized according to creation, as perceived through experience and culture, but also as known through several Old Testament reports — and central to these was the account of the tower of Babel. According to the apartheid interpretation, this was a narrative on how divine grace and mercy divided and separated the peoples at the tower of Babel into different languages, cultures, and communities, not to punish them but in fact to bless them, to force them to experience the wonderful richness and diversity intended for them in the original creation, but against which they revolted in their sinful attempt to unite, bringing together what God created to be separate.

So, according to apartheid theology, creation — in all its richness, variety, complexity, and difference, especially including the differences of race, nation, culture, language, and civilization — should structure re-creation, should determine the form, the structure, the order, the life of salvation, of the new creation in Christ, of the church as the carrier and visible form of re-creation.

Practically, for apartheid theologians, this meant that believers from different cultural, racial, and ethnic backgrounds should therefore form separate churches and separate congregations in order to worship separately. It meant that local congregations could therefore determine for themselves whether they would allow believers from other cultural or ethnic backgrounds to worship with them on occasion or would exclude them under all circumstances — and in the majority of instances and as normal practice, they did the latter, ultimately believing that this was done "according to the Word of God." At the heart of these debates was the question whether the church — the church of Jesus Christ, the church belonging to God in Jesus Christ — should be visibly one, and if indeed, how.

Apartheid theologians fully agreed that the church is one — spiritually, invisibly, with one faith, one hope, one baptism, one bread and wine, one Lord. They denied, however, that this unity should become visible, at least in any structural or organizational form, which according to them belongs to the well-being of the church, and not to its being. Congregations could therefore determine who could become members and who could worship, even based on race and ethnicity, and denominations are associations of congregations who freely organize themselves together because they have something in common, for example being part of and serving the same *volk*.

Hidden behind these seemingly innocent theological positions and these seemingly theoretical ecclesiological arguments were of course different kinds of very real group interests, whether material and financial, cultural and nationalist, classist and elitist, political and economic. These theological viewpoints were ideologically used as powerful social weapons in a very real struggle about human life and death issues.

Very consciously in the tradition of Calvin, classical confessional documents from Reformed theology, and specifically the *Barmen Theological Declaration,* others rejected this ecclesiology, arguing that the church belongs to Jesus Christ alone and that this should also determine the visible structure and order of the church and definitely the worship of the church, including the shared celebration of the one Lord's Supper. At stake in these struggles against the theology and ecclesiology, the worship and spirituality of apartheid, was the conviction that the heart of the gospel and the heart of Christian worship were here being threatened. The very nature and therefore also the transformative and liberating power of Christian worship and spirituality was put at risk.

On Christian Worship

"Christian piety at its best has made a significant contribution to the social transformation of the world," says South African Reformed theologian John de Gruchy, whose wide-ranging contributions to contemporary social theory have their spiritual roots in Christian piety, prayer, and worship. He often dealt with this relationship between social theory and spirituality.[3] The theme runs through all his work.[4] Like several Christian ethicists today,

3. Including his introductory essay, "Christian Spirituality and Social Transformation," in *Cry Justice!* (London: Collins Liturgical Publications, 1986), pp. 23-46, and his essay on "Prayer, Politics, and False Piety," in *When Prayer Makes News,* ed. Allan A. Boesak and Charles Villa-Vicencio (Philadelphia: The Westminster Press, 1986), pp. 97-112, also published as *A Call to End Unjust Rule* (Edinburgh: The Saint Andrew Press, 1986).

4. In particular, notions of seeing, vision, and beauty are intimately related with struggles for justice, both in *Christianity and Democracy* (Cambridge: Cambridge University Press, 1995) and *Christianity, Art, and Transformation: Theological Aesthetics in the Struggle for Justice* (Cambridge: Cambridge University Press, 2001).

he seems convinced that Christian ethics, including Christian participation in public life, depends fundamentally on seeing, on perception, which is not surprising, since Bonhoeffer already claimed that "seeing the world *sub specie Christi* is the paramount theological activity for Christians."[5]

One of the painful effects of apartheid was the fact that South Africans did not "see" in the same way. This was a society in which people lived in different worlds and perceived life, history, and one another in radically diverse ways. They also saw ethical issues in these diverse ways. Even what were regarded as ethical problems and challenges differed drastically. They obviously also disagreed with regard to proper responses to moral challenges but, even before they disagreed about responses and courses of action, they already disagreed fundamentally about what they saw or failed to see, what they experienced and accepted as moral challenges and what they ignored or overlooked. Even popular social theories reflected the diverse and often conflicting visions of those who were looking. But where and how do we learn to see? What determines our vision — of ourselves, of one another, of the world?

Seeing Things Differently is the title of De Gruchy's volume of sermons. "The title," so he explains, "sums up a central theme in the Christian gospel, namely that we are called 'to become like children' in order to see things from a totally different perspective, that is, the perspective of God's gracious reign over the whole of reality."[6] This suggests at least one possible reason why Christian worship is so crucially important for Christian ethics. Christian worship is one of the "social locations," perhaps one of the most important places and occasions where Christian believers learn to see.

The twentieth century taught many Protestant traditions that we should consider the social form of the church seriously, to avoid a form of docetic ecclesiology. One could distinguish at least six such concrete, visible, social forms of the real church, namely worship and the local congregation, denominations and the ecumenical church, and individual believers and voluntary initiatives. At the heart of the church, however, in all its social forms, remains the *worship*. It is not surprising, therefore, that so many recent ethical studies again focused on the relationships between liturgy and life, between worship and ethics, between prayer and lives of commitment and discipleship, between the fundamental activities of be-

---

5. Dietrich Bonhoeffer, *Creation and Fall* (London: SCM Press, 1959), pp. 7-8.

6. John W. de Gruchy, *Seeing Things Differently* (Cape Town: Mercer Books, 2000), p. vii.

ing a worshipping church — baptism, the Eucharist, teaching and preaching, celebration and praise, lament, confession — and the church's response to the cries from within and around us.

In the Reformed tradition since Calvin, it has been customary to give preference for the ear over the eye as the primary human instrument for knowing God. A bias for the visible significantly shaped medieval theology and spirituality. The ultimate religious experience was to be a beatific vision. Calvin brought a major change. We are blind, he repeated. We cannot see. Therefore God speaks to us, and we hear before we can see. And in the worship service, the living God is speaking to us. We hear, and only then do we see.

"The medieval Christian longed for the full vision of God. The Reformed Christian longed for the full coming of the kingdom of God. The medieval Christian sought to approach God. . . . The Reformed Christian sought to respond to the acting God. The Roman tradition tried to see God; the Reformed, to hear God. Their contrasting liturgies are manifestations of these contrasting visions of what it is that we and God have to do with each other," explains Nicholas Wolterstorff.[7]

In hearing, we learn to see. Through sermons, we learn to see differently. This was how Calvin understood the function and the authority of the Scriptures. They become the glasses, the spectacles helping us to see. "The Scriptures are not something to look at but rather look through, lenses that refocus what we see into an intelligent pattern"[8] — and it is primarily the worship service where we listen to and hear God's Word which helps us to see properly.

In twentieth-century Protestantism, Barth is regularly called upon as a major witness in this regard. Already in *Fides Quaerens Intellectum,* his seminal study on Anselm, Barth gave an indication of the importance of faith and prayer for theological reflection. In the lectures on ethics from the same period he made the same point. In the *Church Dogmatics,* already since the first volume, he developed this fundamental conviction systematically. Bromiley remarks that one of the unappreciated aspects of the *Church Dogmatics* is this ultimate orientation of theology to worship.[9]

7. Nicholas Wolterstorff, "Worship and Justice," in *Major Themes in the Reformed Tradition,* ed. Donald McKim (Grand Rapids: Eerdmans, 1992), pp. 311-18.

8. Clifford Green, *Imagining God* (San Francisco: Harper & Row, 1989), p. 107, discussing Calvin.

9. Geoffrey W. Bromiley, *Introduction to the Theology of Karl Barth* (Grand Rapids: Eerdmans, 1979), p. 249.

In Barth's influential publications on the relationship between church and state, he would show that prayer negates itself if it does not become action. In his 1937-1938 Gifford lectures on *The Knowledge of God and the Service of God* in the Reformed tradition, Barth distinguished different forms of the service of God, including the worship of the Christian life, the worship service, and the so-called political worship. He presented the liturgical assembly as "the concrete center" of the church's life and claimed, "The church service is the most important, momentous and majestic thing which can possibly take place on earth." Duncan Forrester comments: "When Karl Barth published his Gifford lectures . . . some English-speaking readers were surprised to discover, in a book which they assumed was about the relation between theology and ethics, substantial discussions of the cultic service of God *(Gottesdienst)* alongside the treatment of the political service of God."[10]

In *The Humanity of God* Barth explicitly endorsed the *lex orandi, lex credendi* principle: "It is imperative to recognize the essence of theology as lying in the liturgical action of adoration, thanksgiving and petition. The old saying, *lex orandi, lex credendi,* far from being a pious statement, is one of the most profound descriptions of theological method."[11] Since the *Introduction to Evangelical Theology,* Barth would make it very explicit that the first and basic act of theological work is prayer.[12] Faith and ethics flow from prayer. Finally, he summarized the proper response to the gospel as prayer, as calling on God, and then interpreted the first petitions of the Lord's Prayer in a moving and powerful way in *The Christian Life.*[13] Indeed, to clasp hands in prayer, according to Barth, is the beginning of an uprising against the disorder of this world.

In the history of the church, the relationship between liturgy and life has often been discussed in terms of this well-known motto of *lex orandi, lex credendi.* Quite literally this expression from the fourth century refers to the relationship between the rule of prayer and the rule of faith, suggesting that the way in which we pray should influence, even determine, the way in which we believe, which means think, speak, and act. During the last century, many theologians have therefore added the words *lex con-*

10. Duncan Forrester, "Ecclesiology and Ethics: A Reformed Perspective," *The Ecumenical Review* 47, no. 2 (1995): 148.

11. Karl Barth, *The Humanity of God* (Richmond: John Knox Press, 1960), p. 90.

12. Karl Barth, *Evangelical Theology: An Introduction* (New York: Holt, Rinehart & Winston, 1963), p. 160.

13. Karl Barth, *The Christian Life (CD IV/4)* (Grand Rapids: Eerdmans, 1981).

vivendi, the rule of our life together, to make it very clear that our actions, our life, the integrity of what we are doing, is also implied in the rule of our faith. Simply put, this means then that our prayers — our worship, our liturgy — should impact the way we believe — think, speak, understand, orientate ourselves — and the way we live — act, behave, conduct ourselves, personally and publicly.

Of course, Christian worship should never be instrumentalized. Christian worship carries its own foundation and purpose. It is not intended to serve moral purposes or ethical, even political, values and aims. In influential recent philosophical traditions — since Kant and Hegel, for example — worship has indeed often been instrumentalized in this way, and in many contemporary liberal societies this is almost taken for granted. Religion, including religious instruction, even in public schools, is then regarded as valuable since it can serve the interests of society and the public life. For that reason religion, including Christianity, but normally all kinds of religion, is tolerated, even supported and used by the authorities. This is obviously an extremely important temptation for the Christian church. The church can benefit in many ways by allowing itself to be instrumentalized — but this would represent a betrayal of Christian worship.

Still, the conviction that worship already involves, almost implies, how and what and whom we believe and therefore also how we should live and why has been present in the Christian faith from the very beginning. Already in the early church, well-known theologians like the North Africans Tertullian and Cyprian already said as much in their respective expositions of the Lord's Prayer. Theodore of Mopsuestia would express these convictions very clearly in his own commentary on Jesus' prayer:

> Every prayer contains teaching of good works. . . . Whoever cares, therefore, for perfection and is anxious to do the things that are pleasing to God, will pay more attention to prayer than to any other thing. . . . Jesus made use of these short words as if to say that prayer does not consist so much in words as in good works, love and zeal for duty. . . . Prayer is by necessity connected with good works, because a thing that is not good to be looked for is not good to be prayed for. . . . This is the reason why here also He uttered the above words to the disciples who had asked Him how to pray, as if He had said to them: If you care for prayer know that it is not performed by words but by the choice of a virtuous life and by the love of God and

diligence in one's duty. If you are zealous in these things you will be praying all your life.[14]

Of course, worship — and prayer — does not directly and immediately lead to specific forms of concrete action and life, whether personal, public, or political. The *lex orandi* influences the *lex convivendi* via the *lex credendi*. The way we pray impacts on the way we believe — the way we think, talk, understand, evaluate, prioritize, see. The way we pray impacts, first of all, who we are before it impacts what we do. The way we pray — Christian worship, Christian prayer — impacts our identity, both our collective and our individual identities; it shapes and forms the church, communities of character, and as part of that, believers, people of Christian character, who then jointly discern and decide, discuss and determine, weigh and opt, choose and act.

Charles Taylor has explained this process in great detail in *Sources of the Self*. We live and act as subjects, says Taylor, because we are situated within "inescapable frameworks," because we are orientated by communities and traditions, because we already inhabit certain "moral topographies," because we are always already at home in "moral spaces," because we have received and accepted certain "moral ontologies." It is in the regular worship of the congregation, above all, in the basic patterns of the worship of the church through the centuries and the vision and values, the memories and expectations, the experiences and commitments of the basic activities during the regular and often repeated worship of the church, that Christians receive this orientation, this framework — which also implies this moral ontology and this moral space.[15]

It is precisely in this way and for this reason that John Webster describes Karl Barth's whole theological project as presenting us with a "moral ontology" — precisely in the sense in which Charles Taylor uses the expression. The influential ethics embedded in Barth's theological work, over the years and in all his diverse theological genres, was nothing else than the implications of this fundamental moral ontology, this alternative vision of reality itself, of the world, of history, of the human project, of politics. In fact, it is possible to argue that worship played a crucial role in Barth's own understanding of the way in which we receive this moral ontology and learn to

14. See H. L. Smith, *Where Two or Three Are Gathered: Liturgy and the Moral Life* (Cleveland, OH: Pilgrim Press, 1995), p. 7.

15. Charles Taylor, *Sources of the Self* (Cambridge, MA: Harvard University Press, 1989).

share and partake in it. It is after all not without reason that preaching played such an important role in his thought and own life.[16]

According to Taylor, alternative moral identities are implied in these moral ontologies. With these ontologies or moral spaces, we receive the opportunity to become moral agents, subjects, or selves in the common sense of the word — people who make decisions and choose options and follow their own ideas and convictions, often thinking that we are totally free. We are able to become agents precisely because and to the extent that we receive such options in the frameworks, the horizons, the spaces which we receive.

> Who am I? This can't necessarily be answered by giving name and genealogy. What does answer this question for us is an understanding of what is of crucial importance to us. To know who I am is a species of knowing where I stand. My identity is defined by the commitments and identifications which provide the frame or horizon within which I can try to determine from case to case what is good, or valuable, or what ought to be done, or what to endorse or oppose. In other words, it is the horizon within which I am capable of taking a stand. . . . What this brings to light is the essential link between identity and a kind of orientation. To know who you are is to be oriented in moral space, a space in which questions arise about what is good or bad, what is worth doing and what is trivial and secondary. . . . Our identity is what allows us to define what is important to us and what not. (Taylor)

Our identity, says Taylor, has got to do with "mattering," with what really and ultimately matters to us. What matters to us, furthermore, is social and historical. It is embedded within the identities of others, within their stories and histories, their memories, suffering, strivings, dreams, hopes, that which finally really matters to them. It is immediately clear why Christian worship is so fundamentally important for the way we believe and the way we live. In a variety of complex ways, the basic patterns and activities of Christian worship obviously impact the way Christians believe — think, speak, understand, trust, orientate themselves — and thereby the way they live.

But how does this actually happen? In recent years, both scholars in-

---

16. John Webster, *Barth's Moral Theology* (Grand Rapids: Eerdmans, 1998); see also John Webster, *Barth's Ethics of Reconciliation* (Cambridge: Cambridge University Press, 1995).

terested in liturgical studies and scholars interested in ethics have shown a renewed interest in the complex relationships between liturgy and ethics. Many interesting and informative studies have already been published, on a variety of related issues. If the question is which processes are at work in the basic patterns of classical Christian worship that could result in moral and ethical implications, many and indeed fascinating answers have already been given.

It is for example possible to reflect on at least eight different processes that may take place during Christian worship, namely (1) processes of subversion or undermining of the everyday life and everyday reality, challenging the power of everyday definitions and exclusions, subverting everyday values and evaluations, dreams and aspirations, re-defining virtues and vices; (2) processes of liberation, involving liberation from guilt, liberation from fear, liberation from the powers, and therefore liberation for hope and for service; (3) processes of communion, *koinonia*, fellowship, solidarity, mutual acceptance and care, building a new family and new relationships and identities, even welcoming strangers and making them feel at home and like people who belong; (4) processes of articulation, of providing worshippers with new language and new insight, with new ways of speaking and expressing themselves, of talking about experiences, events and problems in new ways; (5) processes of calling, of receiving a new and renewed vocation, a task, a purpose, a commitment, which often takes place explicitly during preaching, but could also take place in many other, diverse ways during worship; (6) processes of radical formation and transformation, of up-building, growth and character-formation, but perhaps also of radical change, of conversion and dedication to new ideals and purposes; (7) processes of empowerment, strengthening, encouragement, enabling believers to trust again, to engage life again, to face crises and difficulties, to encounter hardships, to continue on difficult journeys — forms of empowerment that could take place through pastoral and caring experiences, but indeed also through teaching and instruction, through better insight and understanding; (8) processes of explicit, conscious, and deliberate dedication and commitment, of oneself, of time and talent, of possessions and opportunities.

In short, the way we worship impacts who we are and the way we live. The rules of our worship have implications for the ways we understand and see ourselves, for our identities, personal and social, individual and communal, for what matters to us, and these ways in which we understand and see ourselves have implications for our lives, our actions, and our everyday behavior, privately and publicly. Worship is perhaps the primary place where many of us learn to see with Christian eyes — or not. This is what was at stake in the apartheid history.

Worship — and Civil Society?

Christian worship is of extreme importance for Christian faith and for Christian life and therefore also for public life and civil society. Precisely, therefore, this is also the place where everything can go wrong and often does. Christian worship has been and still is an ambivalent phenomenon. In reality it is often more a reflection of society than a critical and creative interruption of society. Worship often legitimates society instead of subverting and interrupting it. Christians often endorse and celebrate the values and virtues of their diverse societies, forming people according to the expectations of their groups and communities, and not according to the gospel. Worship often becomes a merely cultural event, rather than a Christian one — with disastrous effects for ethics and civil society.

The Christian church betrays society when it is no longer the church and when it no longer worships as the church. The Christian church betrays society when it merely becomes a mirror image, a reflection, of everyday life, of reality outside the place of worship, no longer informing social life from the "strangely different" perspective of the gospel.

Such ambiguity, even such betrayal, was sadly but clearly present in Christian worship during the apartheid years. Such betrayal can of course take on many forms, and in South Africa it also took its own peculiar forms, different from the ambiguities and the betrayals in other contexts and cultures.[17] De Gruchy discusses some of the South African characteristics of this ambiguity and betrayal in an essay on "Prayer, politics, and false piety." He argues that false piety takes on many forms, "but it inevitably replaces the God who is beyond human control with a god who can be manipulated to serve and sanction self-interest. False piety reduces God to a *deus ex machina* at our disposal, a god whom we can use for our own

17. An example from the apartheid years demonstrates one form which this betrayal can take. It concerns the influential role of public religious broadcasting during the apartheid years, yet the total lack of any concern in these programmes for what was happening in society at the time. See the alarming findings in B. A. Müller and D. J. Smit, "Public Worship — A Tale of Two Stories," in *The Relevance of Theology for the 1990's*, ed. J. Mouton and B. C. Lategan (Pretoria: HSRC, 1985), 385-408.

ends and one upon whom we can call to sanctify what is in our best self-interest. The god of false piety takes on the characteristics of the particular race, group, or class to which we may belong, and when we enter into battle this god is undoubtedly on our side."

He specifically discusses "two interrelated though apparently opposite manifestations of false piety," namely "its privatization and its patriotic appropriation by the nation or the state." He explains, "The life and worship of churches, and the preaching of its pastors, is often determined in practice much more by popular demands than by biblical and theological integrity. If the church becomes a haven of refuge from responsibility in the world, if sermons are geared to massage the spiritual ego and sanction self-interest, if the liturgy whether traditional or contemporary becomes a mechanism of escape rather than the worship of God as Lord, and if priest, preacher, and people somehow combine or conspire to make it so, then false piety not only flourishes, it becomes the norm."[18] In short, one could argue that what was at risk in the apartheid story was nothing less than the very nature of Christian worship itself.

It is of crucial importance for the church to consider critically the nature of its own worship and to ask continuously whether this remains faithful to the worship of the triune God revealed in Jesus Christ or whether it is "determined in practice much more by popular demands than by biblical and theological integrity" (De Gruchy). The betrayal of the gospel often starts within the worship of the church and often flourishes as a result of the lack of faithfulness to the classic patterns of the worship of the apostolic church.

Worship matters. It is not without reason that major renewals of the Christian church, including the Protestant Reformation, were at heart attempts to renew the worship of the church, the liturgical practices, and the piety expressed in and formed by these liturgical practices.

It is for this reason that the writing of a new *Church Order* for the Uniting Reformed Church in Southern Africa based on the *Belhar Confession* was such a significant moment in the history of the struggle. This *Order* represents the attempt to embody the truth of the gospel, as understood in the historical moment. In ways reminiscent of Calvin, the worship of the local congregation is seen as the heart of the life of the church, but in and through worship the believers are called to serve one another and the world. Its Article 4 reads:

18. De Gruchy, *When Prayer Makes News*, pp. 97-112.

The congregation forms a community of believers in a particular place to serve God, each other and the world. Service of God has a bearing on the whole life of the congregation and therefore includes service to each other and to the world. The heart of this service of God is to be found in the coming together of the congregation round the Word of God and the sacraments, where God is worshipped and praised. God's Word is listened to, the sacraments are received and all needs are brought to God in order to strengthen the believers in their faith and to prepare them for their service to each other and the world. The believers accept mutual responsibility for each other in their spiritual and physical needs. The congregation lives as a family of God in which all are inextricably bound to each other and share each other's joy and sorrow. Each considers the other as higher than him- or herself and no one only cares about her or his own needs, but also about the needs of others. In this way they share each other's burdens and carry out the law of Christ. The congregation's service to humankind and the world consists of proclaiming God's reconciling and liberating acts in and for the world; of living out the love of Christ in the world; of calling humankind to reconciliation with God and mutual reconciliation and peace; of following God, who is in a special way the God of the destitute, the poor and the wronged; by supporting people in any form of suffering and need; and by witnessing and striving against any form of injustice; by calling upon the government and the authorities to serve all the inhabitants of the country by allowing justice to prevail and by fighting against injustice; by witnessing against all rulers and those who are privileged who may selfishly seek their own interests and thus control and harm others.

The painful experience of the apartheid history can almost be heard in the background. The worship of the local congregation is the heart of the life of the church. There believers learn to see how to serve the triune God, one another and society at large. In Article 12 of the *Order,* the church's public responsibility is described, again in typically Reformed fashion, but again also with the apartheid experience, with the claims of *Belhar,* and with contemporary insight into civil society clearly present.

The URCSA sees it as her kingly task to set an example to humankind and society in obedient application of the demands of God's Word in regard to love of neighbour, the exercise of justice and the realization of reconciliation, and the pursuit of true peace in her own life. She sees it as her prophetic task to proclaim these demands of God's Word as they have a bearing on society as a whole and on individual institutions, particularly the state, without respect for persons. She sees it as her priestly task to pray for and intercede for the government and society and to intervene for the suffering, the poor, the wronged, and the oppressed within this society, also by way of organized service.

In short, the apartheid experience has made clear how important worship and therefore ecclesiology and the life and practices of the church may be for public life and for civil society. The apartheid experience left South African Christians with the awareness that questions integral to the nature of Christian worship itself are extremely important and also for our life together in civil society — not because Christian worship may ever be instrumentalized to serve ulterior motives and purposes, but because these questions belong inextricably to the nature and integrity of Christian worship itself.

Are we truly worshipping today in continuity with the apostolic church, in faithfulness to the basic patterns of Christian worship, in congruence with our faith in the triune God? Are we really worshipping together — in spite of our rich and complex cultural particularities and within our wonderful assimilative tradition, do we indeed continuously learn from one another, do we share with one another, do we welcome one another, do we indeed practice the one baptism, the one table, the living presence of the one Lord? Are we — each in our own contexts, in the complexities of our particular social, cultural, economic, political situations — indeed continuously learning to see differently? Does our worship indeed help us, liberate us, empower us, call us, challenge us to see differently — to see one another, our fellow human beings, the world, creation, human history, ourselves, with new eyes, in new perspectives, according to new priorities, with the eyes and the mind of the Spirit of the triune God? And do we then indeed confess what we learn to see in our worship together with our everyday words and with our everyday actions, today, with our talk and with our walk? Or do we perhaps confess one way, yet live another?

Again, that was precisely what was at stake for the churches in the struggle against apartheid — the relationship between the *lex orandi* and the *lex convivendi*, between confession in worship and confession in life, between worship and everyday life in the structures and institutions of civil society.

Trinity, Church, and Society in Brazil

Rudolf von Sinner

Only a few theologians have ventured creatively into the doctrine of the Trinity in Brazil. Although the Trinity is invoked in most churches in every worship service, and although the respective doctrine is part of the compulsory curriculum of any student of theology, there has been a lack of books from the pen of Brazilian authors on the matter.[1] Even Leonardo Boff's seminal book *Trinity and Society* (1986), which will be the prime reference in this article, came primarily out of lectures he gave at the Franciscan Seminary in Petrópolis (State of Rio de Janeiro) and is being widely used as a textbook.[2] Thus, it seems to have been more a response to the need to publish something on the matter for the use of students than a fresh look on the doctrine in the first place. While taking up the systematic

---

1. Much of the material presented here is taken from my doctoral dissertation *Reden vom dreieinigen Gott in Brasilien und Indien. Grundzüge einer ökumenischen Hermeneutik im Dialog mit Leonardo Boff und Raimon Panikkar* (Tübingen: Mohr Siebeck, 2003), pp. 59-195, where numerous bibliographical references can be found. Another important resource is my current research, funded by a scholarship from the Swiss National Science Foundation (www.snf.ch), on the churches' contribution towards *cidadania* (citizenship) in Brazil. A major article on the topic is to be published soon: "The Churches' Contribution to Democratic Transition in Brazil," in *Kirche und Öffentlichkeit in Transformationsgesellschaften*, ed. Christine Lienemann-Perrin and Wolfgang Lienemann (Stuttgart: Kohlhammer, 2006). See also my "Healing Relationships in Society: The Struggle for Citizenship in Brazil," *The International Review of Mission* 93, no. 369 (2004): 238-254; "Religion and Power: Towards the Political Sustainability of the World," *Concilium* 5 (2004): 96-105.

2. Leonardo Boff, *Trinity and Society,* trans. Paul Burns (Tunbridge Wells: Burns & Oates, 1988).

theologians' challenge of dealing with all classical *loci* of theology, however, Boff has been using this task for a rather subtly formulated, but in fact fierce critique, of an oppressive and hierarchical church and society alike. As he was writing, Brazil underwent the final phase of its long transition from authoritarianism to democracy (1974-1989).[3] At the same time, Boff had to observe a year of silence imposed on him by the Roman Congregation for the Doctrine of the Faith, as a consequence of his critical remarks on the church made in his famous *Church, Charism, and Power* (1981).[4] It is, therefore, no wonder that the context in and for which he wrote would be not only the political society, but also the church.

Throughout this article, I shall argue that we have to be wary of simple analogies between the triune God, the church, and the world. In relation to Boff's writing at the time, we also have to recognize that both his own and the Brazilian context have changed considerably in the meantime. I shall, therefore, first give a short introduction into the political history of Brazil as well as the role of civil society and the churches in this country. I shall then explain Boff's elaboration of the doctrine of the Trinity, followed by an evaluation of how a "social doctrine of the Trinity" can "inspire" — a word often used by Boff in this regard — communal interaction.

Politics in Brazil and the Role of Civil Society

The Federal Republic of Brazil *(República Federativa do Brasil)* is the fifth largest country in the world and is ranked thirteenth in economic power (2003).[5] At the same time, Brazil ranks fourth in terms of unequal distri-

---

3. Cf. Thomas Skidmore, "Brazil's Slow Road to Democratization: 1974-1985," in *Democratizing Brazil: Problems of Transition and Consolidation,* ed. Alfred Stepan (New York/ Oxford: Oxford University Press, 1989), pp. 5-42; T. Skidmore, *The Politics of Military Rule in Brazil 1964-85,* reprint ed. (Oxford: Oxford University Press, 1988); Maria D'Alva G. Kinzo, "Transitions: Brazil," in *Democracy in Latin America: (Re)Constructing Political Society,* ed. Manuel Antonio Garretón Merino and Edward Newman (Tokyo/New York/Paris: The United Nations University, 2001), pp. 19-44.

4. Leonardo Boff, *Church, Charism, and Power* (New York: Crossroads, 1986).

5. Cf., for this initial data, von Sinner, *Reden vom dreieinigen Gott,* pp. 78-89 and the literature quoted there; Frances Hagopian, "Politics in Brazil," in *Comparative Politics Today: A World View,* ed. Gabriel Almond et alii, updated 7th ed. (New York: Longman, 2000), pp. 520-574; for the economic ranking, based on the Brazilian Gross National Income of 497.5 billion US-Dollars, see http://www.worldbank.org/data/wdi2005/wditext/Section1.htm, access on June 2, 2005.

bution of wealth.[6] While the richest twenty percent have a share of 64.4% of all income, the poorest twenty percent dispose of a mere two percent (1998). Thirty-five percent of the population live below the national poverty line. In terms of human development, the country is located among the "medium human development" countries, ranking seventy-second in 2002.[7] The Freedomhouse research counts Brazil among the "free" countries with a rating of two in political rights and three in civil rights in 2004.[8]

We do not have much clear evidence about pre-colonial times, but the area was certainly inhabited by numerous ethnic groups, especially in the Amazon region and along the coast, with human presence possibly dating back as far as 12,000 years. On Easter, April 22, 1500, the Portuguese seafarer Pedro Álvares Cabral (1460-1526) landed near today's Porto Seguro in northeastern Brazil. The newly "discovered," or rather conquered, land became a colony under the Portuguese crown, adopting its typical system of *padroado,* in which the crown was responsible not only for the material, but also for the spiritual "well-being" of its subjects. Protestants made their way into the country through French and Dutch intrusions in the sixteenth and seventeenth century, respectively, but their presence remained episodic. In 1807, the Portuguese Court took residence in Brazil, escaping from Napoleon's troops. It returned to Lisbon in 1821, but the Prince Regent remained in Brazil to become the head of the Brazilian Empire, proclaiming independence on September 7, 1822. The first Brazilian constitution was promulgated in 1824, allowing for religious freedom under certain restrictions. The Roman Catholic Church was re-affirmed as the established religion of the Empire.

---

6. Cf. United Nations Development Programme (UNDP) (New York, 2004), pp. 188-91, available at http://hdr.undp.org/reports/global/2004/. The Gini index indicates the location between totally equal distribution (0) and totally unequal distribution of wealth (100). Brazil has had constantly high scores in the last decades; it stands now at 59.1.

7. This is behind neighbouring Argentina (34th), Uruguay (46th) and Venezuela (68th), but ahead of Colombia (73rd), Peru (85th), Paraguay (89th) and Bolivia (114th); *Human Development Report 2004,* pp. 139-141.

8. Data from http://www.freedomhouse.org/research/freeworld/2004/countryratings/brazil.htm, access on 26 May, 2005. Rating is from 1 (free) to 7 (not free), in two categories: political rights and civil rights. Brazil has improved its mark since the return to democracy, rising from a double 5 in 1972 to a double 2 in 1985, but deteriorated between 1993 and 2001 (partly free, 3 and 4, respectively), due mainly to violence, corruption, the ineffectiveness of the judiciary and the police resulting in "public distrust," creating a "climate of lawlessness." These same factors hold Brazil still behind the ideal double 1 rating.

On November 15, 1889, a military coup founded the Republic. The Roman Catholic Church was, subsequently, disestablished, full freedom of worship was introduced, churches were recognized as corporations that could, therefore, acquire goods in their name, and the *padroado* was formally abolished. Thereafter, democratic phases and dictatorial episodes followed each other. A first dictatorial phase of a nationalist-populist kind occurred after the 1930 revolution in the so-called *Estado Novo* (1937-45) under Getúlio Dornelles Vargas (1883-1954). Although under an authoritarian regime, this period saw important advances in labor legislation. After another republican experience, which saw ex-dictator Vargas voted back to the presidency (1951-54) and then, gradually, make a swing to the left, the general confusion led to another "revolution" or coup in 1964. An initially moderate and supposedly transitory military government took power. The hardline generals, however, gradually won over the balance, endowing themselves with virtually absolute power in 1968 and installing a highly repressive regime. Its "legitimacy" was helped by the so-called "economic miracle" which impressed by its high numbers of economic growth even while it seriously indebted the country. As this growth came to an abrupt end with the 1973 oil crisis, more moderate commanders came to power and commenced a slow and controlled transition process in 1974. Peculiarly, despite different kinds of manipulations, direct and indirect elections were always maintained, presidents regularly left office after one mandate, parties continued to exist (even if only two were allowed), and congress, though closed at times, was never dissolved. The military finally handed over power to a civilian government in 1985, but transition could only be considered complete when direct presidential elections were held again in 1989. A Constituent Assembly was created, which produced the 1988 Constitution, the so-called "citizen" Constitution because of its ample catalogue of fundamental rights of the citizen in the seventy-seven paragraphs of its fifth article. With its decentralized structure, popular participation, and ample negotiations that preceded it, the Constituent Assembly is considered by many "the most democratic experience in Brazilian constitutional history."[9]

Today, the country can be considered a fairly consolidated democracy with a presidential system of government. For the first time in over forty years, a democratically and directly elected president, Fernando Henrique Cardoso, handed over the presidential sash to another democratically and

9. Kinzo, "Transitions: Brazil," p. 31.

directly elected president, Luis Inácio Lula da Silva, on January 1, 2003. The ceremony was very moving. Lula, a charismatic metal worker from a humble, northeastern background who became a powerful trade-union and, later, Worker's Party (PT) leader, had been the hope of all those longing for change in the country for three consecutive elections until he made it in the fourth run, conquering common people and entrepreneurs alike with his program of marrying strict economic responsibility with an extensive fight against hunger. In 2004, the country enjoyed considerable economic growth with continued low inflation and a strengthened currency, being applauded by economists within and outside Brazil. While forming new alliances, Lula has had to face strong criticisms, not least from within his own party, for maintaining an austere economic policy and doing far too little for the long overdue redistribution of wealth and income. Having fought for ethically sound politics all along its history, the PT government did not escape from serious corruption scandals in 2005.

Before the 1964 coup, civil society was generally restricted to a limited number of organizations with elitist character. The fifties and sixties, however, were a time of social and cultural effervescence. This was when the great educator Paulo Freire (1921-97) started his work of literacy education and conscientization. Within the Roman Catholic Church, the fifties were a period of fostering social awareness and activity, forming a new generation of progressive leadership. The Catholic Action adopted the French-Belgian model of creating specific organizations for different sectors of society, especially youth organizations for high school students, workers, and university students, among others. Nevertheless, "by 1968, the most innovative Catholic experiment since the French worker-priests had forcibly come to a halt" as the Catholic Action was dismantled.[10] Even so, their heritage remained influential, as many liberation theologians and other church activists emerged from the named organizations, and adopted their method of "see — judge — act," beginning by a social analysis of the context before proceeding to a reading of it in light of faith and turning to subsequent action.[11] The Church Base Communities (CEBs), small groups of church members gathering regularly under lay leadership, were created in the fifties, originally to meet the blatant lack of priests and

10. Ralph Della Cava, "The 'People's Church', the Vatican, and Abertura," in *Democratizing Brazil: Problems of Transition and Consolidation,* ed. Alfred Stepan (New York and Oxford: Oxford University Press, 1989), p. 144.

11. Cf. Leonardo Boff and Clodovis Boff, *Introducing Liberation Theology* (Maryknoll, NY: Orbis, 1994).

to reach members better in religious and social aspects. Gradually, they evolved into politically conscious groups, reading the Bible with eyes open to the context and pressuring for clean water, sewers, education, health services, and the like, mainly at the periphery of great urban centers as well as in rural areas.

During the fiercest period of repression (1968-73), the establishment of an active and organized civil society was virtually impossible. The (very limited) attempts of guerrilla warfare to topple the government had been crushed, important leaders had been tortured and killed or exiled, political parties were reduced to two with little power, trade unions were under fierce control, and the media was under censorship. In the seventies, "the only institution able to assert itself against the military government was the [Roman Catholic] Church."[12]

From 1974 onwards, the Brazilian Bar Association also gained momentum. Like the church, it could count on a well-organized nationwide structure and thus on its own efficient network of communication, not having to rely on the highly censored mass media. The Brazilian Press Association became another organ of opposition. Artists and intellectuals developed ways of indirect criticism through cartoons, poetry, and music, for which the military bureaucrats lacked any sense. By relaxing censorship, President Geisel "was helping to reawaken civil society, but was unprepared to hear what society's voice would say."[13]

At the grassroots, new groups appeared like the CEBs, neighborhood associations, and anti-racist movements, often with women in the leadership. Their concrete influence is difficult to measure due to the frailty, heterogeneity, and limited representativity of social movements, but it is beyond doubt that they made a significant impact since the government was forced to concern itself with them. Strikes (from 1978) and rallies (especially the *Diretas Já* campaign in 1984, claiming direct presidential elections) showed a growing influence of civil society on politics. Associations became important places for the learning of democracy as they tried to pressure the government to fulfil its promise of returning to democracy. We can conclude that civil society has become a much wider and more diversified actor in society through grassroots movements and non-governmental organizations (NGOs), whose creation originated in the phase of transition.

12. Skidmore, "Brazil's Slow Road to Democratization," p. 35.
13. Skidmore, *The Politics of Military Rule in Brazil 1964-85*, p. 188.

A number of serious problems face Brazil after the transition. On the one hand, there is no doubt that significant democratic advances have occurred. *Cidadania,* citizenship, the attribution of rights and duties, has become a key term and is recognized to be something which is to be made effectively available to all sectors of society. On the other hand, there is also no doubt that these advances have not reached all sectors of the population. Apart from the appalling poverty in large parts of the population due to economic factors, there are also problems of political culture.[14] There are, for instance, serious failures in the rule of law which has been unable to effectively contain violence and crime; some have called these failures "disjunctions" in citizenship.[15] Another problem is widespread corruption and clientelism, to which even the ethically pretentious PT government fell prey. Partly due to these undemocratic practices, there is a generalized lack of interpersonal and institutional trust.[16] According to the regular inquiries of *Latinobarómetro,* "most Latin American publics are . . . skeptical — if not actively cynical — about key institutions of democracy, and Latin Americans manifest some of the lowest levels of interpersonal trust observed anywhere in the world."[17] Among institutions, the police, courts, government, and parliament come in very low, while the churches are considered the most trustworthy institutions, a capital of trust they could certainly use constructively for fostering a truly democratic society.[18] We shall try to see how trinitarian thinking could possibly be a Christian answer to the named problems and could foster democ-

14. Cf. Sonia E. Alvarez, Evelina Dagnino, Arturo Escobar, eds., *Cultures of Politics: Politics of Cultures: Re-visioning Latin American Social Movements* (Boulder: Westview Press, 1998); Paulo J. Krischke, *The Learning of Democracy in Latin America: Social Actors and Cultural Change* (Huntington, NY: Nova Science Publishers, 2001).

15. Cf. James Holston and Teresa P. R. Caldeira, "Democracy, Law, and Violence: Disjunctions of Brazilian Citizenship," in *Fault Lines of Democracy in Post-Transition Latin America,* ed. Felipe Agüero and Jeffrey Stark (Miami: North-South Center Press, 1998), pp. 263-296.

16. Cf. Rudolf von Sinner, "Trust and *convivência:* Contributions to a Hermeneutics of Trust in Communal Interaction," *The Ecumenical Review* 57 (2005).

17. Marta Lagos, "How People View Democracy: Between Stability and Crisis in Latin America," *Journal of Democracy* 12, no. 1 (2001): 137; cf. *Latinobarómetro* 2003, download from http://www.latinobarometro.org, accessed on October 2, 2004.

18. Cf. *Latinobarómetro* 2003, p. 27. As to institutions, research done by the World Economic Forum in 2002 shows that the list of trust is headed by the churches (65%), followed by NGOs (61%), the Army (59%) and the Media (58%), with much lower numbers for the Police (40%), Government (38%) and Congress (33%); see *O Estado de São Paulo,* Nov. 8, 2002, p. A17.

racy. First, however, let us have a look at Leonardo Boff's elaboration of the doctrine of the Trinity.

A Social and Cosmic Doctrine of the Trinity

"The Trinity is our true social programme" forms the main line of argument in Leonardo Boff's elaboration of the Trinity. He is heir, among others, to Russian thinker Nikolai Feodorov (1828-1903), already quoted by Jürgen Moltmann in his similar approach to trinitarian theology in relation to society.[19] Boff's position becomes clear by exploring what he is *opposing* and what he seeks to *construct* by trinitarian doctrine.

Boff is clearly opposed to an image of God that denotes a celestial monarch who would be reflected directly in a worldly monarch: One God, One Empire, One King. This opposition stems from the negative experiences he had with hierarchical structures in society and the church, structures that suppress, in their harsh authoritarianism, liberty and creativity. He takes up the strong criticism German theologian Erik Peterson had expressed against this kind of political theology.[20] Although a historical thesis, it was intended to be a contemporary criticism against the rising Nazi Reich and the ideological support it received from thinkers like Carl Schmitt, who held that "all decisive [*prägnanten*] concepts of modern state doctrine are secularized theological concepts."[21] Peterson concluded that the full implementation of trinitarian theology by the Cappadocian Fathers in the fourth century broke radically with any "political theology" which would misuse Christian proclamation to legitimize a political regime or system. There are, according to Peterson, no *vestigia trinitatis* (traces or reflections of the Trinity) in human society. It

---

19. Nikolai F. Feodorov, "The Restoration of Kinship Among Mankind," in *Ultimate Questions: An Anthology of Modern Russian Religious Thought,* ed. Alexander Schmemann (London and Oxford: Oxford University Press, 1977), pp. 175-223; Jürgen Moltmann, *The Trinity and the Kingdom of God* (London: SCM, 1981); see also, from an Indian Orthodox perspective, Geevarghese Mar Osthathios, *Theology of a Classless Society* (Maryknoll, NY: Orbis Books, 1980).

20. Erik Peterson, "Der Monotheismus als politisches Problem: Ein Beitrag zur Geschichte der politischen Theologie im Imperium Romanum [1935]," *Theologische Traktate, Ausgewählte Schriften,* vol. 1 (Würzburg, 1994), pp. 23-81.

21. Carl Schmitt, *Politische Theologie* [1922], 6th ed. (Berlin, 1993), p. 43, translation mine.

is important to add that what both Peterson and his followers point to is, in fact, less a critique of "monotheism" than of a "monarchical" image of God, as a similar kind of theological critique can easily be identified in Israelite monotheism.[22] What they do want to emphasize is that God is a communitarian being-in-relation rather than a monarchical-hierarchical ruler.[23]

More specifically, Boff identifies three forms of monarchical misinterpretations of the Trinity in Latin America. In colonial and rural (feudal) society, he identifies a "religion of the Father alone" centralized in the boss *(patrão)* who holds absolute power. In a more democratic environment, the charismatic leader and warrior comes to the fore, where Jesus would be seen as "our brother" or "our chief and master," constituting the "religion of the Son alone." Finally, where subjectivity and creativity prevail, as in charismatic groups, interiority is stressed and can, in its extreme, lead to fanaticism and anarchism. This latter form would be the "religion of the Spirit alone."[24] Boff stresses that all three aspects are important, seen as relationships to the "above" (origin), to the "sides" (our fellow human beings), and to the "inside" (our own self). Thus, the doctrine of the Trinity could serve as a model of coherence, which we shall explore further below. As Boff turns, however, concrete negative examples into abstract positive aspects, he does not say how these latter could be verified concretely in society.

In a similar way, Boff criticizes the hierarchical model of the Roman Catholic Church as being contrary to God's Trinity. The logic of: One God, One Christ, One Bishop, One Local Church is, then, wrong. The church, as the sacrament of the Holy Trinity, is to be seen as *communio* (communion) and not as *potestas sacra* (holy power). "As a network of communities living in communion with their brothers/sisters and all participating in its

22. Cf. Jan Assmann, *Herrschaft und Heil: Politische Theologie in Altägypten, Israel und Europa* (Munich and Vienna, 2000).

23. On God as communion, more from a philosophical-ontological than political-societal angle, see the work of John Zizioulas, *Being as Communion: Studies in Personhood and the Church* (Crestwood, NY: St. Vladimir's Seminary Press, 1985).

24. Boff, *Trinity and Society,* pp. 13-16. Boff draws heavily on Dominique Barbé's earlier work: *Grace and Power: Base Communities and Nonviolence in Brazil* (Maryknoll, NY: Orbis, 1987), pp. 41-61. However, he modifies its application to be a critique only against the "right," not the "left" side of the political spectrum; thus, any possible self-critique of, for instance, base communities and their internal power structures, which could, according to Barbé, sometimes be like the "religion of the Son alone," is being left aside.

benefits, the church can be built on the model of the Trinity and become its sacrament in history."[25] Different from Peterson, Boff holds that there are, indeed, *vestigia trinitatis* to be found in this world. The triune communion which is communion-in-diversity created the human being as a communitarian being, and indeed all nature as communitarian, releasing them into freedom and receiving them into the communion of the Trinity at the end of times, in the eschaton. This makes it possible (and indeed obligatory) for humans to reflect the triune communion among themselves, a communion which respects differences and fosters communitarian relationships:

> This understanding of the mystery of the Trinity is extremely rich in suggestion in the context of oppression and desire for liberation. The oppressed struggle for participation at all levels of life, for a just and egalitarian sharing while respecting the differences between persons and groups; they seek communion with other cultures and other values, and with God as the ultimate meaning of history and of their own hearts. As these realities are withheld from them in history, they feel obliged to undertake a process of liberation that seeks to enlarge the space for participation and communion available to them. For those who have faith, the trinitarian communion between the divine Three, the union between them in love and vital interpenetration, can serve as a source of inspiration, as a utopian goal that generates models of successively diminishing differences. This is one of the reasons why I am taking the concept of perichoresis as the structural axis of these thoughts. It speaks to the oppressed in their quest and struggle for integral liberation. The community of Father, Son and Holy Spirit becomes the prototype of the human community dreamed of by those

---

25. Boff, *Trinity and Society*, p. 22. Boff has in mind the birth of a new being of the church through an *ecclesiogenesis* from the Church Base Communities. It is, however, an idealistic reading, given that an intimate neighborhood setting cannot simply be translated into a national or even international structure. It can work as salt and leaven in the dough, but no more — and, indeed, no less — than this. The church as sacrament is a thought that has accompanied Boff since his doctoral thesis, precisely on the "Church as Sacrament in the Horizon of the Experience of the World": *Kirche als Sakrament im Horizont der Welterfahrung: Versuch einer Legitimation und einer struktur-funktionalistischen Grundlegung der Kirche im Anschluss an das II. Vatikanische Konzil* (Paderborn: Bonifacius, 1972). A trinitarian ecclesiology in ecumenical perspective can be found in Miroslav Volf, *After Our Likeness: The Church as the Image of the Trinity* (Grand Rapids: Eerdmans, 1998 [translated from the German original, published in 1996]).

who wish to improve society and build it in such a way as to make it into the image and likeness of the Trinity.[26]

Taking up the ancient notion of *perichoresis* (interpenetration), Boff describes how the three persons of the Trinity, Father, Son, and Holy Spirit, are at the same time united in their love for one another and different in their "individuality." Evidently, this immediately opens the strenuous debate on the concrete meaning of "person" and the relationship between the "individual" and the "collective." The very terms and their diverging connotations indicate that we cannot easily deduce the shape of human society by describing God as society, nor induce God's being from human society. There is, I contend, a double analogy here: not only are the three persons of the Trinity related to their divine unity like (and not equal to) human persons to their community, but the very notion of diversity and unity is analogous. Divine *perichoresis* and human *perichoresis* — if the term is at all adequate to denote human community — are not univocal, but analogical. This is necessary to emphasize for both sides, to preserve God as God and humans as humans. Therefore, if, as Peterson and his followers contend, God is not to be used as legitimizing a monarchical government, he cannot grant divine character to the three powers in representative democracy either, as suggested by some authors in the fifties.[27] Furthermore, the same analogy had been used to legitimize a triple monarchy in the Byzantine period, which clearly demonstrates the arbitrariness of such direct analogies.[28] While these remarks

---

26. Boff, *Trinity and Society*, pp. 6-7.

27. The theoretical bridge for this interpretation had been Carl Gustav Jung's doctrine of archetypes, which is also often used by Boff. See Hans Marti, *Urbild und Verfassung: Eine Studie zum hintergründigen Gehalt einer Verfassung* (Bern and Stuttgart: H. Huber, 1958); Max Imboden, *Die Staatsformen: Versuch einer psychologischen Deutung staatsrechtlicher Dogmen* (Basel: Helbing and Lichtenhahn, 1959). Kant had already applied Montesquieu's division of powers in the state in a "moral" way to God, whose Trinity he described as holy legislator, good governor, and just judge. See Immanuel Kant, *Die Religion in den Grenzen der blossen Vernunft* [1794], Werkausgabe, vol. 4 (Darmstadt: Wissenschaftliche Buchgesellschaft, 1998), pp. 806ff. On trinitarian political analogies in general, see David Nicholl, *Deity and Domination. Images of God and the State in the Nineteenth and Twentieth Centuries* (London: Routledge, 1994).

28. In 669/70, Byzantine soldiers proclaimed Constantine IV's brothers to be co-emperors, with reference to the Trinity: "In the Trinity we believe, three emperors we crown," according to Gisbert Greshake, *Der dreieine Gott: Eine trinitarische Theologie* (Freiburg/Basel/Vienna: Herder, 1997), p. 470, note 95.

impose serious restrictions on analogies, they do not invalidate them altogether.

Another important aspect, developed more explicitly in later works by the same author, is the cosmic dimension of the interrelatedness of all being. Boff has been occupying, with his ecological-cosmological reflections, a pioneering role in a time which is characterized by economic globalization and its, for many, disastrous social and ecological consequences. In connection with the 1992 UN Conference on the Environment in Rio de Janeiro, Boff emphasized the urgency of ecological issues. Relating them to Teilhardian cosmology, the findings of a number of scientists, and the doctrine of the Trinity, he has raised this issue in Brazil through a number of widely read books.[29] This in itself is very important, given that, despite environmental threats like deforestation in the Amazon region having been known for a long time, ecological awareness is still rarely to be found among the population. At the same time, it is an important feature of Boff's work that he seeks, again and again, to view humanity within the whole of creation, the wholeness of its past and future. What he presents is the view of a planetarian community of nature and humanity, of humans among themselves, of humanity and God; it is (national) citizenship, cocitizenship, and citizenship of the earth.[30]

> The Trinity, as mystery of communion of the three Divine Persons, has always given herself to creation as well as to the life of every single human being, and has revealed herself — under the forms of sociability, mutual openness, love and self-giving, but also accusation and protest against the lack of such values — to the communities of humanity. Whole humanity is the temple of the Trinity, independent of time, space, and religion. All humans are sons and daughters in the Son, all humans are under the energy of the Spirit, and all humans are being drawn up by the Father.[31]

Boff insists on God's participation in the world and the world's participation in God: "The world has an eternal destiny; it will be the body of

29. See for instance Leonardo Boff, *Ecology and Liberation: A New Paradigm* (Maryknoll, NY: Orbis, 1995); *Cry of the Earth, Cry of the Poor* (Maryknoll, NY: Orbis, 1997).

30. Leonardo Boff, *Depois de 500 anos: Que Brasil queremos?* (Petrópolis: Vozes, 2000), pp. 25-28, 51-53.

31. Leonardo Boff, *Gott kommt früher als der Missionar. Neuevangelisierung für eine Kultur des Lebens und der Freiheit,* 2nd ed. (Düsseldorf: Patmos, 1992), p. 43; translation mine.

the Trinity, in its cosmological, personal and historical-social dimen-sion."[32] The relationship between God and world is, then, not only an ana-logical one in terms of the trinitarian God being a model for human soci-ety and for the church, but also an ontological one. As creation proceeds in the beginning from the Father through the Son in the power of the Holy Spirit, "starting with the transforming power of the Spirit, through the lib-erating action of the Son, the universe will finally come to the Father."[33]

Trinity, Church, and Civil Society

The search for a concrete molding of society and the church inspired by the triune God is a legitimate and, indeed, important contribution offered by Boff, not only for Brazil, but for a globalized world. As stated earlier, the question is how such trinitarian "inspiration" can be applied to the forma-tion of structures in society and the church. Boff himself does not go be-yond claiming, in general terms, the need for a "basic democracy":

> It is not the theologian's task to devise social models that best approxi-mate to the Trinity. Nevertheless, if we take basic democracy in the sense that the ancient Greeks (Plato, Aristotle and others) took it, as not so much a definite social structure as the principle underlying and providing inspiration for social models, then we should say that the values implied in this constitute the best pointers to how to respect and accept trinitarian communion. Basic democracy seeks the greatest possible equality between persons, achieved by means of progressive development of processes of participation in everything that concerns human personal and social existence. And beyond equality and partic-ipation, it seeks communion with transcendent values, those that de-fine the highest meaning of life and history. The more such ideas are put into practice, the more will divine communion be mirrored among men and women.[34]

Following on the reflections presented in this article, trying to com-bine the critical and constructive ("inspiring") function of a *perichoretic*

---

32. Boff, *Gott kommt*, p. 169.

33. Boff, *Trinity and Society*, p. 230.

34. Boff, *Trinity and Society*, pp. 151f. It is, however, questionable if Plato and Aristotle are adequate references here given their very critical view of democracy, outrightly rejected by Plato and relativized by Aristotle.

trinitarian doctrine and the challenges of Brazilian society, I shall emphasize four aspects which I believe are fundamental aspects for the churches' contribution towards democracy, motivated by faith: otherness, participation, trust, and coherence. As it is a widely participatory democracy which is aimed at by civil society, and as the churches are part of civil society, trinitarian thinking in relation to society as a whole may indeed encourage and inspire actors of civil society. In the line of what has been argued above, we are not seeking simplistic deductions or inductions, but features of God as Trinity which are fundamental for human beings not only to coexist, but to interact in communion.[35]

A first central aspect is *otherness*. Plurality implies diversity, and community in a democracy is unthinkable without recognizing the uniqueness of each member of society. Therefore, the respect of otherness, the acknowledgement of difference and the right to be different, is essential. In Latin American theology, this originated among those who were in close contact with indigenous peoples, but has received wider attention in recent times. In my view, this respect for otherness also cautions against so-called *macro-ecumenism*.[36] Denying the value of the other's faith is wrong, but so is presuming that "God is anyway the same," which tends to lead to indifference. A sensitive hermeneutic of the other is necessary to preserve each person's uniqueness and her right to difference, including religious difference.[37] It preserves mystery and seeks understanding, as

35. The Brazilian word for such communal interaction is *convivência*, conviviality, which goes much beyond mere coexistence; cf. Ivan Illich, *Tools of Conviviality* (New York: Harper & Row, 1973); Theo Sundermeier, "Konvivenz als Grundstruktur ökumenischer Existenz heute," in *Ökumenische Existenz heute,* ed. Dietrich Ritschl, Theo Sundermeier, Wolfgang Huber (Munich: Kaiser, 1986), pp. 49-100; von Sinner, "Trust and *convivência*."

36. The term "macro-ecumenism" was coined in the 1990s in Latin America and denotes an ecumenism extended beyond Christianity to other religions. It can be found especially among Roman Catholic dialogue activists and tends to leave out Christian, interconfessional dialogue. I fear that it is, in the end, little more than a simplistic way of inclusion, which amounts to disrespecting otherness.

37. I have tried to explain this further in Rudolf von Sinner, "Inter-Religious Dialogue: From 'Anonymous Christians' to the Theologies of Religions," in *The God of All Grace: Essays in Honour of Origen Vasantha Jathanna,* ed. Joseph George (Bangalore: Asian Trading Corporation/United Theological College, 2005), pp. 186-201. German literature tends to describe the "other" as "stranger," not in a derogatory way, but in order to safeguard the always remaining difference which cannot, and must not, be overcome completely, and also to indicate the difficulty to understand the other; see for instance Theo Sundermeier, *Den Fremden verstehen: Eine praktische Hermeneutik* (Göttingen, 1996), and the contributions in Andrea Schultze, Rudolf von Sinner, and Wolfram Stierle, eds., *Vom Geheimnis des Unterschieds: Die*

happens in theology trying to unveil and, at the same time, respect the mystery of God as tri-une, unity in difference.

A second aspect is *participation*. This concept is central to the discourse on civil society. In Brazil, it is implied in the struggle for *cidadania*, citizenship. *Cidadania* is, in the first place, the "right to have rights" in a situation of "social apartheid."[38] In a broader sense, as most authors use it, this concept includes the real possibility of access to rights and the awareness of one's duties, as well as the constant molding and extension of the citizens' participation in the social and political life of their country. Aspects of the citizen's effective participation are, then, becoming central, as is the political culture by which such participation is encouraged or hindered. The churches, as part of civil society, have an important role to play in this encouragement of citizen participation, and indeed do so in different ways. In fact, the Brazilian churches can count on much larger membership and participation than any other kind of voluntary organization. Ideally, they function as schools for democracy, as they train people within their own structures, promote collaboration with the state, for instance in councils involving state and civil society on youth matters or issues of food security, and contribute to discourse in a critical-constructive way.[39] In terms of trinitarian theology, the aspect of participation well describes the idea of interpenetration, *perichoresis*.

A third aspect is the need for *trust*. As mentioned above, the disfunctions and disjunctions in Brazilian democracy are not only a matter of corruption and clientelism among politicians and state clerks but of a lack of trust in democracy as a system, as well as in the persons who carry it, which is the whole of society. Of course, historical experience has not done much to give the impression that things could work better and that state and system would indeed be worthy of trust. Trust, however, is something which needs to be invested prior to knowing what the result will be. In a democratic society, it becomes necessary to trust persons in a rather abstract way because I shall never know the majority of my fellow citizens. If democracy is to work, I have to presuppose that others have a similiar

---

Wahrnehmung des Fremden in Ökumene-, Missions- und Religionswissenschaft (Münster: LIT, 2002).

38. Evelina Dagnino, "Os movimentos sociais e a emergência de uma nova noção de cidadania," in *Anos 90. Política e Sociedade no Brasil,* ed. E. Dagnino (São Paulo: Editora Brasiliense, 1994), pp. 108, 105.

39. Cf. Rudolf von Sinner, "Healing Relationships in Society" and "The Churches' Contribution to Democratic Transition in Brazil."

interest in the functioning of democracy.[40] If such common interest cannot be taken for granted, and if a good number of fellow citizens, especially those who hold more power than I do, fail in proving to be trustworthy, a deeper reason is needed in order to still be ready to invest trust. Such reason can be given by faith, which essentially means trust — not in oneself, but in God. Lutherans are accustomed to thinking of the human being as similarly just and a sinner. We know that we cannot trust ourselves and each other for our own sake and merit but for God's sake and merit. God seen as tri-une can give good reasons to invest trust in democracy even where it is "disjunctive"; Godself preserves continuity in the midst of different, highly ambiguous historical situations where he manifests Godself, most centrally in the cross at Golgotha, and empowers persons to live their lives seeking to be just while knowing they are inescapably sinners.

Finally, a fourth necessary element is *coherence:* to have a project for the whole of society and not just for oneself or one's peer group or even for one's church. As this depends on a specific perception of both society and of faith, what is needed is *a hermeneutics of coherence.*[41] The highly competitive religious market, with an ever-increasing diversity of churches and religious movements, is giving a very sad testimony of such (in-)coherence. Theologically speaking, insisting on God as Trinity could help to prevent restrictive misunderstandings, as if God were only Holy Spirit and not also Son, made human in Jesus Christ, and Father, as creator. This balance of a unity and diversity in God is prone to foster *koinonia,* the ecumenical key word for community among the different members of the body of Christ.[42] In terms of society as a whole, such integration of unity and diversity could, if well succeeded, be an important contribution of churches to a pluralist society. This presupposes that Christians and churches do not, as is sadly the case with many evangelical politicians in Brazil,[43] primarily seek to gain advantages for their respective churches, but see their mission as a testimony of service *(diakonia)* to the whole of society.

40. Cf. Claus Offe, "How Can We Trust Our Fellow Citizens?" in *Democracy and Trust,* ed. Mark Warren (Cambridge: Cambridge University Press, 1999), pp. 42-87.

41. Cf. Commission of Faith and Order, *A Treasure in Earthen Vessels: An Instrument for an Ecumenical Reflection on Hermeneutics* (Geneva: World Council of Churches, 1998), p. 9 and passim.

42. Cf. Jean-Marie R. Tillard, "Koinonia," in *Dictionary of the Ecumenical Movement,* ed. Nicholas Lossky et al., 2nd ed. (Geneva: World Council of Churches, 2002), pp. 646-52.

43. Cf. Paul Freston, *Evangelicals and Politics in Asia, Africa and Latin America* (Cambridge: Cambridge University Press, 2001), pp. 11-58.

In this way, not in direct deductions or inductions, but in identifying characteristics of God as Trinity, the doctrine of the Trinity, namely the metaphor of *perichoresis* which points to a loving, dynamic, and coherent God, can serve as a powerful theological resource for the churches to contribute meaningfully, as part of civil society, towards the construction of a respecting, participatory, trusting, and coherent society. In the words of the letter to the Ephesians, a witness to the triune God and presenter of an inter-personal ethics in a nutshell:

> I therefore, the prisoner in the Lord, beg you to lead a life worthy of the calling to which you have been called, with all humility and gentleness, with patience, bearing with one another in love, making every effort to maintain the unity of the Spirit in the bond of peace. There is one body and one Spirit, just as you were called to the one hope of your calling, one Lord, one faith, one baptism, one God and Father of all, who is above all and through all and in all.

Beyond the Culture Wars:
Contours of Authentic Dialogue

Paul Louis Metzger

Toward a Trinitarian Model of Authentic Dialogue

The tragic and fatal shooting in 2003 of an African American woman by a white police officer in the city of Portland led to an outcry from the African American community, including the following protest from one of my friends, a leading African American pastor in the city: "When will a black woman's blood be viewed as having the same value as a white man's?" The outcry and the divergent responses from other communities exposed Portland's long-standing divisions and wounds.

As a result of the tensions, the Portland Police Department in cooperation with The National Conference for Community and Justice initiated several dialogue circles. These dialogue circles were made up of representatives from the Portland Police Bureau as well as religious leaders from a variety of traditions, including Buddhist, Jewish, and Christian, and were intended to break down barriers and build mutual understanding and respect between those of different walks of life. I was invited to participate and found the whole experience enlightening and refreshing, even provoking further thought on a question that has interested me for some time. That question is, "How can the Christian community engage in authentic dialogue in search of the mutuality so necessary for civil society and yet remain true to the particular truth claims of the Christian faith?" This paper attempts an answer to this question by setting forth a Trinitarian model of authentic dialogue, one that pursues mutuality while preserving the particularity of the Christian truth claims. It will even be argued that the

Christian community is called and enabled to pursue such mutuality *because of* the particularity of the Trinitarian faith.

This is no easy task for the North American church. For one, the political tradition of democratic liberalism exhorts the church to be tolerant of "competing" institutions yet refuses to tolerate the church and its particular claims in the public sphere.[1] Such "anti-religious" intolerance leads to fear of the homogenizing and dehumanizing influence of the purportedly pluralistic secular state. It is also a difficult task in that from the other side the Christian Religious Right often plays politics for power at the center, void of concern for mutuality and authentic dialogue, instead of portraying Christ's power through weakness and his concern for "the other," including "the other" on society's fringe.[2] Its manifest destiny ideology and rhetoric of "taking back America" lead to fear of the homogenizing and dehumanizing influence of the allegedly Christian Religious Right.

Adherents of both sides fail to see the homogenizing and dehumanizing tendencies of their respective camps. Moreover, secular liberalism fails to see how religious it is whereas the Religious Right fails to see how secular it is. Overcoming the blinding barriers to authentic dialogue from

---

1. Stanley Hauerwas critiques this state of affairs in *After Christendom,* with a new preface by the author (Nashville: Abingdon Press, 1999). In *Democracy and Tradition,* Jeffrey Stout argues that religion is not inherently a political "conversation-stopper," contrary to Richard Rorty (Jeffrey Stout, *Democracy and Tradition* [Princeton: Princeton University Press, 2004], p. 10). While challenging Hauerwas's brand of theological traditionalism, he appreciates Hauerwas's concerns about the secular liberal democratic enterprise and its proponents like Rorty for whom religious beliefs are best privatized (see pp. 10-11).

2. This orientation is evident in the following statements from Gary North and Randall Terry: "The long-term goal of Christians in politics should be to gain exclusive control over the franchise. Those who refuse to submit publicly to the eternal sanctions of God by submitting to His Church's public marks of the covenant — baptism and holy communion — must be denied citizenship, just as they were in ancient Israel. The way to achieve this political goal is through successful mass evangelism followed by constitutional revision." Gary North, *Political Polytheism: The Myth of Pluralism* (Tyler, TX: Institute for Christian Economics, 1989), p. 87. "I want you to just let a wave of intolerance wash over you. I want you to let a wave of hatred wash over you. Yes, hate is good. . . . Our goal is a Christian nation. . . . We have a biblical duty, we are called by God, to conquer this country. We don't want equal time. We don't want pluralism." Randall Terry; quoted in Bob Caylor, "Terry Preaches Theocratic Rule: 'No More Mr. Nice Christian' Is the Pro-Life Activist's Theme for the '90s," in *The News Sentinel,* Fort Wayne, IN, Aug. 16, 1993. Presently the Tea Party movement often speaks of "taking back America." See Kate Zernike, Carl Hulse, and Brian Knowlton, "At Lincoln Memorial, A Call for Religious Rebirth," in *The New York Times,* August 28, 2010; nytimes.com/2010/08/29/.../ (accessed on 10-29-10).

the left requires unmasking the unnamed deity of secular liberalism and bearing witness to the personal name of the triune God. Overcoming the blinding barriers to authentic dialogue from the right requires disclosing to the Right the triune action of the one true God in beloved community, and reclaiming this God, which the Right has "hijacked" for less than sacred aims. Both moves assist in promoting authentic dialogue. In the following section, we will seek to unmask the unnamed deity and then move on to reclaim the hijacked God.

In Search of Particularity

Unmasking the Unnamed Deity

Every society has a deity, named or unnamed, that impacts human well-being positively or negatively. The secular state advances a nameless deity, which, by its namelessness, assists in advancing imperial political agendas. Unmasking secular pluralism's unnamed deity and its impact on society promotes authentic dialogue — dialogue that accounts for particular truth-claims and safeguards the well-being of "the other."

Every society's acknowledged or implicit deity bears upon society's self-ordering. In *The Promise of Trinitarian Theology*, Colin Gunton writes,

> . . . something will perform the function of a deity. God, some god, is thus indispensable, in the sense that all societies have one as a kind of ideal or focus of social unity. But the deity a society worships, whether that deity be avowed or unconscious, makes much difference to its life, so that much hangs on which god it is that we hang our hearts.[3]

Appealing to Lesslie Newbigin, Gunton claims that our pluralistic society is not truly plural. By "relegating" religion to the private sphere, "modern societies effectively emasculate religious interests so that they cease to be truly constitutive of what a society really is." While this move makes "religion a kind of option in the marketplace," it "conceals the fact that modern commercial and technological forces are exerting a homogenizing and therefore unifying pressure on the way our social order takes shape."[4] This

3. Colin E. Gunton, *The Promise of Trinitarian Theology*, 2nd edition (Edinburgh: T&T Clark, 1997), p. 168.
4. Gunton, *The Promise of Trinitarian Theology*, pp. 162-163.

particular pluralistic orientation leads to homogeneity (as does the revived Christendom of the Religious Right, albeit from a different frame of reference), eroding public faith commitments and the intermediate communities between the individual and the state so vital to individual and societal wellbeing.[5]

Now the religious pluralist certainly wishes to safeguard against homogeneity and oppression, and has served the church well in pointing out abuses committed in the name of the Triune God. So, I grant John Hick's claim that a conservative Christian perspective often hinders a compassionate existence.[6] There is certainly evidence to support Hick's charge in the current wave of culture wars, including the way in which the Religious Right engages the broader domain. Nonetheless, even though the Religious Right can be and often is oppressive, wishing to turn America into a theocracy, the religious pluralist inadvertently assists the state and market in manipulating and commodifying human life. How so?

According to R. Kendall Soulen, whether it is ancient Egypt and Rome, the present day nation-state, or the WTO and the ever-expanding market, imperial powers advance a nameless deity that serves to advance their own political ambitions. In developing his argument, Soulen quotes Edward Gibbon: in the time of the Caesars, all the religions were "considered by the people equally true, by the philosophers equally false, and by the magistrates equally useful." A nameless deity submits to the political powers, failing to check the market's extension and human life's commodification. As Soulen puts it, "The pluralist theology of religion unwittingly provides a spiritual rationale for the unlimited dominance of the marketplace, for the commodification of all things, including religion, and indeed, human life itself."[7] A nameless deity falls prey to commodification. "A proper name," on the other hand (especially when it is the name of the personal God revealed in Jesus Christ), "is the very opposite of a commodity."[8]

Soulen believes that, just as Jewish slaves insisted that Moses tell them the name of the God who sent him to them, those enslaved by present day empires will increasingly demand of those who hope to liberate

---

5. Gunton, *The Promise of Trinitarian Theology,* p. 163.

6. John Hick, *God Has Many Names* (Philadelphia: The Westminster Press, 1982), pp. 19-20.

7. R. Kendall Soulen, "'Go Tell Pharaoh' Or, Why Empires Prefer a Nameless God," in *Cultural Encounters: A Journal for the Theology of Culture,* vol. 1/2 (Summer 2005): 53.

8. See Soulen, "'Go Tell Pharaoh,'" p. 57.

them, "Who is it that sent you? What is his name?"[9] Only a name-bearing God can bear their burden and adequately resist commodification. And only such a God can give back to them their personal identity and value.

A nameless God and nameless people go hand in hand. By reducing the transcendent, personal God to a nameless function or quantity, it reduces everyone to a nameless function or quantity. For Trinitarian theology (which is not reducible to discussions of functions and quantities), the naming of this God promotes personal identity for the Jewish slave of old and the present-day black woman and her blood in the face of the commodifying advance of the seemingly omnipresent state and market.

Moreover, the naming of this God promotes particularity and concern for the other. For the triune God revealed in Jesus has relational space for otherness. The divine personal name, to which the church bears witness and from which personal particularity flows, is triune. For as the New Testament shows, Jesus exegetes the divine name (see John 1:18). As triune, God has relational space for otherness within the divine being. As a result, this God has relational space for otherness when engaging the creation. In his discussion of divine omnipresence in the *Church Dogmatics,* Karl Barth addresses the inherent danger of "the absolute non-spatiality of God" doctrine. Barth writes, "Non-spatiality means existence without distance, which means identity." In contrast to this model, he claims, "God possesses space, His own space, and that just because of His spatiality, He is able to be the Triune, the Lord of everything else, and therefore the One in and over all things."[10]

The church bears witness to the named triune God, who has space within his own being for relational otherness, and so makes space for the other. Moreover, the church is called to be a community that makes space for otherness within its own being, for it is a community constituted and shaped by this triune God through Word and Sacrament by the Spirit, bearing witness to the world of the recapitulation of all things in the crucified, resurrected, ascended, and returning Christ. Thus, the church points beyond the depersonalizing state and the market to this higher, interpersonal power to which the state and market must give account. Far from being merely a voluntary association of religious individuals, the church is what William Cavanaugh calls the Eucharistic community,

9. See Soulen, "'Go Tell Pharaoh,'" p. 55.

10. Karl Barth, *Church Dogmatics,* vol. II/1, *The Doctrine of God,* ed. G. W. Bromiley and T. F. Torrance (Edinburgh: T&T Clark, 1957), pp. 468-469.

which "participates in the life of the triune God, who is the only good that can be common to all." Its reality is global and eternal, anticipating "the heavenly polity on earth."[11] Public faith commitments and intermediate communities between the individual and the state such as the church are necessary for safeguarding against homogenization and dehumanization. The church's public confession of the triune God and communal practices rooted in the Eucharist call into question the state's and market's messianic pretensions to commodify all of life. But what about the church's own messianic pretensions?

The church is by nature a witnessing community. As such, it is not only called to point beyond the state and market. It is also called to point beyond itself to the revelation of this triune God.[12] In this way, it creates space for alternative views and encourages dialogue with other communities making particular claims. So, the church's particular identity as one of witness to the Word made flesh — who makes space for us — makes space for other voices to be heard. The church is not the kingdom, but is a fundamentally important witness to the kingdom in view of its proclamation of the Christ to whom it submits and whom it cannot submit to itself. Such distancing of Christ from the church means that the church can never circumscribe or capture Christ, and so manipulate him to advance a crusader-like agenda to kill the "infidel," whoever that may be.

Such distancing does not imply any incapacity to disclose. God in Christ gives himself to be known in and through the church, yet without the church circumscribing God through its speech. This view of the church as witness upholds the pluralist conviction that human concepts cannot domesticate God, yet without sacrificing the all-important orthodox claim that God gives himself to be "identified," as Soulen argues.[13] God will not allow either human conceptualities or divine ineffability to imprison him.[14] The true church dwells within this dialectic and so is a confessing church. As the confessing church, it does not compel but appeals to the Word made flesh, who in keeping with his nature as the Word,

---

11. William T. Cavanaugh, "Killing for the Telephone Company: Why the Nation-State Is Not the Keeper of the Common Good," *Modern Theology* 20, no. 2 (April 2004): 269.

12. Barth himself relativizes Christian religion as a series of human contrived abstractions on God in favor of the revelation of the triune God to humanity to which the church is called to bear witness. See Karl Barth, *Church Dogmatics*, vol. I/2, *The Doctrine of the Word of God*, ed. G. W. Bromiley and T. F. Torrance (Edinburgh: T&T Clark, 1956), pp. 328-331.

13. Soulen, "'Go Tell Pharaoh,'" p. 56.

14. Soulen, "'Go Tell Pharaoh,'" pp. 56-57.

rules by appealing, by serving, not by lording it over his fellows.[15] As the primary witness to this Word, the church is able to enter into authentic dialogue and make space for a plural society to be genuinely plural while upholding its particular faith claims.

The confessing church centered round the Word and Sacrament bows its knee to Jesus, not to Pharaoh, Caesar, the WTO, or a divine despot. Unlike the fallen powers, Jesus reveals God's name in history by humbling himself to death on a cross in order to bring down "the mighty from their throne and" exalt "those of low degree" in his resurrection from the dead. Unfortunately, this point is often lost on the Christian community, which all too often fails to bear witness to this triune God, but instead confesses an oppressive deity, and so becomes a fallen power, too. As stated in the introduction, the Christian Religious Right often plays politics for power at the center instead of portraying Christ's power through weakness and his concern for "the other," including "the other" on society's fringe. It is necessary to reclaim the God of Moses and Jesus, which the Right has hijacked with its claim that this God is on its side, by paying greater attention to God's triune being at work in beloved community in the world, and by reminding the North American church of its true calling to witness, far removed from the increasingly vitriolic rhetoric of the culture wars.

Reclaiming the Hijacked God

In *Exclusion and Embrace,* Miroslav Volf claims,

> The single personal will and the single impersonal principle or law — two variations of the transcendent "One" — enforce unity by suppressing and subsuming the difference; the crucified Messiah creates unity by giving his own self. Far from being the assertion of the one against many, the cross is the self-giving of the one for many.[16]

Gunton writes, "Insofar as there is a political programme in the divine economy it is realized by the gathering of a community around the crucified and risen Lord. Insofar as it depicts a mode of human action, it is

---

15. Karl Barth speaks of how the Word appeals and does not compel in *Against the Stream: Shorter Post-War Writings, 1946-1952* (London: SCM Press, 1954), p. 214.

16. Miroslav Volf, *Exclusion and Embrace: A Theological Exploration of Identity, Otherness, and Reconciliation* (Nashville: Abingdon Press, 1996), p. 47.

manifestly non-coercive."[17] For Gunton, ". . . the church is indispensable to society as a minority community calling upon the wider world also to worship, and prepared to pay the price for that witness." The church does not compel worship or acceptance of its vision; rather, it embodies it. Its most effective means of operation

> in the modern world is as a church, perhaps generally a minority church, which does not trim its teaching to the fashions of the present but actively orients its life to the cross and resurrection of the incarnate Lord. This means that the church as an institution has to learn the lesson that the best way to gain its political life and influence is to lose it.[18]

Two American Christians who epitomize well this theo-political orientation, and whose lives call Christ's community to account, are Martin Luther King, Jr. and John M. Perkins. In his recent book, *The Beloved Community,* Charles Marsh provides a fascinating theological explanation of the American civil rights and community development movements, and convincingly shows that faith commitments inspired and sustained King, Perkins, and others. In contrast to secularist historiography, which sees the beloved community program as a "secular movement that used religion to its advantage,"[19] King's vision of beloved community in which all people are one "was theologically specific: beloved community as the realization of divine love in lived social relation."[20] Biblical faith supplies a fitting arsenal of hope for resisting the enemies of justice through Christ's compelling sacrificial love.

Marsh revisits the beginnings of the beloved community, its eventual "fragmentation and disillusionment,"[21] and its reemergence through the "more modest, yet more enduring" community development movement led by Perkins. This latter group has advanced the vision of beloved community in terms of concrete community transformation.[22] Marsh leaves the reader with the welcome news that in our "violent time," "the same spiritual vision that animated the civil rights movement remains a vital

17. Gunton, *The Promise of Trinitarian Theology,* p. 173.

18. Gunton, *The Promise of Trinitarian Theology,* p. 177.

19. Charles Marsh, *The Beloved Community: How Faith Shapes Social Justice, from the Civil Rights Movement to Today* (New York: Basic Books, 2005), p. 4.

20. Marsh, *The Beloved Community,* p. 2.

21. Marsh, *The Beloved Community,* p. 4.

22. Marsh, *The Beloved Community,* pp. 4-5.

source of moral energy and social discipline for the present age."[23] Such words provide inspiration to face a contemporary challenge: many North American Christians "have surpassed all competitors in" the "booming business" of trivializing faith, which fails to remember the fundamental difference between "discipleship and patriotism," and in reifying the American way of life.[24]

Marsh's account of King and Perkins makes clear that there are indeed exceptions to the rule. Most of us know the exceptional story of how King — like the Christ he followed — sacrificed his own body and future (and not his oppressors') not simply to win rights but to win reconciliation between the oppressed and oppressors. Most of us, though, are not as familiar with Perkins' equally exceptional story, and so I will tell a bit of it now.

Perkins visited Portland a few years back to speak on behalf of The Institute for the Theology of Culture: New Wine, New Wineskins, which I direct at Multnomah Biblical Seminary. One of his speaking venues was at Reed College. Now Perkins is a self-professed Evangelical Christian. Reed College, on the other hand, was listed in the Princeton Review in 2006 as receiving the highest score among universities for "ignoring God on a regular basis."[25] Perkins and the Reedies are poles apart in more ways than one, but the Reedies were attracted to Perkins because of his lifelong work as a civil rights leader and community development activist.

Perkins shared his personal story the night he spoke at Reed. Born the son of a sharecropper from Mississippi, a teenage Perkins witnessed the fatal shooting of his older brother — a decorated war veteran, who had recently returned home — at the hands of a white police officer because of the color of his skin. Perkins left Mississippi for California, convinced that Christianity was the white man's religion, which he used to oppress blacks. Certainly, North American Christianity often hijacks and distorts the image of Christ. But the real Jesus was free to pursue Perkins, and later disclosed himself to Perkins in California. Perkins realized that Jesus was everyone's God, not simply the white man's, but his God, too; and so, Perkins entrusted his life to him.

In the late 1950s, sometime after Perkins met Christ, God impressed upon him his people's need back in Mississippi. Perkins told his wife that

---

23. Marsh, *The Beloved Community*, p. 7.
24. Marsh, *The Beloved Community*, p. 7.
25. Robert Franek, with Tom Meltzer, et al., *The Best 361 Colleges: The Smart Student's Guide to Colleges*, 2006 Edition (New York: Princeton Review, 2005).

he believed God was calling them to leave California and return to Mississippi to help African Americans oppressed by poverty and injustice. He and his wife decided to move the family to Mississippi in 1960. They made a big impact, helping his people with community development. The local authorities took note and decided to make a little impact of their own. One night, some white police officers set a trap for Perkins and his associates and threw them inside a police station prison, where they set about beating Perkins nearly to death. Those police officers shredded some of Perkins's vital organs with their punches and kicks. They also forced a fork up his nose and down his throat.

The now elderly Perkins told the Reed students that as he was lying there in blood on that prison cell floor, looking up into those white police officers' faces as they beat him, he felt only pity for them, no bitterness. How could they hate him so? Something horrible must have happened to each one of them, causing such hatred. Perkins recounted how God took all that hatred unleashed on him that night and used it as a catalyst — unleashing Perkins to a life of racial reconciliation. An overwhelming sense of compassionate justice rolling down from the divine mountains spread through his life, and through the Reed auditorium that evening.[26] You could feel it in the air. In Perkins, the Reed students had come face to face with the Crucified God's ambassador, not an impostor easily fit into Evangelical stereotypes. They responded with a two-minute standing ovation for a life so well lived.

One of the most beautiful things about Perkins is that he creates the space to be heard because he inhabits or embodies his claims. His particular truth claims of the transcendent are immanent in his practice. The Word has truly become flesh in his life by the indwelling Spirit. Perkins makes it possible for those outside to hear him — and to see Christ. Perkins and that minority Christian community centered around the crucified and risen Christ do not compel worship of Christ but embody its messianic vision. They are willing to pay the price for their witness. Like Jesus before them, they gain political influence by losing it. As Jesus himself said, "A kernel of wheat must fall to the ground and die if it is to bear much fruit" (John 12:24).

For Perkins, and for King before him, the church is called to embody the great redemptive event of the cross, which, according to Marsh, makes

---

26. Perkins retells his story in John M. Perkins, *Let Justice Roll Down* (Ventura: Regal Books, 1976).

"free space for redemptive community."[27] Perkins's and King's lives, like Christ's, create space for dialogue, fostering and nurturing the beloved community. Christian individuals and communities create space to be heard when they suffer compassionately the other's existence, suffering compassionately with and for the other, seeking after reconciliation.

The Religious Right could benefit greatly from reflecting upon Trinitarian orthodoxy and its accompanying practices, such as the compassionate suffering of Christ, King, and Perkins. Jesus did not marginalize liberals and lesbians but instead identified with those the dominant culture marginalized. Moreover, Jesus crossed the barrier imposed by those at war with God rather than build it higher. In fact, he invited to his banquet those on the inside, though they excluded him, and all the others despised as unsound and insignificant by those inside the camp.

King and Perkins would not limit the beloved community to Christians. Nor would they say Christians alone aspire to a compassionate form of existence. For example, the Zen Buddhist tradition resonates with Perkins's particular brand of Evangelical Christian faith illustrated above. Both forms of faith affirm compassionate existence, patient acceptance, and identification with the other. Such communities should come together in solidarity in the present hour, for the increasingly vitriolic rhetoric on both the left and right threatens the cultivation of the beloved community in American society, as perhaps never before.

If conservative Christians really wish to reinvigorate the American way of life and revive the church, we need to anticipate the future fulfillment of Christ's peaceable kingdom here on earth through the Spirit's compassionate long-suffering of the other, not through the fleshly "taking back" of America from the other for privileged lifestyles of leisure and moralistic utopias. We need to partner with others to re-create and cultivate again civic practices such as town-hall meeting places where everyone's voice can be heard. This historic enterprise has been missing from the current political and cultural landscape, driven away by the mass-market, mass media, individualism, and non-local virtual spaces of many Internet chat rooms and competing blogs. We cannot afford to write one another off, nor allow the mass media to oversimplify respective movements and over-dramatize the differences. Historic faith communities have a vital part to play individually and collectively, drawing from long-standing traditions and practices of compassionate existence to provide

27. Marsh, *The Beloved Community,* p. 45.

meeting places in neutral zones to negotiate peace between the warring factions made up of adherents brainwashed by the polarizing propaganda of the oversimplified Left and Right.

After the November 3, 2004 national and state elections in the United States, a Zen Buddhist priest who had taken part in the same dialogue circle mentioned earlier in this essay contacted me and asked if we could restart discussions. My friend was deeply troubled by the anger and fear within his own community concerning the religious and political divisions locally and nationally. Their anger and fear arose from a perceived or real Religious Right take-over of America. He hoped that we could work together — beginning in our own religious communities — to build mutual understanding and to foster civil discourse. I was struck by my friend's insight into the anger, fear, and pain, not only of his own community, but also of mine, which the warring sides incite and inflict on one another through their overcharged and oversimplified rhetoric. He was also concerned that such violent rhetoric and propaganda might lead to violence, as one of his members threatened. Sticks and stones often break bones, and words will often lead there.

And so, my Buddhist priest friend invited me to speak at his temple about Evangelical Christianity. Many in his community feel threatened by Evangelical Christianity (the Left and Right seem to be unaware of the fact that both sides not only resent one an*other,* but also are afraid of one an*other*). The threat — real or imagined — is that the Religious Right wishes to take back America and is succeeding. The supposed role Evangelicals had in helping President Bush win re-election along with helping ban Gay marriage in liberal Oregon has convinced many that the Right has already taken back America. Thus, the news at the Zen temple that an Evangelical Christian leader was coming to speak naturally awakened fear and anger in many of them.

During the talk, I defined Evangelicalism, drew attention to the Scopes Monkey Trial and the longstanding Fundamentalist-Modernist controversy, noted red flags, and spoke of ways to break down barriers and create partnerships between those from the opposing sides. I also shared the story of Perkins at Reed. At the end of my talk, a Buddhist lay monk exclaimed, "If anyone has a corner on compassion, it should be you guys with your belief that God came down to earth and became one of us, to identify with us in our brokenness. What happened?" Perkins' particular brand of Christian witness spoke volumes to these people, shining light on the compassion sitting in Christianity's corner. How I long for that compassion to come out of the corner and into the center of Evangelical Christianity's public profile and posture more often, impacting our rhetoric and particular engagement of the other for the sake of building a civil society and a world for all.

Christ, the Dharma, and the Power of Mutual Persuasion

Dialogue circles like the one noted at the outset of this essay are powerful means for building understanding between those of different perspectives and persuasions. However, sheer dialogue does not lead to true mutuality but keeps us separate from one another. For dialogue to be truly authentic, it must go beyond mutual understanding. For true mutuality to exist, we must seek after mutual persuasion.

Neither Christians nor those from other persuasions have all that it takes. All of us are broken. And so, we should seek to persuade one another to go together beyond where we currently are. We should also invite the society at large, secularist and non-secularist alike, to go there with us. While the Zen priest and I view the transcendent differently, our respective views on compassion help us affirm one another's dignity and show one another respect.

From the standpoint of Trinitarian theology, the particular and public claims of Christian faith promote authentic dialogue in pursuit of mutuality. From my perspective, Jesus is the center and circumference, the ground, grid, and goal of creaturely life. As such, Jesus inhabits the space between the extremes, and makes it possible for people from all sides to meet in the middle.

Christians need to be more keenly aware of how Christ operates in the world. The night I spoke on Evangelical Christianity at the Buddhist temple, members of the Buddhist community solicited the thoughts of my students who had accompanied me. The Zen Center newsletter recorded the students' reflections:

> They said that they were impressed by the compassion, thoughtfulness and sincerity of those of us associated with the Zen Center, and that this actually deepens their appreciation for how profoundly Christ operates in the world. (The students simply smiled when, in response, someone said that the evening's events had deepened their own appreciation for how profoundly the *Dharma* operates in the world.)[28]

28. Domyo Sater, "Building Bridges: An Evening of Meaningful Dialogue Between

My students and I certainly gained a greater appreciation for how profoundly Christ operates in the world the day the Buddhist priest came to speak to an Evangelical Christian audience at Multnomah where I teach. The Buddhist priest drew attention to the harsh rhetoric from the Left toward the Right, called it deplorable, and then apologized for it — even though he himself had not uttered such statements. His authenticity and vulnerability *moved* me and persuaded me to stand up and apologize to him and his fellow Buddhists gathered there for the harsh rhetoric from the Right aimed at the Left. We are just beginning this dialogue and have a long way to go.

We may not persuade one another to become Buddhists or Christians. But we are persuading one another to go more deeply into our respective traditions in view of what we learn from one another in search of sources that will advance further a compassionate form of shared existence. Beginning with these town-hall-like meetings involving our respective faith communities, we have begun to inhabit more complex public spaces than simply the state or market. They provide space for the individual person against the encroachment of the state and market. Not only will such intermediate and mediating communities of public faith meeting together mediate the individual to the state and market, but also they will provide a safe haven so that those from the Left and Right can put down their arms to encounter one another beyond what they stereotypically read and see and hear of one another from the headline news. It is my hope that we will stop trying to corner one another or to steer society to the left or to the right but will together go in search of compassion at the center. That is where we will find it. For even if the Christian community has the corner on compassion, we will find that when we conservative Christians finally return to "take back" that corner, the left-of-center Buddhists sitting there will be pointing us to Jesus and away from the not-so-Religious Right in search of a world for all.[29]

Liberal Zen Buddhists and Conservative Evangelical Christians," *Still Point* 24, no. 4 (July-August 2005): 7.

29. My ongoing dialogue and partnership with Zen Buddhist priest, Kyogen Carlson, is chronicled in Sallie Jiko Tisdale's feature story, "Beloved Commuity," in *Tricycle: The Buddhist Review* (Fall 2006): 54-59, 114-15 (with accompanying sidebars).

Epilogue

On "the Global" in Global Civil Society: Towards a Theological Archaeology of the Present

J. Kameron Carter

> Which came first, history or geography? The latter is the foundation of the former, because occurrences have to refer to something. History is in never relenting process, but things change as well and result at times in a totally different geography. Geography is therefore the substratum.
>
> Immanuel Kant

> The word "globalization" is . . . the most accomplished form of the *imperialism of the universal.* . . .
>
> Pierre Bourdieu

> Having been rescued from the rule of this world, [we] have now become Christ's own. . . . [In him] I am deprived of my immediate relationship to the given realities of the world since Christ the mediator and Lord has stepped in between me and the world. . . . [This] break with the world is absolute. It requires and causes our *death.*
>
> Dietrich Bonhoeffer

Introduction: The Global as a Theological Problem

This book has as its stated task, as the editors have put it in the introduction to Part II, of offering "a hitherto unexplored *via media* between the proponents of the social analogy [of the trinity] and their critics," *and* of bringing this *via media* to bear on a pressing question of contemporary social theory and of the humanities more broadly. This is the question of how we might theologically, and more specifically in trinitarian terms, envision life together on a world-wide scale and as unbounded by the constraints of nations, and thus in international or global terms. In other words, this book is a collective effort to theologically engage the idea and practice of *global* civil society and to press toward a true internationalism or, better still, a transnational vision of the human and practice of human existence. The work of theorizing global civil society has been left, in the main in this collection, to John Keane, whose essay in this volume furthers his wide-ranging corpus on the topic. The other essayists in this collection, working within the varied subfields of Christian theology, have drawn on the Christian doctrine of God's triune identity to engage the global in theological terms.

I want to use this epilogue to suggest the next steps to be taken in a theological research program that would interact with the realities of late-modern global existence. In what follows I begin to develop an archaeology of "the global" in global civil society. That is to say, I examine how the global, as the spatial complement of that other category of modernity, the temporal, has functioned to constitute the present. My basic claim is that the global names a spatially uneven reality constituted between "the West and the rest." Moreover, I contend that such a vision of the global, which I fear remains at work in the notion of *global* civil society, has its origins in a problematic Christian social imagination. Thus, the problem of the global is the problem of modern theology itself — the problem of theology's role in producing an uneven global present and the problem of whether it can be extricated from the very problem it had no small role in producing.

At the heart of what is problematic about modern globality — and here I am using the notion of globality, the global, and globalization in close conceptual proximity — is its (often repressed) linkage to colonial and postcolonial history, and thus to the missionary project of civilization. Central to this project was implanting western rule throughout the globe as the rule of white men. Within such a framework, the global names a mode of social organization and relations. It is a spatial consciousness that is planetary in scope, universal in reach, and violent in practice, a consciousness that has come to be written into, as Michel de Certeau has argued, "the practices of everyday life."[1] Thus, Immanuel Kant, no insignifi-

---

1. Michel de Certeau, *The Practice of Everyday Life* (Berkeley: University of California Press, 1984).

cant cultural theorist and thinker of modernity, was on to something when he said just before launching his massive critical enterprise that spatiality or "geography is the substratum" of the modern world. But what becomes apparent when the full sweep of Kant's corpus is taken into account, from the early work in geography and anthropology to the critical philosophy on into his late political and religious writings, is that his statement about geography is unintelligible when severed from the wider colonialist architecture of the western civilizing project as a global project. Within this structure is a spatial rift between the West and the rest and a hierarchical arrangement within which the human has been imagined.

I am unable to unpack here all of the layers of this claim.[2] Instead, as a concluding word for this collection that points towards future steps in this research agenda of theologically engaging globality, I limit myself to a more focused examination of the theological architecture of the notion of the global, behind which is the problem of "the imperialism of the universal," as Pierre Bourdieu has called it. I take up the specific problem of the universal and the global in the first part of what follows. It is here that I sketch the relationship between the universal and the global in the making of modern social space as a set of power relations. In examining the problem of the universal, I draw on recent work in the field of comparative literature and its key concept of global or "world literature" *(Weltliteratur)*.

I then take up the matter of how the theological came to function inside of and as an iteration of the problem of the universal. As I show, a discourse of God as Trinity has aided and abetted the problem of the universal. It is in this section that my argument poses the greatest challenge to the theological efforts carried out in this volume. For it is here that I profile the fact that theology, more generally, and the discourse of God as Trinity, more specifically, has been part of the problem of the universal as a structure of domination and uneven global development. I carry out this part of the argument through a consideration of developments in theology and Christianity's social performance in the fifteenth century and as consolidated in 1492. This is the archive for the argument I develop here.

Now, it is important that I am as clear as possible on what I seek to accomplish. My concern in this section — and throughout this epilogue,

---

2. I do some of this unpacking in my *Race: A Theological Account* (New York: Oxford University Press, 2008), and a groundbreaking development of aspects of this claim is accomplished by Willie James Jennings in *The Christian Imagination: Theology and the Origins of Race* (New Haven: Yale University Press, 2010).

for that matter — is not just historical. Rather, my argument functions in close proximity to genealogy and archaeology. "Genealogy," said Foucault, "is gray, meticulous, and patiently documentary."[3] As such, it is an extension of archaeology in that the genealogist must descend into the archives of "documents that have been scratched over and recopied many times."[4] As such genealogy "does not oppose itself to history." Rather, "it opposes itself to the search for 'origins'" and, for that matter, to destiny.[5] Foucault was keenly aware that history in the mode of a quest for origins and destiny "often involves a consideration of [how] race and social type" are made to bear the weight of origins and destiny.[6] Genealogy, by contrast, refuses such a project. It "does not map the destiny of a people." To be a genealogist is "to discover that truth or being does not lie at the root of what we know and what we are, but the exteriority of accidents."[7] This epilogue is a consideration of a significant thread in the network of such accidents. That thread is the production of social space as a global set of power relations refracted through a discourse of western civilization.[8]

In this epilogue, then, I'm concerned fundamentally with the present and with the accidents or contingencies involved in how theology came to function to produce a global order of things. Trinitarian theology had no small part in this. Indeed, I suggest that it may be the case that the contemporary vogue in trinitarianism, whether by social analogy trinitarians and now more so by trinitarian classicists, might be symptomatic of a late-modern melancholy, a nostalgic wistfulness, for a "unity" that once was. It is this unity of "once upon a time" that I want to surface in this archaeology of global existence as tied to the western project of civilization.

After exploring the archive of 1492, I turn to the final part of this epilogue, which is also the most schematic. Here I argue that future work in the direction of theologically engaging global existence must turn to Christology and the vision of the human built into his Jewish flesh. In his flesh space is reconfigured away from an identification of Christianity with

3. Michel Foucault, "Nietzsche, Genealogy, History," in *The Foucault Reader*, ed. Paul Rabinow (New York: Pantheon, 1984), p. 76.
4. Foucault, "Nietzsche, Genealogy, History," p. 76.
5. Foucault, "Nietzsche, Genealogy, History," p. 77.
6. Foucault, "Nietzsche, Genealogy, History," p. 81.
7. Foucault, "Nietzsche, Genealogy, History," p. 81.
8. It should be clear in laying out matters this way that my arguments are diametric to Samuel P. Huntington's in *The Clash of Civilizations and the Remaking of World Order* (New York: Simon & Schuster, 1998) and to those who argue in a similar vein.

western civilization and its pretensions to global control. Such pretensions are crucified in his body. To be Christian is to exist inside of this crucifixion. My chief theological interlocutor for sketching this out is Dietrich Bonhoeffer.

The Universal and the Global: The World Republic of Letters

I want to begin with the problem of the universal in the making of modern global and social space, and for this I want to consider recent work done in the field of comparative literature. This field has been marked by Johann Wolfgang von Goethe's idea of "world literature" *(Weltliteratur)*. Goethe considered this idea, which he formulated in the beginning of the nineteenth century, to be a central component of the process of intra-European cultural exchange that would enrich national cultures and literatures by means of struggles, arguments, and critical comparisons.[9] I have found that the analyses of the problem of the universal (and the particular) that

---

9. Goethe uses the term *Weltliteratur* directly in only a few places, though he invokes the concept in other phrasings in numerous places. Here are a couple of instances that point to what he means by the notion. In a letter to his friend Adolph Friedrich Carl Streckfuss, dated January 27, 1827, Goethe wrote, "I am convinced that a world literature is in process of formation, that the nations are in favor of it and for this reason make friendly overtures. The German can and should be most active in this respect; he has a fine part to play in this great mutual approach" (quoted in Fritz Strich, *Goethe and World Literature,* trans. C. A. M. Sym [London: Routledge, 1949], p. 349). In July of the same year, 1827, Goethe again wrote, "This is the great advantage that world literature affords, one that in time will become more and more obvious. Carlyle has written the life of Schiller and has estimated him throughout as it would have been difficult for a German to do. On the other hand, we can judge Shakespeare and Byron and know how to evaluate their merits perhaps better than the English themselves" (quoted in Strich, *Goethe,* p. 349). And later again that year, on October 12, 1827, in a letter to Sulpiz Boisserée, Goethe wrote: "In this connection it might be added that what I call world literature develops in the first place when the differences that prevail within one nation are resolved through the understanding and judgment of the rest" (quoted in Strich, *Goethe,* p. 349).

For some recent theoretical considerations of the idea of "world literature," see Franco Moretti, "Conjectures of World Literature," *New Left Review* 1 (2000): 54-68; Stefan Hoesel-Uhlig, "Changing Fields: The Directions of Goethe's *Weltliteratur,*" in *Debating World Literature,* ed. Christopher Prendergast (London: Verso, 2002), pp. 26-53, along with the other essays of this volume; David Damrosch, *What Is World Literature?* (Princeton: Princeton University Press, 2002); and Emily Apter, *The Translation Zone: A New Comparative Literature* (Princeton: Princeton University Press, 2006).

have been taking place in this field of the humanities are relevant to the theological archaeology of the global present I seek to outline here.

Research in this field has been calling renewed attention to how the global is a field of contestation and bitter struggle, how it is constituted by means of a wide-ranging contest for literary recognition. What does literariness mean? It means having one's national writings recognized and ultimately consecrated, by means of literary prizes (like the Nobel Prize in Literature, for example). Consecrated writings are deemed to be of more than national significance. Stated differently, to have one's work deemed literary is to have it recognized, as Goethe put it, as belonging to humanity as such. "It is to be hoped," he wrote in his journal *Propyläen* in 1801, at the dawn of the nineteenth century,

> that people will soon be convinced that there is no such thing as patriotic art or patriotic science. Both belong, like all good things, to the whole world, and can be fostered only by untrammelled intercourse among all contemporaries, continually bearing in mind what we have inherited from the past.[10]

And so, to have one's art deemed literary is for it to be deemed, beyond a purely patriotic art or parochial science, for and of the world. It is to be "cosmopolitan" and ultimately "universal." Hence, the notion of *world* literature.

While several theorists have weighed in on the question of the invention of "literature" and have analyzed how the notion of "the world" in comparative *world* literature functions, I want specifically to engage the recent work of French literary theorist Pascale Casanova on these matters, for internal to her analysis of the making of world literary space is an account of how struggle, and indeed "the imperialism of the universal," as Bourdieu put it, defines globality as a structure of uneven development. Moreover, her analyses show that a central feature of the world literary space and globality is annexation or assimilation to the universal. I want to engage her work here, even if in a necessarily cursory manner, with a view to highlighting this problem as central to the problem of the universal. But finally, my engagement with Casanova on these matters will help me set up what I seek to do in the rest of this epilogue, which is consider the theological operations, tied as they have historically been to a trinitarian imagining of the Christian God, that have made the global what it is.

10. Quoted in Strich, *Goethe*, p. 35.

In her extraordinary work, *The World Republic of Letters,* Casanova analyzes the complex field of modern world literature and the emergence of world literary space. She indicates three phases to its evolution: the Renaissance phase from the sixteenth to the eighteenth centuries; the phase of western nationalism during the long nineteenth century through World War I; and the phase of globalization, which took off in earnest with decolonization after World War II.

The first phase in the making of world literary space "saw the exclusive use of Latin among educated men give way first to a demand for intellectual recognition of vulgar tongues [and] then to the creation of modern literatures claiming to compete with the grandeur of ancient literatures."[11] The demand for the recognition of vulgar tongues was led by the French, who were at the forefront of "the vernacularizing thrust of print capitalism."[12] On this point, the manifesto of the French poet Joachim du Bellay (1522-1560), *The Defense and Illustration of the French Language* (1549), along with his involvement in the establishment of the French Renaissance Pléiade, a consortium of French men of letters, is quite significant for an understanding of the early accumulation of "literary capital" in the French language and for understanding how French became the standard bearer of literary universality. Du Bellay's *Defense* was the Pléiade's manifesto of this transformation. It was their call to arms, their call to literary arms. It was their call for the rise of the French language — and by extension, the French people and all things French — to acquire the status of being not merely French but universal or for all people. Du Bellay and the Pléiade sought nothing short of the "devouring" of Latin and that the French language stand in the place Latin once stood. Such are the modern beginnings, in the first phase of the invention of world literature, the inauguration of a new imperialism of the universal. This linguistic imperialism had everything to do with the *"littérisation"* of the French language, of its transformation into the sign and index of universality.

The many twists and turns, detailed by Casanova, by which over the subsequent two centuries a "French *imperium*" of language replaced a

11. Casanova, *World Republic of Letters* (Cambridge, MA: Harvard University Press, 2004), p. 47.

12. Benedict Anderson, *Imagined Communities: Reflections on the Origins and Spread of Nationalism* (London: Verso, 1983), p. 66. Quoted by Casanova, *World Republic of Letters,* p. 47. But still, Latin exerted an immense influence in the West even after and through the rise of the vernaculars. On this see the important work of Françoise Waquet, *Latin; or, the Empire of a Sign: From the Sixteenth to the Twentieth Centuries* (London: Verso, 2001).

"Latin *imperium*" of language, need not bog down and thus obstruct my argument. The critical point thus far is this: during this first phase in the formation of world literary space, "the French had come so fully to believe in the definitive victory of their language over Latin, and moreover had so completely succeeded in causing it to be believed by others (with the result that the authority of the language was acknowledged by all other elites in Europe)" — remember the Prussian Frederick the Great's concession of this point in his 1780 document, written significantly in French, *De la littérature allemande* — "that the use of French was quickly to spread throughout the continent."[13] In fact, so ubiquitous had French become that it was virtually "a second mother tongue in aristocratic circles in Germany and Russia . . . a sort of second language of conversation and 'civility'." French was more than a national language and, by extension, the French people were more than just a national people. It and they had transcended their borders to become cosmopolitan.[14] Casanova, in this regard, observes that the French language was "curiously '[denationalized]' and thereby rendered international."[15] It had become the linguistic sign or index of the universal, having detached itself, under the push of men and women of (French) letters, "from [political] dependency on the king, and then subjection to the national cause."[16] Du Bellay's vision had come to pass. Moreover, after the French Revolution of 1789, waged as it was in the name of the "rights of man" and in the name of a liberty bigger than just the freedom of the French but the liberty of all citizens of the world (hence, those connected with the Haitian Revolution could invoke the French Revolution for their cause), French universality came to be spatially identified with Paris as the literary-political capital of the world.[17]

13. Casanova, *World Republic of Letters*, p. 67.
14. Casanova, *World Republic of Letters*, pp. 67-68.
15. Casanova, *World Republic of Letters*, p. 68.
16. Casanova, *World Republic of Letters*, p. 69.
17. Casanova's narrative goes quite far in explaining why African Americans during the Harlem Renaissance and beyond sought freedom by going to Paris. One thinks here of a string of African and African American intellectuals from Josephine Baker and Alioune Diop to Richard Wright and James Baldwin. For a consideration of this phenomenon, see for example, Bennetta Jules-Rosette, *Black Paris: The African Writers' Landscape* (Urbana: University of Illinois Press, 1998); Theresa A. Leininger-Miller, *New Negro Artists in Paris* (Rutgers, NJ: Rutgers University Press, 2001); Jeffrey H. Jackson, *Making Jazz French: Music and Modern Life in Interwar Paris* (Durham, NC: Duke University Press, 2003); and Brent Hayes Edwards, *The Practice of Diaspora: Literature, Translation, and the Rise of Black Internationalism* (Cambridge, MA: Harvard University Press, 2003). What has been true of black

What is evident already in this first phase of the evolution of world literary space is that "world literature" emerged to function like an alternate "society," indeed as a form of social life that exceeded the nation and the politics of the state. Insofar as this is the case, it presaged something like global civil society. In imitation of Latin, or as part of its gesture to "devour" Latin, and thus take over Latin's one-time function of uniting the social, ecclesial, and political worlds, modern world literature functions as a kind of imperialism. This imperialism linguistically absorbs all things into itself by virtue of the demand that the dominated speak, and thus be absorbed or translated into, the language of the dominant. This universalism is marked by the need for the dominated to enter into a relationship of cultural and linguistic dependence. This is what was at stake in the transition from the Latin to the French *imperium*.

This brings me to the second phase in the development of world literary space and thus of the modern universal. In this second phase "the vernacularizing thrust of the print capitalism" was extended beyond the French language to incorporate the other "smaller" languages at the time of Europe. The key figure in this revolution is the German polymath Johann Gottfried von Herder (1744-1803). It was he who broke from the judgment of Frederick the Great of Prussia — it was Frederick who acceded to French cultural and linguistic superiority — to enlarge modern literary space and the very geography of the universal. Goethe, whom I referred to at the beginning of this section, brought to culmination the gestures of Herder. Refusing to kowtow to the cosmopolitan power of French preeminence, Herder changed the rules of the international literary game by arguing in several works that a nation's own language and its unique popular and folk traditions, which are the seat of their national spirit or "soul" *(Seele)*,[18] are the source of their own literary genius. *Das Volk* is the source of a people's

---

intellectuals is true of other intellectuals and writers as well. One thinks of Henry James and Gertrude Stein in the U.S. and beyond the U.S., James Joyce, Danilo Kiš, E. M. Cioran and others, each of whom set out on an odyssey of being "translated men." Casanova considers each of these writers. To undergo the processes of translation is to undergo the process of trying to acquire universal recognition and to speak as and from the universal. The other side of the translation process is crushing out or suffocating and thus killing one's mother tongue. As Casanova puts it, this is "the tragedy of translated men."

18. Not coincidentally, it is precisely this sense of "soul" that the African American intellectual W. E. B. Du Bois invoked in the title of his central text of African American and American letters, *The Souls of Black Folk* (1903). Du Bois was well versed in the German Romantic tradition, particularly through his acquaintance quite possibly with Friedrich

cultural capital. There was no need to pass through the French or any other people. In building his case against French cultural-linguistic domination, Herder turned to the English, celebrating William Shakespeare as the linguistic and cultural conservator of all things English. Shakespeare, contended Herder, is not reducible to the French. Rather, he is iconic of Englishness and from his particularity contributes to humanity as such. Herder then used his analyses of Englishness and of Shakespeare to begin the process of literarily constituting the genius of "Germanness" and calling on the German-speaking peoples to produce a specifically German literature out of the "authenticity" of its own traditions. The nineteenth-century German Romantics took up this call, with the twentieth-century philosopher Martin Heidegger, arguably, theorizing it through his philosophical notion of German rootedness or situatedness *(Bodenständigkeit)* in its own blood and soil and its self-assertion *(Selbstbehauptung)* as a people on the basis of this rootedness and situatedness.[19] The English, for their part and in turn, drew on Herder and his interpretation of Englishness and of Shakespeare to carve out their own space beyond French cultural, literary, and linguistic domination of the world republic of letters. Western literary, and at the same time political, internationalism was thus taking shape at this time in ways still recognizable today.

In short, Herder set in motion a revolution that would have wideranging effects, what Casanova calls "the Herder effect." "Henceforth, all the 'little' nations in Europe and elsewhere were able, on account of their ennoblement by the people, to claim an independent existence that was inseparably political and literary" because it was rooted in *their* language.[20] The little nations of Europe, too, could now stake a claim to universal significance for the development of civilization and high culture. The Germans had as much to contribute to universality as did the English as did the French, and so forth. All could struggle for recognition and international acceptance.

Schleiermacher when he was a student of Wilhelm Dilthey, but certainly through his careful reading of the works of Goethe both at Fisk University and during his studies abroad as a doctoral student at the University of Berlin during the late nineteenth century.

19. See the quite important work by Charles Bambach, *Heidegger's Roots: Nietzsche, National Socialism, and the Greeks* (Ithaca: Cornell University Press, 2003). See also the readings of Heidegger in Claudia Koonz, *The Nazi Conscience* (Cambridge, MA: Belknap Press of Harvard University Press, 2003) and in Mark Lilla, *The Reckless Mind: Intellectuals in Politics* (New York: New York Review of Books, 2001).

20. Casanova, *World Republic of Letters*, p. 77.

But two things are critical to note here for my purposes. The construction of literary internationalism at this point in the evolution of world literary space was consolidating "the idea of Europe" and of Europeanness.[21] Later in the nineteenth century the U.S. would add to this consolidation as its political and cultural capital increased. Thus, internationalism, as my discussion so far shows, was a western project, a firming up of the project of civilization. The second matter worth bearing in mind is something I have already said in my consideration of the first phase of world literary development. And that is this: the second phase once again shows the universal to be a field of contestation, a space of competitive struggle. The genesis of international space lay in this struggle. Herder's significance is that he gave to nations who found themselves in subordination to a given literary capital (as the Irish, for example, were to London and the English; as the English in turn were, along with the Germans, to the French; and as the Czech Republic and the Prague Circle, which included the Yiddish writer Franz Kafka, were in relationship to Berlin) the intellectual tools culled from their own peoplehood for their literary and political legitimacy. "Before the twentieth century in Europe, this struggle [for legitimacy] took the form of an attempt to nationalize language and literature."[22]

The third phase in the making of world literary space extends the Herder effect beyond the "little" nations or powers of Europe to the politically even smaller, newly independent nations of Africa, Asia, and Latin America. This phase took off with the rise of decolonization efforts after the Second World War. Struggle is also indicative of this phase of the making of the social geography of world literature. Indeed, if the making of an international literary sphere that transcended the borders of Western nations and their politics was fraught with struggle due to unevenness in power arrangements, then struggle and unevenness have proven to be even more so the case in the global situation. This is because the global situation is not dissociable from the colonial situation, a fact more easily hidden in

21. That "Europe" was an idea that had to establish itself as what we now know spatially as Europe has been the subject of scholarly investigation. See, for example, Denys Hay, *Europe: The Emergence of an Idea* (Edinburgh: Edinburgh University Press, 1968); Anthony Pagden, *The Idea of Europe: From Antiquity to the European Union* (Cambridge: Cambridge University Press, 2002); and Roberto Dianotto, *Europe (in Theory)* (Durham, NC: Duke University Press, 2007).

22. Pascale Casanova, *The World Republic of Letters*, trans. M. B. DeBevoise (Cambridge, MA: Harvard University Press, 2004), p. 79.

the prior two phases. The global situation is tied to the history of colonial domination, to the history, as the cultural theorist Stuart Hall remarked, of "the West over the rest."[23]

And this too, that is, the colonial order of things, was tied to the empire of language, for language was the vehicle of imperial domination at the quotidian level of everyday life. As Antonio de Nebrija, who wrote the first published grammar of any modern European language, Castilian or Spanish in particular (and here Nebrija predates du Bellay's efforts regarding the French language), said in the grammar's Introduction: "Language has always been the companion of empire."[24] Not insignificantly, these words were spoken the same year as Christopher Columbus, in the name of the West, began the conquest of the Americas in 1492, thus setting in motion the problem of globality (more on this below).

What the third moment of the development of world literary space discloses is that the international empire of language or the problem of French *imperium* in the first stage of world literary space was only an aspect of a wider problem, the problem of making world literary space a set of global, and not just western, international power relations. The third moment discloses that from the beginning of the making of such space, the problem of the global was already at work as a field in a ferociously violent contest over the universal — who could be admitted into it and thus represent it and who could not, and finally who could mediate it to others. In this contest, certain languages and ultimately peoples, "for language is above all a means of designating the group speaking it,"[25] are crushed because they are deemed inferior on the basis of a certain calculus of and hierarchy within the notion of the human presupposed in universalist thinking and the civilizing mission. In the third phase of the evolution of world literary space, writers from once colonized zones have sought to enter into the universal as part of a strategy of linguistic decolonization and recognition. Bilingualism has played no small role in their strategies. In describing precisely this situation of the bilingual shuttle between their crushed or dominated native tongue or peoplehood and the dominant languages out of which they must speak for the sake of universal recognition, ultimately

---

23. Stuart Hall, "The West and the Rest: Discourse and Power," in *Modernity: An Introduction to Modern Societies,* ed. Stuart Hall, David Held, Don Hubert and Kenneth Thompson (Cambridge, MA: Blackwell, 1996), pp. 184-227.

24. Quoted in Todorov Tzvetan, *The Conquest of America: The Question of the Other* (Norman, OK: University of Oklahoma Press, 1999), p. 123.

25. Tzvetan, *The Conquest of America,* p. 123.

as human, Albert Memmi acutely captures the tragic dimensions of postcolonial globality:

> The mother tongue of the colonized [writer] . . . has no dignity in [his own] country or in the concert of people. If he wishes to practice a trade, make a place for himself, exist in public life and in the world, he must first submit to the language of others, that of the colonizers, his masters. In the linguistic conflict that goes on inside the colonized [writer], his mother tongue ends up being humiliated, crushed. And since the contempt has an objective basis, he ends up sharing it himself.[26]

While there is much more that could be said in reflection on Casanova's deft analyses of the making of world literary space, I hope my point is sufficiently clear. And that point is this: as a set of power relations, the global is a field of struggle tied to the universal — who can enter into it and who cannot; who is seen as its "natural" denizen and who is not; who can mediate it to others (and thus function as "savior") because they speak from the universal, and who cannot. Moreover, I have sought to show through engaging Casanova that the uneven power relations that mark world literary space and that have been exacerbated under the late-modern conditions of global existence are linked to an unevenness built into the modern notion of the human, that is, into the notion of "Universal Man" as "Western Man." When world literary space is interpreted in relationship to colonial history, this anthropological unevenness, which is ultimately racial and ethnic in character, is produced of the spatial fragmentation that splits social reality between the West and the rest. Casanova's consideration of the evolution of world literature in significant ways brushes up against this anthropological problem *qua* spatial problem. What I want to do now is drill further into the problem of late-modern global existence through a consideration of the theological operations that worked to produce the global as the spatial complement to modernity/coloniality in the first place. For this I turn to what I would like to call the political theology of 1492.

26. Quoted in Casanova, *World Republic of Letters*, pp. 258-59.

The Trinitarian Deformation of the World:
The Political Theology of 1492

In turning to the archive of 1492 to explore the archaeology of the global present, and importantly to explore its theological character, I seek to do two things. First, I want to press those accounts of global civil society, like the account given by Keane in this volume, to consider the theological make-up of global existence today and how the vision of the global built into their notions of global civil society may in fact reproduce in secular, non-theological terms the problematic vision of the global from which theologians functioned at the dawn of the modern/colonial world. But second, in turning to the archive of 1492, which I am reading as in fact a theological archive, I am pressing contemporary theologians who have sought to engage global existence today for a deeper account of how a certain Christian social imagination, upheld and theorized by theologians, produced the space of the global as a space of uneven development that placed Europe, Euroamerica, and the western civilizing project at the center of the order of things. Max Stackhouse's essay in this volume edges in this direction, as does Alexander Brodie's essay, which considers the theological and homiletic background out of which civil society discourse arose in the Scottish Enlightenment, though he leaves unaccounted for the wider global architecture of the Scottish Enlightenment itself and how that might bear on civil society rhetoric. My claim is that only against the backdrop of the story of how Christianity became bound up with the western civilizing project, the very project that produced the global as a structure of uneven development, which is undergirded by a particular way of conceiving the human, can a contemporary theological engagement envision an engagement with global existence today that would not, unwittingly perhaps, reproduce theology's original mistake of producing a world in which all social relations are mediated by western culture as Christian culture with a built-in anthropology of the universal, self-sufficient "Man."

The story of how Christianity's social vision came to be identified with the project of western civilization and its global and universal ambitions is indeed a painful tale, but a tale in many respects yet untold. It is a tale lost to view in the revival of Augustinianism and Thomism in many quarters of contemporary theology, Catholic and Protestant alike.[27] I say

27. Much of the work done under the banners of Radical Orthodoxy and Narra-

this because the revival of the medieval or the making of what might be called a "medieval modernity" that is operative inside of contemporary theology suggests a condition of melancholy, a nostalgic longing to construct a future of social wholeness by reconstructing "the monuments of the [a theological] past."[28] The nostalgic effort to theologically reconstitute the past by laying claim to a would-be medieval wholeness is envisioned as the antidote to the social fragmentation indicative of a broken world.[29] The Church, which stood at the pinnacle of the "empire of Latin," mediated this wholeness in the medieval era, before the rise of vernacular or vulgar fragmentation in the fifteenth and sixteenth centuries. The story of Christian social performance in the fifteenth century is very much the story of how medieval wholeness or universality sought to encompass the globe as European wholeness or universality. What I want to point out is how inside of all of this was a peculiar theological operation.

A central figure in this story is the fifteenth-century French cardinal Pierre D'Ailly (1350-1420), the central theological voice at the Council of Constance (1414-1418). It was in his medieval and in many ways Thomist theological vision that a proto-racial account of the human received its first articulation. It was proto-racial and not yet fully racial because, while his thought made one of the earliest claims that human beings could be grouped according to essences that determined who they were quite apart from the contingencies and exigencies of history, D'Ailly nevertheless located these differences within a framework of theological differences. That is to say, D'Ailly fully integrated a proto-racial vision of the human into his theological account of the differences between Christians, Jews, and "Saracens," as Muslims were then called. These theological differences connoted for him anthropological differences. And so, with D'Ailly *theological* anthropology morphs into an *anthropological* theology, within which a prior essence of some sort (let's call it a "racial" essence) explains the Christian difference from and supremacy over Jews and Muslims. Human difference grounded in what we would now call racial character does

---

tive Theology succumb to the problem I am talking about, as does a bit of the work by Roman Catholic theologians under the banner of *Ressourcement* or return to the sources of the tradition.

28. Svetlana Boym, *The Future of Nostalgia* (New York: Basic Books, 2001), p. 41.

29. It is precisely with such a metaphor of fragmentation that Alasdair MacIntyre opened his celebrated work *After Virtue: A Study in Moral Theory* (Notre Dame: University of Notre Dame Press, 1984). This is the problem, the problem of the loss of a unifying tradition that must be solved.

important, explanatory work for D'Ailly within Christendom's crusader imaginary.[30]

A crucial development happens in the middle of the fifteen century. This development might be called the genesis of globality as we have it. The Portuguese Prince Henry the Navigator took up D'Ailly's theological and political, or theopolitical, medievalist vision regarding the crusades. Through his transatlantic travels and his "discovery" of inhabitants in sub-Saharan Africa, then called Guinea, he would be pivotal in the transition from D'Ailly's protoracial vision of anthropological theology to a fully racial theological aesthetic. This racial-theological aesthetic of the human was also a spatial aesthetic of global existence. It was, in other words, a way of configuring spatial relations as power relations. The catalyst for the transition from a protoracial to a racial vision of the human was the opening up of the transatlantic commercial circuit, led by Prince Henry, who incorporated or annexed the inhabitants of sub-Saharan Africa into the medieval proto-racial imaginary. This was utterly new as the crusader imaginary morphed into a global one and as the Atlantic Ocean came to displace the Mediterranean Sea as the locus for organizing the social, political, and religious worlds. But note how Prince Henry annexed Africa. He did it by designating Africans as racially black. Indeed, race is being constituted in this very moment with a complete hierarchy of light to dark into which other peoples could later be inserted. Moreover, whiteness itself is what is ultimately being invisibly brought into being in this social moment as the driving force behind globality. The following quotation by Zurara, Prince Henry's chronicler, sustains this claim. Documenting the Prince's exploits of valor in capturing Africans who would be the first racial slaves to land in Europe, thus inaugurating the modern slave trade, Zurara paints a harrowing scene of their seizure:

These people [the captured Africans], assembled together on that open place, were an astonishing sight to behold. Among them were

30. I am drawing on the critical Spanish edition of Pierre D'Ailly's *Tratado sobre el acuerdo entre la verdad astronómica y la narración histórica* among other of his writings in developing these claims. For this text, see Pierre D'Ailly, *"Ymago Mundi" y otros opúsculos*, ed. Antonio Ramírez de Verger, Juan Fernández Valverde and Francisco Socas (Madrid: Alianza Editorial, S.A., 1992). I am also quite indebted to two important critical engagements with D'Ailly: Laura Ackerman Smoller, *History, Prophecy, and the Stars: The Christian Astrology of Pierre D'Ailly, 1350-1420* (Princeton: Princeton University Press, 1994) and Nicolás Wey Gómez, *The Tropics of Empire: Why Columbus Sailed South to the Indies* (Cambridge, MA: MIT Press, 2008), which has an extended engagement with D'Ailly's theological outlook.

some who were quite white-skinned, handsome and of good appearance; others [Berbers or 'tawny Moors'] were less white, seeming more like brown men; others still were as black as Ethiopians, so deformed of face and body that, to those who stared at them, it almost seemed that they were looking at spirits from the lowest hemisphere. But what heart, however hardened it might be, could not be pierced by a feeling of pity at the site of that company? Some held their heads low, their faces bathed in tears as they looked at each other; some groaned very piteously, looking towards the heavens fixedly and crying out aloud, as if they were calling on the father of the universe to help them; others struck their faces with their hands and threw themselves full length on the ground; yet others lamented in the form of a chant, according to the custom of their native land, and though the words of the language in which they sang could not be understood by our people, the chant revealed clearly enough the degree of their grief.[31]

This passage points to a racial aesthetic and a racial hierarchy through which to interpret, theologically no less, the human. It is an aesthetic that is explicit about the lower end of the hierarchy. Zurara identifies this lower end as black, which is to say, as grotesque or "deformed." But this lower end of the aesthetic register has theological content inasmuch as for Zurara racial blackness is a theological signifier of the demonic. This comes out in Zurara's comments that to gaze upon the facial appearances of these Africans on an auction block was to gaze upon visitors from hell or "spirits from the lowest hemisphere."

Later still in the fifteenth century, with his "discovery" of the Americas in 1492, Christopher Columbus in effect extended what Prince Henry of Portugal started, making even more pronounced the theological circuits of the trans- or Black Atlantic. Columbus's writings, many of which were edited by Father Bartolomé de las Casas, display a deep trinitarian spirituality within which he situated his narrative theological vision of the world. In his letter of March 3, 1493 to the sovereigns Isabella of Castile and Ferdinand of Aragon, a letter written on the return leg of his first voyage in which he "discovered" the Caribbean Islands or the Americas, Columbus gives the mission he has just accomplished a trinitarian framing. At one point in the letter he says:

---

31. From Azurara's *Chronicles of the Conquest of Guinea* as recorded in Peter Russell, *Prince Henry 'the Navigator': A Life* (New Haven: Yale University Press, 2000), pp. 242-43.

Most powerful sovereigns: all of Christendom should hold great celebrations, and especially God's Church, for the finding of such a multitude of such friendly peoples, which with very little effort will be con-
verted to our Holy Faith, and so many lands filled with so many goods
very necessary to us in which all Christians will have comfort and
profits, all of which was unknown nor did anyone speak of it except in
fables. Great rejoicing and celebrations in the churches [text dam-
aged]. . . . Your highnesses should order that many praises should be
given to the Holy Trinity [text damaged] your kingdoms and domains
because of the great love [the Holy Trinity?] has shown you, more than
any other prince.[32]

Columbus concludes the letter with a prayer: ". . . may the Holy Trinity
guard and make your Highnesses' royal estate. Written in the sea of Spain,
on the fourth day of March of the year fourteen ninety-three. At sea."[33]

But sandwiched between these invocations of God as Trinity are references to the various peoples found on the islands. These peoples are interpreted in ethnographic, which is to say, racial terms. But what is critical
here is that racial ethnography functioned inside of a trinitarian frame of
reference. And to render matters more complex, it must also be said that
Columbus's racial-ethnographic outlook made race the refracting optic
for gender too. He writes,

Wherefore your Highnesses should know that the first island of the
Indies, closest to Spain, is populated entirely by women, without a
single man, and their comportment is not feminine, but rather they
use weapons and other masculine practices. They carry bows and ar-
rows and take their adornments from the copper mines, which metal

32. I draw on both the restored letter and a translation of it provided in Margarita
Zamora, *Reading Columbus* (Berkeley: University of California Press, 1993), p. 195. The theo-
logical reading of Columbus's mission to the "Indies" is informed by several historical engagements with the issue of the discovery and conquest of the Americas. Here are just a few
of those I have found most important: Alain Milhou, *Colón y su mentalidad mesiánica*
(Valladolid: Casa-Museo de Colón, 1983); P. M. Watts, "Prophecy and Discovery: On the
Spiritual Origins of Christopher Columbus's 'Enterprise of the Indies,'" *American Historical
Review* 90 (1985): 73-102; Leonard Sweet, "Christopher Columbus and the Millennial Vision
of the New World," *Catholic Historical Review* 72 (1986): 372-81; William D. Phillips, Jr. and
Carla Rahn Phillips, *The Worlds of Christopher Columbus* (Cambridge: Cambridge Univer-
sity Press, 1992); and Djelal Kadir, *Columbus and the Ends of the Earth: Europe's Prophetic
Rhetoric as Conquering Ideology* (Berkeley: University of California Press, 1992).

33. Zamora, *Reading Columbus*, p. 197.

they have in very large quantity. They call this island Matenino, the second Caribo, [blank] leagues out from this one. Here are found those people which all of the other islands of the Indies fear; they eat human flesh, are great bowmen, have many canoes almost as big as oar-powered *fustas,* in which they travel all over the islands of the Indies, and they are so feared that they have no equal. They go about naked like the others, except that they wear their hair very full, like women.[34]

This passage shows how gender articulates race at the colonial site of empire in the modern world.[35] But when read in light of other comments in the March 1493 letter and from the logs of the first voyage, what is also clear is this: the racial interpretation of the Amerindians through protocols of gender is as such an interpretation of them in terms of how they socially organize themselves. Here is a passage from the logs of the first voyage that establishes this point: "These people are very gentle and timid, naked as I said before, without weapons and *without law*."[36] Here is another passage from the letter of March 4, 1493 that also makes the point:

All of them, women and men alike, go about naked like their mothers bore them, although some of the women wear a small piece of cotton or a patch of grass with which they cover themselves. They have neither iron nor weapons, except for canes on the end of which they place a thin sharp stick. Everything they make is done with stones. I have not learned that any of them has private property, because while I was spending a few days with this king in the village of La Navidad, I saw that all of the people, and the women in particular, would bring him *agís,* which is the food they eat, and he would order them to be distributed; a very singular sustenance.[37]

Columbus immediately draws religious conclusions from his interpretation of what he takes as the deficiencies of Amerindian social order. They are "without law" and "weapons" and without the notion of "private property." He then says both in the logs and in his 1493 letter that the Amer-

---

34. Zamora, *Reading Columbus,* p. 196.

35. This is an issue carefully examined in Anne McClintock, *Imperial Leather: Race, Gender, and Sexuality in the Colonial Contest* (New York: Routledge, 1995).

36. Samuel Eliot Morison, ed., *Journals and Other Documents on the Life and Voyages of Christopher Columbus* (New York: The Heritage Press, 1963), p. 88. Italics mine.

37. Morison, ed., *Journals and Other Documents,* p. 192.

indians are "without religion."[38] That is to say, they are outside of the umbrella of Christianity/Christendom.

Columbus's conclusion is that to bring the Amerindians into the order of Christendom, which he represented, was to bring them into a kind of global civil order. The March 1493 letter makes clear that this order is theologically sanctioned by a trinitarian vision of God. That is to say, a trinitarian theological outlook upholds the social order. It did this by placing a racial overlay onto human bodies, thus constituting the human as a racial being in which Europeanness stands at the pinnacle to mediate salvation and broker authentic human existence. The racial order of things that brought *homo racialis* into being is operating inside of a trinitarian imagination.

In fact, Columbus's trinitarian sensibility only increased with time. Indeed, Columbus's naming on his third voyage of the island of "Trinidad" is tied directly to his trinitarian outlook on the world. As recorded in Bartolomé de Las Casas's abstract of the logs of Columbus's third voyage, Columbus says:

> On the seventeenth day of the fair weather, which was bearing them along, the Admiral hoped to sight land on account of the said indications from the birds they had seen. And as he did not sight on Monday, on the next day, Tuesday, 31 July, since there was already a shortage of water, he decided to change his course toward the west, and to turn to the starboard hand, and seek to pick up the island of Dominica or one of the Carib islands. So he gave orders to steer to the N by E, and he continued on this course until midday. "But, as His Divine Majesty," says he, "ever showeth mercy towards me, fortuitously and by chance a seaman from Huelva, my servant named Alonso Pérez, climbed to the crow's nest and saw land to the west, distant 15 leagues, and it appeared to be in the shape of three rocks or mountains." These are his words. He named this land "The Island of Trinidad" because he had determined that the first land he should discover would be so called [or given the divine name]. "It pleased our Lord," he [Columbus] says,

---

38. In the letter Columbus says, "Nowhere in these islands have I known the inhabitants to have a religion, or idolatry. . . ." Zamora, *Reading Columbus*, p. 192. And at one point in the logs he says, "I believe that they [i.e., the Amerindians] would easily be made Christians, because it seemed to me that they belonged to no religion. I, may it please Our Lord, will carry off six of them at my departure to Your Highnesses." Morison, ed., *Journals and Other Documents*, p. 65.

"that on the first sight there were three rocks, I mean mountains, all in a group, all at once and in a single view. May his almighty power guide me by his charity," he says, "in such wise that he will be served and Your Highnesses have much pleasure, for it is certain that the finding of this island in this region was a great miracle, as great as the Discovery of the First Voyage." These are his words.[39]

How does trinitarianism function in all of this? It does the work of enacting the relationship between a "civilized" West and the rest of the "racially inferior" world. But it does so by reconfiguring space itself. That is, the Caribbean islands are spatially placed inside of and thus annexed to trinitarian social space. But here trinitarianism is made to work in concert with Columbus's will to annexation and thus his will to constitute global existence by assimilating the Caribbean islands to the Western imagination. In this way, trinitarianism gives theological warrant to the universal aspirations of the West.

The sixteenth-century theologians at the University of Salamanca in Spain would take it as their task to reflect theologically on what had happened in the "discovery" of the Americas and its inhabitants. They would theorize the social order that was emerging in the wake of the discovery. In this regard, perhaps the central figure among the Salamancan intellectuals was the Thomist theologian Francisco de Vitoria, a central figure in the formulation of a discourse of "the rights of the people."[40] Vitoria made a significant contribution to the emergence of a discourse of international law, which sought to establish the rights of nations on the new global scene. Arguably, the Salamancan deliberations were the forerunner to what in the Enlightenment would become a discourse on cosmopolitanism and global civil society. But again, the formulation of international law and a discourse of "the rights of the people," discourses that are central to the notion of global civil society, were in critical ways tied to the racial-ethnographic imagination that had come to ground the modern world and that had come to be internal to the discourse of theology in producing the modern world.[41]

What I seek to do here in probing this disturbing archive in the making of global existence and a modern/colonial world is to point out the in-

39. Samuel Eliot Morison, ed., *Journals and Other Documents*, p. 265.
40. Walter Mignolo, "The Many Faces of Cosmo-polis: Border Thinking and Critical Cosmopolitanism," *Public Culture* 12, no. 3 (2000): 723.
41. Anthony Pagden, *The Fall of Natural Man* (Cambridge: Cambridge University Press, 1982).

debtedness the notion of the global has to a deformed Christian theological imagination that was at once a problematic social imagination. This is something that Keane does not rigorously enough address. (On this point, my comments join those of Kristin Deede Johnson's in her contribution to this volume.) But also, I want to indicate why it is not easy to simply return to a trinitarian engagement with global existence given the complicity of trinitarian and theological discourse in the production of a world structured by global and anthropological unevenness (something that contemporary theologians have not rigorously enough addressed). And finally, my point has been to provide a backdrop for raising the following question: If what I have sketched here has any merit, then the question that remains is whether it is even possible for theology to engage the notion of global civil society in such a way as *not* to reenact western hegemony precisely inside of the rhetorics of theology — be those rhetorics "orthodox" or "liberal." What was it about theological discourse, and the discourse of God's triune life in particular, that allowed it to midwife an ethnographic vision of the human that came to house an account of the universal centered in the mediating authority of the West over the rest of the world as a centerpiece of its civilizing project? To answer this I want now to turn from the doctrine of the Trinity to a consideration of the identity of Jesus (Christology) and to the politics of his identity (atonement), for it is with the doctrine of Jesus' identity that the deepest issues regarding the universal and the formation of the global present lie.

The Global; or, the Christological Problem Revisited

What I have started to outline here are the theological operations by which an ethnographic gaze started to take shape as the orienting center of a Christian imagination. I've argued that these are the very operations by which the West constituted itself as the West in relationship to the non-western world. Let me be clear: these were excruciatingly violent processes which were tied also to the common realities of everyday life. And yet, as life-depriving as they were, they were envisioned as bringing "salvation" to those considered less than civilized. This "salvation" consisted of their annexation to civilization. All of this happened inside of a trinitarian outlook. Moreover, implied in what I've shown is that social analogy trinitarianism and classical trinitarianism meet in this process. They are not alternatives to each other. This is because Columbus' trinitarianism, which in the strictest sense was "orthodox" or was in keeping with the Church's confession of his day, functioned materially to construct a social world, as analogical trinitarians would have. Columbus was both of these.

Thus, the issue may be insufficiently framed if the choice is between social analogy or classical trinitarianism or something even on and thus still inside of this continuum. The question that must be confronted is this: how was the vision of God that was at work in the archive I've overviewed here able to function instrumentally to bring forth, at the hands in no small part of theologians and other serious Christians like Columbus, a world of global unevenness? How did it happen? To cut to the answer, it was due in significant part to this: the confession of God as Trinity was articulated in independence of Jesus as Israel's ongoing Messiah and as the one into whom all others must enter. With this lost to view, a world was constructed in which Europe in due course positioned itself as the universal and as the mediator of reality and within the social world.

In this regard the trinitarian confession functioned in a double way. First, in keeping with the crusader mentality of the fifteenth century, the trinitarian confession functioned as an anti-Jewish (and anti-Islamic) confession. And thus, the trinitarian theopolitics of 1492, though "orthodox," did not point as it should have to Israel's covenantal interaction with YHWH as the primary and ongoing story into which, through Jesus as Israel's Messiah, non-Jewish Christians have entered and to which they bear witness. Trinitarian thinking is to aid Christians in their intellectual and social witness to this reality. Instead of this — and here is my other side of how the trinitarian confession functioned — trinitarianism redounded back to the West and its civilizing project. It came to function inside the western order of things to sanctify it through its way of conceiving of God. Within this framework Jesus could not be viewed as Israel's Messiah with the Church being a weak witness to their Messiah. Rather, Jesus was seized as the cultural property of the West and therefore as the one who religiously superintends a global order in which the West was positioned as universal mediator. In short, inside of the problem of globality is the problem of Christian supersessionism, albeit now deployed to do ethnographic work in shaping a global order centered in the West as universal.

To ground my claim that inside of the problem of the global is the christological problem of the identity of Jesus and that within this lies the problem of the refusal of Jesus' Jewish covenantal existence, I refer once again to Christopher Columbus, particularly, to the prologue he appended to the logs of his first voyage. Margarita Zamora has persuasively argued that the prologue was originally a stand-alone document, a letter written by Columbus to the Spanish sovereigns on the departure leg of his trip across the Atlantic. It was only later appended to the logs as its prologue by Bartolomé de las Casas.[42] The prologue, then, is a pre-discovery document that functions in effect as the opening bookend for the voyage. It lays out from Columbus's perspective the intention and meaning of the enterprise as he saw it as it was getting underway and before he "discovered" anything or anybody. It is within this document that the enterprise is given its christologico-supersessionistic framing and is positioned within a medieval crusader imaginary. Its opening words are "In the Name of Our Lord Jesus Christ." From there it proceeds to interpret the significance of the year 1492. It is worth quoting at length:

> Because, most Christian and very Exalted, Excellent and mighty Princes, King and Queen of the Spains and of the Islands of the Sea, our Lord and Lady, in the present year 1492, after Your Highnesses had made an end to the war with the Moors [the Muslims] who ruled in Europe [that is, in Iberia], and had concluded the war in the very great City of Granada, where in the present year, on the second day of the month of January, I saw the Royal Standard of Your Highnesses placed by force of arms on the towers of the Alhambra (which is the citadel of the said city). . . .
>
> And thus, after all the Jews had been exiled from your realms and dominions, in the same month of January your Highnesses commanded me that with a sufficient fleet I should go to the said regions of India. . . . And I departed from the city of Granada on the 12th day of the month of May of the same year 1492, on a Saturday, and came to the town of Palos, which is a seaport, where I fitted for sea three vessels well suited for such an enterprise, and I departed from the said harbor . . . and took route for the Canary Islands of Your Highnesses . . . that I might thence take my course and sail until I should reach the Indies and give the letters of Your Highnesses to those princes, and thus comply with what you had commanded.[43]

While a full analysis of this passage and its significance cannot be given here, what is important for my purposes is Columbus's reference to the expulsion of the Jews from Castile in 1492 and the position he gave to

42. Zamora, *Reading Columbus*, pp. 21-38.
43. Morison, ed., *Journals and Other Documents*, pp. 47-49.

this event in his interpretation of his enterprise. In this passage Columbus establishes what might be called an interpretive conjunction between three events, all taking place in "this present year of 1492." The first event was the defeat of the Moors or the Saracens in Granada, which many (including Columbus) interpreted as a turn of fortunes for Christendom in the crusades, particularly since the fall of the eastern Christian outpost of Constantinople to Islam in 1453.[44] It was Columbus's hope to complete the defeat of Islam, and thus conclude the crusades, by retaking Jerusalem itself.[45] The search for India by way of the Atlantic was part of a theopolitical military strategy to accomplish this. However, the effectiveness of the strategy required, many believed, not only that Christendom's external enemy be dealt with, but that it be purged of its chief internal enemy as well. In other words, the defeat of the external enemy, the enemy beyond the realm of Christendom (i.e. the Saracens or Muslims), required purification from a contaminant or an enemy within the realm of Christendom. This enemy within was the Jews.[46] Columbus interpreted the second great event of 1492, the expulsion of the Jews from Castile, which took place in March of that year (not January as he erroneously says in his Prologue or in the pre-discovery letter) as addressing the Jewish problem. In other words, the presence of Jews within the realms of Christendom was interpreted as what stood in the way of striking the final defeat of the Saracens, or taking back Jerusalem from them, in the crusades.

The third event of 1492 that Columbus refers to is his Orientalist mission to evangelize India, for with a partner in the Indies (and with its resources) Christendom would be better positioned to defeat the Moors, to retake Jerusalem, and thus to bring about an apocalypse that would be the harbinger of an eschatological age, the Kingdom of God.[47] Columbus

44. Roger Crowley, *1453: The Holy War for Constantinople and the Clash of Islam and the West* (New York: Hyperion, 2005).

45. Columbus says in his letter of March 4, 1493 to Isabella and Ferdinand: "I conclude here: that through the divine grace of Him who is the origin of all good and virtuous things, who favors and gives victory to all those who walk in His path, that in seven years from today I will be able to pay your Highnesses for five thousand cavalry and fifty thousand foot soldiers for the war and conquest of Jerusalem, *for which purpose this enterprise was undertaken.*" Zamora, *Reading Columbus*, pp. 194-95; italics mine.

46. For a quite insightful theorization of how Jews and Muslims functioned as Christendom's theopolitical double-enemy, see Gil Anidjar, *The Jew, the Arab: A History of the Enemy* (Stanford: Stanford University Press, 2003).

47. Given this, Edward Said's "orientalism" thesis requires supplementation. Cf. Edward Said, *Orientalism* (New York: Vintage, 1979). Orientalism as a scientific discourse may

interpreted the expulsion of the Jews, which signified the purification of Christianity of its Jewish infection, as the key event. It was seen as the event that put the victory of Christendom within reach. What was hindering Christendom to this point, so the logic went, was that it was being handicapped by a Jewish parasite within the body (politic) of the West. Such is how the theological problem of Christian supersessionism materially displayed itself in giving birth to the modern world.

Columbus's pre-discovery letter of 1492, which was appended to the logs of his first voyage, begins with an invocation of "the Name of Our Lord Jesus Christ." This invocation was meant to be one that announced the purity of Christian faith and the purity of its central figure, Jesus Christ, from external (Islamic) and even more so internal (Jewish) contamination. But what does a purified Jesus mean? It means a Jesus cut off from the covenantal people of Israel and now tied to the West as its possession and thus its religious symbol.

A second quotation will help me elucidate this point. It comes from the document that closes the logs of Columbus's first voyage. The passage is found near the beginning of the letter of March 4, 1493 in which Columbus tells of his naming of the islands as he encountered them and their inhabitants on the voyage. He says:

> I found innumerable people and very many islands, of which I took possession in Your Highnesses' name, by royal crier and with Your Highnesses' royal banner unfurled, and it was not contradicted. To the first [island] I gave the name San Salvador, in memory of his Supreme Majesty [Jesus Christ], to the second Santa María de la Concepción, to the third Fernandina, to the fourth Isabela, to the fifth Juana. . . .[48]

What this passage records is Columbus's first act of expropriation.[49] By expropriation I mean that Columbus does not merely lay claim to the islands through a linguistic process of naming. This would simply be appropriation. In naming the islands as he did, he was drawing them into the imaginary of Christendom and the global social order that, through

---

have its origins in the nineteenth century, as Said has rightly said. But its deeper impulse lay in the fifteenth century in the late medieval and early Renaissance birth of the modern world.

48. Zamora, *Reading Columbus*, p. 190.

49. The following explanation of "expropriation" is informed by the discussion of this term in Luis N. Rivera, *A Violent Evangelism: The Political and Religious Conquest of the Americas* (Louisville: Westminster/John Knox, 1992).

these very events, was in the process of being constituted as the West. We considered Columbus's naming of the island of "the Trinity" (Trinidad) in his third voyage in the previous section of this epilogue. Here we see that his first event of naming on the first voyage was not trinitarian. It was Christological; it concerned the identity of Jesus. Moreover, it was Soteriological; it concerned the politics of his identity. The islands are "named" into the death of Jesus, which as such is their incorporation, their being configured into, Columbus's Christian imagination. In other words, the names given to the islands so as to "invent" them as the "Americas" or as a global extension of Europe, were at their crux the first act of theological expropriation. And it was staged as a christological-soteriological event. The later trinitarian naming of the island of Trini-dad on the third voyage happens inside of the "christological" event of the first voyage. For Columbus says, "To the first [island] I gave the name San Salvador," or Holy Savior, "in memory of his Supreme Majesty [Jesus Christ]." In naming the first island after the Holy Savior, Jesus Christ, Columbus lodges the events of his "India Mission" and "Jerusalem En-terprise" within a soteriological framework. One might say that the global social order that is under production in the events of discovery is one that figures the West in soteriological terms. The global, then, is a horizon of redemption as all things accede to becoming tied to the West or absorbed into it. The West and the social order it represents occupies the position of "Savior."[50]

The image in Figure 1 (on p. 325) aesthetically symbolizes this read-ing of the surrounding documents to the logs of Columbus's first voyage. Columbus saw himself as carrying out a christological mission. As his name, "Christopher," suggests, he took himself in accordance with the Greek etymology of his name as the "christos-ferens," the bearer or the

50. While there may be similarities between what I am saying here and the arguments developed by William T. Cavanaugh about "the myth of the state as savior" — see his *Theopolitical Imagination* (London: T&T Clark, 2002) — it would be a mistake to conflate the two. For the glaring oversight in Cavanaugh's argument is that he does not address the colonial dimensions of modern statecraft. Because he does not do this, he has no way of ad-dressing how the problem of race is internal to modern statecraft. Moreover, he has no way of addressing how theology itself, indeed theology of the Eucharistic sort that he proposes as a solution to the problem, was an instrument within the production of the modern state and its self-identity as savior. Thus, in an unintended way (and I stress here unintended), Cavanaugh can be read as offering a theological solution to the soteriological myth of the state as savior that represents a regression to the origins of the problem.

**Figure 1: Detail of Colum-
bus as Christoferens from
the map of Juan de la
Cosa.** Frontispiece reproduced from R. H. Major,
ed., *Select Letters of Christopher Columbus* (London,
1870)

bringer of Christ to the Indies and thus as the inaugurator of a "New
World." This image is a profound representation of the problem: Christ is
so identified with Columbus that Columbus stands between Christ and
the world. In this sense, Columbus as symbol of the West, a point that the
U.S. poet Walt Whitman concedes and celebrates in *Leaves of Grass*, is messianic.[51] Moreover, that Columbus in this image stands in the waters of the

51. In "Passage to India," Whitman envisions the American project of Manifest Destiny in the nineteenth century as saving the western civilizing project started by Columbus
in 1492, which he imagined as in decline. He says:

> The medieval navigators rise before me,
> The world of 1492, with its awaken'd enterprise;
> Something swelling in humanity now like the sap of the earth in spring,
> The sunset splendor of chivalry declining.
> And who art thou, sad shade?
> Gigantic, visionary, thyself a visionary,
> With majestic limbs, and pious, beaming eyes,

Atlantic means that his mediation is global, spanning the emerging trans-atlantic waterways, the (theological) circuits of the "Black Atlantic." I say that these circuits were global because they were not only triangulated be-tween Europe, Africa, and the Americas. Through the seafaring of the Por-tuguese, they extended eventually around the Cape of Good Hope and into the Indian Ocean and Far East Asia. In short, the Black Atlantic was the global Atlantic. It is the symbol of global existence. Columbus took his messianic role in the midst of this with utter seriousness. So serious did he

> Spreading around, with every look of thine, a golden world,
> Enhuing it with gorgeous hues.
> As the chief histrion,
> Down to the footlights walks, in some great scena,
> Dominating the rest, I see the Admiral himself,
> (History's type of courage, action, faith;)
> Behold him sail from Palos, leading his little fleet;
> His voyage behold — his return — his great fame,
> His misfortunes, calumniators — behold him a prisoner, chain'd,
> Behold his dejection, poverty, death.

But Whitman gives all of this trinitarian and christological basis, just as Columbus did, which in the broad sweep of his politics is tied to his own complex commitments to Ameri-can Manifest Destiny.

> After the seas are all cross'd, (as they seem already cross'd,)
> After the great captains and engineers have accomplish'd their work,
> After the noble inventors — after the scientists, the chemist, the geologist,
>   ethnologist,
> Finally shall come the Poet, worthy that name;
> The true Son of God shall come, singing his songs.
> Then, not your deeds only, O voyagers, O scientists and inventors, shall be
>   justified,
> All these hearts, as of fretted children, shall be sooth'd,
> All affection shall be fully responded to — the secret shall be told;
> All these separations and gaps shall be taken up, and hook'd and link'd together;
> The whole Earth — this cold, impassive, voiceless Earth, shall be completely
>   justified,
> Trinitas divine shall be gloriously accomplish'd and compacted by the true son of
>   God, the poet,
> (He shall indeed pass the straits and conquer the mountains,
> He shall double the Cape of Good Hope to some purpose;)
> Nature and Man shall be disjoin'd and diffused no more,
> The true son of God shall absolutely fuse them.

I have quoted from *Walt Whitman: Complete Poetry and Collected Prose*, ed. Justin Kaplan (New York: Library Classics of the United States, 1982), pp. 536, 534-35.

Figure 2: Columbus's
signature

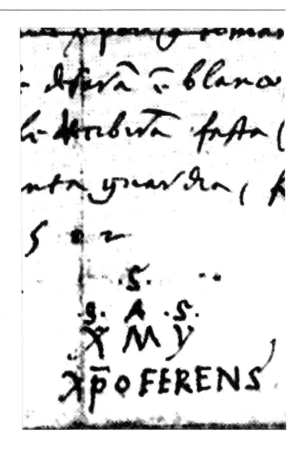

take his messianic role that that after his first voyage he started signing
documents with the name "Christo-ferens" (see figure 2 above).

Conclusion: Towards a Christological Re-Formation of the World

Given the archaeology that I have sketched here, what is the way forward? I
suggest that a trinitarian engagement with the realities of late-modern and
post-colonial global existence demands a reimaging of the identity of Jesus. The quotation by Bonhoeffer in the epigraph to these reflections
points to what I mean. Bonhoeffer suggests that Jesus is an alternate spatial
reality. In his flesh social space is reconfigured, such that in him "the rule
of this world" is disrupted. In him, we are deprived of our "immediate [re-
lationships] to the given realities of the world" inasmuch as in his lordship

328

Christ "[steps] in between me and the world."⁵² The death of Christ is Jesus' bringing to death (in his death) a world order centered in anyone other than him. As a result of his reflections on German National Socialism and on Hitler and the Nazi regime, Bonhoeffer became increasingly clear that Christ's death entailed the death of "God," where "God" here was a western order, refracted in his specific case through Hitler, that took itself to be the global mediator and thus the center of the world. This order of things and vision of reality had been judged in his flesh, with the verdict of death pronounced over all other mediation but his own, and so that his resurrected life could come after it. Bonhoeffer's wager was that the twentieth-century destabilization of the West from the World Wars to decolonization and the struggles of once colonized and marginalized peoples to be in the world without "God," the quest to be "secular," was the bringing to naught of a previous global order organized through the western universality or mediation.

Moreover, Bonhoeffer already started to see inside of the secular unrest of the twentieth century and the reconfiguration of global realities the emergence within Christian theology of a reactionary melancholy. On the eve of his death in Tegel, he started to discern a nostalgic longing in theology, a yearning for a bygone symbolized by the Middle Ages. He started to see a return to the medieval. What was being held up about the Middle Ages and medieval theology was a vision of God that could unify the world through the mediating and thus unifying capacities of Christian civilization as western civilization. But in a letter to his friend Eberhard Bethge from the prison in Tegel dated July 16, 1944, Bonhoeffer judged such melancholy mistaken:

> Anxious souls will ask what room there is left for God now; and as they know of no answer to the question, they condemn the whole development that has brought them to such straits. I wrote to you before about the various emergency exits that have been contrived; and we ought to add to them the *salto mortale* [death-leap] back into the Middle Ages. But the principle of the Middle Ages is heteronomy in the form of clericalism; a return to that can be a counsel of despair, and it would be at the cost of intellectual honesty. It's a dream that reminds one of the song *O wüsst' ich doch den Weg zurück, den weiten Weg ins*

---

52. Dietrich Bonhoeffer, *Discipleship*, vol. 4, Dietrich Bonhoeffer Works (Minneapolis: Fortress Press, 2001), pp. 207-08.

Kinderland [If only I knew the way back, the long way back to childhood]. There is no such way — at any rate not if it means deliberately abandoning our mental integrity; the only way is that of Matt. 18:3, i.e., through repentance, through *ultimate* honesty.[53]

Repentance for Bonhoeffer is the only way forward, and repentance is a christological event. It is to turn from the "godly" world and to enter into the absolute break (sounding somewhat like the early dialectical Karl Barth) Jesus has inaugurated in his flesh. This break is the judgment on the world as now "godless." The illusion of the western possession of God on its shoulders is shattered, its pretensions to global mediation withered in Christ and in the politics of his flesh. Such is the late-modern, global condition. The only orientation now is repentance, which means embracing Christ as the center and embracing his death as our death and as the death of the western rule and the will to effect reconciliation on its terms. The religionless and godless Jesus "directs us to God's powerlessness and suffering; [for] only the suffering God can help. To that extent we may say that the development toward the world's coming of age . . . , which has done away with a false conception of God, opens up a way of seeing the God of the Bible, who wins power and space in the world through his weakness."[54] The space the godless, the religionless, and secular Jesus wins in the world is a space in which Christianity is uncoupled from the western civilizing project. It is now one in which he speaks as the center but from places of displacement, from the cross. Only from him can the global be engaged. Indeed, only he can engage the global and, in that engagement, crucify every other will to seize the center and be universal. This is the politics of Jesus' identity from which a new reformation can happen, the reformation of the globe and of the world.

53. Dietrich Bonhoeffer, *Letters and Papers from Prison* (New York: Collier, 1972), p. 360. Matthew 18:3 says, "Unless you turn and become like children, you will never enter the Kingdom of heaven."

54. Bonhoeffer, *Letters and Papers*, p. 361.

Contributors

Daniela C. Augustine is Assistant Professor of Theological Ethics at Lee University, Cleveland, Tennessee. She is the co-founder of the Bulgarian Theological College in Stara Zagora, Bulgaria, where she served as Academic Dean and Vice President for Academic Affairs. Dr. Augustine is also the co-founder and an Executive Committee member of the Civic Association "Project Antioch" in the Czech Republic. Prior to joining the faculty of Lee University, she lectured for the International Program of the Protestant Theological Faculty of Charles University, Prague, and the Pentecostal Theological Seminary, Cleveland, Tennessee. Her research and publications are on the topic of public theology and social transformation, postmodernity, and globalization. She is the author of *At the Cross-roads of Social Transformation: An Eastern European Theological Reflection* (Saarbrücken, Germany: LAP Publishing Co., 2010). Dr. Augustine is a member of the Center of Theological Inquiry, Princeton.

Alexander Broadie is an Honorary Professorial Research Fellow and Emeritus Professor of Logic and Rhetoric at the University of Glasgow. He is a leading scholar of the Scottish philosophical tradition, including the Scottish Enlightenment. His many publications in this field include *The Tradition of Scottish Philosophy* (Edinburgh: Polygon/Edinburgh University Press, 1990), *The Scottish Enlightenment: An Anthology* (Edinburgh: Canongate Books, 1997), *The Scottish Enlightenment: The Historical Age of the Historical Nation* (Edinburgh: Birlinn, 2001), the edited volume, *The Cambridge Companion to the Scottish Enlightenment* (Cambridge: Cambridge University Press, 2003), *A History of*

Scottish Philosophy (Edinburgh: Edinburgh University Press, 2009), and "The Rise (and Fall?) of the Scottish Enlightenment," in *The Oxford Companion to Modern Scottish History*, ed. T. Devine and J. Wormald (Oxford: Oxford University Press, forthcoming).

J. Kameron Carter is Associate Professor of Theology and Black Church Studies at Duke University Divinity School. His publications include *Race: A Theological Account* (Oxford: Oxford University Press, 2008), "Race and the Experience of Death: Reappraising American Evangelicalism," in *The Cambridge Companion to American Evangelicalism* (Cambridge: Cambridge University Press, forthcoming), and "Theology, Exegesis, and the Just Society: Gregory of Nyssa as Abolitionist Intellectual," *Ex Auditu* 23 (2007). For the 2006-07 academic year, Dr. Carter was a fellow at the National Humanities Center at Research Triangle Park, NC.

Peter J. Casarella is Professor of Catholic Studies, DePaul University, and founding Director of DePaul's Center for World Catholicism and Intercultural Theology. He has written numerous essays in scholarly journals on a variety of topics, including medieval Christian Neoplatonism, contemporary theological aesthetics, and the Hispanic/Latino presence in the U.S. Catholic Church. He has co-edited two volumes of essays: with Raúl Gómez, S.D.S., *Cuerpo de Cristo: The Hispanic Presence in the U.S. Catholic Church* (New York: Academic Renewal, 2003), and with George Schner, S.J., *Christian Spirituality and the Culture of Modernity: The Thought of Louis Dupré* (Grand Rapids: Eerdmans, 1998). In March 2006, The Catholic University of America Press published his edited volume, *Cusanus: The Legacy of Learned Ignorance*. In 2003-2004, he held the J. Houston Witherspoon Research Fellowship in Theology and Natural Science at the Center of Theological Inquiry in Princeton, NJ. He also serves as President of the American Cusanus Society and as a member of the Wissenschaftliche Beirat of the Cusanus-Gesellschaft.

William J. Danaher, Jr. is Dean of the Faculty of Theology at Huron University College. His publications include *The Trinitarian Ethics of Jonathan Edwards* (Louisville: Westminster John Knox Press, 2004); *Image in the Fragments: Theological Engagements with Popular Literature, Art and Film* (Lanham, MD: Cowley Publications, forthcoming); "'Laces Just Right': Frank Griswold and the Ethics of Reconciliation," in *I Have Called You Friends: Reflections on Reconciliation in Honor of Frank Griswold* (Lanham, MD: Cowley Publications, 2006); "Renewing the Anglican Moral Vision: What Called to

Common Mission Offers Anglican Moral Theology," *Anglican Theological Review* 85, no. 1 (Winter 2005); "The Politics of Repentance," *Sewanee Magazine* (July 2004); and "Pacifism, Just War, and the Limits of Ethics," *Journal of Lutheran Ethics* (April 2003). He is a member of the Center of Theological Inquiry, Princeton.

Kimberly Hutchings is Professor in International Relations at the London School of Economics and Political Science (LSE). Her research interests include international and global ethics. She is the author of many books and articles on global civil society and citizenship, including the co-edited work (with Roland Dannreuther) *Cosmopolitan Citizenship* (Basingstoke: Palgrave Macmillan, 1999), *International Political Theory: Rethinking Ethics in a Global Era* (London: Sage Publications, 1999), "Feminism and Global Citizenship," in *Global Citizenship: A Critical Reader,* ed. Nigel Dower and John Williams (New York: Routledge, 2002), "Subjects, Citizens or Pilgrims? Citizenship and Civil Society in a Global Context," in *The Idea of Global Civil Society: Politics and Ethics in a Globalizing Era,* ed. Randall Germain and Michael Kenny (London and New York: Routledge, 2005), *Time and World Politics: Thinking the Present* (Manchester: Manchester University Press, 2008), and *Global Ethics* (Cambridge: Polity Press, 2010).

Kristen Deede Johnson is Assistant Professor of Political Science and Associate Director of the CrossRoads Project, Hope College. Her research lies in the areas of political thought, theology, and culture, and her publications include *Theology, Political Theory, and Pluralism: Beyond Tolerance and Difference* (Cambridge: Cambridge University Press, 2007).

John Keane is Professor of Politics at the University of Sydney, Australia, and at the Wissenschaftszentrum Berlin (WZB). In 1989, he founded the Centre for the Study of Democracy (CSD). Among his many books on civil society and democracy are *Democracy and Civil Society* (London: Verso Books, 1988; rev. ed., University of Westminster Press, 1998), *Civil Society: Old Images, New Visions* (Cambridge: Polity Press, 1998), *Vaclav Havel: A Political Tragedy in Six Acts* (New York: Bloomsbury Publishing PLC, 1999), *Global Civil Society?* (Cambridge: Cambridge University Press, 2003), *Violence and Democracy* (Cambridge: Cambridge University Press, 2004), and the first major history of democracy in a hundred years, *The Life and Death of Democracy* (New York: Simon and Schuster, 2009).

Nico Koopman is Professor of Systematic Theology and Ethics, Director of the Beyers Naudé Centre for Public Theology, and Dean of the Faculty of Theology at the University of Stellenbosch. His work focuses on various themes in the field of public theology. This is done in a variety of local and international partnerships. One of his publications is a book on ethics which is co-authored with his colleague, Robert Vosloo: *Die ligtheid van die lig. Morele oriëntasie in 'n postmoderne tyd* (Wellington: Lux Verbi, 2002). This book won the Andrew Murray Prize for theological literature. Two recent articles on public theology are "After Ten Years: Public Theology in Postapartheid South Africa. Lessons from a Debate in the USA," *Nederduitse Gereformeerde Teologiese tydskrif (NGTT)* 46/1, 2 (2005), and "Theology and the Fulfillment of Social and Economic Rights," in *Theories of Social and Economic Justice*, ed. A. Van der Walt (Stellenbosch: Sunmedia, 2005). Dr. Koopman was public theologian in residence at the Center of Theological Inquiry, Princeton, 2007-2008, and the first Chair of the Global Network for Public Theology, 2007-2008, on behalf of CTI.

Christoffel Lombard is Professor of Theology and Ethics, and Chair of the Department of Religion and Theology at the University of the Western Cape. His publications include (with P. Isaak): "The Impact of Religion on Namibian Society," in *Namibia, Sociology, Society*, ed. V. Winterfeldt, T. Fox, and M. Pimpelani (Windhoek: University of Namibia Press, 2002); *The Ethics of Listening* (Windhoek: Ecumenical Institute for Namibia, 1999); "Namibian Perspectives on Academic Cooperation in a Globalized World," UNITWIN Publication (1999); and (editor with J. Hunter), *Multi-party Democracy, Civil Society and Economic Transformation in Southern Africa* (Windhoek: SAUSSC, 1991). Professor Lombard was also the editor of the *Journal of Religion and Theology in Namibia* (1999-2003). He is a member of the Center of Theological Inquiry, Princeton.

Paul Louis Metzger is Professor of Christian Theology and Theology of Culture and Director of The Institute for the Theology of Culture: New Wine, New Wineskins, Multnomah Biblical Seminary. His publications include *The Word of Christ and the World of Culture: Sacred and Secular through the Theology of Karl Barth* (Grand Rapids: Eerdmans, 2003); the edited volume *Trinitarian Soundings in Systematic Theology* (London and New York: T&T Clark International, 2005); *Consuming Jesus: Beyond Race and Class Divisions in a Consumer Church* (Grand Rapids: Eerdmans, 2007); and the co-authored work (with Brad Harper), *Exploring Ecclesiology: An Evangelical and Ecumenical Introduction* (Grand Rapids: Brazos, 2009). He is the editor of *Cultural Encoun-*

ters: A Journal for the Theology of Culture and a member of the Center of Theological Inquiry, Princeton.

Petr Pokorný is Professor of New Testament Exegesis at Charles University and Director of the Centre of Biblical Studies in Prague. His publications include: *The Genesis of Christology* (London and New York: T&T Clark, 1987; reprint 1994, transl. from German); *Colossians: A Commentary* (Peabody, MA: Hendrickson 1991, transl. from German); *Jesus in the Eyes of His Followers* (North Richland Hills, TX: BIBAL, 1998); *Theologie der lukanischen Schriften* (Göttingen: Vandenhoeck & Ruprecht, 1998); editor together with Jan Roskovec: *Philosophical Hermeneutics and Biblical Exegesis* (Tübingen: Mohr-Siebeck, 2002). He holds honorary doctorates from Bonn and Budapest and is a member of the Center of Theological Inquiry, Princeton.

J. Jayakiran Sebastian is H. George Anderson Professor of Mission and Cultures and Director of the Multicultural Mission Resource Center at the Lutheran Theological Seminary, Philadelphia. His publications include ". . . *baptisma unum in sancta ecclesia . . .*": *A Theological Appraisal of the Baptismal Controversy in the Work and Writings of Cyprian of Carthage* (Verlag an der Lottbek, Peter Jensen, 1997/ISPCK, 1997) and *Enlivening the Past: An Asian Theologian's Engagement with the Early Teachers of Faith* (Piscataway, NJ: Gorgias Press, 2009). He is a member of the Center of Theological Inquiry, Princeton.

Rudolf von Sinner is Professor of Systematic Theology, Ecumenism and Inter-religious Dialogue, Escola Superior de Teologia (Lutheran School of Theology), São Leopoldo, Brazil. His publications include *Reden vom dreieinigen Gott in Brasilien und Indien: Grundzüge einer ökumenischen Hermeneutik im Dialog mit Leonardo Boff und Raimon Panikkar* (Mohr Siebeck, 2003); "Religion and Power: Towards the Political Sustainability of the World," in *Concilium* 40/5 (2004); and "Trust and convivência: Contributions to a Hermeneutics of Trust in Communal Interaction," in *The Ecumenical Review* 57, no. 3 (2005). Prof. von Sinner was awarded the University of Basel's Amerbach Prize in 2002. He is a member of the Center of Theological Inquiry, Princeton.

Dirkie Smit is Professor of Systematic Theology at Stellenbosch University, South Africa, and is active in its Beyers Naudé Center for Public Theology and in the Reformed and ecumenical church. He has published more than 300 scholarly works, in journals, dictionaries, encyclopedias, and edited volumes, as well as authored or co-edited more than 30 popular books, and he has a weekly column in *Die Burger.* His publications include essays on public theology and on worship, as well as a trilogy on the Nicene Creed, *Wat Here is en lewend maak* (Wellington: Lux Verbi, 2001), *Lig uit lig* (Wellington: Lux Verbi, 2001) and *Vernuwe! — na die beeld van ons Skepper* (Wellington: Lux Verbi, 2003). He is a member of the Center of Theological Inquiry, Princeton.

Max L. Stackhouse is the Rimmer and Ruth de Vries Professor of Reformed Theology and Public Life Emeritus at Princeton Theological Seminary, where he was the founding Director of the Kuyper Center for Public Theology. He has served as President of the Society for Christian Ethics and the American Theological Society. His many publications include *Public Theology and Political Economy* (Grand Rapids: Eerdmans, 1984; repub. New York: Parthenon, 1998), *On Moral Business: Classical and Contemporary Resources on Ethics and Economic Life* (Grand Rapids: Eerdmans, 1995), and the four-volume edited series, *God and Globalization* (London: Continuum, 2000, 2001, 2003, 2007), including his own final monograph in the series, *Globalization and Grace: A Christian Public Theology for a Global Future* (London: Continuum, 2007). He is a member of the Center of Theological Inquiry, Princeton.

William F. Storrar is the Director of the Center of Theological Inquiry, Princeton, and a Professor Extraordinary of the University of Stellenbosch, South Africa. He served as Convener of Common Cause, a civil society forum on Scotland's democratic future, 1992-2000. His publications in the field of public theology and ethics, the church and civil society, include *Public Theology for the 21st Century,* co-edited with Andrew R. Morton (London: Continuum, 2004); *God and Society: Doing Social Theology in Scotland Today,* co-edited with Peter Donald (Edinburgh: Saint Andrew Press, 2003); "2007: A Kairos Moment for Public Theology," *International Journal of Public Theology* 1, no. 1 (2007); and "Scottish Civil Society and Devolution," in *The Future of Christian Social Ethics,* ed. Elaine L. Graham and Esther Reed (London: Continuum, 2004). He chairs the editorial board of the *International Journal of Public Theology* (Brill) and initiated the formation of the Global Network for Public Theology, 2007. He was formerly the Professor of Christian Ethics and Practical Theology, and Director of the Centre for Theology and Public Issues, at the University of Edinburgh. He is a member of the Center of Theological Inquiry, Princeton.

Index